Dismantling the Cold War

CSIA Studies in International Security

Michael E. Brown, Sean M. Lynn-Jones, & Steven E. Miller, series editors
Teresa J. Lawson, executive editor
Center for Science and International Affairs (CSIA)
John F. Kennedy School of Government, Harvard University

Published by The MIT Press:

Nuclear Weapons and Arms Control in the Middle East, by Shai Feldman (1996)

The Greek Paradox: Promise vs. Performance, Graham T. Allison and Kalypso Nicolaïdis, eds. (1996)

The International Dimensions of Internal Conflict, Michael E. Brown, ed. (1996)

Avoiding Nuclear Anarchy: Containing the Threat of Loose Russian Nuclear Weapons and Fissile Material, Graham T. Allison, Owen R. Coté, Jr., Richard A. Falkenrath, & Steven E. Miller (1996)

The Arms Production Dilemma: Contraction and Restraint in the World Combat Aircraft Industry, Randall Forsberg, ed. (1994)

Shaping Europe's Military Order: The Origins and Consequences of the CFE Treaty, Richard A. Falkenrath (1994)

Published by Brassey's, Inc.:

Damage Limitation or Crisis? Russia and the Outside World, Robert D. Blackwill and Sergei A. Karaganov, eds. (1994)

Arms Unbound: The Globalization of Defense Production, David Mussington (1994)

Russian Security After the Cold War: Seven Views from Moscow, Teresa Pelton Johnson and Steven E. Miller, eds. (1994)

Published by CSIA:

Cooperative Denuclearization: From Pledges to Deeds, Graham Allison, Ashton B. Carter, Steven E. Miller, and Philip Zelikow, eds. (1993)

Soviet Nuclear Fission: Control of the Nuclear Arsenal in a Disintegrating Soviet Union, Kurt M. Campbell, Ashton B. Carter, Steven E. Miller, and Charles A. Zraket (1991)

Dismantling the Cold War

U.S. and NIS Perspectives on the Nunn-Lugar Cooperative Threat Reduction Program

John M. Shields and William C. Potter, eds.

CSIA Studies in International Security

The MIT Press
Cambridge, Massachusetts
London, England

Library of Congress Cataloging-in-Publication Data

Dismantling the Cold War : U.S. and NIS perspectives on the Nunn-Lugar Cooperative
Threat Reduction Program / John M. Shields & William C. Potter, editors.
    p.   cm. — (CSIA studies in international security)
Includes bibliographical references.
ISBN 0-262-69198-1 (alk. paper)
    1. Nuclear disarmament—Former Soviet republics.   2. Technical assistance, American—
Former Soviet republics.   3. Weapons of mass destruction.   I. Shields, John M.   II. Potter,
William C.   III. Series.
JX1974.7.D66   1997
327.1'74'094709049—dc21   96-39444
                                                                                                                                              CIP

10 9 8 7 6 5 4 3 2 1
Printed in the United States of America

Edited by Mary Albon

Contents

Case Studies of CTR Projects

Conclusions, Next Steps, and Future Directions

Acknowledgments

This volume is the product of a year-long research initiative of the NIS Nonproliferation Project at the Monterey Institute of International Studies. It has benefited enormously from the assistance and support of several individuals and organizations. First drafts of most of the book chapters were presented at a conference on the Nunn-Lugar Cooperative Threat Reduction Program held in Monterey on August 20–22, 1995. The conference was sponsored by the Center for Nonproliferation Studies of the Monterey Institute of International Studies, in cooperation with Harvard University's Center for Science and International Affairs. The research and conference were made possible by generous support from the Carnegie Corporation of New York, the Ford Foundation, the John D. and Catherine T. MacArthur Foundation, the John Merck Fund, the Ploughshares Fund, the Rockefeller Brothers Fund, and the W. Alton Jones Foundation.

The project profited enormously from the guidance and encouragement of Oleg Bukharin, Matthew Bunn, Richard Combs, Richard Falkenrath, Gloria Duffy, Rose Gottemoeller, Bill Hoehn, Michael Newlin, Joseph Pilat, and Steven Miller. Emily Ewell and Erin Hammel were instrumental in organizing and implementing the August 1995 conference, and its success was a direct result of their labors. Kseniya Yershova, Anna Mikheeva, John Lepingwell, Michael Lysobey, Adam Moody, and Holly Porteous provided editorial and translation assistance for many of the NIS contributions to this volume. The editors are also very grateful to the invaluable conference assistance and manuscript preparation provided by Allene Thompson and Meg Benjamin, and wish to thank Mary Albon for her copyediting of the final manuscript. Special thanks are due to Teresa Lawson for overseeing the production of the book manuscript for publication.

—*John M. Shields*
—*William C. Potter*

Foreword

Changing Threats in the Post-Cold War World

Senator Sam Nunn

Why is nonproliferation so important? For the first time in the history of the world, an empire has disintegrated containing 30,000 nuclear weapons, at least 40,000 tons of chemical weapons, and a robust biological weapons capability. We do not have to be hypothetical about the threat. We have witnessed two bombings in the United States, one in New York City at the World Trade Center and one at the Oklahoma City Federal Building, that produced terrible tragedies with conventional weapons. You can imagine what would have happened had those been weapons of mass destruction. We also have seen small-scale use of a weapon of mass destruction when a chemical device was used by terrorists in a Tokyo subway. So we do not have to be hypothetical, but allow me to be hypothetical for a moment.

Assume it is 1997. A diplomatic pouch comes into New York City containing 30 pounds of a lethal, binary chemical agent. The pouch leaves New York City in the trunk of an automobile and is driven to Washington where it is delivered to a group of Middle Eastern terrorists. These individuals have procured a radio-guided drone aircraft. The president of the United States is scheduled to make his State of the Union address. The terrorists pull up in a van near the Tidal Basin, about a mile or so from the Capitol. They strap the lethal chemicals under the wings of the drone aircraft and guide it toward the Capitol. Will we be ready for such an incident?

Let us take another hypothetical case. Assume it is 1997. Ten kilograms of highly enriched uranium are missing from a Russian

---

This Foreword is based on remarks delivered by Senator Nunn in a keynote address at a conference on "The Nunn-Lugar Cooperative Threat Reduction Program: Donor and Recipient Country Perspectives," which took place August 20–22, 1995, at the Monterey Institute of International Studies, Monterey, California.

laboratory. Law enforcement authorities in Russia suspect organized crime and they begin an intensive hunt. In early 1998 the president of Russia receives a message as follows: "Two nuclear weapons with timing devices are hidden securely in the basements of Moscow buildings. We demand full Chechnya independence, announced within 48 hours on television by the president. The clock is ticking." Will we be ready?

I use the term "we" because we are all in this together. We have a mutual stake in averting such incidents. The question of whether we will be ready depends on whether we work together and whether we as a team of concerned individuals around the world are able to coordinate our efforts.

One of our most important tools for combating proliferation is the Nunn-Lugar Cooperative Threat Reduction Program. This program was born in the U.S. Senate in the fall of 1991. Since then, Congress has made available $1.27 billion out of the Department of Defense budget to help the states of the former Soviet Union handle responsibly weapons of mass destruction and cope with problems related to these weapons.

The program has several broad purposes, which include: (1) consolidation of weapons of mass destruction in safe areas away from areas of conflict; (2) careful inventory and accounting of these weapons; (3) safe handling of them at a time of considerable domestic turmoil in the former Soviet Union; (4) safe disposition of these weapons, as called for by arms control agreements and also by common sense; and (5) assistance in gainfully employing literally thousands of former Soviet scientists who know how to make weapons of mass destruction—who know how to build missiles that can carry weapons of mass destruction around the globe but who often do not know where their next paycheck is coming from and are in great demand for employment by rogue nations and terrorist groups.

I think it is particularly important that the conference in Monterey was able to gather together so many top officials from the recipient countries—from Belarus, Kazakstan, Russia, and Ukraine—many of whom I have come to know over the years and worked with, and who have done an excellent job in this program. This volume contains several chapters in which these experts and officials share their insights and experiences with the Nunn-Lugar Program. Criticism of the program is voiced, sometimes sharp criticism. But that is what we need, because we require constant feedback from the people who are absolutely essential in making this program work at the receiving end.

There are several criticisms of the Nunn-Lugar Program on the U.S. side that I think have some merit. The program got off to a slow start in terms of obligating funds. The money was there, but initially was not spent very rapidly. Most American taxpayers would argue that spending money slowly was a fine thing. But in the Washington budget cycles and even in the news media, it is taken as a cardinal sin if money is appropriated and not spent immediately. There were several reasons for the slow obligation rate. First, the program was passed by Congress during the Bush administration and was greeted by some in that administration with the "not invented here" syndrome. They did not oppose the program, but neither did they embrace it with real enthusiasm. The second reason was bureaucracy: bureaucracy is difficult enough to deal with in one country, but when you are dealing with several newly independent countries, obviously it takes a long time to reach agreements, particularly agreements in such a highly sensitive area. And third was the phenomenon of reprogramming: since this was a congressional initiative, there was no money for the program already in the budget submitted by the Bush administration. To get the legislation passed, we did not put new money in and cancel other programs. Rather, we gave the executive branch the authority to reprogram money from existing accounts. This meant that the Department of Defense had to find activities to cancel or reduce in order to transfer funds to this new, unanticipated account.

With all of this said, I think we have to keep the matter in perspective. Those of us in America know how much money we have spent for national defense over the last 40 or 50 years. We have spent literally trillions of dollars defending our nation and helping to defend our allies against what we perceived to be a very large threat posed by the Soviet Union and the Warsaw Pact. How much would we have been willing to pay in those days to eliminate all nuclear weapons in three Soviet Republics? How much would we have paid to deactivate 2,825 Soviet nuclear warheads and destroy 630 launchers and bombers? How much would we have paid to help shift thousands of scientists, dealing in military activities and military procurement programs, to civilian endeavors? The Nunn-Lugar Program has contributed to these accomplishments for less than $1.27 billion. That is the perspective, I think, that we need to bring to this problem and this challenge. In my view, given the history of 40 years of confrontation, of animosity and of brinkmanship, we are off to an amazingly productive start.

This program has, I believe, helped to focus the leadership of these newly emerging countries on the key problem of weapons of mass destruction at a time when they have had many critical things to consider, when this was only one of many urgent priorities. One of the first things the Russians did, for example, was to bring all of their tactical weapons back to Russia from literally all corners of the former Soviet Union. Many of these weapons were deployed in areas where armed conflict has since erupted—such as Armenia, Azerbaijan, and Georgia. So that initiative was most timely and has been, I think, a tremendous success.

How have Nunn-Lugar funds been used? They have been used both for incentives and for specific results. First, to consolidate the storage of nuclear weapons in Russia away from possible areas of conflict. Second, to break technical logjams relating to weapons of mass destruction in each of the cooperating countries. This funding is not simply given to governments as cash. Rather, it is awarded to American companies for services and equipment that are then furnished to the recipient countries. More than 90 percent of all Nunn-Lugar assistance is in that category. The kinds of things that have been provided in terms of services and equipment include software for inventory and account-ing purposes, emergency response equipment for coping with an accident in the transportation or storage of these weapons of mass destruction, specially reinforced rail cars for transporting these weapons from one locale to another within the former Soviet Union, fissile material containers to make sure that the transport of warheads is conducted safely, protective clothing for those working in this area, and even bulletproof kevlar blankets that are put over certain weapon containers before they are transported.

My commitment to cooperative threat reduction goes back many years, to the first trip I made to NATO headquarters in the early 1970s. Senator John Stennis, who was then chairman of the Armed Services Committee, was along in years and unable to travel abroad as often as he would have liked. He asked me as a newly elected senator to go to NATO, spend two or three weeks there, and then submit a report to the Armed Services Committee.

One of the things I focused on during that visit was the storage and deployment sites for our tactical nuclear weapons. It is important to keep in mind that this was shortly after the Vietnam War, when the mood and morale of the U.S. military were somewhat comparable to the present mood and morale of the Russian military. I remember very well visiting with U.S. generals who explained to me that all of our tactical nuclear weapons were secure. Everything was wonderful. We had perfect security. There was no problem. After one of those briefings, as I was leaving an area where tactical nuclear weapons were stored, I shook hands with a sergeant, and as I took his hand I felt a piece of folded paper, which I slipped into my pocket. When I had an opportunity a little later, I took a look at the paper. The sergeant had written: "Senator Nunn, please meet me at the barracks around 6:00 tonight after work. I have very important information for you."

Well, I was experienced enough, having been an enlisted man myself, to know I had better find out what the sergeant had in mind. So I did. He and three or four of his fellow sergeants related a horror story to me. A story of a demoralized military. A story of drug abuse. A story of alcohol abuse. A story of U.S. soldiers actually guarding tactical nuclear weapons while they were stoned on drugs. The horror story went on and on for over two hours. I came out of that session thoroughly shaken and determined to try to do something about the matter.

When I returned to Washington, I went directly to see then Secretary of Defense Jim Schlesinger and told him that we had a real problem in Germany. I related to him how the soldiers guarding our tactical nuclear missiles thought that it would take no more than a group of six to eight well-trained terrorists to gain control over one of our tactical nuclear compounds in the middle of Western Europe. Such an incident, even if it lasted only a few hours, would have had a devastating effect on European public opinion. We had a major problem, one that grew out of the psychological trauma of the Vietnam War, and it was a problem that was not being acknowledged. Secretary Schlesinger saw to it that steps were taken in the next few months and over the next few years to remedy the situation.

The second personal experience that I had in the field of cooperative threat reduction stemmed from years of asking questions about the ways a nuclear war could start. I studied various horrible scenarios in which the Soviet Union or the United States might somehow conclude, in an insane moment, that it would be to its advantage to launch a first strike, or perhaps commence an escalation that could result in a first strike. I pondered such scenarios in my own mind, and it never really made sense to me that any set of national leaders could be so insane.

Yet I fully realized that we had to consider such scenarios for purposes of prudent planning if for nothing else.

I started asking questions about accidental launch. What would we do if there was an accidental launch, missiles started coming toward the United States, and the leader of the Soviet Union got the president of the United States on the hot line and said, "I'm sorry, we've had an accidental launch, and ten Soviet missiles are heading your way. Please apologize to your people." What would we do about that? What would we do about an unauthorized launch in which some renegade member of the Soviet military, perhaps a submarine commander—as we have seen in the movies—decided on his own to launch a nuclear strike from his submarine? What about a launch from some Third World country?

I recall visiting the Strategic Air Command in Omaha, Nebraska, when the late General Dick Ellis, whom I greatly admired, was in charge. I talked to General Ellis at length about the kind of scenario that might unfold if a third country launched a nuclear strike, maybe eight or ten missiles, against the Soviet Union or perhaps the United States, and wanted it to appear to one superpower that the launch had come from the other superpower. What could we do under such circumstances? Could we detect the origin of that strike? Would we know that it did not come from the Soviet Union; or would Moscow know that it did not originate with us?

General Ellis, at my request, put his top team at the Strategic Air Command headquarters on these questions, primarily to determine how capable we would be at determining the origin of an accidental, third country, or terrorist strike. The study was highly classified—I suppose most of it is still classified—but the fact was that the United States at that time was not very good at detecting the origin of that kind of strike. And the even more depressing news was that the Soviet Union was probably worse than we were. It was quite revealing to have the head of the Strategic Air Command tell you privately that we had a real stake in the Soviet Union's ability to detect the origin of a nuclear strike. We had a real stake in the Soviet Union's ability to understand that a flock of geese heading toward Moscow was not a missile attack launched by the United States.

I began to realize that each superpower had a vital stake—a stake that continues to exist today—in the other superpower's ability to detect the origin of an attack and to know when there was a false alarm. Can you imagine the horror of having the Russian military falsely interpret some of their intelligence data to indicate a strike may be coming, then by terrible coincidence finding something on their radar indicating that a strike may be coming, and then having a senior general report to the political leadership that a nuclear strike appears to be incoming and Russia's only choice is to launch immediately a retaliatory strike?

Such things are so horrible that you hate even to contemplate them. And yet we have to contemplate them, even after START I and START II are completely implemented. We are going to have a unique relationship with Russia for many years ahead, because we are the only two countries in the world that can destroy each other completely in the span of a few hours. Unfortunately, this will remain true even after all pending arms control agreements are fully implemented. So each of us must understand that we have a unique relationship.

What resulted from all of this? I will not go into great detail, but the concept of "risk reduction centers" was one thing that came out of it. Senator John Warner and I went to President Reagan and his national security advisor, Bud McFarland, to propose establishing risk reduction centers in Moscow and in Washington that would alert each side about any kind of military maneuver, missile test, or any similar activity. Bud McFarland accepted about half of our proposals, and today we do have risk reduction centers up and running in Moscow and in Washington.

Another thing that came out of my concern over accidental launch scenarios was a proposal to Secretary of Defense Dick Cheney, some years later, that we enter into a bilateral agreement with the Russians—without verification, without enforcement, with only an understanding on each side—that each of us would undertake an intensive, internal study of our ability to deal with an accidental nuclear launch. Secretary Cheney did not accept that idea, although he did agree with the need to conduct an internal review of the accidental launch problem. Jeane Kirkpatrick headed this effort, which produced a number of mostly classified safety measures that have improved our ability to deal with that kind of situation.

The third personal experience that strengthened my conviction about the importance of cooperative threat reduction occurred during an unusual visit to Moscow in 1991. This visit took place immediately after the unsuccessful coup attempt against Soviet President Mikhail Gorbachev, during which he had been under house arrest in the Crimea. I had a personal meeting with Gorbachev just after his return to Moscow, and one of the key things on my mind was the status of the nuclear briefcase, the nuclear control device in the personal possession of the head of the country. Had Gorbachev really been in command throughout the coup attempt? Did he maintain total control over the Soviet Union's nuclear weapons? I had met with Gorbachev on a number of previous occasions, and his answers to these questions did not have the same ring of conviction as his statements during our earlier meetings. It seemed to me that either he was not himself clear about the status of command and control of nuclear weapons during that crucial period, or he was not comfortable discussing the matter candidly with me.

In either event, upon my return to Washington, I concluded that the Soviet Union was in great peril. In particular, I believed that we needed to do everything we could to help the Soviet authorities gain control and keep control over their own nuclear weapons. At about the same time, Chairman of the House Armed Services Committee Les Aspin had proposed a humanitarian aid package for the Soviet Union. Both the House and the Senate had already passed the defense authorization and appropriation bills. The Senate Armed Services Committee, which I then chaired, and the House Armed Services Committee were already in conference on our respective defense authorization bills. This was in September 1991. Les Aspin and I decided to do something very unusual. We decided to try to put his humanitarian aid package and my concerns about weapons of mass destruction together in a conference initiative, even though nothing of this nature appeared in either the House or the Senate bill.

In a word, we did not get away with it. We encountered angry protests from some of our respective committee members, we received tepid support from the Bush administration, and we had to withdraw our provision or face defeat of the entire conference report on the Senate and House floors.

At this juncture, Senator Richard Lugar entered the picture. I went to Senator Lugar and asked him if he would be willing to join me in this effort, and he agreed to do so. We had already been working together on a nonproliferation project for Dr. David Hamburg, president of the Carnegie Corporation of New York. We agreed to organize a breakfast meeting with 15 or 20 key senators, featuring a briefing by Dr. Ashton Carter of Harvard's Center for Science and International Affairs, which had just completed a study of the Soviet Union's nuclear weapons.[1]

---

1. Kurt M. Campbell, Ashton B. Carter, Steven E. Miller, and Charles A. Zraket, *Soviet Nuclear Fission: Control of the Nuclear Arsenal in a Disintegrating Soviet Union,* CSIA Studies in International Security (Cambridge, Mass.: Center for Science and

This was a timely study, supported by the Carnegie Corporation, that outlined in an analytical, scholarly format the dangers of nuclear command, control, and safety in an unstable Soviet Union.

In short, within a few weeks we were able to pass legislation in the Senate and then in the House, almost without opposition, that addressed my core concerns and those of Les Aspin. The legislation was in the form of amendments to an unrelated bill. It amounted to $400 million in the nuclear control area, which later became known as the Nunn-Lugar Program, and $100 million in humanitarian aid. This was the origin of the Nunn-Lugar Cooperative Threat Reduction Program, which was signed into law by President Bush in December 1991.

In reviewing the events since that time, a few conclusions are possible. First, I believe that the world has been brought out of a period that, while characterized by a high risk of nuclear conflict, was also a period of high stability because of the fear of use of these weapons. We have entered a new period of low risk, which unfortunately is accompanied by low stability. The danger of a calculated, massive nuclear exchange between the two superpowers has now diminished greatly. We have officially declared the U.S.-Russian relationship to be one of partnership, and in fact we are working together daily on many cooperative endeavors. So, in comparison to the Cold War period, the overall nuclear risk is low. Yet the new period is also one of low stability because of the intensification of tribal conflicts, ethnic conflicts, religious conflicts, and class conflicts in the absence of global superpower rivalry. This hatred is pouring out of our television sets every day from places like Bosnia, Somalia, Rwanda, and many other hot spots around the globe. It is almost as though humanity's house has come through a massive earthquake without being touched, but now we find that the foundation is being steadily eaten away by termites.

As enemies for 40 years, the United States and the Soviet Union engaged in brinkmanship, confrontations, and contests all around the globe. Yet we avoided nuclear war. We avoided the use of any weapon of mass destruction. The key question that faces us as the century draws to a close, and will face us for years to come, is whether the United States and Russia, now as partners and as friends, can keep the world safe from weapons of mass destruction as we reduce our arsenals and

International Affairs, Harvard University, November 1991).

as Russia and the other nations of the former Soviet Union strive for free-market economies and for democracy.

If we are to accomplish this, we must use to maximum benefit all of the tools available to us. First, the Nunn-Lugar Program. It is in great difficulty on Capitol Hill. For some reason, it has come under attack as if it were a foreign aid program. In addition, some in Congress seem to think Nunn-Lugar assistance gives the United States great leverage over Russian actions. For example, some members of Congress have been inclined to tell the Russian side that if Russia does not halt the reactor sale to Iran—and I do not myself think this sale is a good idea—the United States should stop helping Russia dismantle the missiles aimed at the United States.

The logic of this argument is something out of a Marx Brothers movie, in which the bad guys are coming across the room and one of the brothers puts a gun to his own head and shouts: "Come one step closer and I'll pull the trigger!" That is the sort of logic we are encountering. So we need help on Capitol Hill from people who understand this program, from interested citizens who understand that this is one of the best defense expenditures we can possibly make.

We also need stronger export controls and border controls. We need to make sure we can regulate effectively exports involving critical materials as well as scientific and technical know-how. This will require a high degree of international cooperation. While it will be difficult for our respective intelligence communities, we need to coordinate and exchange relevant intelligence information in all of the nonproliferation areas. We are doing some of that now. We need to do much more, both with intelligence and with analysis. We need to intensify and focus cooperative diplomatic efforts on nonproliferation. We need to strengthen law enforcement, in particular because criminal elements with no particular political philosophy but with enormous greed are beginning to enter this picture. We need to launch an all-out, joint effort in the fight against organized crime in the former Soviet Union, in the United States, and throughout the world.

We need to beef up, expand, and reorient the risk reduction concept that I described above. Again, risk reduction centers are already in place in Washington and Moscow. Let me repeat the same recommendation that Senator Warner and I made ten years ago, without success, to Bud McFarland. These risk reduction centers should be given specific responsibility to develop jointly contingency planning for dealing with the use, or threat of use, of weapons of mass destruction by terrorists or by rogue Third World nations. In other words, we should prepare ourselves now for terrible incidents that may occur in the future. We should have confidence that we can work effectively with our friends and allies around the globe on such problems.

Finally, the United States and Russia have the awesome joint responsibility to dismantle the most powerful arsenals of destructive power in history. In spite of our inevitable differences, we will continue to share this responsibility for a long time to come. For the United States' part, in the next few years there are going to be serious efforts to develop missile defenses. In fact, that effort is under way in Congress now. We confront many threats. We face a chemical terrorism threat; we have suitcase bomb threats; we have threats of nonconventional Third World strikes; and we have threats of proliferation of missile technology. As I have noted, we have moved from a period of high risk and high stability to a period of low risk but low stability. The magnitude of the overall risk has gone down, but the number of relatively small risks has increased.

In this environment, missile defense development—both theater missile defense, which is not covered by the Anti–Ballistic Missile (ABM) Treaty, and national missile defense, which is covered by the ABM Treaty—is an important priority for America's security. However, I believe we must think this through very carefully, and our approach must be to keep the Russians, our allies, and other interested parties fully informed. Any decision to deploy a national missile defense system should be based on effectiveness, on affordability, on the potential threat, and on our obligations under the ABM Treaty, which was entered into in the early 1970s. We should make it clear that America's goal is to provide protection against accidental or unauthorized launches and against a limited missile attack by Third World countries or terrorist groups. We must also make it clear to the Russians that we will seek modest, and I emphasize modest, amendments to the ABM Treaty by mutual agreement to allow both the United States and Russia to protect their respective national territories against limited missile attack.

Most important, we should make clear that we do not seek to develop or deploy a defensive system which, combined with our offensive power, would give us even a theoretical first-strike capability against Russia. This is vital and we must strive for clear understanding on this point. If Russia comes to the conclusion that we are seeking such a system, then it is very likely that Russia will stop dismantling its weapons pursuant to START I and START II. The result would be a net decrease in American security, with thousands of warheads, scheduled to be dismantled under START I and START II, still aimed at the United States. So this is a subject of great importance, under debate now in Washington.

We need responsibility from the United States on such issues; we also need responsibility by Russia. The Conventional Forces in Europe (CFE) Treaty that has entered into force and currently is being implemented must not be viewed by either nation as written in a sacred script. I think the same is true for the ABM Treaty. But the CFE Treaty, as well as the ABM Treaty, must be implemented by the signatories until changed by mutual agreement. This will require hard efforts in the diplomatic field and good faith by all parties.

It is also essential that Russia come into full compliance with the 1972 Biological Weapons Convention. We must resolve together outstanding issues in implementation of the Wyoming Understanding of 1989 regarding chemical weapons and the bilateral chemical weapons agreement of 1990. These are important matters which will have a major impact on Capitol Hill and on U.S.-Russian cooperation across the board.

As I mentioned at the outset, in my view, proliferation of weapons of mass destruction clearly is the number one national security challenge we face. Our friends and colleagues from Ukraine, Kazakstan, Belarus, and Russia should be congratulated for their efforts. We could not have made the progress that we have made without the cooperation and understanding that has been demonstrated by each of those countries. I applaud the ideas and products generated as a result of the conference and I congratulate the Monterey Institute for the splendid work it is doing in this area and many others.

Chapter 1

Introduction

Assessing the Dismantlement Process

William C. Potter & John M. Shields

Prior to the collapse of the Soviet Union, little attention was given to the possibility that war, revolution, or a coup d'état might suddenly lead to the proliferation of nuclear weapons.[1] Although Soviet decision-makers began to recognize the vulnerability of their tactical nuclear warheads by early 1990 after the escalation of the Nagorno-Karabakh conflict and the declaration of Lithuanian independence, no immediate action was taken to redeploy those forces.[2] Only after the failed August 1991 coup, when a group of hard-line Communists attempted to seize power from Soviet President Mikhail Gorbachev, did the security of the vast Soviet nuclear arsenal emerge as the subject of sustained high-level attention in Moscow and Washington.[3]

As the Soviet Union disintegrated, initial concerns in both capitals about the diminution of central political control over nuclear weapons and the dangers of accidental or inadvertent nuclear use soon turned

---

1. One exception was the prescient study by Leonard S. Spector, *Going Nuclear* (Cambridge, Mass.: Ballinger, 1987); see esp. pp. 15–63.

2. A proposal reportedly was made in 1990 to remove nuclear forces from the non-Russian republics, but the plan was rejected. See Alexei Arbatov, "Security Issues in Soviet Successor States," *Russia and her Neighbors Symposium Report*, RAND/ UCLA Center for Soviet Studies (May 20, 1992), p. 2.

3. Shortly after the failed coup, on September 27, 1991, President Bush announced that the United States would unilaterally destroy all of its land-based tactical nuclear warheads after withdrawing those based overseas. This step made it possible for President Gorbachev to announce similar measures the following week. Gorbachev also proposed to move air-launched tactical warheads to central storage. The rapid pace with which these redeployments took place indicates prior planning for this contingency on the part of the military.

to worries about proliferation. At least three different kinds of proliferation threats were apparent.[4]

The first pertained to the devolution of political power to the republics, and the attendant risk of nuclear inheritance by Soviet successor states. This potential threat in August 1991 appeared to be realized by the end of the year when the Soviet Union ceased to exist, replaced by 15 newly independent states, four of which inherited the entire Soviet strategic nuclear arsenal. Ukraine, for example, became, virtually overnight, the host of the world's third largest stockpile of intercontinental ballistic missiles and strategic bombers. Although Russia retained control over most, if not all, of this stockpile,[5] its long-term stewardship was by no means assured. Given Ukraine's extensive nuclear and missile infrastructure, which included a large and diverse civilian nuclear power program, uranium mines, plants for processing uranium ore, key dual-use nuclear-related commodities, and the world's largest missile factory, the prospect of Ukraine's accession to the Non-Proliferation Treaty (NPT) was at best uncertain.[6] At the end of 1991, policymakers in Washington and Moscow were confronted with similar concerns about the nuclear ambitions of Belarus and Kazakstan, in addition to the problem of retrieving thousands of tactical nuclear weapons that had been dispersed in at least 14 of the Soviet republics.[7]

---

4. These basic categories of threat were first identified and analyzed in the extraordinarily influential volume by Kurt M. Campbell, Ashton B. Carter, Steven E. Miller, and Charles A. Zraket, *Soviet Nuclear Fission: Control of the Nuclear Arsenal in a Disintegrating Soviet Union*, CSIA Studies in International Security (Cambridge, Mass.: Center for Science and International Affairs [CSIA], 1991), pp. ii–iii.

5. See Martin J. DeWing, "The Ukrainian Nuclear Arsenal: Problems of Command, Control, and Maintenance," CNS Working Paper No. 3, Monterey Institute of International Studies (October 1993).

6. For an analysis of the nuclear assets of the post-Soviet states and their proliferation tendencies, see William C. Potter, "The Politics of Nuclear Renunciation: The Cases of Belarus, Kazakstan, and Ukraine," Stimson Center Occasional Paper No. 22 (April 1995). See also Mitchell Reiss, *Bridled Ambition: Why Countries Constrain Their Nuclear Capabilities* (Washington, D.C.: Woodrow Wilson Center Press, 1995), and *Nuclear Successor States of the Soviet Union: Nuclear Weapon and Sensitive Export Status Report* No. 4, Monterey Institute of International Studies and Carnegie Endowment for International Peace (May 1996).

7. Turkmenistan may not have had any nuclear weapons on its territory.

The second proliferation danger was the risk that in a period of political disintegration and social and economic upheaval, nuclear weapons and/or their components might fall into unauthorized hands. One scenario, popular in the Western press, involved the seizure of nuclear weapons by a renegade military unit. Older tactical weapons without "permissive action links" (PALs) to protect their unauthorized use were particularly attractive targets, as were warheads stored in facilities that had been constructed for conventional munitions, and warhead components from dismantled weapons that were kept at interim storage sites.[8] These items also were vulnerable to theft by disgruntled former or active-duty Russian Special Operations (*spetsnaz*) troops who were trained to use atomic demolition weapons and who may have had knowledge of, and access to, nuclear weapons storage depots. In addition, warhead security during transportation was a source of official concern. Some Russian authorities also confided in private that security was suspect at warhead disassembly facilities.[9] Indeed, the general state of disarray and economic malaise in the Russian military and nuclear weapons complex was such that one could not dismiss out of hand stories that one would hope were apocryphal. Illustrative of this genre were reports of the sale of tactical nuclear weapons from Kazakstan to Iran and the temporary desertion of a crew of an SS-25 nuclear missile battery as it searched for food.

Yet another proliferation danger, only dimly recognized at the time of the Soviet Union's demise, but subsequently the subject of great attention, involved what has come to be known as the problem of "loose nukes" or "nuclear leakage."[10] At issue was the prospect of a global surge in proliferation due to the diversion and export from the former

---

8. Many of these sites had less than adequate protection. See Thomas B. Cochran, "Testimony before the Military Application of Nuclear Energy Panel of the House Armed Services Committee," April 19, 1994, p. 2.

9. On this point see William C. Potter, "Before the Deluge? Assessing the Threat of Nuclear Leakage from the Post-Soviet States," *Arms Control Today* (October 1995), p. 13.

10. This threat is discussed in detail by Graham T. Allison, Owen R. Coté, Jr., Richard A. Falkenrath, and Steven E. Miller in *Avoiding Nuclear Anarchy: Containing the Threat of Loose Russian Nuclear Weapons and Fissile Material*, CSIA Studies in International Security (Cambridge, Mass.: MIT Press, 1996). See also John Holdren, "Reducing the Threat of Nuclear Theft in the Former Soviet Union," *Arms Control Today*, March 1996, pp. 14–20; and Potter, "Before the Deluge?"

Soviet nuclear complex of not only weapons, but also sensitive material, technology, equipment, and expertise. Although the international news media initially distorted the problem by repeatedly "crying wolf" over black market nuclear transactions involving the states of the former Soviet Union, proliferation-significant diversions did occur as early as 1992, and since then have grown in terms of both the frequency and size of the fissile material contraband. More difficult to estimate, but equally threatening from the standpoint of nonproliferation, was the specter of an exodus of underpaid and/or unemployed nuclear weapons specialists. Literally tens, if not hundreds, of thousands of scientists and technicians with experience in the design and manufacture of nuclear weapons and related technology worked in the huge Soviet nuclear weapons complex. At the time of the breakup of the Soviet Union, reportedly 100,000 scientists, engineers, and officials had nuclear security clearances equivalent to the U.S. Department of Energy's "Q" clearance.[11] Although there was no evidence to suggest that most of these individuals were anything but loyal citizens, it also was clear that their dedication would be severely tested in an environment of job insecurity, food and housing shortages, plummeting prestige, continuing political turmoil, and lucrative offers from abroad.

The Origins and Scope of U.S.-NIS Cooperation

The end of the Cold War and the disintegration of the Soviet Union presented U.S. policymakers with a number of major new proliferation challenges and nonproliferation opportunities. Fortunately, the need to take rapid action to meet these denuclearization challenges was recognized by a bipartisan coalition in the U.S. Congress led by Senators Sam Nunn (Democrat–Georgia) and Richard Lugar (Republican–Indiana). As a consequence of their initiative, in November 1991, three months after the failed Moscow coup, new legislation was introduced to accelerate the timetable for destruction of the strategic

---

11. See *Nuclear Fuel*, October 28, 1991, p. 15. See also William C. Potter, "Exports and Experts: Proliferation Risks from the New Commonwealth," *Arms Control Today*, January/February 1992, pp. 32–37.

weapons being eliminated under the START I Treaty,[12] to assist the return to Russia of all strategic and tactical nuclear weapons, and to ensure the safe and secure storage of these weapons pending their dismantlement. This legislation, initially called the Soviet Nuclear Threat Reduction Act and renamed in subsequent years the Cooperative Threat Reduction (CTR) Program, was commonly known as the "Nunn-Lugar Program."

As originally designed, the CTR Program provided the Department of Defense (DOD) with the authority to fund assistance to the Soviet Union (and subsequently, to eligible post-Soviet states) to dismantle and destroy weapons of mass destruction; to strengthen the security of nuclear weapons and fissile materials in connection with dismantlement; to prevent proliferation; and to help demilitarize the industrial and scientific infrastructure that supported weapons of mass destruction in the newly independent states (NIS) of the former Soviet Union. Specific program objectives, as established by Congress, were to cooperate with NIS republics to:

- destroy nuclear, chemical, and other weapons of mass destruction;

- transport, store, disable, and safeguard weapons in connection with their destruction;

- establish verifiable safeguards against proliferation of such weapons;

- prevent diversion of weapons-related expertise;

- facilitate demilitarization of defense industries and conversion of military capabilities and technologies;

- expand defense and military contacts between the United States and the NIS;

- convert defense industrial facilities to commercial uses; and

---

12. Under the terms of the 1991 Soviet Strategic Arms Reduction Talks (START I) Treaty, both sides agreed to reduce their strategic forces to no more than 1,600 delivery vehicles armed with no more than 6,000 warheads.

- facilitate environmental cleanup of nuclear contamination in the Arctic Ocean.

The CTR Program continues to provide services, tools, and technology required to assist the NIS with the elimination or reduction of weapons of mass destruction and to modernize and expand safeguards against proliferation within these states. Summarizing the purpose of the program he co-sponsored, Senator Nunn observed in 1992, "I know of no more urgent national security challenge confronting our nation. Nor do I know of any greater opportunity ... to reduce the dangers confronting us."

Since its inception, the CTR Program and parallel initiatives sponsored by the Departments of State, Energy, and Commerce, have claimed notable accomplishments. Ongoing or recently completed technical work underwritten by these programs has been instrumental in meeting key post–Cold War U.S. objectives of arms reduction, nuclear security, nonproliferation, and environmental remediation. Projects pursued in cooperation with U.S. partners in the NIS have supported the safe and secure transport of nuclear warheads from non-Russian republics to consolidated storage in Russia; assisted destruction of strategic nuclear delivery vehicles such as long-range bombers, ballistic missiles, and submarines; improved physical protection and accounting of fissile materials at several NIS nuclear facilities; helped develop the organizational and technical basis for export controls of weapons-related items across Russian and other NIS borders; and generated gainful employment and commercial research and development (R&D) opportunities for redundant Soviet weapons scientists, reducing the incentives for these personnel to seek weapons work elsewhere.

U.S. threat reduction and nonproliferation assistance has also yielded important indirect benefits that have been underappreciated. U.S. efforts to assist the non-Russian Soviet successor states with the burdens of demilitarization played a central role in the decisions by these countries to adhere to arms control agreements signed by the Soviet Union, to renounce their claim to nuclear weapons, and to commit themselves to a non-nuclear future. U.S. Nunn-Lugar commitments to Ukraine, for example, were a key incentive for Kiev to sign the Trilateral Statement with Russia and the United States in January 1994, by which Ukraine agreed that nuclear weapons deployed on its territory would be withdrawn to Russia for dismantlement, a *sine qua non* for further progress on strategic arms control. Nunn-Lugar assistance further encouraged Kiev to sign the NPT as a non-nuclear weapon state, a prerequisite for START I entry into force.

In the five years since the CTR Program was initiated, as U.S. and NIS personnel have worked together to address a complex set of military-technical problems, the program's organization, funding, and priorities have been modified significantly. These adjustments have been, in part, a response to the changing circumstances on the ground in post-Soviet republics. Some more urgent, short-term tasks, such as warhead transport back to Russia, were implemented relatively rapidly, while others have been sufficiently complex to require support over a much longer period. In some cases, moreover, U.S.-NIS cooperation has revealed additional needs requiring assistance that were unanticipated by the original Nunn-Lugar mandate.

Other changes over the life of the CTR Program are a reflection of bureaucratic and political pressures and competing budgetary priorities. One of the most important domestic influences on the program, for example, has been the radical shift in political priorities brought about by the 1994 congressional elections. This event brought to power a number of legislators who were antagonistic to foreign aid spending in general and to aid for the former Soviet Union in particular. An immediate consequence of the change of personnel in Washington was the reduction or elimination of some CTR activities while responsibility for others was shifted from DOD to other U.S. government agencies.

CTR assistance efforts since 1991 have been forced to navigate many financial, bureaucratic, and political obstacles. Nonetheless, the momentum generated by the CTR Program has also laid the foundation for a broad array of programs sponsored by other U.S. agencies and pursued multilaterally with U.S. allies. Just as the CTR Program's promise of assistance has had a ripple effect, encouraging non-Russian NIS to renounce nuclear weapons and abide by arms reduction commitments, the CTR Program has had a programmatic ripple effect as well, spawning a number of supporting initiatives. The CTR Program is now one tool in a robust tool kit of measures supporting threat reduction and nonproliferation in Soviet successor states. The U.S. Department of Energy (DOE) has now taken over principal responsibility for helping Russia and other NIS to improve fissile material protection, control, and accounting (MPC&A) procedures and technologies at some of the most high-risk nuclear facilities in these states. DOE cooperates directly with Russia's Ministry of Atomic Energy (Minatom) at the government-to-government level. At the grass-roots level, DOE laboratories such as Los Alamos, Livermore, and Sandia have initiated contacts with similar nuclear research institutes in the NIS to design, develop, and install MPC&A improvements at these facilities. The State Department currently funds U.S. assistance to the NIS to improve export controls of sensitive technologies and materials. It also has taken the lead in coordinating multilateral support to science and technology centers in Moscow and Kiev that provide commercial research opportunities for former Soviet weapons scientists and engineers. The Commerce Department, in a similar initiative to support nonproliferation goals in the NIS, provides training, equipment, and other assistance to these republics to improve customs controls along NIS borders.

The Changing Context of U.S.-NIS Cooperation

The strong political consensus in the United States that supported assistance to the Soviet Union in 1991 was matched by a mood of optimism and cooperation in bilateral relations generally. However, over time, this optimism has given way to growing disagreements and sometimes overt antagonism between the United States and Soviet successor states, particularly Russia. The erosion or failure of key economic and political reforms in Russia, the emergence of nationalistic political groups and the rehabilitation of Communist Party forces antagonistic to the West, anti-democratic measures taken by Russian President Boris Yeltsin, and allegations of continued Russian biological weapons research have renewed concerns among U.S. officials, legislators, and other observers as to Russia's future political direction and military intentions. Several bilateral disputes have also soured the early promise of U.S.-Russian relations and raised alarms on both sides. Among the most contentious are U.S. proposals to expand NATO to include former Warsaw Pact states, Russian military action against a separatist movement in Chechnya, Russian sales of reactor technology to Iran, and Russia's reluctance to meet its obligations under the Conventional Forces in Europe (CFE) Treaty.

Although the deterioration of U.S.-Russian relations has been arrested, at least temporarily, by President Yeltsin's electoral victory in July 1996, prior disputes have eroded legislative and popular support in the United States for cooperative assistance to Russia and, to a lesser degree, to all former Soviet republics. To be sure, senior administration officials and key legislators continue to make a compelling argument that helping these states destroy their strategic weapons and secure their bomb-making technologies is clearly in the U.S. national interest regardless of other actions or policies taken by Moscow. Nonetheless, a growing number of legislators and conservative nongovernmental analysts have come to reject this view, and have begun to do so in a very vocal and public manner.

For some of these critics, the rallying call is "CTR is foreign aid under another name."[13] Although foreign aid in general is under growing scrutiny, assistance to Russia is especially suspect in light of the war in Chechnya. In the words of one CTR critic, aid to the NIS is "a \$3 billion hobby horse."[14] A corollary criticism is that the CTR encompasses activities that have little direct relevance to U.S. defense requirements. CTR projects such as defense conversion and the provision of housing for NIS missile officers, for example, are portrayed as an illegitimate use of defense funds that might better be expended on U.S. military equipment.[15] At a time when the United States is grappling with the economic consequences of defense cutbacks, assistance that is perceived as enhancing the quality of life in the former Soviet Union is particularly subject to attack. A related criticism is that the CTR Program has departed from its original mission, narrowly characterized as weapons dismantlement.[16]

Still other critics have suggested, based on recent political and military moves by Moscow, that aid of any kind to the former Soviet Union is now not merely wasteful but dangerous as well. Such aid, these critics argue, is a fungible commodity. CTR and other programs,

---

13. For a critical analysis of this proposition, see Richard S. Soll, "Misconceptions about the Cooperative Threat Reduction Program," Director's Series on Proliferation No. 8, Lawrence Livermore National Laboratory (June 1, 1995).

14. Charles Flickner, "The Russian Aid Mess," *The National Interest*, No. 38 (Winter 1994/95), p. 13, cited in ibid., p. 35.

15. See, for example, Rich Kelly, "The Nunn-Lugar Act: A Wasteful and Dangerous Illusion," Foreign Policy Briefing, Cato Institute (March 18, 1996); and Baker Spring, "The Defense Budget for Defense: Why Nunn-Lugar Money Should Go to the B-2," Executive Memorandum, Heritage Foundation (August 1, 1995).

16. On this point see Soll, "Misconceptions about the Cooperative Threat Reduction Program," pp. 36–37.

by providing funds to help Moscow meet its arms control obligations, merely free more of Russia's own resources to maintain its military forces and prop up its weapons development programs. Disclosure in spring 1996 of a massive Russian project to construct an underground military complex in the Ural Mountains has fueled this argument.[17]

Much of the U.S. criticism leveled at the CTR Program is predictable, if unfounded, and relates to basic philosophical differences about the nature of the post-Soviet threat and the appropriate U.S. response to post–Cold War security challenges. Because the criticism is well understood, even if misdirected, a bipartisan coalition in the U.S. Congress has managed, to date, to beat back most domestic attacks and to preserve the core elements of the CTR Program. It remains to be seen whether this coalition can be maintained after the retirement from the U.S. Senate of one of the most, if not the most, important CTR proponents, Senator Sam Nunn.

An equally difficult challenge to the CTR Program, and one that was poorly understood and unanticipated, was the harsh criticism of the program's implementation by the NIS recipients. Despite a number of demonstrative benefits, Russian and other NIS aid recipients have become increasingly suspicious of U.S. motives for providing demilitarization assistance, and are outspoken in their criticism of the management of these programs. Unofficial and sometimes official complaints have criticized the slow and bureaucratic implementation of projects by U.S. agencies, the lack of timely and consistent information as to the status of various projects, and the imposition of intrusive and sometimes bizarre accounting rules, work plans, and schedules by U.S. program managers. Particularly irksome from the perspective of these republics is the use of mostly U.S. contractors and U.S.-supplied equipment to perform CTR tasks, often at higher cost and with longer delays than equally qualified NIS contractors and suppliers, thousands of whom remain out of work.

These specific criticisms are embedded in more general laments about post-Soviet economic, political, and social ills and the failure of the West to ameliorate these conditions. Although criticism of the CTR Program is most pronounced in Russia, where the political mood is increasingly anti-Western and xenophobic, officials in Belarus,

---

17. See Michael R. Gordon, "Despite Cold War's End, Russia Keeps Building a Secret Complex," *New York Times*, April 16, 1996, pp. A1 and A6.

Kazakstan, and Ukraine also acknowledge that denuclearization cooperation with the United States has become more difficult to defend at home. Early expectations of the program have been disappointed not only because of problems of implementation, but because of unrealistic views of the goals and scope of U.S. assistance. Particularly troubling to officials and the public at large in post-Soviet states is the "failure" of U.S. assistance programs to address the tremendous social and economic dislocation arising from demilitarization. To the extent that popular political opinion in the NIS is aware of cooperative programs with the United States, the dominant mood is increasingly one of cynicism. In the 1996 Russian presidential election campaign, for example, anti-Western moods were tapped to gain political ground, and the CTR Program was presented and often perceived as a means for the United States to disarm NIS states militarily and to erode their technological and industrial base. Congressional attempts to use CTR and other assistance to compel Russian behavior in other areas of bilateral relations have only antagonized these suspicions.

Objectives of this Study

Although the target of frequent criticism, until recently the CTR Program has not been the subject of very thorough or systematic assessment.[18] Notably absent from any public evaluation is an analysis

---

18. The most comprehensive critique of U.S. denuclearization policy, including but not limited to the CTR Program, is provided by Allison, Coté, Falkenrath, and Miller, *Avoiding Nuclear Anarchy*. A brief and very critical evaluation of the Nunn-Lugar assistance effort is provided in "Weapons of Mass Destruction: Reducing the Threat from the Former Soviet Union," Report to Congressional Requesters, U.S. General Accounting Office (U.S. GAO), October 1994, updated June 1995. A useful description of the Cooperative Threat Reduction Program is provided by Theodor Galdi, "The Nunn-Lugar Cooperative Threat Reduction Program for Soviet Weapons Dismantlement: Background and Implementation," CRS Report for Congress, Congressional Research Service (CRS), Washington, D.C. (December 29, 1993, updated June 8, 1995). A particularly influential early analysis and set of recommendations is provided by Graham T. Allison, Ashton B. Carter, Steven E. Miller, and Philip Zelikow, eds., *Cooperative Denuclearization: From Pledges to Deeds*, CSIA Studies in International Security (Cambridge, Mass.: Center for Science and International Affairs, Harvard University, January 1993). Other relevant studies include Steven J. Kosiak, "Nonproliferation & Counterproliferation: Investing for a Safer World?" Defense Budget Project (April 1995); Dunbar Lockwood, "The

of the "in-country" implementation of the program and an assessment from the vantage point of the various recipient countries. In order to correct, at least in part, this deficiency, the Center for Nonproliferation Studies at the Monterey Institute of International Studies launched a year-long comparative analysis of the major CTR activities in Belarus, Kazakstan, Russia, and Ukraine. Drawing extensively upon scholars and materials from the former Soviet Union, the research project sought to identify:

- What activities have been most effective in terms of the program objectives, and why?

- What activities have been least successful, and why?

- What accounts for delays in program implementation, and how can future assistance be expedited?

- What should be the priorities for future denuclearization assistance?

- How can a new consensus be forged for cooperative threat reduction?

The preliminary findings of this project were presented at a conference in Monterey, California, in August 1995. The conference, sponsored by the Monterey Institute of International Studies, in cooperation with Harvard University's Center for Science and International Affairs, brought together legislators who had developed early threat reduction legislation, senior U.S. and NIS government officials who had worked together to develop joint demilitarization projects, military and technical personnel responsible for executing many of these projects, and a number of governmental and nongovernmental specialists in the field. The participants at the August 1995 conference provided both a critical review of progress and problems in U.S.-NIS

Nunn-Lugar Program: No Time to Pull the Plug," *Arms Control Today*, June 1995, pp. 8–13; and Jason D. Ellis, "Dollar Diplomacy and Nuclear Nonproliferation: The Case of Nunn-Lugar," paper presented at the annual conference of the International Studies Association, San Diego, Calif. (April 16–20, 1996).

cooperation to date, and identified specific ways in which such cooperation could be improved.

This volume provides a selection of the most significant presentations at the August 1995 conference, as updated to take account of more recent developments. Several additional chapters by distinguished U.S. analysts who represented different institutional players in the CTR process also are included. The two principal objectives of the volume are: (1) to assess the effectiveness of U.S.-NIS denuclearization efforts; and (2) to specify means to improve those efforts. Central to the latter task is the identification of measures—programmatic, political, fiscal, organizational, and otherwise—that will enable the United States and its NIS partners to carry out critical threat reduction initiatives despite domestic political opposition and strains in U.S.-Russian relations. As such, a major goal of this study also is to suggest how a new consensus—domestic and international—can be forged with respect to cooperative threat reduction.

The point of departure for this attempt at consensus-building is a set of propositions distilled from the CTR study and developed at length in this volume.

COOPERATIVE THREAT REDUCTION HAS MADE A SIGNIFICANT CONTRIBU-
TION TO U.S. AND NIS NATIONAL SECURITY

A wealth of information is presented by contributors to this study which supports the conclusion that the CTR Program and related initiatives have directly and indirectly contributed to the nonproliferation of weapons of mass destruction. The CTR Program has been especially effective in mitigating the danger of nuclear inheritance, one of the three principal threats arising from the disintegration of the Soviet Union. It also has provided a framework in which to begin to tackle a number of other pressing proliferation challenges.

DENUCLEARIZATION INITIATIVES ARE AT A CRITICAL JUNCTURE, AND
MUCH MORE REMAINS TO BE DONE

Despite the many tangible accomplishments to date of the CTR Program and associated initiatives, the overall denuclearization assistance effort remains very much a work in progress. The reality today in Soviet successor republics is that thousands of tons of weapons-grade uranium, plutonium, and other critical bomb-making materials are housed in poorly safeguarded facilities overseen by a shrinking work force of underpaid, underequipped personnel. Tens of thousands of tons of chemical agents in munitions sometimes dating to World War II are awaiting destruction at Russian facilities with little or no means of containing potential accidents. At NIS nuclear research centers and military R&D bureaus, thousands of highly skilled scientists, engineers, and technicians are being cut from employment rosters and are being actively recruited by countries hoping to develop indigenous weapons programs.

Although joint U.S.-NIS efforts addressed many of the immediate dangers arising from the breakup of the Soviet Union, in other areas, months or years of logistical and organizational preparation are only now beginning to yield dividends. CTR initiatives to dispose of Russian chemical weapons stockpiles and DOE-sponsored MPC&A improvements at NIS nuclear facilities are two examples of complex, capital-intensive programs that have required particularly long lead times to develop the organizational basis for technical cooperation. Seeing these and other efforts through to completion will require additional time and resources. This study examines how follow-on efforts might be reorganized or redesigned to make better use of time and resources and to better anticipate other problems. In working with their NIS partners in these endeavors, U.S. officials have naturally modified and reworked these programs many times, in an ad hoc manner, to meet emerging needs or fix unexpected problems. This study represents a more comprehensive and systematic attempt to develop a common set of U.S.-NIS priorities, to identify threat reduction activities that are in need of additional support, and to propose organizational and other changes to make more efficient use of scarce resources.

THE FATE OF THE CTR PROGRAM AFFECTS THE FUTURE OF U.S.-NIS RELATIONS

Relations between the West and the fledgling democracies of the former Soviet Union are at a crucial, and painful, stage of development, from which point they may mature productively or revert to their adversarial past. A central theme of this study, reiterated by both U.S. and NIS contributors, is that threat reduction and demilitarization assistance will play a key role in how these relations develop. The contributors to this volume paint a stark picture of the consequences of allowing bilateral disputes or other problems to derail critical threat reduction cooperation. The immediate impact of reductions or elimination of assistance would be to dramatically increase the danger that nuclear and other weapons materials, technologies, and expertise would be diverted to the global arms market. It would also have a direct impact on the ability of these countries to complete political, military, and economic reforms. Although this study looks for ways to insulate nuclear security and nonproliferation cooperation from the "bumps in the road" of U.S.-NIS relations, it also emphasizes that cooperative assistance programs can be designed and implemented in a way that strengthens U.S. relations with the post-Soviet states.

The Target Audience

This volume is addressed to multiple audiences, including especially scholars and analysts of post–Cold War U.S.-NIS security relations, specialists on Russia and the former Soviet Union, and nonproliferation analysts. It also targets policymakers in these issue areas, as well as students of public policy.

Scholars and analysts interested in the major security challenges of the post–Cold War world will find much new information on U.S.-NIS security relations, especially as they relate to problems of nuclear security and cooperative threat reduction. The perspectives on these issues by high-ranking Russian and other post-Soviet policymakers and analysts are particularly noteworthy as they have not appeared elsewhere in any language.

Students of Russia and other post-Soviet republics should find very revealing the accounts of domestic political incentives and constraints on national security policymaking in the former Soviet Union. They also should profit from new insights provided about bureaucratic politics, organizational processes, and policy implementation in the NIS. Thanks to the policymaking positions held by many of the volume contributors during the immediate post-Soviet period, the reader will be introduced to heretofore untold stories of policy decisions and will be able to reconstruct previously obscure but important events. These insights are important not only for Russian/NIS area specialists, but for nonproliferation analysts who hope to fashion broader theories of the politics of nuclear renunciation and restraint.

Finally, students of public policy in general, as well as specialists on the U.S. and NIS policy processes, will find a fascinating case study of the origins and implementation of a major foreign policy program. The story of the Nunn-Lugar Cooperative Threat Reduction Program is also a tale of agenda-setting, policy controversy, domestic and bureaucratic politics, and individual personalities. Most significantly, it is a story of policy implementation by parties in the United States and the NIS who, by virtue of their positions as executors of policy, were able both to further and, at times, frustrate the objectives of those who conceived the program.

Organization of this Study

This study is divided into three sections: (1) U.S. perspectives on the CTR Program; (2) perspectives from the recipient NIS countries on program implementation; and (3) case studies of particular demilitarization and nonproliferation activities associated with the cooperative threat reduction effort. Individual chapters offer perspectives from senior U.S. and NIS government officials who have conceived and managed these program activities, military and technical personnel who have implemented these programs, and other specialists who have assessed particular aspects of these initiatives.

The three chapters in the first main section of the book offer contrasting U.S. perspectives on the origins, successes, problems, and future agenda of U.S. demilitarization assistance to the NIS by three individuals who were instrumental in developing and implementing the CTR Program. Gloria Duffy, former Deputy Assistant Secretary of Defense and Special Coordinator for Cooperative Threat Reduction, describes how CTR embodies a new U.S. approach to security policy— preventive defense. Reviewing the accomplishments of the CTR Program, she directly counters the arguments of many of the program's critics, and identifies future dangers and opportunities for denuclearization assistance. The difficulty of forging and maintaining domestic political support for such assistance is the focus of the study by Richard Combs, Senior Legislative Assistant to Senator Sam Nunn at the time of the conception of the Nunn-Lugar Program. In his chapter, Combs reviews the impact of U.S. domestic politics on the CTR Program and the prospect for future support of this and similar programs in a Republican-controlled Congress. Rose Gottemoeller, former Director for Russia, Ukraine, and Eurasia on the National Security Council staff responsible for denuclearization, also focuses on the politics of nonproliferation assistance, but with more attention to the interagency dimension of the process. Her chapter includes a cautionary tale of how bureaucratic-organizational pressures can conspire to undermine the effectiveness of U.S. assistance, and she offers prescriptions for strengthening future CTR initiatives.

The middle third of the book contains analyses of U.S. and other Western cooperative assistance from several perspectives in NIS recipient countries. Among the six contributors to this discussion are senior officials from NIS governments who have coordinated program activities with U.S. officials, military personnel charged with executing the demilitarization programs, and scholars and public policy analysts from the post-Soviet republics who have closely followed the program's implementation. Russia, by virtue of the size of its nuclear infrastructure, has commanded the bulk of U.S. and other Western assistance. The structure of this section of the book reflects this reality and begins with three chapters devoted to CTR implementation in Russia, each written from a distinct point of view.

Vladimir Orlov, Director of the Center for Policy Studies in Russia (PIR Center) and editor of the journal *Yadernyi Kontrol* (Nuclear control), surveys key Russian decision-makers who have directed Russian nuclear security and demilitarization policies. Regarding cooperative U.S.-Russian threat reduction, Orlov provides an overview of the opinions of these decision-makers and outlines the political pressures that have influenced these perspectives. Alexander Pikayev, Director of the Committee for Critical Technologies and Nonproliferation in Moscow, provides a detailed analysis of Nunn-Lugar programs and spending. Comparing the U.S. assistance effort to Russia's own spending on its demilitarization and nuclear security requirements, Pikayev identifies a number of areas where U.S. assistance might be put to more effective use. Moreover, as an advisor to the Russian Duma on national security issues, Pikayev offers a number of insights on the Russian legislature's views on these issues. A third perspective on U.S.-Russian demilitarization cooperation is provided by General Evgenii Maslin, Head of Strategic Forces of the 12th Directorate of Russia's Ministry of Defense. General Maslin was instrumental in implementing the most time-urgent and sensitive areas of U.S.-Russian cooperation—safe and secure transport of nuclear weapons from non-Russian republics and consolidation of these weapons in Russia. General Maslin provides an assessment of the problems and achievements of U.S. cooperative assistance in this area from an operational perspective.

Subsequent chapters in this section provide analyses of the CTR Program from each of the three non-Russian republics that inherited portions of the Soviet nuclear weapons complex. Kostyantyn Hryshchenko, Ukraine's Deputy Foreign Minister, assesses the CTR

Program's impact on his country's efforts to dismantle its nuclear weapons infrastructure. Vyachaslau Paznyak, Director of the International Institute for Policy Studies in Minsk, outlines Belarus's demilitarization priorities and the impact of the CTR Program on implementing these plans. Finally, three leading Kazakstani analysts, Oumirserik Kasenov, Dastan Eleukenov, and Murat Laumulin, discuss the problems and prospects of Kazakstan's defense conversion, nuclear security, and nonproliferation agenda, and the role played by U.S. assistance in achieving these objectives.

The last portion of this volume more closely examines and assesses seven specific cases of U.S.-NIS cooperation under the CTR Program. These case studies cover the full range of U.S.-NIS technical and political cooperation.

Three of these selections focus on activities directed at Russian nuclear scientists. Oleg Bukharin, a physicist currently affiliated with Princeton University's Center for Energy and Environmental Studies, provides a detailed analysis of the structure and activities of Russia's Ministry of Atomic Energy. After reviewing the mixed U.S. record of interaction with this key but highly secretive ministry, he suggests how one might establish a more productive relationship for technical cooperation. Katherine Johnson, a Department of Defense official previously on assignment with Los Alamos National Laboratory, describes the Department of Energy's laboratory-to-laboratory program of cooperation between U.S. and Russian nuclear research facilities. She recommends a number of ways in which that program's very successful grass-roots or "bottom-up" approach to denuclearization assistance might be applied more broadly to government-to-government programs. Adam Moody of the Monterey Institute's Center for Nonproliferation Studies provides a detailed review and assessment of the multilateral initiative, funded in part by the CTR Program, to provide former Soviet weapons scientists with non-military research opportunities.

A second set of case studies focuses on CTR activities involving the threat of nuclear material diversion and export. Ambassador Michael Newlin, a former career diplomat involved in implementing export control aspects of the Nunn-Lugar Program in the NIS, discusses ongoing legislative and technological measures in Russia, Ukraine, Belarus, and Kazakhstan to control the flow of critical nuclear and nuclear-related dual-use materials and technologies across national borders. Jessica Stern, a former staff member of the National Security

Council, depicts the institutional problems associated with fissile material controls in former Soviet states and assesses the progress to date of government-to-government and lab-to-lab programs to improve physical protection, material control, and accounting at key NIS nuclear facilities. William Potter, Director of the Monterey Institute's Center for Nonproliferation Studies, indicates both the opportunities and challenges of post–Cold War diplomacy in his recounting of "Project Sapphire," a joint U.S.-Kazakstani effort to remove hundreds of kilograms of weapons-grade uranium from Kazakstan to more secure storage in the United States.

The section of case studies concludes with a review of the progress made and problems remaining in the chemical weapons demilitarization component of the CTR Program. Former Russian diplomat Igor Khripunov examines the technical, bureaucratic, and political obstacles to U.S.-Russian cooperation in this sphere, as well as the international security implications should cooperation falter.

This volume concludes with a set of lessons learned from the CTR Program. A review of those CTR activities that were most successful suggests the importance of a symmetry of interests and objectives between U.S. and NIS participants. It also highlights the need for shared, equal, and active involvement by U.S. and NIS parties, as partners rather than donors and recipients. Other factors that contribute to CTR successes are the opportunity for frequent and routine communication between U.S. and NIS participants and the presence of incentives to foster bureaucratic flexibility and cost-consciousness. It is imperative that these lessons inform future cooperative threat reduction efforts if preventive defense is to remain a viable nonproliferation strategy.

U.S. Perspectives on the CTR Program

Chapter 2

Cooperative Threat Reduction in Perspective

Gloria Duffy

Ukraine's shipment of the last of some 1,600 strategic nuclear warheads on its territory to Russia for dismantlement on June 1, 1996, was the dramatic finale to an extraordinary process. This event, and many other positive developments related to the security and dismantling of weapons of mass destruction in the former Soviet Union, are the result of a very unusual cooperative effort since 1992 between the United States and four governments of the newly independent states (NIS) to prevent the proliferation of nuclear weapons, weapons-usable fissile materials, and other sensitive weapons, materials, and expertise.

For the United States, this process, known as cooperative threat reduction (CTR), funded and organized beginning in the fall of 1991 through the Nunn-Lugar program, is a novel departure from normal means of pursuing security policy in general, and nonproliferation in particular. While certain historical analogs exist—the Marshall Plan is sometimes cited as economic assistance in the service of political or national security goals—the Nunn-Lugar effort goes considerably beyond the traditional methods of diplomatic exhortation, threats, pressure, cartels, or other means that have been used to pursue nonproliferation goals.

As the Soviet Union began to disintegrate in the fall of 1991, the United States and the world community were faced with the danger of 30,000 strategic nuclear weapons on Soviet territory, 3,200 of them outside Russia. In addition, there existed in this region the equivalent of 100,000 nuclear explosive charges in the form of tons of plutonium and highly enriched uranium, thousands of nuclear scientists with

---

The author would like to thank the John D. and Catherine T. MacArthur Foundation and the Center for International Security and Arms Control at Stanford University for supporting work on this chapter.

weapons-related expertise, scores of industrial enterprises producing components for weapons of mass destruction, ballistic missiles and other delivery systems, and a vast array of other weapons and strategic materials left behind when the Soviet Union collapsed.

The United States faced similar challenges in the aftermath of the Cold War: controlling and dismantling a huge stockpile of weapons of mass destruction, and converting a large infrastructure of weapons scientists and defense production capacity to peaceful purposes. But it faced these challenges from the secure base of a robust economy and stable political administration. The NIS, however, confronted these problems amid rapid political change and economic privation. With the possible exception of Ukraine, the non-Russian republics in particular had no direct experience in controlling, dismantling, or otherwise dealing with nuclear weapons, their components, and the infrastructure supporting them.

The U.S. effort to encourage the NIS toward certain types of actions to secure, dismantle, and convert the weapons complexes on their territories, and to aid them in taking those steps, has been absolutely unique. It is important to remember how unprecedented it was for the former Cold War adversaries, within three years of the fall of the Berlin Wall, to be collaborating in the disposition of the most sensitive military capabilities of the former Soviet Union. It has required cooperation of the most unusual sort both within the U.S. government and between the United States and the NIS governments, breaking down patterns of thought and behavior entrenched during decades of hostility. It is easy to take this cooperation for granted, but to do so obscures the pathbreaking nature of this effort.

To borrow a phrase from Dick Combs, "how well the dog can dance is not so remarkable as the fact that the dog can dance at all." A number of "dogs," including the Pentagon, the Russian Ministry of Defense, the new governments of Ukraine, Belarus, and Kazakstan, and U.S. and foreign companies, have been dancing in remarkable ways to make the Nunn-Lugar program work during the past five years. There have naturally been glitches and unrealized potential in an enterprise this unusual. However, it is essential to keep in mind the unprecedented and demanding nature of the effort in any evaluation of how this program has performed.

The cooperative threat reduction approach has unquestionably been highly successful. There are many qualitative and quantitative indicators of its success in safeguarding and reducing nuclear weapons.

It played an important role in the decisions of Ukraine, Belarus, and Kazakstan to forgo nuclear weapons capabilities, and in their abilities to carry out those decisions. CTR is assisting in the dismantlement of thousands of strategic launchers. It has led to the creation of over 50 joint projects between former adversaries, ranging from chopping up Russian strategic bombers more efficiently to work involving the United States, Russia, and Kazakstan to permanently seal the test tunnels at the former Soviet nuclear weapons test site at Semipalatinsk.

What particularly stands out about this enterprise is that the U.S. goals of encouraging the newly independent former Soviet states to dismantle and safeguard nuclear weapons could not have been accomplished by any other means, either by traditional diplomacy or by military force. The U.S. offer of assistance to the NIS to undertake projects deemed important by the United States introduced U.S. concerns about nonproliferation—which in many ways reflected the concerns of the international community—into decision-making processes in the NIS. Assistance also supported those individuals and organizations within the NIS who wished to bring these issues closer to the top of the policy agenda of these new and beleaguered nations.

The approach represented by the Nunn-Lugar program is in fact a fundamentally new method of pursuing U.S. national security objectives, and it foreshadows an important future security strategy for the United States. It is an approach that can be called "preventive" or prophylactic, rather than reactive, defense. It relies upon the United States utilizing its economic and technical resources to become directly engaged in shaping the outcome of events in various regions of the world to prevent the emergence of serious security threats before they require a more costly and demanding response by military means. U.S. Secretary of Defense William Perry has been the leader not only in practicing this preventive approach to defense but also in giving it a broader conceptualization.

Preventive defense is an important case in point of the Clinton administration's foreign policy strategy of engagement. It is a prudent future direction for U.S. security policy simply because the security problems the United States faces today are less and less susceptible to solution through traditional approaches of military force, deterrence, or even standard diplomacy.

The dangers of proliferation in and from the former Soviet Union are a perfect example of this new security environment. It is clear from a review of the more traditional tools of security policy that none of

these methods could have accomplished the same goals that cooperative threat reduction has achieved. Diplomatic or economic pressure
placed on would-be proliferators in the past—Pakistan being a prime
example—has generally backfired, and possibly even created a greater
siege mentality in the target country, increasing the probability of
nuclearization. Early attempts by the United States to use these
traditional methods with the NIS, especially Ukraine, were not
productive either.

Besides embodying a new approach to U.S. security policy,
cooperative threat reduction has played a unique role in opening up
communication and establishing a base for the relationship between the
United States and the countries of the former Soviet Union. In the cases
of Ukraine, Belarus, and Kazakstan, the Nunn-Lugar program negotiations and discussions were essentially the first in-depth direct channel
of communication begun between these governments and Washington.
This makes sense, because before the United States and these emerging
republics could build a new, post–Cold War basis for their relationships, it was natural to meet on the common ground of dealing with the
aftermath of the Cold War—the weapons, bases, scientists, and defense
production complexes that each side had built to defend against the
other. The United States and the NIS shared the experience of the Cold
War buildup and then, from necessity, shared the experience of
dismantling the weapons and their infrastructure.

Seen in this light, some of the most important aspects of the Nunn-
Lugar effort are those that established a more lasting basis for the
relationship between the United States and Russia, Belarus, Ukraine,
and Kazakstan. Funded at only a fraction of the total Nunn-Lugar
budget, the program of military-to-military contacts under this
initiative is establishing ongoing contacts between the uniformed and
civilian defense structures of the United States and the NIS.

Ranging from high-level consultations on defense policy to
meetings on guarding borders, the military-to-military contacts
program moves beyond the nuclear weapons issues to establish the
basis for a relationship between the United States and the NIS. The
program supports consultations on matters of common concern
between the U.S. and NIS societies, such as the organization of defense
ministries in a democracy. The program has also been the vehicle for
planning joint peacekeeping exercises. The military-to-military
dialogue is extraordinarily important in the establishment of multilevel
and positive relationships between the United States and the NIS,

where none existed previously. In 1995 alone, the United States engaged in over 100 joint military activities of this kind with Russia, Ukraine, Belarus, and Kazakstan.

Another general benefit is that through the Nunn-Lugar program, the United States has begun to develop a habit of openness with its partners in Russia, Ukraine, Kazakstan, and Belarus that did not exist during the Cold War years. The exchange of baseline information about military practices and procedures, frequent updates and progress reports on joint projects, and regular meetings and consultations are all important aspects of moving beyond the closed and secretive ways of the Cold War. These new habits have given former adversaries the benefit of learning from each other and understanding each other's practices and experiences.

For example, through Nunn-Lugar consultations, the United States and Russia have exchanged very useful comparative information on how the two countries provide security for nuclear weapons during transport and storage. This exchange has worked both ways, with the United States providing information on its procedures, as well as Russia on its own practices. This information exchange has been extremely useful for designing effective Nunn-Lugar programs on nuclear weapons security. Moreover, the knowledge each side now has of the other's procedures will be helpful should a crisis occur in either country in which a nuclear facility was under attack or sabotaged or a nuclear weapon was stolen, diverted, or otherwise misused. The United States and Russia will now be able to consult on cooperative measures to deal with such a crisis based on better knowledge about the situation in each other's country.

Similarly, the much maligned Nunn-Lugar defense conversion program has a larger role to play in the establishment of positive relations between the United States and its former adversaries. It has interested U.S. companies in becoming involved in commercial projects in the NIS where they would otherwise have been unwilling to take the risk. It has also been a channel for communicating important information about the operation of a market economy, as well as specifically converting defense production capabilities to civilian production.

In evaluating the Nunn-Lugar program's specific achievements, it is easy to lose sight of these larger roles played by the program. But in many ways, these often unspoken roles and effects of the Nunn-Lugar effort are its most significant outcomes.

Accomplishments of the Program

These general benefits alone would be worth the $1.5 billion (0.2 percent of the annual U.S. defense budget) that the Nunn-Lugar program has so far cost U.S. taxpayers. But of course, the Nunn-Lugar program has also registered important specific successes for denuclearization and demilitarization in the former Soviet Union.

There is no need here to enumerate in detail the specific successes of the Nunn-Lugar program because they are so avidly chronicled and debated elsewhere in this volume. Nonetheless, a few major accomplishments bear mentioning.

The first, of course, is the role the Nunn-Lugar program played in encouraging the decisions of Ukraine, Belarus, and Kazakstan to renounce nuclear weapons and become non-nuclear weapons state parties to the Non-Proliferation Treaty (NPT). Some people challenge the notion that Nunn-Lugar did play an important role in these decisions, and question how this process really worked.

Ukraine offers the clearest example of how the availability of assistance made a difference. U.S. offers of assistance first opened the door in the summer of 1993 for the U.S. government to discuss the nuclear weapons in Ukraine with the Ukrainian Ministry of Defense. And in the end, as Kostyantyn Hryshchenko notes (Chapter 8 in this volume), the Ukrainian Rada made the receipt of adequate U.S. denuclearization aid one of the conditions in November 1993 for ratification of START I and the removal of all nuclear weapons from Ukrainian soil. Until this condition was fulfilled, START I could not go into effect. Until Ukraine became committed to START, NPT accession was impossible. In Ukraine, from the beginning to the end of the process, the relationship between U.S. assistance and denuclearization was quite clear.

This is not in any way to diminish Ukraine's independent decision to become a non-nuclear state. The decision was a courageous one made by Ukraine's leaders alone, and they deserve a great deal of respect for making this choice. It was a choice of world wide significance for nonproliferation. One shudders to think how different and negative the atmosphere would have been at the 1995 NPT Extension Conference had Ukraine just decided to join the nuclear club as one of its most well-armed members, instead of becoming a non-nuclear party to the NPT.

Many of the advances brought about through cooperative threat reduction are quite concrete. Here I will simply give some examples of the more than 50 joint projects undertaken by the United States together with Russia, Kazakstan, Belarus, or Ukraine:

- providing Russia with equipment to speed the dismantling of launchers and delivery systems;

- helping Ukraine to safely store the heptyl propellant from de-activated SS-19 intercontinental ballistic missiles (ICBMs) so that deactivation could continue on schedule;

- working together with Russia to design a secure facility to store fissile material from dismantled nuclear weapons;

- collaborating with Belarus to create a model of how to clean up and reuse a nuclear base for civilian purposes;

- helping Belarus destroy the launch pads for SS-25 mobile missiles, in an environmentally sound manner;

- cooperating through the International Science and Technology Center (ISTC) with all four nuclear NIS as well as the European Community (EC) and Japan, with nearly $100 million in funding from the United States, the EC, and Japan, to provide alternative employment for NIS scientists who have designed weapons of mass destruction;

- working with Kazakstan to dismantle the SS-18 silos in that country;

- providing a contractor to Russia to help develop a strategy for disposing of Russia's stockpile of 40,000 tons of chemical weapons and eventually to help design facilities for its disposal;

- working together with Russia, albeit with some difficulty, to better protect stockpiles of weapons-usable fissile materials from misuse or diversion;

- cooperating with Russia, very productively, to improve security of nuclear weapons in Russia during storage and transport by providing computers for keeping real-time data on the weapons, diagnostic railcars to assess the condition of railway tracks, and other equipment;

- assisting Ukraine to dismantle strategic missiles and launchers;

- working jointly with Kazakstan and Russia to permanently seal the test tunnels at the former Soviet nuclear test site at Semipalatinsk;

- collaborating with all four countries to convert defense enterprises to civilian purposes, resulting in the creation of more than 20 projects involving conversion of defense plants to civilian production;

- assisting Ukraine and Russia to build housing for the Strategic Rocket Forces troops demobilized as a result of the reduction in deployed nuclear weapons, including housing in Russia for demobilized troops responsible for guarding nuclear weapons;

- establishing direct communications links between the United States and Ukraine, Belarus, and Kazakstan; and

- working with Kazakstan, via Project Sapphire, to remove 600 kilograms of poorly secured, highly enriched uranium from Ulba to secure storage at Oak Ridge, Tennessee.

The list of projects continues at some length, today representing a very extensive range of cooperation in dismantlement, conversion, and demilitarization of weapons of mass destruction, their delivery systems, and the complex of plants and scientists that supported their development, manufacture, and maintenance.

One might argue that the number of projects begun is less important than how effective they have been at reducing the threat of proliferation, and whether the interests of all parties—the United States, the four recipient NIS, and the international nonproliferation regime—have been met through this effort. The following section addresses this question.

Critiques of the Program

The Cooperative Threat Reduction program has been criticized from all sides, in the U.S. Congress, by the U.S. General Accounting Office (GAO), and not least of all by some of the U.S. partners in recipient countries. The criticisms have covered the waterfront. Some members of Congress have charged that the Nunn-Lugar program has not brought about concrete results for dismantlement and denuclearization. Some, such as Representative Norman Dicks (Democrat–Washington) have worried that assistance to Russia liberates Moscow to spend funds on further military developments that could threaten the United States or the international community.

The GAO has charged that funds provided to Russian scientists for research on the environment or health sciences are underwriting their continued work on nuclear weapons, since the funding provided through the ISTC does not in all cases pay for 100 percent of weapons scientists' time. Meanwhile, observers from the recipient countries complain that the program has been slow to perform, that funds are expended slowly, that projects do not meet their interests, and that, in implementing CTR projects, the United States buys U.S. technology that is readily available in the NIS rather than purchasing it locally.

This chapter will not address all of these critiques. But it is important to note that many of the critics of the Nunn-Lugar program understandably see the effort from their own, sometimes narrow, institutional or national perspectives. It is rare to find an overview of the entire program, its objectives, and performance. Many of the critiques stem from what appears to be an incomplete understanding of the program; many of the flaws that are pointed out by various analysts of the program are approaches that exist for a reason, even if an arcane one peculiar to the American system of government. A few examples of this phenomenon are described below.

One example of a criticism stemming from incomplete information about the CTR program is the frequent complaint of both U.S. analysts and representatives of recipient countries about the U.S. practice of contracting domestically rather than in the NIS for much of the assistance to be provided to the NIS. It is correctly pointed out that this practice creates resentment, does not create a strong economic interest in the program in the recipient states, and may lead the United States to spend more than is necessary on the items provided. The congressional mandate to work through U.S. technology and technicians whenever possible is cited as the main reason for this contracting preference. And the U.S. Defense Department is sometimes criticized for an overly rigid interpretation of contracting procedures.

In fact, with the exception of defense conversion projects, it is inaccurate to argue that the United States has required contracting for Nunn-Lugar assistance to be with U.S. firms. What the United States is required to do by law is to operate by the principles of "free and fair competition" in its federal procurement activities. The U.S. government cannot simply choose to buy goods from a particular company, be it domestic or foreign, but must submit contracts to bid, just as any municipal government must do for street maintenance contracts.

This means that any company, foreign or domestic, is free to bid on a contract for a Nunn-Lugar project. To win, the company must be able to leap the hurdles of the contracting process to present the most attractive bid. Firms in the NIS have been eligible to bid on Nunn-Lugar contracts, and in a number of cases representatives of the NIS governments have sat with American contracting officers in Washington as part of the contractor selection process. The largest single Nunn-Lugar contract—for intermodal railcars to transport liquid rocket fuel in Russia—is actually held by a French firm, not an American company, which won the contract in competitive bidding. NIS firms, for various reasons, either have not bid or have not been very successful in bidding for CTR program contracts. There are exceptions, however. Contracts have been awarded to private firms in Kazakstan, and both private firms and a government agency in Ukraine, for dismantlement activities.

There is an alternative to "free and fair competition": "sole source" contracting. This means that for urgent national security reasons, the United States can decide to simply pick a single source for a contract. The Defense Department on a number of occasions did decide to obtain Nunn-Lugar goods through sole sourcing to a Ukrainian, Russian, or Kazakstani firm. Examples are the purchase of cranes and heptyl storage tanks in Ukraine in 1994 and contracting in 1995 with two Kazakstani firms for some of the work to dismantle the SS-18 silos.

But each time the U.S. government did this, it took a risk that the strategy would backfire. If the government awards a sole-source contract, companies that believe they have a right to bid on the contract can lodge a protest and put the project on hold for weeks or months while the issue is adjudicated. Protests have in fact been lodged in a few Nunn-Lugar cases, putting some projects on hold. And so the preference has been, where possible, to proceed with the normal, competitive contracting procedures to avoid unnecessary delays.

In Fiscal Years (FY) 1996 and 1997, Congress has begun to provide some latitude in the wording of Nunn-Lugar legislation which encourages purchase of equipment in the NIS. The United States should definitely take advantage of this wherever possible to procure more of the assistance locally in the NIS. But the prudence of avoiding legal challenges to the program remains valid.

Another understandable misconception is the complaint that less than half of the total Nunn-Lugar funds allocated to the NIS have actually been spent to date. This is hardly surprising if one understands that all Nunn-Lugar agreements are multiyear projects, with the expenditure of funds planned over a period of several years as both parties to a project proceed with the work. There was never an intention to spend all the funds in the first year or two of most of the projects, and indeed, to do so would in many cases be wasteful or unwelcome by the NIS government agencies involved in the projects.

With regard to implementation of CTR projects, the pace may seem slow to recipient countries. But it is actually somewhat extraordinary that only about a year elapsed from the time when strategic launcher dismantling agreements were reached with Russia, Ukraine, and Kazakstan to the time when equipment was procured, shipped, and put to use in these countries. In some cases, the time that passed between agreement on a project and arrival of the assistance in a recipient country was considerably shorter.

The review of attitudes in various agencies in Russia toward the CTR program, provided by Vladimir Orlov elsewhere in this volume, is very helpful. However, it is curious that this survey does not mention, or assess the views of, the agency that is the largest recipient of CTR assistance in Russia. This is the Ministry (formerly State Committee) for Defense Industries (MDI), which has responsibility for dismantling bombers, silos, land-based and sea-based strategic launchers, and in general the tasks of dismantling strategic delivery systems in Russia. In Russia, it is to MDI that the United States has provided the most Nunn-Lugar equipment and supplies for dismantling strategic systems.

The MDI has always expressed a very positive attitude toward its cooperation with the United States in the CTR program, and has always been a practical, positive collaborator with the United States. Certainly the views of senior MDI officials such as Minister Zenoviy Pak, former

Chairman Viktor Glukhikh, or dismantlement program director Nikolai Shumkov should be taken into account in a survey of Russian government attitudes. Sometimes the agencies that express the greatest concerns about the program, such as Russia's Ministry of Atomic Energy (Minatom), are not those that have the broadest or deepest working relationship with the United States in the Cooperative Threat Reduction program.

These clarifications are not intended to criticize those who raise concerns about the program. The United States should make every effort to address the concerns of recipient countries and agencies, including speeding the delivery of assistance and making sure it is provided in a form and at times that are most useful to the recipients. The U.S. government owes this not only to the recipient countries, but to the U.S. taxpayer as well. But it is important to keep an overview of the effort in mind, and to keep a sense of perspective about how unusual and complex these activities are. It takes time to get these efforts moving, and inevitably there will be some false starts and mistakes. Good communication, of exactly the sort represented by the dialogue in this volume, is essential to making the cooperation between the United States and its NIS partners more effective.

It is also important for the American audience to remember that the Nunn-Lugar effort can do some things very well, such as most of the projects that have been undertaken jointly with the NIS governments to date. But there are some accomplishments of which cooperative threat reduction is not capable. These include converting the entire excess nuclear weapons complex of Russia, Ukraine, Belarus, and Kazakstan to peaceful purposes, and supporting the transition to peaceful research and development (R&D) of the entire group of Soviet weapons scientists who have been involved in developing weapons of mass destruction. There are not enough funds in the U.S. Treasury to accomplish such feats. Thus there will always be questions about whether the problems of retraining weapons scientists, converting defense industries, and protecting weapons or fissile material in the recipient countries have been completely solved.

Cooperative threat reduction can act as a catalyst, as a partner in the efforts the NIS are themselves making, and can reduce the probability that weapons, material, or know-how will proliferate from the NIS. But this approach cannot by itself solve many of these problems.

For example, one project that has been a perennial headache for both U.S. and Russian officials is the attempt to construct a centralized, secure storage facility in the Ural Mountains at Mayak for plutonium from dismantled nuclear weapons. Beyond some systemic difficulties for the U.S. and Russia in working together on a project in the sensitive area of nuclear weapons, I believe the core of the problem has been the lack of sufficient financial resources from either the United States or Russia to move ahead and complete the project. The United States has allocated $90 million to the project from CTR funds. The total price tag is probably about four times that amount. The Russian government, in this case Minatom, has been unwilling to make a commitment to proceed with the project because in their lean financial circumstances they cannot with confidence commit several hundred million dollars from the Russian state budget to this effort.

And so the two countries are engaged in a dance involving small steps forward, long delays while each side waits for the other to make further financial commitments, and a frustratingly slow pace of progress toward the goal. The fundamental problem is the lack of combined financial resources to bring this project to fruition. In this case, the solution is probably to turn to other donor countries, perhaps Japan in particular, to contribute additional funds to the effort. The storage facility project is an example of the limitations of the CTR program to solve entirely and by itself large and costly nuclear security problems.

The fact that not all problems can be completely solved by the CTR effort seems obvious, but it often appears as though certain individuals and groups, particularly members of the U.S. Congress, have unreasonably high expectations for what the United States can do with relatively small sums of money.

What has made cooperative threat reduction succeed has been the willingness of the United States and its NIS partners to work through their differences and the burdens of Cold War attitudes to find common ground. Finding a balance of common interests has made possible every agreement, project, and cooperative effort undertaken through the CTR effort. In some cases, finding common interests has meant that the United States has addressed the social, economic, or environmental concerns of the recipient country, when they have been connected to demilitarization or denuclearization, as part of a project in pursuit of U.S. goals of dismantlement or denuclearization. In other cases, the NIS, particularly Russia, have taken steps to break down barriers of secrecy rooted in the Cold War era, when these habits stood in the way of undertaking a common project.

As General Evgenii Maslin notes (Chapter 7 in these pages), much has depended on the relationships formed between those working together on behalf of the United States and the NIS. General Maslin himself has stood out as a man with a clear sense of the higher interests involved in the joint work between the United States and Russia, and, as a consequence, the cooperation between the U.S. Department of Defense and the Russian Ministry of Defense has been particularly productive.

The Future

As positive as the CTR effort has been in general, both dangers and opportunities lie ahead for the program. A great deal of public attention has focused on the problem of unprotected, weapons-grade fissile material located in the former Soviet Union, particularly in Russia. This is indeed a major threat, as terrorists and rogue states seem ever more likely to seek weapons of mass destruction. Doing something about this problem is probably the single most important challenge for the CTR program in the next few years.

Quite rightly, a major emphasis for CTR in 1997 and beyond is in helping the NIS, particularly Russia, to improve the security of fissile material. This effort is being pursued through both government-to-government cooperation, and the less formal lab-to-lab collaboration. While the government-to-government program has made some progress at Russia's national labs, the lab-to-lab approach has been more effective in actually putting in place physical security for fissile materials at other laboratories, production plants, storage sites, processing facilities at Russia's military facilities which are closed to Western access, and other sites.

It is unlikely that any of the technical measures now under way to deal with security of fissile materials will be fully effective until the Russian scientific and industrial community takes full responsibility for the problem of possible leakage of fissile material and becomes self-policing. There is precedent for this type of scientific responsibility in Russia; Andrei Sakharov was a resounding voice to the scientific community to undertake such responsibilities. Preventing fissile material, or even chemical weapons, from falling into the hands of terrorists is a moral imperative equal to those of human rights and disarmament which Sakharov exhorted his colleagues to embrace.

The United States should continue to support scientists and government officials in Russia in improving the security of fissile materials, and encourage them in every possible way to take this threat seriously. The U.S. Congress should provide adequate funding for this effort, even in a climate when foreign aid, including the Nunn-Lugar program, is under attack. We are working against time to secure these materials against the very present danger that terrorists are attempting to gain access to them. What could be a more self-interested priority for U.S. foreign assistance?

The CTR program can also help in the future with high-priority weapons dismantlement efforts in the NIS that are beyond the scope of current projects. For example, one of the factors that will influence Russia's decision about whether to undertake the obligation of acceding to START II will be whether adequate economic resources are available to implement the treaty. CTR funds can help with the tasks of START II implementation, such as building a plant for the elimination of solid rocket motors, and perhaps help to alleviate one of the hesitations the Russian Duma has about ratifying the treaty.

In fact, there is no shortage of constructive projects that could be undertaken through Nunn-Lugar cooperation. The real question is whether the CTR program will survive the challenges of a shifting political environment in Russia and the continuing fragility of support for the program in the U.S. Congress.

An unusual level of cooperation and transparency has been achieved through Nunn-Lugar programs with Russia. However, as Yeltsin's democratic, reformist government is challenged by both Communists and nationalists, suspicions may continue to grow about U.S. objectives in pursuing openness, particularly when it involves militarily sensitive Russian facilities, weapons, and programs. This may curtail some aspects of CTR cooperation, particularly those related to fissile material security, nuclear weapons security, defense conversion, and reemployment of scientists from the weapons labs on civilian projects. The United States and Russia have "pushed the envelope" over the past few years, engaging in reciprocal visits to each other's nuclear weapons facilities. They have moved beyond the Cold War limits of secrecy, but this evolution is not supported by all constituencies, either in Russia or the United States.

This effort should continue, toward a regime of greater transparency and accountability in U.S. and Russian nuclear facilities and stockpiles of weapons and fissile materials. Pursuing this regime is in the interests of the United States and Russia, particularly in an international environment where both countries face threats from terrorists and rogue states in pursuit of weapons of mass destruction. The more familiar each side is with the other's assets and procedures, the more each coordinates with the other and takes better account of weapons and fissile material on each side's territory, then the better both countries will be able to deal with these external threats. And the more progress that the United States and Russia make toward reciprocal transparency and accountability, the more solid ground they will be on when they ask other countries to open their facilities and weapons programs to outside examination.

But continuing to develop the regime of cooperation and transparency will present a challenge in the current environment, and strong vision and leadership will be required by U.S. and Russian leaders to continue to make progress. The challenge will grow more acute as NATO moves toward expansion, which is sure to create some negative feelings in Russia, particularly among those constituencies that are already skeptical about U.S. objectives in the CTR program and the level of U.S.-Russian cooperation.

But the greater threat to CTR cooperation may be in the United States. Support for the Nunn-Lugar program has gone from a strong, bipartisan consensus in the first two years (although, as Dick Combs notes, the program was almost stillborn in 1991), through a trough of skepticism and discord in 1994–95. This is a bit strange since during the first 18 months little was accomplished through the program, but beginning in 1993 real progress toward its objectives began to occur.

There are many different agendas at work in U.S. congressional attitudes toward the CTR program. Some members of Congress have problems with U.S. foreign aid in general. Others do not wish to see federal monies spent on defense industry conversion abroad when they are not spent on industry conversion at home. Still others believe that defense budget dollars in particular should not be spent on such a nontraditional approach to defense.

One thing seems clear, however: the debate over whether the CTR program is a valuable expenditure of U.S. tax dollars is an "inside the Beltway" issue. By all indications, the American people instinctively understand that preventive defense measures such as the CTR program make sense for the United States and are well worth the expenditure of funds. A common reaction from members of the public, when learning about the CTR program, is to say that it is the best use they have ever heard of for U.S. tax dollars. Members of Congress who oppose this approach would do well to consult their constituents, because the voters understand it and support it.

In leaving the Senate, Senator Sam Nunn made a wise effort to embed the FY 1997 CTR program in a larger legislative package, including measures to deal with potential terrorist use of nuclear, chemical, or biological weapons within the United States. The approach taken in legislation sponsored by Senators Nunn, Lugar, and Domenici, sometimes referred to as "Nunn-Lugar II," makes substantive as well as political sense since the challenges of dealing with proliferation at home and abroad are related, and both can be approached through preventive measures.

But the very fact that Senator Nunn and his colleagues had to go to such lengths to interweave CTR with domestic programs in order to generate support for the concept demonstrates that this unique and successful avenue is still not fully legitimated as a valid approach to U.S. defense. It is still regarded as something of a stepchild—not "real" defense.

As stated at the outset, the traditional tools of security policy are ever less appropriate for the security challenges that the United States faces now and will face in the future. How could military force, deterrence, or even traditional diplomacy have persuaded Ukraine to become non-nuclear or North Korea to stop operating nuclear reactors producing bomb-grade nuclear material? Preventive defense will be a central, not peripheral, approach to dealing with such threats in the future. What is needed in the Congress is a paradigm shift that brings preventive approaches like the CTR effort more into focus as mainstream defense strategies.

While it is necessary for now to legitimate the Nunn-Lugar program by connecting it to programs with more domestic support, in the long run the best way to solidify its support will probably be to broaden the concept, to apply the CTR idea to other security problems worldwide, and hence to demonstrate the general validity of the approach.

Chapter 3

U.S. Domestic Politics and the Nunn-Lugar Program

Richard Combs

Government officials in the nuclear successor states of the former Soviet Union (FSU) who have been the recipients of U.S. assistance through the Cooperative Threat Reduction (CTR) Program and other initiatives, have, in the past, demonstrated little understanding of the political context surrounding these programs. Many of these officials assume that the Nunn-Lugar CTR Program enjoys broad, bipartisan support in the U.S. Congress. They tend to assume, therefore, that the problems they have experienced with the program are due to the way in which bureaucrats within the U.S. administration have implemented the program's provisions. While the latter assumption is arguable, the former assumption is wholly wrong, particularly as it applies to congressional consideration of Nunn-Lugar legislation for Fiscal Year (FY) 1996.

Officials and the public at large in CTR recipient countries need to have a fuller understanding of why many of their concerns about the program have not been satisfied by the U.S. executive branch. They need to appreciate the role that Congress and congressional politics have had in creating, shaping, and continuing the Nunn-Lugar effort, even if this aspect of the program's history may be somewhat unsettling. While other chapters of this volume have focused on the execution of the CTR Program in particular countries or in specific project areas, the purpose of this chapter is to examine the legislative history behind the CTR initiative and derivative threat reduction programs. This chapter attempts to describe how domestic political factors in the United States have played a role in U.S. assistance programs for the former Soviet Union. In doing so, its goal is not only to give government officials in CTR recipient countries a fuller understanding of the political forces that have shaped assistance to their countries, but also to provide policymakers in both the United States and these recipient states a template for future action.

This chapter begins with a review of the key personnel and events surrounding early legislative attempts to provide demilitarization and denuclearization assistance to the Soviet Union and the eventual development of the Nunn-Lugar initiative. It then traces the progress of this initiative from FY 1992 until the present and considers how the program has changed or was shaped to meet a number of competing political pressures. Moreover, it examines how two administrations—one Republican, one Democratic—have used the initiative in their policies toward the Soviet Union and, subsequently, toward former Soviet states. Particular attention is given in this chapter to the implications of the "Republican revolution" in November 1994. The change in congressional leadership in that year had a dramatic effect on the CTR Program and brought to light some fundamental differences within the Congress over the purpose and scope of CTR and similar endeavors. This assessment concludes by considering how lessons learned from the CTR Program's fractious political history may help guide future efforts to carry out its ambitious nonproliferation and demilitarization goals.

Legislative Origins of the Nunn-Lugar Program

The CTR Program came very close to defeat during the initial attempts to develop it in the fall of 1991. In response to deteriorating political, military, and economic conditions in the Soviet Union, Senator Sam Nunn (Democrat–Georgia), then chairman of the Senate Armed Services Committee (SASC), and Congressman Les Aspin (Democrat–Wisconsin), then chairman of the House Armed Services Committee (HASC), attempted in that year to assemble a legislative initiative that would provide Moscow with emergency food and medical supplies as well as with technical assistance to safely transport, store, and dismantle its nuclear and chemical weapons. The Nunn-Aspin initiative also attempted to provide assistance for conversion of Soviet defense production facilities to civilian uses, environmental cleanup of sites contaminated by decades of Soviet weapons development, and occupational retraining and housing for decommissioned Soviet Strategic Rocket Forces officers.

House and Senate Republicans adamantly opposed the threat reduction package assembled by Nunn and Aspin. Several Republican members of the Senate Armed Services Committee went so far as to hold a press conference to criticize the officer housing and training aspects of the package. The legislation nonetheless was approved by the two defense authorization committees and added to the FY 1992 defense authorization bill, but only after straight party-line votes in both committees. The Bush administration did not oppose this initiative but was not enthusiastic about it, saying only that the administration would not oppose the Nunn-Aspin legislation so long as it was discretionary (i.e., that it made possible but did not mandate assistance to the Soviet Union).

However, just before the defense authorization bill reached the Senate floor, Harrison Wofford, a Democrat, won a formerly Republican Senate seat in a special Pennsylvania election, largely on the basis of an "America first" platform. Wofford's successful dark horse candidacy sent an anti-foreign aid shock wave through the House and Senate. This development, added to Republican opposition to specific aspects of the package and the absence of active White House support, caused the Democratic leadership in both the House and Senate to remove the Nunn-Aspin legislation from the FY 1992 defense authorization bill. The program was effectively killed, at least for the 1991–92 budget cycle.[1]

Shortly after this legislation was withdrawn, Senator Nunn joined Senator Richard Lugar (Republican–Indiana) for an informal briefing in Senator Lugar's office on the subject of the security of strategic nuclear weapons in the Soviet Union in the midst of political and military turmoil there. The briefer, Dr. Ashton Carter of Harvard University's Center for Science and International Affairs, had, together with several Harvard colleagues, recently completed a detailed study of this problem.[2] Their conclusion was carefully reasoned and profoundly disturbing: political and economic instability in the Soviet Union could have grave consequences for the safety and security of Moscow's nuclear arsenal, particularly if the Soviet Union divided into autonomous republics. At the time, this division appeared highly

---

1. Fiscal years run from October 1 of the current year to September 30 of the subsequent year.

2. Kurt M. Campbell, Ashton B. Carter, Steven E. Miller, and Charles A. Zraket, *Soviet Nuclear Fission: Control of the Nuclear Arsenal in a Disintegrating Soviet Union*, CSIA Studies in International Security (Cambridge, Mass.: Center for Science and International Affairs, Harvard University, 1991).

probable, and, in fact, within two months of Carter's briefing, at the end of December 1991, the Soviet Union was formally dissolved.

The Harvard study reinforced Senator Nunn's conviction that it was in the national security interest of the United States to assist the Soviet Union, which appeared to be on the brink of total collapse, to secure and control its vast stocks of weapons of mass destruction. Senator Lugar, a respected Republican foreign affairs specialist, was also impressed by Carter's briefing and agreed to join Senator Nunn in a concerted effort to revive the key parts of the abortive Nunn-Aspin legislation. Dr. Carter pledged that he and his Harvard colleagues would do all they could to assist.

Over the next several weeks, the two senators constructed a solid bipartisan consensus in the Senate in support of a slimmed-down legislative package that would provide $500 million for the safe transportation, storage, destruction, and nonproliferation of Soviet weapons of mass destruction. The Nunn-Lugar legislation—cosponsored by 24 senators, including Robert Dole (Republican–Kansas) and Jesse Helms (Republican–South Carolina)—was offered in the Senate as an amendment to an unrelated bill, the Arms Export Control Act, in late November 1991. It was adopted by a roll call vote of 84–6. The House approved the measure by voice vote, and President George Bush signed it into law on December 12, 1991.[3]

However, the Senate Appropriations Committee had the last word regarding Nunn-Lugar funding. For reasons that were never clearly articulated (perhaps little more than a demonstration of their carefully guarded control of the country's purse strings), the Senate appropriators decided to provide $400 million rather than the $500 million recommended by Senators Nunn and Lugar and their 24 Senate cosponsors. Although the provisions of the Nunn-Lugar amendment were to be overseen by the Department of Defense (DOD), the amendment did not represent a new appropriation. It was not "new money" that added $400 million to the Defense Department account. Rather, the amendment was an authorization that allowed DOD to transfer (or "reprogram") up to $400 million from other categories in the existing DOD operating budget to this new program. The authority to reprogram was discretionary, not obligatory.

---

3. The legislation, commonly referred to as the "Nunn-Lugar amendment," was formally titled "The Soviet Nuclear Threat Reduction Act of 1991" (Title II, Public Law 102-228).

In bringing together this impressive Senate coalition, Senators Nunn and Lugar had to accommodate numerous concerns voiced by House and Senate Republicans. These included: designating the Department of Defense rather than the Department of State as the program's implementing agency; specifying that, "where feasible," U.S. technology and expertise should be utilized for all Nunn-Lugar activities (the so-called "buy American" provision to which recipient FSU countries have so strenuously objected); requiring prior notification to Congress of any commitment of reprogrammed funds to projects in the FSU; and establishing several performance criteria that recipient countries were required to meet before receiving Nunn-Lugar funding. These criteria included observance of internationally recognized norms of human rights, observance of arms control obligations, and facilitation of U.S. verification that U.S. funds were in fact utilized as agreed by the United States and the recipient country.

EARLY GROWING PAINS

Following a March 1992 trip to the former Soviet Union, Senators Nunn and Lugar—who had been accompanied by Senators John Warner and Jeff Bingaman, as well as by Ashton Carter of Harvard, defense conversion specialist William Perry of Stanford University, and Carnegie Corporation President David Hamburg—succeeded in adding authority for defense conversion, environmental cleanup, and housing assistance for displaced Soviet strategic weapons officers to the FY 1993 Nunn-Lugar legislation. Many House Republicans and some Senate Republicans were unhappy about this new authority to use Defense Department funds in the former Soviet Union. But the Democrats at that time were the majority party in Congress and had sufficient votes to overcome Republican objections. SASC Chairman Nunn added authority for these programs to the FY 1993 Defense Authorization Bill, and the other three committees of Congress (the House Armed Services Committee and the House and Senate appropriating committees) acquiesced in this initiative.

It should be noted that the trip report produced by the March 1992 Nunn-Lugar congressional delegation included numerous recommendations for U.S. assistance to the former Soviet Union beyond cooperative threat reduction. The senators briefed Secretary of State James Baker, National Security Adviser Brent Scowcroft, and later President Bush on their findings and recommendations. These briefings helped the Bush administration to appreciate the importance of cooperative threat reduction. In addition, they provided the impetus and much of the substance of the Bush administration's initial, comprehensive assistance package for the countries of the former Soviet Union, which became known as "The Freedom Support Act."[4]

Since the FY 1993 legislative year, the Nunn-Lugar Program has been an integral part of the annual defense authorization bill. During the Bush administration, the Nunn-Lugar provisions remained a congressional initiative. They were not part of the administration's budget request to Congress, and they continued to authorize, not mandate, spending on threat reduction activities. Once the Nunn-Lugar legislation was established in the annual defense authorization bill, four congressional committees became essential to its annual legislative fate. These were the two "authorizing" committees, the Senate Armed Services Committee and the House Armed Services Committee, which were responsible for writing the basic law and for recommending annual funding levels. The other two committees were the defense "appropriating" subcommittees of the Senate and House Appropriations Committees, responsible for providing actual funding for all components of the defense budget. Each year, each committee meets to "mark up" defense legislation for the coming fiscal year. Then the two Senate defense bills, authorizing and appropriating, are separately debated and voted on by the full Senate. The same process takes place in the House. Finally, the two pairs of committees—the Senate and House defense authorizers and the Senate and House defense appropriators—meet in conference to resolve their differences and report an agreed bill back to the Senate and House for final passage. Once that happens, the two bills are sent to the president for his signature or veto.

---

4. "The Freedom Support Act of 1992" was submitted to Congress on April 3, 1992. After extensive amendment by Congress, it was approved in the Senate on July 2 (by a vote of 76–20) and by the House on August 6 (by a vote of 255–164). It was signed into law as Public Law 102-511 on October 24, 1992. The law authorized $505.8 million in FY 1993 for humanitarian and technical assistance, exchange programs, and State Department as well as U.S. Information Agency expenses for the region. The U.S. Agency for International Development (USAID) was designated as executive agent for most of these programs.

Enter the Clinton Administration

From the beginning of its term of office in 1993, the Clinton administration demonstrated a great deal of enthusiasm for the Nunn-Lugar Program. This came as no surprise. The new secretary of defense, Les Aspin, had cosponsored the 1991 attempt to provide demilitarization assistance to the Soviet Union. Deputy Secretary of Defense William Perry was a strong supporter of the Nunn-Lugar concept and was particularly enthusiastic about U.S. assistance for converting Russian defense production facilities to civilian production. The assistant secretary of defense responsible for Nunn-Lugar policy was Dr. Ashton Carter of Harvard, who had been instrumental in the revival of the first, failed legislative effort of 1991. This enthusiasm intensified when William Perry became secretary of defense. The State Department, the National Security Council staff, the Vice President's office, and the administration coordinator for the former Soviet Union, Ambassador Strobe Talbott, were all supportive as well.

The program, termed "cooperative threat reduction" by the Clinton administration, for the first time was included in the administration's budget request when the Clinton White House submitted to Congress its defense budget for FY 1994. The original discretionary transfer, or reprogramming, approach, which had been a congressional initiative for FY 1992 and FY 1993, was discarded.

The Clinton administration inherited the difficult problem of persuading the newly independent states of Belarus, Kazakstan, and Ukraine to become non-nuclear weapon states by voluntarily returning to Russia the strategic nuclear weapons that each possessed when the Soviet Union disintegrated in December 1991. On March 23, 1992, the presidents of Belarus, Kazakstan, and Ukraine signed the Lisbon Protocol, whereby they became party to the START I Treaty in return for their pledge—subject to parliamentary ratification in each country— that each of their respective countries would adhere to the Non-Proliferation Treaty (NPT) as non-nuclear states "in the shortest possible time." But as of early 1993 the Ukrainian Parliament indicated that it had major reservations about giving up "Ukraine's" nuclear weapons, and it was unclear what the Kazak Parliament would do. In contrast, the Belarusan Parliament proceeded apace with ratification of the Lisbon Protocol and the START I Treaty.

One "carrot" that the Clinton administration offered to Kazakstan and Ukraine in return for prompt denuclearization and ratification of

START I was considerable CTR assistance—including housing and retraining for Strategic Rocket Force officers, environmental cleanup, and defense conversion. This was in keeping with the letter of the Nunn-Lugar legislation, but it set an important precedent that deviated significantly from congressional understanding of the program. It created expectations in Belarus, Kazakstan, and Ukraine that their willingness to give up strategic nuclear weapons—which their governments had already pledged to do in return for becoming party to the START I Treaty—entitled them to Nunn-Lugar funds as an appropriate reward for good behavior. Few members of Congress objected to this use of the Nunn-Lugar Program. The result, nonetheless, was a marked departure from the original congressional understanding, as of the fall of 1991, that the program was intended to advance U.S. national security interests by helping the Soviet Union and its successor states overcome selected technical bottlenecks in securing and destroying their weapons of mass destruction.

A similar development was the proposal by the Clinton administration in 1993 to use Nunn-Lugar funds for defense conversion in Russia. A committee on defense conversion was created by the administration under the umbrella of the Gore-Chernomyrdin Commission, which had been established at the first Clinton-Yeltsin summit meeting in Vancouver in April 1993 to oversee U.S.-Russian cooperation. The U.S. chairman of this defense conversion committee was Deputy Secretary of Defense Perry, who retained this responsibility even when he became secretary of defense following Secretary Aspin's untimely death in 1994. Perry's Russian counterpart was First Deputy Defense Minister Andrei Kokoshin.

In the summer of 1993, when the defense authorization bill was in conference, Perry personally persuaded the two authorizing committees to create and capitalize a U.S. "Defense Enterprise Fund" as part of the Nunn-Lugar provisions in the FY 1994 defense bill. The fund was to operate as a semiautonomous, eventually self-financing investment organization to foster defense conversion in the former Soviet Union. Republicans, particularly in the House, had qualms about this approach to assisting the Russian defense sector at a time when the U.S. defense sector was anxious to receive financial help from Washington.

During the first two years of the Clinton presidency, the four congressional committees with jurisdiction over the Nunn-Lugar CTR Program varied in their enthusiasm for the program. Not surprisingly, the Senate Armed Services Committee, chaired by Senator Nunn, with

Senator John Warner of Virginia the ranking Republican member, was the most stalwart supporter of the program (Senator Lugar was not a member of either Senate committee directly involved with the legislation, although he played an active supporting role nonetheless). The Defense Subcommittee of the Senate Appropriations Committee, led by Senator Daniel Inouye (Democrat–Hawaii), with Senator Ted Stevens of Alaska as ranking Republican member, generally followed Senator Nunn's lead.

The House Armed Services Committee, chaired by Congressman Ron Dellums (Democrat–California), with Congressman Floyd Spence of South Carolina as ranking Republican, was less enthusiastic about the program, largely because there were few outspoken supporters among Democratic committee members and many critics among the Republican minority. Least enthusiastic was the Defense Subcommittee of the House Appropriations Committee, chaired by Congressman John Murtha (Democrat–Pennsylvania), with Congressman Bill Young of Florida as ranking Republican member. Murtha's staff considered Nunn-Lugar reprogramming authority to be overly generous when measured against the Pentagon's slow spending rate of available Nunn-Lugar funds. As of the end of FY 1993, the Defense Department had actually used only $470 million of the total $800 million in transfer authority it had been given for CTR activities. Based on its staff's recommendation, the House Appropriations Committee voted not to renew the $330 million in transfer authority that expired at the end of FY 1993. Moreover, it voted not to appropriate any of the $400 million requested by the Clinton administration for FY 1994. This decision was reversed only by strenuous lobbying efforts by the Clinton administration and by Senators Nunn and Lugar personally.

Others legislators sitting on the House Appropriations Committee, including influential committee member David Obey (Democrat–Wisconsin), argued that several Nunn-Lugar programs should not be administered by the Defense Department. Deputy Secretary of Defense John Deutch, who had led the administration's lobbying effort for CTR funding in 1994, decided that the future of the program required some accommodation of this congressional concern. Deutch won interagency agreement to move three major programs out of the DOD budget beginning in FY 1995 and henceforth to fund them from the budgets of other departments.

A cooperative program between U.S. national laboratories (primarily Los Alamos, Sandia, and Lawrence Livermore) and their

Russian counterpart organizations on improving fissile material security measures in Russian nuclear facilities was shifted to the budget of the Department of Energy (DOE), which funds and oversees the U.S. nuclear laboratories. A smaller program of government-to-government cooperation, between the Department of Energy and the Russian Ministry of Atomic Energy (Minatom), was also moved to DOE's budget. Because the Energy and Water Subcommittees of the House and Senate had appropriating authority over the DOE budget, this shift in departmental authority gave these subcommittees oversight over these programs in Russia. A third program, the International Science and Technology Center (ISTC), which provided former Soviet weapons scientists with opportunities to be involved in nonmilitary research, was shifted from the DOD budget to the Department of State, as was a program to help Soviet successor states develop more robust export controls over critical technologies. The State Department's involvement in threat reduction activities now meant that the foreign relations authorizing committees and the foreign operations appropriating committees in the House and Senate became involved in the annual CTR budget debate. The total funding for these four programs was about $85 million.

REVENGE OF THE REPUBLICANS

When the "Republican revolution" of November 1994 brought Republican majorities to both the Senate and the House, it also brought Republican chairmen to the four committees with principal jurisdiction over the Nunn-Lugar Program. Republican members of Congress who had been unenthusiastic and sometimes hostile toward expenditure of U.S. defense dollars on cooperative threat reduction for countries of the former Soviet Union finally had the votes in their respective committees and in the full Senate and House to translate their concerns into law.

Despite vigorous lobbying by Defense Secretary Perry and his staff, the 1995 legislative cycle (which produced defense authorization and appropriations legislation for FY 1996) was not kind to the Nunn-Lugar Program. The House Armed Services Committee, renamed the House National Security Committee (HNSC) and chaired by Congressman Spence, voted to authorize only $200 million of the $371 million requested by the Clinton Administration in its FY 1996 Defense Department budget for Nunn-Lugar activities. Of the $171 million in total cuts:

- all of the requested $104 million for chemical weapons destruction was eliminated;

- $23 million of the requested $29 million for a fissile material storage facility was cut;

- all of the $40 million requested for defense conversion initiatives through the Defense Enterprise Fund was eliminated; and

- overall operating expenditures were reduced by $4 million.

The Defense Subcommittee of the House Appropriations Committee followed suit, making available only $200 million.

In addition, the HNSC added numerous legislative restrictions to the program. For example, each program element was subjected to a specific funding cap. All funding authority for defense conversion was eliminated, and the legislative authority for Secretary Perry's Defense Enterprise Fund was rescinded altogether. Moreover, the criteria that Soviet states were required to meet to be eligible for CTR funding were tightened significantly. The original legislation stated that a recipient country must be "committed" to meeting six criteria. The HNSC voted to eliminate this somewhat subjective phrase, thereby requiring full compliance with each of the six criteria.

Moreover, when the House authorization bill moved from the HNSC to the House floor, the full House voted by a two-to-one margin for an amendment offered by Congressman Robert Dornan (Republican–California) to suspend all CTR funding for Russia until the U.S. president certified that Russia was in compliance with its obligations under the Biological Weapons Convention (BWC) of 1972. Congressman Dornan and his supporters knew that the administration had evidence of a continuing Russian biological weapons offensive research program and therefore could not certify Russian compliance with the convention, which prohibits such research (but does not provide for an inspection regime or for sanctions).

The Senate Armed Services Committee, chaired by 92-year-old Strom Thurmond (Republican–South Carolina), presented the SASC Democrats with a take-it-or-leave-it CTR funding level of $200 million, which clearly had been coordinated with the HNSC Republican majority. The specific cuts proposed by the SASC Republicans were virtually identical to those enacted by the HNSC Republicans. Thanks to strenuous efforts by Senator Nunn and his fellow Democrats on the committee, the SASC in the end recommended an overall CTR funding level of $300 million, with a $50 million reduction in CTR funding for Russia, pending presidential certification of Russian compliance with the BWC. These recommendations by the SASC were approved by the full Senate without opposition, although Senator John Kyl (Republican–Arizona) added an amendment on the Senate floor requiring additional certifications by the administration before all of the funds for chemical weapons destruction could be released.

The Senate Appropriations Committee cut the $300 million CTR funding level recommended by the SASC to $298 million, arguing without specific prejudice to the CTR Program that all accounts had to be reduced in the name of fiscal responsibility. In a surprise move, they also stipulated that no FY 1996 funds could be allocated to the Defense Enterprise Fund, although a small amount of prior-year funding could be used to keep the fund alive. These recommendations also were approved by the full Senate.

The annual defense authorization bills also have jurisdiction over the defense-related functions of DOE, although the appropriation of funds for these purposes is made by the Subcommittees on Energy and Water rather than by the Defense Subcommittees. The HNSC cut these programs, including lab-to-lab and government-to-government fissile material security cooperation and associated programs, by about 16 percent ($15 million was cut from the total request of $92.2 million). The general justification for this cut was that such non-weapons-related programs had to be reduced to provide badly needed resources for maintenance of the U.S. nuclear weapons stockpile. The specific rationale for the cut, however, was that these programs had been poorly planned. The SASC Republicans insisted on exactly the same cut, for the same reasons. A last-minute effort by DOE to increase lab-to-lab cooperation by $25 million over the requested $70 million was ignored by both authorizing committees. However, the SASC position on DOE's Nunn-Lugar activities was reversed by the full Senate, thanks to a coalition led by SASC Democrats and moderate Republicans such as Pete Domenici (Republican–New Mexico) and Richard Lugar. The Energy and Water Subcommittee, chaired by Senator Domenici, voted to appropriate full funding and was supported by the full Senate.

The final stage in the FY 1996 CTR legislative process involved conferences between the counterpart committees in the Senate and the House. In the appropriations conference between House and Senate, the

Senate prevailed, winning an increase from $200 million to $298 million for the Defense Department's CTR programs, and an amount for DOE's CTR-related programs that was much closer to what DOE had requested.

The conference between the two authorizing committees, the SASC and the HNSC, was unusually disorganized, prolonged, and partisan. There were major differences over the CTR provisions. These included a difference of $171 million in authorized CTR funding, the "committed to" language regarding eligibility criteria, the Dornan BWC restriction on funding for Russia, elimination of authority for the Defense Enterprise Fund, and specific funding caps on each CTR Program element. In addition to the disagreement over the CTR Program, deep differences existed on such issues as national missile defense, the Anti-Ballistic Missile (ABM) Treaty, the placing of U.S. military forces under foreign command, and the availability of abortions for military personnel and their dependents. Although unrelated to CTR, these issues cast a partisan shadow across the entire conference.

In the end, the two authorizing committees agreed to the Senate funding level of $300 million. Of this total, $65 million was withheld from CTR programs in Russia until the president certified that Russia was in compliance with the Biological Weapons Convention, with the proviso that the funds withheld from Russia could be used for CTR programs elsewhere in the former Soviet Union. The key phrase "committed to" was left in law, as was authority for the Defense Enterprise Fund. Funding caps were preserved but made more flexible. Finally, the HNSC acquiesced to the Senate position on full funding for DOE's CTR-related activities.

The saga of the FY 1996 CTR legislation did not end at this point, however. Because of language in the authorization act approved by both houses of Congress signaling a U.S. intention to abrogate the ABM Treaty, President Clinton vetoed the entire FY 1996 Defense Authorization Act.[5] In addition, the official "Statement of Administration Policy" on the act noted specifically that the administration had serious concerns about the "onerous certification requirements for the use of

---

5. The FY 1996 Defense Authorization Act specified that it should be the policy of the United States to deploy multiple ABM sites. However, the ABM Treaty allows only one ABM site in the United States and one in the Soviet Union. The president's veto did not apply to the FY 1996 defense appropriations bill, which contained no such language.

Nunn-Lugar Cooperative Threat Reduction funds, as well as sub-limits on specified activities and elimination of funding for the Defense Enterprise Fund." However, when the Senate and House Republicans agreed to drop the objectionable language on the ABM Treaty, President Clinton signed the amended bill without further modification of its Nunn-Lugar provisions.

The Political Context for Cooperative Assistance

The battles fought over FY 1996 CTR legislation are instructive for several important trends that they reveal—trends that are likely to have an enduring impact on the Nunn-Lugar Program and related efforts.

The most significant trend concerns the impact of the "Republican revolution" of November 1994. The new majority, particularly in the House, was determined to show that its agenda was different from that of the old Democratic majority and was more in tune with the genuine concerns of the American people. The Republicans, with those elected in November 1994 in the forefront, believed they had a clear mandate to balance the federal budget and shrink the size and power of the federal government. Foreign and national security policy was a secondary concern, amounting to little more than a general Republican feeling that the Clinton administration had cut U.S. defense capabilities too deeply and too quickly and was prone to engage the United States in foreign problems that did not involve vital U.S. national interests.

At the same time, there was little Republican consensus on a single overarching concept of U.S. foreign policy. For that matter, there was little consensus on this score among congressional Democrats and no consistent set of foreign policy priorities articulated by the Clinton administration. Various administration themes, such as "aggressive multilateralism," "neo-Wilsonianism," and "enlarging democracy," took root neither in the Congress nor in the country.

The danger of accidental or unauthorized use of nuclear weapons, and the related danger of proliferation of weapons of mass destruction, were acknowledged by most congressional Republicans but were not given high priority. Neither was the Nunn-Lugar legislation, which had been crafted to address these particular threats. Secretary of Defense Perry's conviction that proliferation posed a major national security challenge to the United States did not resonate among the Republican majority in Congress. Their preference was to respond to the prolifera-tion threat defensively, by building national as well as theater missile defense systems and by strengthening U.S. offensive military capabilities across the board.

A related trend was the belief of veteran Senate and House Republicans that they at last had the votes to correct what they considered to be flawed policies of the former Democratic majority. In particular, Republicans in the SASC and the HNSC believed that Democratic defense policy had weakened military readiness and that the annual defense budget under Democratic leadership had become a "cash cow" for an increasing number of nonmilitary activities.

Several key Republican members of the HNSC believed that much of the Nunn-Lugar Program was not "real" defense and therefore did not belong in the Defense Department budget. Dismantling nuclear warheads and launchers aimed at the United States in their view merited some U.S. financial assistance. But most other Nunn-Lugar activities—including defense conversion, environmental cleanup, and military housing—were regarded as foreign aid which, if merited at all, should be funded elsewhere. The interagency agreement brokered by Deputy Secretary of Defense Deutch to move oversight of selected CTR activities to DOE and the State Department was meant to address these concerns. However, in the view of the new Republican majority, the administration had not gone far enough in moving "non-defense" CTR programs out of the DOD budget. These Republicans were unswayed by Secretary Perry's insistence that the Nunn-Lugar Program elements that remained in the DOD budget, such as development of a fissile material storage facility in Russia, in fact were "defense by another means."

Moreover, several influential Republican members of the SASC and HNSC believed that the Democratic majority in the two committees, led formerly by Chairman Nunn and Chairman Dellums, had thrown money into Nunn-Lugar programs without exercising careful oversight of these programs. Combined with the Republican concern to strengthen U.S. military capabilities, this belief caused the new Republican majority in both committees to look skeptically at each aspect of the Clinton administration's FY 1996 Nunn-Lugar budget request.

Finally, some influential Republicans in both the House and Senate were concerned that Russia remained a potential enemy of the United States and was still engaged in suspect military activity. These members, led by Robert Dornan in the House and John Kyl in the Senate, frequently questioned the wisdom of using the U.S. defense budget to help dismantle Russia's older strategic weapons, while Russia simultaneously devoted its resources to developing new strategic systems.

Future Prospects for U.S.-FSU Cooperation

Senator Richard Lugar's unsuccessful attempt to highlight the dangers of proliferation of weapons of mass destruction in his 1995–96 campaign for the presidency demonstrates that this issue remains of low political salience for most American voters—even after the use of chemical weapons by a Japanese terrorist group and the use of massive conventional explosives at the New York World Trade Center and the Oklahoma City Federal Building. The lesson seems to be that, barring a tragedy in the United States involving nuclear, chemical, or biological weapons, U.S. public opinion is unlikely to become concerned about the dangers of the proliferation of these weapons. In the absence of any strong public opinion regarding the proliferation dangers remaining in the former Soviet Union, it is likely that, as in the past, the correlation of political forces inside Washington will determine the fate of the Nunn-Lugar Program.

The fundamental political question, where the CTR Program is concerned, is whether the Republican assault on the program during the FY 1996 budget cycle will be repeated in FY 1997 and beyond. Republican antipathy toward U.S. funding of Russian defense conversion, Russian officer housing, and environmental cleanup from the pollution caused by weapons of mass destruction is unlikely to change substantially. Similarly, Republican concern over Russian actions that seem incompatible with the letter or with the spirit of the Nunn-Lugar legislation is likely to continue to play a role in the budget process. Doubts expressed over the past two years about Russian compliance with the Biological Weapons Convention have not been satisfied. Congressional unhappiness over the lack of Russian cooperation with the United States on eliminating chemical weapons production facilities is an enduring problem as well. New problems are also likely to arise. For example, media reports of a "mammoth underground military complex" in the Ural Mountains[6] may provoke a new Republican-

---

6. See, for example, Michael Gordon, "Despite Cold War's End, Russia Keeps Building a Secret Complex," *New York Times*, April 16, 1996, p. A6.

sponsored stipulation that Nunn-Lugar funding for Russia be withheld until the U.S. president certifies to Congress that this military complex has no offensive military significance.

At the same time, there are some positive signs within Congress for the future of the Nunn-Lugar legislation. First, Republicans on the Senate Armed Services Committee may have had second thoughts about their relatively confrontational approach to the FY 1996 budget process, which brought about a presidential veto and raised the possibility that there would be no defense authorization bill for FY 1996. In this case, the defense appropriations bill would govern, and the Senate Armed Services Committee, along with the House National Security Committee, would be greatly reduced in influence. Few Republican members of either committee wish to see this happen. Among other things, the favored projects of these legislators would not become the law of the land.

The close collaboration on the defense budget between the SASC chairman and ranking member that was generally characteristic of Senator Nunn's tenure as chairman and Senator John Warner's tenure as ranking Republican member did not characterize the FY 1996 budget cycle, when Senator Strom Thurmond became chairman and Senator Nunn became ranking Democratic member. This was not because of ill will or an uncooperative attitude on Chairman Thurmond's part. In fact, the relationship between these two senators had long featured mutual respect and friendship. The problem stemmed from the overall impact of the Republican revolution, and was magnified by partisan attitudes on the part of some SASC Republicans who became chairmen of the SASC's subcommittees. The problem also stemmed from relatively inexperienced Republican staff members, in their first year as the majority party and in many cases in their first year in the Senate.

Chairman Thurmond has since named a new SASC majority staff director experienced in both the substance and the mechanics of the budget process. And Republican members of both authorizing committees may have concluded from the experience of the FY 1996 legislation that a more cooperative approach to the Democratic minority and to the Democratic administration in the end will help bring about a defense authorization bill more favorable to Republican interests.

Another positive sign is that Senators Nunn and Lugar have attempted to renew congressional and public interest in cooperative threat reduction and nonproliferation through a series of open Senate hearings on various facets of the problem. Senator Lugar, in his capacity as chairman of the European Subcommittee of the Foreign Relations Committee, began the series in August 1995. Senator Nunn, in his capacity as ranking member of the Permanent Subcommittee on Investigations of the Governmental Affairs Committee, continued the process with fall 1995 hearings on the proliferation of chemical and biological weapons and with spring 1996 hearings on the proliferation of fissile material.

At the conclusion of these hearings, both senators announced their intention to build a bipartisan Senate coalition around the need for new legislation and new funding for cooperative threat reduction, nonproliferation, and the ability of the United States to detect and respond to an incident of nuclear, chemical, or biological terrorism on U.S. territory. This was difficult enough in the fall of 1991, when the Democrats were in the majority in both houses of Congress and when the Soviet Union clearly was facing disintegration. It will be even more difficult to accomplish in the aftermath of the Republican revolution, which will continue to shape the House and Senate until at least the 1996 elections, and when Russia seems to be turning toward renewed nationalism and self-assertiveness. Yet Senators Nunn and Lugar are highly respected members of Congress, are widely admired for their sincerity and expertise regarding foreign policy and national security issues, and showed in 1991 that their leadership on such issues can produce important results. So their efforts in 1996 cannot be taken lightly.

It is impossible to forecast the political future of the Nunn-Lugar Program beyond the November 1996 elections. The existence of the CTR Program and much of its success to date are due, in large measure, to the energy and personal diplomacy of several key individuals. One of the leading congressional advocates of the program, Sam Nunn, will retire from the Senate at the end of 1996, although the current term of his CTR collaborator, Richard Lugar, will not end until the year 2000. It is unclear whether the Democrats will be able to regain a majority in either the House or the Senate. Nor, of course, can the outcome of the U.S. presidential elections be predicted. And should President Clinton gain a second term, it is unclear whether the leading senior advocate of cooperative threat reduction in the current Clinton administration, Secretary of Defense Perry, will continue in his current position.

A related question is whether the next U.S. president will regard nonproliferation of weapons of mass destruction as a high national security priority. While Secretary Perry consistently has ranked this problem at the top of his list of national security challenges, the Clinton administration as a whole has not in practice treated nonproliferation as a high-priority concern. Neither the funding level nor the executive branch organization for nonproliferation has changed significantly from the Bush years.

As of mid-1996, Republican presidential candidate Robert Dole appears to have a pragmatic rather than a visionary approach to foreign and national security affairs. Should he become the next U.S. president, many observers speculate that he will delegate most of the foreign and national security agenda to tested Republican practitioners. If so, the future of cooperative threat reduction and related programs will depend largely on the views of his individual senior advisors, whose identities are presently unknown.

Lessons to be Learned

Several suggestions for future activities emerge from this review of the history of Nunn-Lugar CTR legislation and its implementation. First, recipient countries could help sustain and perhaps even expand CTR programs by becoming more familiar with the political context of this legislation and taking a more active role on Capitol Hill in voicing their interest in CTR as well as their concerns about it. Their testimony could provide dramatic evidence to a perhaps skeptical Congress of the continued need for nonproliferation assistance in these countries. More important, it could provide U.S. lawmakers with more tangible evidence that U.S. funding was producing real threat reduction and nonproliferation results in the former Soviet Union. This holds true for the daily work of the Belarusan, Kazakstani, Russian, and Ukrainian embassies in Washington. It also pertains, where appropriate, to visiting officials from these countries who are able to schedule meetings with members of Congress and congressional staff. U.S. officials in DOD, the State Department, DOE, and other governmental agencies involved in CTR implementation should be alert to suggest calls on Congress to such visitors and to direct them toward appropriate members and staff.

Second, the executive branch should consider further steps to move CTR programs from the Department of Defense to other agencies, following the successful example of the transfer from DOD to DOE of the lab-to-lab and government-to-government programs for fissile material security. For example, programs involving defense conversion might be transferred to the Department of State, which already has funding and oversight responsibilities for the International Science and Technology Center in Moscow and its fraternal twin in Kiev, the Science and Technology Center in Ukraine, the purpose of which is to assist former Soviet weapons scientists to move from military to civilian research.

Third, as CTR programs are decentralized, coordination among the involved executive branch components becomes correspondingly more essential. The Nunn-Lugar-Domenici legislation currently before Congress (referred to on Capitol Hill as "Nunn-Lugar II"), calls for designation of a senior member of the administration as overall coordinator of all aspects of the nonproliferation effort. Since the fundamental purpose of the Nunn-Lugar effort is to prevent the proliferation of weapons of mass destruction, it would be sensible to make the new coordinator responsible for coordination of all Nunn-Lugar CTR activities. If this element of the proposed legislation is not enacted, existing coordination from within the National Security Council should be reviewed and strengthened.

Finally, the executive branch might also consider characterizing the overall Nunn-Lugar CTR effort more as a nonproliferation program and less as a "threat reduction" activity. Admittedly, this is largely a matter of semantics. Yet most members of Congress, most U.S. opinion leaders, and most American voters do not regard present-day Belarus, Kazakstan, Russia, and Ukraine as posing serious military threats to the United States. It should be more persuasive to portray the CTR Program as an extremely cost-effective nonproliferation measure, given that the best way to prevent proliferation is to protect against the spread of fissile material and other components of weapons of mass destruction at their source.

Of course, we also must be concerned about export policy and border controls, including our own, as well as detection, neutralization, and event response capabilities, should attempts be made to use weapons of mass destruction against the United States and particularly from inside the United States. Nonetheless, while we cannot afford to rely entirely on cooperative threat reduction in our nonproliferation strategy, the most cost-effective first line of defense against proliferation from the former Soviet Union remains safe storage, transportation, and destruction of weapons and weapon components at their current locations within the former Soviet Union.

Chapter 4

Presidential Priorities in Nuclear Policy

Rose Gottemoeller

The Nunn-Lugar Program was a powerful tool in accomplishing the denuclearization of Ukraine, Kazakstan, and Belarus. Ensuring that the nuclear weapons that remained in these three countries as they became independent were removed and destroyed (or in the case of Belarus, redeployed to Russia) was a top foreign policy priority of the Clinton administration during its first years in office. This goal was achieved with spectacular success, and a key reason was that the White House exercised full flexibility to use the Nunn-Lugar Program—together with other tools of diplomacy and inducements—to secure progress.

Today, denuclearization would be more likely to fail, for Nunn-Lugar and other related assistance have dispersed and disappeared into the government departments responsible for implementing the programs—the Departments of Defense, Energy, and State. The White House does not today have at its disposal the means to build another large and comprehensive strategy to tackle major issues of nuclear, biological, and chemical proliferation. Diplomacy, the marshaling of incentives, and strategic policy planning all reside in different government locations and are brought together on increasingly rare occasions.

One might argue, of course, that with the denuclearization job completed in a decisive manner, there are no longer any big strategic nonproliferation objectives to be achieved. Instead, the focus should be

---

The analysis here is based largely on the author's personal observations as the Director for Russia, Ukraine, and Eurasia on the National Security Council staff with responsibility for denuclearization, from January 1993 to December 1994. Added to these observations are comments and analyses by other observers in both the executive and legislative branches of government, as well as nongovernmental specialists. Where appropriate, their work is cited here. However, the author wishes to stress that this chapter is a highly personal view of the situation surrounding nonproliferation assistance to the countries of the former Soviet Union. Any errors of fact or analysis are solely the responsibility of the author.

on implementing programs against problems that are already well defined and well understood—nuclear material safety and security, for example, or energy replacement so that production of plutonium from power plants will cease. The problem ceases to be strategy and becomes one of implementation, best achieved through departmental action unencumbered by interagency coordination and White House direction.

Although there are successful implementation programs under way that should continue under the day-to-day supervision of their agencies, it seems premature to say that strategic policy planning and direction are no longer necessary. At least three reasons can be cited. First, precedents are inadequately established for working on complex problems that may recur, such as nuclear material transfers to safe storage sites on the model of Project Sapphire. Second, tough and unprecedented diplomacy is on the horizon, particularly with regard to warhead dismantlement and destruction. The ready capability to marshal incentives will be important to facilitate the dismantlement process and supplementary activities such as transparency. Finally, response to emergency situations will be hampered if resources and the flexibility to use them are held solely in the agencies. Such emergencies need not be only in the most crisis-ridden situations such as the April 1995 Tokyo subway gas attack. They also should apply to the rapid emergence of new threats, such as efficient new export routes for nuclear contraband through countries to the south of Russia, which could be quickly countered through the infusion of export control and customs assistance into the region.

This chapter develops these themes, stressing that the president and the White House must be the focal point of strategic planning and policy for how the United States works with Russia and the countries of the former Soviet Union to address the universe of problems involving weapons of mass destruction since the breakup of the Soviet Union. Where the traditional realm of arms control negotiations is concerned, this focus is not at risk, for here interagency cooperation under White House direction has a strong history and continues operating to this day. More problematic are the areas where precedents are being set in managing the residual arsenals, either because Russia and the United States have never tried to tackle the issue before in an arms control negotiation (warhead control and accounting), or because our experience is too new (Project Sapphire), or because we cannot fully comprehend what threats and emergencies might arise—and how quickly. For these reasons, this chapter argues that only central coordination through the White House will give the United States the capability to respond with flexibility, rapidity, and coherence to unforeseen proliferation threats.

The chapter first recounts briefly the success that was achieved in the denuclearization arena by the Nunn-Lugar effort, then describes the circumstances under which the White House receded as a focal point of strategic planning and policy. Finally, in discussing the current situation, it suggests how best to establish a mix involving both the efficient and continued implementation of successful programs by the agencies responsible for them, and restoration of an effective centralized tool for achieving critical policy goals in the nonproliferation arena.

Consensus and Its Limits

The Nunn-Lugar Program was launched with much fanfare. Although it was a congressional initiative and was not in the administration's defense budget request in either 1992 or 1993, the early publicity did much to assuage public concerns that the United States government was doing nothing about the threat of "loose" nuclear weapons in the former Soviet Union. It added to the public impression that the Bush administration was taking energetic action to counter these potential problems, for at the same time then Secretary of State James Baker was personally involved in the high-stakes diplomacy that led to the completion of the Lisbon Protocol to the START I Treaty in May 1992.[1]

Following this activist period, however, Bush, Baker, and the Republican administration turned to a reelection campaign in which the president's foreign policy accomplishments were seen to be a liability. Implementation of the Lisbon Protocol went on the back burner in the summer of 1992, and early implementation of the Nunn-Lugar Program proceeded in a low-key but steady manner, entrusted to an interagency group chaired by the National Security Council's Defense and Arms Control Directorate. This group developed a creditable list of early projects for the program. Some of these, such as

---

1. The Lisbon Protocol was designed to draw Ukraine, Kazakstan, and Belarus into the START I Treaty, thereby acquiring an instrument to enable them to eliminate the nuclear forces on their territories; it also called for them to become non-nuclear states under the Non-Proliferation Treaty.

a storage facility for fissile materials removed from nuclear weapons and the International Science and Technology Center (ISTC) to provide project work to former Soviet nuclear scientists, were big-ticket or high-visibility projects meant to serve as flagships, i.e., to symbolize the particular "denuclearization" role of U.S. assistance. Other projects, however, were more prosaic "off-the-shelf" purchases meant to address near-term difficulties that the Russians might encounter in transporting or dismantling their weapon systems.

It was around this second group of projects that the easiest bureaucratic consensus developed. The Nunn-Lugar legislation essentially required a "buy American" strategy that was readily served by off-the-shelf purchases; these were also more easily accomplished through the Department of Defense (DOD) procurement rules which that agency saw as necessary to implementation of the program. As long as the program was sending equipment that was readily acquired—some of it from excess U.S. stocks—the strain on the defense procurement and budget process was not serious and the interagency community could be satisfied that it was accomplishing some of the Bush administration's denuclearization goals. However, no agreement could be reached at this time on spending for the big-ticket programs such as the nuclear materials storage facility, in part because there was no interagency consensus about how the project could or should be implemented.

Lack of a robust U.S. interagency consensus was not the only reason that the bigger projects did not go forward. The Russian government was experiencing the new sensation of talking to Westerners—especially Americans—about the problems brought about by the breakup of the Soviet nuclear arsenal. Their hesitancy to admit problems to their former enemies, combined with the overall confusion and crisis of confidence that the Soviet breakup produced, created a slow and complicated negotiation and implementation process.

Early Successes and Problems of the Clinton Administration

The Clinton administration arrived on the scene eager to take up the denuclearization effort but not fully aware of these two problems: that the consensus supporting the program inside the professional bureaucracy was fragile, and that working with the Russians would be time-consuming and, in the end, would further erode the consensus in the Washington agencies—especially in the Department of Defense.

Table 4-1. Strategic Nuclear Launchers and Warheads Deployed in Belarus, Kazakstan, and Ukraine, 1991–92.

	ICBMs & warheads		Bombers & warheads		Total warheads
Belarus	80	80	–		80
Kazakstan	104	1,040	40	320	1,360
Ukraine	176	1,240	41	328	1,568

SOURCE: These estimates are based on information provided in International Institute for Strategic Studies (IISS), *The Military Balance* 1991–92 (London: Brassey's Ltd. for IISS, 1991); and IISS, *The Military Balance 1992–93* (London: Brassey's Ltd. for IISS, 1992). The systems included are those that would be accountable under START counting rules.

Nevertheless, President Clinton entered office in January 1993 with implementation of the Lisbon Protocol and denuclearization of Ukraine, Kazakstan, and Belarus as a key foreign policy goal. Clinton was ultimately successful with his denuclearization diplomacy, for the three countries all acceded to the Non-Proliferation Treaty (NPT) and START was brought into force by December 1994. Throughout the negotiations with each of these three countries, the Nunn-Lugar Program was the most consistent and productive tool available to U.S. diplomats. The program acquired a special importance for the countries seated opposite the United States at the negotiating table. They saw it as a symbol of continuing U.S. commitment to their independence, national well-being, security, and a non-nuclear future. They also judged the status of their relationship to the U.S. relative to the amount of Nunn-Lugar assistance that they had been promised. The program became, for good or ill, a measure of their national success in attracting U.S. attention and support.

During this period, the Nunn-Lugar Program was the most important means that the Clinton team had available to accomplish the president's foreign policy priority of ensuring that Ukraine, Kazakstan, and Belarus did not maintain a hold on nuclear weapons. All told, these countries deployed over 3,000 warheads that were in danger, over time, of falling into disrepair, improper maintenance, and eventually, perhaps, entering illicit markets for nuclear goods. The nuclear deployments in each country at the time of the Soviet Union's demise are detailed in Table 4-1.

Using the Nunn-Lugar Program to reward denuclearization progress was an area of continuing interagency consensus: assistance to Ukraine was doubled in recognition of its decision to let go of its warheads under the Trilateral Statement (for a total of $350 million through Fiscal Year [FY] 94); $100 million was extended to Belarus as the first country to fulfill its Lisbon Protocol commitments at the time of Clinton's trip to Minsk in January 1994; and by February 1994, when President Nazarbaev came to Washington, $160 million had been extended to Kazakstan. These figures were established with broad U.S. interagency agreement on what the sums would be spent for, but specific implementation agreements on the projects on which the money would be spent had to be negotiated with the countries involved.

Often, these negotiations became frustrating exercises in trying to rectify what the country wanted—usually housing, officer training, or environmental cleanup—with what the U.S. government believed the assistance could be spent on—with an emphasis on the nitty-gritty denuclearization goal of eliminating weapons, launchers, and basing sites. Officially, the U.S. side continued to stress off-the-shelf American technology and products, while the countries involved began to protest that their own manufacturers could provide more appropriate equipment at lower costs. Because of these differences, implementation of many Nunn-Lugar projects stalled or never got off the ground.

Thus, the fragile U.S. consensus over the program had to confront the reality that the countries involved wanted other uses for the monies, and when they could not get them, they became increasingly recalcitrant in negotiations and complained publicly about the ineffectiveness of the program. This negative trend in turn produced a reaction inside Washington, and the fragile interagency consensus about the Nunn-Lugar Program began to come apart as broader concerns emerged about the effectiveness of the aid program to Russia as a whole.

Across the board, the Congress and many outside observers were complaining about implementation of the U.S. aid program, and problems in the implementation of Nunn-Lugar seemed to be a visible example. When the Republican Party succeeded at the polls in November 1994, this effect picked up momentum amid an overall attack on foreign assistance in the new Republican-dominated Congress. Despite its success as a tool of denuclearization, the program became a magnet for criticism on Capitol Hill, which found a clear resonance among some in the executive branch, especially the Defense Department.

Defense Criticism and the Remedies

From the program's inception, key DOD bureaucratic actors were concerned about the program. The Joint Chiefs of Staff were concerned about the impact that skimming DOD budget resources would have on operations and maintenance, while some Office of the Secretary of Defense professionals were not keen to see DOD budget resources discussed and divided up in a process involving other agencies. These tensions were kept under control during the Bush administration by the nature of the projects under way in the early days of the program. The high degree to which they depended on off-the-shelf products, some of which were excess DOD equipment, ensured continued, albeit guarded, acquiescence inside the department.

When the Clinton administration took office, a strongly pro–Nunn-Lugar team arrived in the Pentagon. Les Aspin, Clinton's first secretary of defense, had, with Senator Sam Nunn, sponsored an unsuccessful House-Senate bill for Soviet denuclearization assistance prior to the successful legislation sponsored by Senators Nunn and Richard Lugar. Following Aspin's departure from DOD, Secretary William Perry, who replaced him, spoke up often in public forums in support of the Nunn-Lugar Program, and used a number of highly publicized trips to the former Soviet states to emphasize its successes. Assistant Secretary of Defense for International Security Policy Ashton Carter had provided the conceptual underpinnings for the program through his work at Harvard prior to joining the Clinton administration. Dr. Gloria Duffy became the special coordinator for cooperative threat reduction, a position carrying the rank of deputy assistant secretary and meant to symbolize the high degree of importance that the Clinton Defense Department invested in the program.

The Clinton DOD team was quick off the mark in working with other agencies to devise strategies for negotiations with Ukraine, Kazakstan, and Belarus. They were also invaluable to the implementation of key policy initiatives. An example was the approach made to Russia and Ukraine to launch negotiation of the Trilateral Statement: In June 1993 during a trip to Garmisch-Partenkirchen, Les Aspin first approached his Russian counterpart, Pavel Grachev, with the idea that the missiles in Ukraine might be demobilized gradually, with warheads—once removed from the missiles—remaining in storage in Ukraine for a temporary period.[2] Although Grachev reacted in a strongly negative way, Aspin then went on to Kiev, where he stressed to his Ukrainian counterpart, Konstantin Morozov, that such an approach would make it possible for Ukraine to begin the process of demobilizing the missiles without appearing to bow to Russian demands.

But despite its success in helping to advance highly desirable U.S. policies, the Clinton DOD team came increasingly to face critics of the Nunn-Lugar Program inside DOD who felt that it was placing too much of a strain on the defense budget. These included not only individuals with long-standing concerns in the professional civilian and uniformed bureaucracies, but also Clinton appointees with budget responsibilities, especially in the comptroller's office. These critics of the program inside the department came into a kind of tacit alliance with critics of the program on Capitol Hill. They believed that if the Nunn-Lugar Program could be scaled back or its impact on the defense budget could be clearly circumscribed or limited in time, the department would benefit. Thus, in DOD, a kind of tension came into being between those who saw the defense budget being too heavily impacted by the program, and those who thought it could bear the strain.

Clinton's DOD leadership attempted to repair the breach in the department in several ways, at the same time addressing some of the criticisms of the program that had been directed at it from the outside. The first step was to streamline Nunn-Lugar implementation by establishing a program office with responsibility for overseeing the Defense Nuclear Agency (DNA). DNA had for several years come under criticism for slowing program implementation by insisting that the letter of DOD procurement rules be fulfilled. Once the policy machinery had agreed to a project and negotiated an agreement with counterparts in the target country, implementation then disappeared from view. The project would frequently only resurface as a complaint from a U.S. contractor trying to wrestle with DNA. These complaints

---

2. For accounts of these discussions, see Michael R. Gordon, "Aspin Meets Russian in Bid to Take Ukraine's A-Arms," *New York Times,* June 6, 1993, p. 16; Michael R. Gordon, "Russians Fault U.S. on Shifting Ukraine's Arms," *New York Times,* June 7, 1993, p. 2; R. Jeffrey Smith, "Russian Rebuffs U.S. Plan on A-Arms," *Washington Post,* June 7, 1993, p. 16; R. Jeffrey Smith, "Ukrainians Endorse Arms Plan," *Washington Post,* June 8, 1996, p. 16.

found resonance among critics of the program on Capitol Hill, with the result that the program was blamed once more for "not delivering."

The program office, headed by Roland LeJoie, a retired general well experienced in dealing with the former Soviet Union, took on the task of streamlining the procurement process, smoothing in-country implementation, and presenting the public case for Nunn-Lugar's effectiveness as an aid program. The idea was a good one, and seems to have had a positive impact on perceptions of the program and on its performance.

Balkanization

The second step, however, was more radical and negative in its impact in that it involved shedding or attempting to shed portions of the program for which the agency could find no internal consensus. This "balkanization" of the program unfolded in the late fall of 1994, after a bruising budget battle on Capitol Hill that impressed the Clinton Defense Department team with the criticisms of the program and the need for improved implementation, but also hardened opinion inside DOD about the strain it imposed on the defense budget process.

In an attempt to strike a balance between Perry's high-level support and the critics of the program inside the department, then Deputy Secretary of Defense John Deutch devised a deal that permitted DOD to divest itself of the less palatable—from the perspective of the defense budget hawks—aspects of the program. The balkanization involved moving certain programs, particularly nonmilitary nuclear material protection, control, and accounting (MPC&A), outside the orbit of the Nunn-Lugar Program and into the Department of Energy. Energy was to receive a one-time payment from Nunn-Lugar to support its MPC&A projects in FY 1995. Thereafter, it would find its own budget resources for MPC&A and the Defense Department and the Nunn-Lugar Program would be out of the business. A similar deal was made with the State Department for the ISTC and export control assistance.

The Departments of Energy and State agreed to this approach at a high level and it was enthusiastically supported by some specialists outside the government. The results in at least one sense have been positive. The deal clearly has had a good effect on budgets for certain programs, in particular the MPC&A programs run by the Department of Energy on a lab-to-lab basis with Russia.[3]

For that reason, it can be said that balkanization has been a successful strategy for forcing the Departments of Energy and State to step up to the budget requirements inherent in maintaining support for expensive and challenging nonproliferation programs. A major frustration of the Defense Department—as well as the Office of Management and Budget (OMB) in the White House—had been that the other agencies had tended to treat the Nunn-Lugar Program, and the defense budget underpinning it, as a kind of "cash cow" for programs that they should have been willing to fund themselves.[4]

Nevertheless, this achievement has been at major cost to the president's ability to pursue his nonproliferation policy goals. As the nuclear safety, security, and dismantlement activities have become increasingly fragmented among agencies, they have rapidly sunk out of sight in the bureaucracies involved, thus endangering White House efforts to set coherent nonproliferation priorities and then achieve them.

These risks emerged just as the president, having successfully completed his efforts to implement the Lisbon Protocol, declared that dismantlement of warheads and protection of the materials being taken out of them would become a top priority of U.S. policy. Warhead dismantlement and material protection, control, and accounting would be a major focus of U.S. joint efforts at the highest level: President Clinton, Vice President Al Gore, and their counterparts President Boris Yeltsin and Prime Minister Viktor Chernomyrdin in Russia. With the balkanization of Nunn-Lugar and other nonproliferation assistance, however, the most coherent tool with which to effect this policy was disappearing, calling into question the government's potential to fulfill this top presidential priority.

---

3. This case is made well in Jason Ellis, "Nunn-Lugar's Mid-Life Crisis," *Survival* (Spring 1997).

4. In late 1994, the OMB launched a revealing exercise in which it asked agencies to describe in budgetary terms precisely the resources that they were willing to apply to the warhead dismantlement and material control problems. Whereas agencies could describe in programmatic terms what they would like to see done to tackle these issues, they had no ready funds available. The answer to the budget problem, whatever the project or the agency initiating it, tended to be "Nunn-Lugar."

Balkanization sprang from some real frustrations with the implementation of the program, and it is worth addressing them in order to consider how the Nunn-Lugar Program might be handled in the future. The interagency consensus on what projects were wholly acceptable, as noted above, really only extended to a few areas, especially missile elimination involving off-the-shelf technologies and products that could be bought from U.S. companies. Many of the more challenging and innovative projects that involved constraining the potential flow of nuclear materials into illicit hands required working with the Russian Ministry of Atomic Energy (Minatom), the minister of which, Viktor Mikhailov, was a difficult and powerful man who at times seemed bent on preventing U.S.-Russian cooperation in whatever ways he could.

The Department of Defense, having developed an excellent working relationship with its own counterpart ministry over the years, saw no reason in the end to break its head on Mr. Mikhailov's iron gate, and asked the Energy Department to do so. Energy, having had success in working with Russian weapons laboratories at a grass-roots level, saw no reason not to try to develop that success. A similar story can be told with regard to the State Department and its inherited oversight of the ISTC and export control programs. Both Energy and State, furthermore, had become weary of trying to work with the Defense Department, where the weak support for the Nunn-Lugar Program at the working level continued to put up road blocks to implementation, which in turn created more criticism of the program outside.

At the same time—the end of 1994—the NSC failed to exert discipline on the process, for its convening power at the working level unraveled. Several reasons can be cited for this, key among them movement or departure of personnel. It was then that the meetings took place among the Departments of State, Defense, and Energy to broker balkanization.

The Future of the Program: Making the Case

The problems of balkanization and the frustrations that led DOD as well as the other agencies to pursue it point to the necessity of developing a long-range concept for Nunn-Lugar that reinstates the sense of the program as a profoundly important swords-into-plowshares program. It is a reality that the defense budget is the natural target in any swords-into-plowshares initiative, but ways must be developed to make that reality more palatable to the Defense Department and its backers on Capitol Hill. Many in Congress are more comfortable with increasing expenditures on defense procurement than on taking apart the Cold War nuclear arsenal of Russia.

That said, it behooves the rest of the government not to treat DOD as a source of ready cash with no limits to the demands that can be placed on it. Resources in the program will always be limited, and other agencies should routinely shoulder part of the budget responsibility by applying their own resources to the nonproliferation task. Seeking a wider group of agencies willing to put budget resources into the safe and secure dismantlement of nuclear weapons in the former Soviet Union is a legitimate goal under any circumstances, and it is especially needed to create a wider U.S. budget base for such projects.

But the critics of the program must also be answered, and the Department of Defense and the Clinton administration have put some effort into this since 1994. It has not quieted the critics, however, who continue to argue that the Nunn-Lugar Program not only does not live up to its promise, but milks the defense budget in the bargain. The evidence of diplomatic and programmatic successes does not seem to make a difference to these critics.

Thus, if the Nunn-Lugar Program is to survive, a convincing long-term rationale for it must be developed. That rationale should be married to a clear set of other assistance efforts involving weapons of mass destruction so that Nunn-Lugar remains the valuable tool that it is, but does not serve as an excuse for other agencies not to act. In early 1996, positive steps in this direction were taken on Capitol Hill, when Senators Nunn, Lugar, and Domenici convened a set of hearings to examine the need for new funding in the program. Their hearings focused not only on the "supply side" proliferation of weapons of mass destruction—control, protection, accounting, and elimination in the former Soviet Union—but also on domestic preparedness in the United States.

With terrorist attacks emerging as a real problem inside U.S. borders—e.g., the World Trade Center and Oklahoma City bombings—preparedness was an important issue by which to make the case for the program to Congress. The strategy proved successful. The senators offered an amendment to the defense appropriations bill, "Defense Against Weapons of Mass Destruction Bill of 1996," which called for further funding, including $124 million for domestic projects.[5] The amendment was passed by the Senate by a vote of 93 to 0 (with 7 abstentions)—putting on record a high degree of support for the program.

Programmatic Goals

The essential rationale for the program must be joined to specific goals to improve its performance, for that too will be important in assuaging the critics. In particular, a better programmatic case must be made for Nunn-Lugar assistance each year. In the first three years of the program, the sum of $400 million per year had a certain mantra-like quality that was not always backed up by well-thought-out projects. As a result, projects took a long time to mature, implementation was slow, and monies were not spent. In some cases, funds were lost when Congress revoked the spending authority for them.

The yearly programmatic case should be joined to a long-term sense of what project priorities will continue to be developed and what new priorities will be introduced: a new emphasis on chemical and biological weapons-related projects could be developed, for example, assuming Russia will resolve outstanding concerns about past activities in these areas.

More difficult is trying to build the case for the programs that are frequently the touchstone for the denuclearizing countries in the region: programs to move the human resources out of the nuclear business and into civilian life. The case has been made with difficulty for the ISTC, which addresses the "brain drain" problem of former Soviet nuclear scientists. The case has not been made with regard to the military officers who man the missile sites and deploy aboard the submarines. But Ukraine, Kazakhstan, Belarus, and Russia see programs to retrain these personnel and provide housing for them as a key means to retain the social consensus for denuclearization.

For many in Congress, such "transformation" funds are a poor use of DOD resources, especially, they argue, because the Russian government continues to provide considerable resources for the modernization of the Russian armed forces. Most damning, in the eyes of these

---

5. Discussion Draft, Title XIII, Sections 1301–1356, Amendment to S. 1745, "Defense Against Weapons of Mass Destruction Act of 1996," June 24, 1996.

critics, are the expenditures for new submarines and strategic nuclear weapons, and for the deep-underground site in the Urals that is thought to be a command center for the Russian leadership in the event of nuclear war.

Making the Case in Moscow

The modernization issue must be dealt with in a straightforward way if any case is to be made for long-term Nunn-Lugar support of projects that help nuclear officers. In this effort, the Russian government and defense establishment must lend a hand, both in providing the rationale for the programs, and in expressing the need for social welfare projects in a straightforward way. Because of Russia's long history of secrecy, this will be difficult, but it is necessary. This need also applies to the larger case for the Nunn-Lugar Program, for congressmen are concerned that the funds are being used to destroy older systems while more capable ones are being built.

U.S. and other analyses of Russian defense plans can play a role in this effort, for they are more likely than Russian analyses to illustrate clearly the impact of the continuing programs. The SS-25 single-warhead missiles and Russia's new submarine systems, for example, can both be supported on stability grounds: the whole point of the START negotiations, from the U.S. perspective, was to remove the great Soviet preponderance of multiple-warhead heavy intercontinental ballistic missiles (ICBMs). If the United States demanded that Russia stop modernizing, it would keep these less-stable systems, a development that would work against U.S. strategic interests. The Russians also make the argument that the older systems are less safe, which applies equally to U.S. weapons and is an accepted reason for their modernization. Addressing such issues and putting them in context can begin to build a long-term rationale for the Nunn-Lugar Program.

The context should also focus on the way in which the Nunn-Lugar Program helps to dismantle the nuclear legacy in each of the countries involved, not only in Russia. When a nuclear base closes down in Ukraine, Kazakstan, or Belarus and its weapons go back to Russia for destruction, the country should be helped to fulfill its promise to stay out of the nuclear business forever. If the nuclear officers are simply thrown out on the economy, they will have no place to go and may be tempted to turn to illicit nuclear weapons-related business.

This threat points to the heart of the difficulty: Nunn-Lugar funds can now pay for elimination of the hardware of nuclear weaponry without too much difficulty; they can also pay (through the ISTC) for moving some of the brainpower behind the weapons into other spheres. It also should be able to pay for moving the operators, those who know the weapons inside and out, into other business. Thus, the "denuclearization" of a former Soviet missile base should in concept include disposing of the hardware, transforming the manpower, and transferring the base to other uses.

Such an approach to the whole problem would be optimum, and it is a goal for which the Clinton administration has striven in trying to work with Nunn-Lugar partner countries. Politically, however, pursuing this course is difficult, for many in the U.S. Congress cannot accept that the United States would pay to civilianize old Soviet missile bases at a time when the U.S. government is having difficulty finding the money to close down and convert bases at home. To respond to this concern, it is important to stress the theme of the wider problem: the leftover excess of the nuclear age is inherently dangerous and is among the top priorities that the United States must deal with in these early years of the post-Soviet transition. The specter of riots at Strategic Rocket Forces bases, as occurred in Kazakstan in 1993, should not be repeated.

Spreading the Responsibility

Beyond building this context, it must be stressed that DOD and its budget should not stand alone in providing support to Russia, Ukraine, Kazakstan, and Belarus. Other agencies also need to be seen as taking budgetary responsibility for nonproliferation and denuclearization efforts, for the key underlying reason that drove DOD to dismember Nunn-Lugar was a frustration that other agencies were not willing to help carry the load in dealing with the legacy of the old Soviet nuclear arsenal. This issue became especially relevant when the U.S. priority shifted from denuclearization of Ukraine, Kazakstan, and Belarus through implementation of the Lisbon Protocol, to addressing the problem of material control, accounting, and protection as warheads were dismantled and their materials had to be stored.

It should be noted that the Department of Energy has at times taken the tack that it is facing the enormous budgetary responsibility of dealing with the U.S. nuclear legacy, including the huge cost of cleanup at some sites, and should not be in the first rank of those working on the Russian problem. At the same time, DOE has managed one of the most successful projects to date in dealing with Russia—the lab-to-lab program—and has special knowledge of, and responsibility for, warhead dismantlement and material disposition. It therefore has a natural place in addressing this set of problems and arguably is better positioned to make the case about the threat and the need to Congress.

If the balkanization "grand bargain" was needed to accomplish the budgetary division of labor among the Departments of Defense, Energy, and State, then perhaps it was necessary as a temporary tactic. However, balkanization as a continuing fixture of government is undesirable, since it enables agencies to remove themselves from White House-directed action in the formulation of critical national policy, practically assuring that the president's nonproliferation priorities cannot be met.

Restoring the White House Role

The most important step to ensure a coherent policy and process is to restore the high-level focus on the problem in the White House. Clear precedents exist, for denuclearization policy toward Ukraine, Kazakstan, and Belarus was supported by a strong interagency consensus that a White House-led process was necessary to accomplish the task. The traditional arms control agenda—START, the Conventional Forces in Europe (CFE) Treaty, the Comprehensive Test Ban Treaty—continues to be handled by an NSC-chaired interagency group, the activities of which are well established and accepted.

The dissipation of the consensus on denuclearization and nonproliferation in the aftermath of the Lisbon Protocol success had much to do with the White House failing to establish the universe of remaining problems as a new high-priority goal. The threat of nuclear, chemical, and biological proliferation attracted high-level rhetorical support in the White House, but did not produce an effort to engage the interagency community in the same way it had been involved in policy toward Ukraine, Kazakstan, and Belarus. As a result, the agencies drifted away from the authority of the White House and commenced to cut their own deals, such as the balkanization arrangement.

Perhaps the new range of tasks—among them, countering terrorism, dealing with the emergence of a nuclear black market, addressing warhead dismantlement, improving safety and accountability at nuclear facilities, providing for material disposition—was simply too amorphous to attract an easy bureaucratic consensus. Indeed, more agencies would have to be involved in the mix, including some considerable heavyweights such as the Federal Bureau of Investigation.

Various critics have attributed the White House failure to assert authority to the split in responsibilities among NSC directorates: the Lisbon Protocol work was established in the Russia, Ukraine, and Eurasia Directorate; MPC&A in the Nonproliferation Directorate. However, that split seems an unlikely cause because the division of labor among the directorates was smooth and the working relationship was good.

Rather than a fissure in the NSC, the cause was more likely that the White House never chose to pursue a special, high-profile and high-level assignment to accomplish the president's security priority with Russia, warhead dismantlement, material control and accounting, and related denuclearization and nonproliferation problems. That solution was put forward by a special study of the President's Committee of Advisers on Science and Technology (PCAST), which concluded that a presidential directive was needed to ensure that the security of nuclear weapons and fissile materials would be a top national security priority for federal agencies and the U.S. national laboratories. This directive was signed by President Clinton in September 1995. It reiterated that the National Security Council would oversee coordination of U.S. government programs and initiatives in the nuclear materials area, and noted that an NSC staff director for nuclear materials security had been appointed.[6]

That individual, Kenneth Fairfax, succeeded in restoring momentum in the formulation of U.S. policy toward MPC&A in the prelude to the Moscow summit on nuclear security issues held in April 1996. However, the question remains as to whether his purview and authority over the issues were broad enough. The safe and secure handling of nuclear materials was an important issue, but equally important were other measures devised to ensure that the clean up, control, accounting, and destruction of former Soviet weapons of mass destruction were accomplished.

---

6. See White House Statement and Fact Sheet, "Nuclear Materials Security in the Former Soviet Union," September 24, 1995.

This requirement to chart strategy for a larger universe of issues having to do with weapons of mass destruction argues for a senior figure with broad authority and scope of action. Late in 1994, this need was articulated by several agencies, most powerfully DOE, who argued that a White House "tsar" for nuclear warhead and material issues was required to place some order and strategic vision on the process.

The tsar concept was reiterated in mid-1996, when the new legislation sponsored by Senators Nunn, Lugar, and Domenici to underpin a second stage of denuclearization and nonproliferation assistance called for the establishment of a high-level position in the White House to manage and direct policy in this arena. This national coordinator for nonproliferation matters was to chair a new NSC Committee on Nonproliferation tasked with reviewing and managing all federal programs and policies related to nonproliferation of weapons of mass destruction, terrorism, and international organized crime.[7]

Although this idea properly refocused attention on the issue of White House authority, it probably would not have solved the underlying problem of getting the agencies to work well together under effective strategic direction. Tsars have sometimes been successful at moving presidential goals forward, but they more frequently have served as a White House excuse to undertake agency responsibilities and supplant agency authority—an outcome to be avoided since the results have been mixed (and, at times, illegal). The solution is more likely to be one that already exists, that is, to use established arrangements in the White House hierarchy.

Role of the Vice President

The Clinton White House has enjoyed a steady rhythm of summit meetings with the Yeltsin administration in Moscow, both because of regular presidential meetings, and because a relationship and process have been established between Vice President Gore and Prime Minister Chernomyrdin. The Gore-Chernomyrdin Commission[8] has been a

---

7. Discussion Draft, Title XIII, Subtitle D, Sections 1341–1344.

8. The official name, although rarely used, is the U.S.-Russian Joint Commission on Economic and Technological Cooperation. It was officially established at the Vancouver summit in April 1993 and meets approximately twice a year, alternating

partial means of ensuring that the White House has a clear grip on the problems associated with nuclear, chemical, and biological weapons because a focus on the issues has become a norm for commission meetings. While no leader's position is assured forever in either Moscow or Washington, the utility of the process is well enough established that the commission seems likely to continue in some variant and for some time—regardless of who occupies the Kremlin or the White House. The United States and Russia will thus retain in place a system established at the highest levels to work on problems associated with their weapons of mass destruction.

In Washington, the commission has an established practice, that is, not so much to establish a new "tsarist" system, as to make the best use of the system in existence. To accomplish this goal, symbiosis between the president's and vice president's staff is important. Through the 1993–94 period, when the Gore-Chernomyrdin Commission was being developed, an integral link between the National Security Council and the vice president's office was maintained, with NSC staff dual-hatted as key figures in the Gore-Chernomyrdin Secretariat. This system worked well and was especially important as the rhythm built up between the Gore-Chernomyrdin meetings and the Clinton-Yeltsin summits: the two presidents would take an important political step forward, and three or four months later the vice president and prime minister would agree to the terms of the concrete implementation or resolve difficulties that had emerged in the course of trying to initiate implementation. The NSC staff, working closely with the vice president's staff, was the medium that permitted issues to progress smoothly from one meeting to the next.

The White House system, therefore, already contains two of the necessary ingredients for effective work on the issues. The first is engaged principals, one of whom, Vice President Gore, has long-standing interest and expertise in nuclear and other weapons of mass destruction issues. The second ingredient is staff who are organized in a way that will move issues effectively between those principals. The third ingredient is one requiring work, namely, reconnection of the White House to the relevant agencies in a way that will permit strategic planning and policy formulation for weapons of mass destruction.

---

between Russia and the United States.

Interagency leadership need not be a complicated affair, however. An optimum arrangement would be to ensure that an NSC senior director with responsibility for chairing the interagency group on weapons of mass destruction would also chair the Gore-Chernomyrdin Secretariat group preparing the agenda for the vice presidential meetings. The NSC group, it should be stressed, would have under its planning and coordination purview not only projects funded by Nunn-Lugar, but projects funded by all agencies. At the same time, a senior staff member from the Office of the Vice President should be a key member of the NSC interagency group on fissile material issues. This individual should also be a co-chair of the Gore-Chernomyrdin Secretariat group.

The key to these arrangements, which seem complicated at first glance, is to use the engagement of the vice president and the established momentum of the Gore-Chernomyrdin process as the focal point for reconnecting the White House to the rest of the government on these issues. The NSC and the Office of the Vice President would be integrally and cooperatively linked; the rhythm of presidential and vice presidential summits makes that possible.

Restoring the strategic level of planning and policy formulation must be highlighted as the key goal requiring attention: it is perhaps the single most important step that can be taken to ensure the success of U.S. policy toward cooperative threat reduction and, in the end, to ensure survival of the Nunn-Lugar Program and related assistance programs. As long as the White House remains disengaged from the problem, then the president's clearly stated priorities will go unfulfilled and the program will remain in trouble on Capitol Hill. All of the other steps listed here—articulating a long-term rationale for the program, setting the programmatic priorities each year, getting the Russians to make the case for their defense expenditures—are necessary but not sufficient for these goals to be accomplished. Only visibly engaging the White House and ensuring its authority over a broad policy agenda will do so.

But restoring White House involvement should not usurp the authority and control of the agencies that will be involved in these assistance programs. Indeed, the effect should be quite the opposite, for with the power of the presidency coherently engaged, the agencies should find enhanced their ability to negotiate and implement policy toward nuclear and other weapons of mass destruction in Russia.

The greatest success for U.S. policy will be achieved if a rightful division is restored between the budget and implementation burdens of the agencies and a coherent White House process backed by full presidential support. The Nunn-Lugar Program was the successful tool of just such a vigorous division of labor, which enabled the United States to prevent the emergence of new nuclear powers following the breakup of the Soviet nuclear arsenal. If this threat had not been dealt with, the post–Cold War security environment would have rapidly worsened and acquired a nuclear complexion. The Nunn-Lugar Program was the most important tool in preventing this horrific outcome, but it should not stand alone in the future. Other agencies need to share the costs, and they have done so effectively in recent times. The current focus must be on restoring strategic leadership to the process.

Recipient Country
Perspectives
on the CTR Program

Chapter 5

Perspectives of Russian Decision-makers and Problems of Implementation

Vladimir A. Orlov

The Cooperative Threat Reduction (CTR) Program, better known in Russia as the Nunn-Lugar Program, is designed to provide the Russian Federation and other newly independent states of the former Soviet Union (Ukraine, Belarus, and Kazakstan) with technical assistance to eliminate strategic offensive arms, reduce the risks of weapons proliferation, retrain and employ former weapons scientists and engineers, improve nuclear emergency response capabilities, destroy chemical weapons stockpiles, enhance capabilities for fissile material protection, control, and accounting (MPC&A), stimulate conversion of defense industrial enterprises for commercial purposes, and develop systems of export controls within and among the republics. In dollar terms, the Russian component of the CTR Program is the largest; politically, it is also considered the most important. Out of a total of $1.24 billion in assistance proposed under the CTR Program as of the beginning of 1996, the Russian share has been $612 million.[1]

However, several obstacles to effective implementation of the CTR Program in Russia have been encountered. By late 1995, actual disbursements to Russia amounted to about $212 million, or 34 percent of total CTR spending for Russia notified to the U.S. Congress by the U.S. Department of Defense (DOD). Unofficial estimates of the amounts actually received under the CTR program in terms of real goods and services arriving in Russia are even lower. One such estimate in mid-1995 calculated that Russia had received only 22 percent of promised CTR obligations from the United States.[2] There are at least four dimensions to the problem of CTR implementation in Russia: inter-

---

1. U.S. Department of Defense, CTR Program Office, *CTR Funding by Country*, December 18, 1995, pp. 1–2. EDITORS' NOTE: For CTR funding by country see Appendix to this volume.

2. Unofficial estimate by the Presidential Administration of the Russian Federation.

national politics, domestic politics, financial constraints, and technical issues. This chapter focuses primarily on the domestic political issues and events, both in Russia and the United States, that have slowed CTR implementation.

Domestic Political Moods and the CTR Program

U.S.-Russian agreements were concluded at an unfortunate time from the standpoint of Russian domestic politics. Proposals for cooperation were almost immediately criticized by Russian parliamentarians. The CTR umbrella agreements first came under attack in December 1992 in hearings held by the Congress of People's Deputies of the Russian Federation during its plenary session. Sergei Baburin, Gennadii Sayenko, Mikhail Astafiev, and other influential deputies criticized the bilateral agreements because they "contradicted the Russian Constitution" and "violated Russian sovereignty." Moreover, in a report by the Committee on Foreign Affairs of the Russian Parliament, Committee Chairman Yevgenii Ambartsumov suggested that the agreements violated some of Russia's legal norms and that "the U.S. side [could] use the agreements to export illegally important materials from Russia, avoiding Russian customs control." At the time, however, Ambartsumov pledged not to overturn or obstruct the agreements, acknowledging that the negative consequences of doing so outweighed the ill effects he foresaw in cooperating with the United States. Instead, he promised to address outstanding problems through an exchange of official letters between U.S. and Russian foreign offices.[3]

During these same hearings, a crucial voice of support was the head of Russia's Ministry of Atomic Energy (Minatom), Viktor Mikhailov, who responded to the sharp criticism of the deputies, insisting, "U.S.-Russian cooperation in the nuclear field is extremely important for us, and we should protect it, not attack it." In response to questions of possible ulterior motives on the part of the United States in providing assistance, Mikhailov argued, "they [the United States] are afraid that there can be an accident during the transportation or storage of nuclear

---

3. The December 1992 committee deliberations and report and the statements by Chairman Ambartsumov are all reported in *Sovietskaia Rossiia viet* (Russia), December 19, 1992, p. 14.

weapons in Russia. They also are afraid that Russia won't be able to follow the START I Treaty because of a lack of financial resources."[4]

As a result of testimony by Mikhailov and others, a majority of the deputies came to the conclusion that the CTR agreements did not compromise Russian national security and that the United States was motivated not by espionage but by, in the words of Foreign Affairs Committee Chairman Ambartsumov, "reasonable self-interest." At the same time, some observed, as Astafiev did, that "Germany in 1945 was also disarmed free of charge."[5] Since this early, heated debate, the CTR issue has not been debated publicly in Russia. Neither legislators from the State Duma nor the mass media have paid much attention to the issue of cooperative demilitarization. At the same time, the positions of both proponents and opponents of the agreement have not changed radically.

The high-level support that the CTR Program received during this period was the result of the bottom-line understanding among Russian policymakers that U.S. funding and technical assistance were crucial to Russian military efforts to destroy strategic weapons in accordance with START time lines, reduce the risk of accidents during nuclear warhead dismantlement, and minimize proliferation risks by assisting development of a modern system of MPC&A. As Colonel-General Evgenii Maslin, head of the 12th Main Directorate of the Russian Ministry of Defense (MOD), has observed, "We would like to carry out the process of nuclear warhead dismantlement by ourselves, but we should be realists—there is a lack of financial resources in Russia."[6]

Russian officials continue to acknowledge the importance of U.S. assistance for demilitarization and other goals. However, the strong support of General Maslin and other realists in Russia's top decision-making circles on the overall goals of the CTR Program has been muted by the increasingly vocal differences between the United States and Russia on CTR implementation as well as a variety of unrelated political and military issues.

---

4. Ibid.

5. Ibid.

6. Evgenii Maslin, "Poka chto ni odin yadernyi boepropas v Rossii ne propodal i ne byl pokhishen" (Thus far, not a single nuclear device has disappeared or been stolen in Russia), *Yadernyi Kontrol* (Nuclear control), No. 5 (1995), p. 12.

Growing Anti-Americanism

Implementation of demilitarization projects pursuant to Nunn-Lugar legislation has been hampered by shifts in the political climate in both the United States and Russia. Illustrative of this change was the vote, on June 14, 1995, by the U.S. House of Representatives (224–180) in favor of an amendment to the CTR legislation that would freeze any further assistance to Russia pending its cessation of biological weapons research.[7] Although the amendment was subsequently modified to allow some CTR funding for Russia, this provision has nonetheless had a very negative impact on the U.S.-Russian dialogue on nuclear security and nonproliferation issues. Similarly, the attempt by the Republican majority in Congress to adopt a law freezing CTR assistance to Russia if it continues its nuclear commerce with Iran (including construction of nuclear reactors at Bushehr)[8] has been met in Russia with significant disappointment and even irritation. Russian officials, in private conversations, maintain that some influential forces in the United States must be trying to provoke Russia to reject CTR assistance. Although this is not yet an official position, the reality is that more and more Russian officials share this view.

Since 1995, there have been increasing signs in Russia of anti-Americanism among not only legislators, but also governmental officials, analysts, and diplomats. This anti-American mood is not as aggressive as it was during the Cold War. Nonetheless, it demonstrates that "the honeymoon is over" and that the euphoria over the end of the Cold War has officially passed. It now appears that U.S.-Russian relations may be entering a time of "cold peace." This new dimension to Russian foreign policy has made Russian officials much more critical of U.S. initiatives, and it has had a special impact on the CTR Program.

In economic affairs, for example, Russia's policy has been evolving toward more active support for Russian industry and national enterprises. In this context, the focus of criticism of the CTR Program is that it is primarily a means for the U.S. government to support U.S. business, not Russia. Some Russian political leaders and managers of industrial enterprises have become vocal critics of the CTR Program for its resistance to using readily available equipment, manpower, and

---

7. Associated Press, June 14, 1995.

8. Associated Press, May 24, 1995.

materials from local enterprises in Russia to perform even basic demilitarization activities. Imports of heavy-lift cranes, cutting tools, and other low-technology equipment at higher cost and with frequent delays compared to indigenous supplies, these observers claim, have wasted CTR funds and made poor use of Russia's own demilitarization resources. This criticism is likely to become even sharper in the future as Russian economic conditions worsen. Even now, Russian entrepreneurs from military-industrial enterprises assert, for example, that "if the Nunn-Lugar money had been given directly to them they would have created equipment tens times cheaper than Americans do, in a shorter amount of time, without bureaucratic waste, with the same or higher quality, and with tens of thousands of highly qualified Russian workers and engineers saved from unemployment."[9]

Growing anti-Americanism may also play a part in Russia's current arms control policies. The Russian leadership appears to be in no hurry to ratify START II[10] even though it has talked about the possibility of concluding a START III Treaty in the near future.[11] For example, Sergei Karaganov, one of Russian President Boris Yeltsin's key foreign policy consultants, has argued that "Russia, according to its current geopolitical situation, should not agree to any further cuts of nuclear weapons."[12] Ratification of the START II agreement has been a glacial process. According to Russian law, the president is responsible for initiating the ratification process, yet it was only on June 21, 1995, that President Yeltsin, after a series of inexplicable delays, finally offered START II to the State Duma for ratification.

Conversations on arms control issues with key Duma legislators, including many who sit on the Committee on Defense and the Committee on Foreign Affairs, reveal a generally favorable view of

---

9. Author's interview with Yuri Skokov, November, 1994.

10. Author's interview with an official in the president's office, June 1995. See also Yuri Fedorov, "Chto stoit za torgom vokrug SNV-2?" (What is behind the haggling over START II?) *Moskovskie novosti* (Moscow news), No. 42 (June 1995), p. 14.

11. Television interview with Andrei Kozyrev, ORT Channel, April 21, 1995.

12. Sergei Karaganov, quoted in *Nezavisimaia Gazeta* (Independent newspaper), June 12, 1994.

START II ratification.[13] However, considerable obstacles to ratification remain, even if these committees give their approval. In the words of one observer:

It is not the right time for ratification. The president does not want to confront the legislators on this particular point, and at the same time, he does not want to start public, and long-lasting, hearings. For him, the better way would be to slow down the ratification process while still following internationally and bilaterally recognized Russian obligations. It is the same as it was for a long time with the budget: the government has it, but the Duma has not approved it, so the government uses the acting budget for implementation.[14]

Recent U.S. moves to expand NATO membership to former Warsaw Treaty Organization (WTO) states have also had a chilling effect on U.S.-Russian arms control efforts and cooperation at large. In the words of Vladimir Lukin, chairman of the Duma Committee on Foreign Affairs, "There are considerable questions as to how we would ratify START II when the political situation in Europe has changed and when the biggest military machine in the world [NATO] has made attempts, successful enough, to reach the Russian border. We would not be able to explain this paradox to the Russian people."[15]

This kind of rhetoric notwithstanding, there is still a clear understanding, at least among governmental experts, that continued support from the United States is required for Russia's efforts to dismantle nuclear weapons and improve fissile material protection and controls.

---

13. Author's interviews with Sergei Yushenkov, chairman of the Committee on Defense; Vladimir Lukin, chairman of the Committee on Foreign Affairs; and Vyacheslav Nikonov, chairman of the Subcommittee on Arms Control. All three represent the "liberal" wing of the parliament.

14. Author's interview with representative of the presidential administration, July 1995.

15. Lukin is quoted in *The Economist*, April 8, 1995. Even if the Duma votes for ratification, the ratification process cannot be completed without the approval of the Federation Council, the upper chamber of parliament. In a vein similar to those of his Duma colleagues, Vladimir Shumeiko, the speaker of the Federation Council, has publicly insisted on establishing, by law, linkage between START II ratification and NATO expansion: "Only if there is no expansion of NATO," he has said, "would the ratification of the START II Treaty be possible." See *Kommersant Daily*, April 2, 1995, p. 1.

Any anti-Americanism among Russian officials and parliamentarians is balanced by the realization that there is no real alternative to assistance from and cooperation with the United States, at both the lab-to-lab and government-to-government levels. A more general problem, particularly at the parliamentary level, is the apparently decreasing interest in arms control problems, the bilateral relationship with the United States, and other international issues. In the months before and after the Russian parliamentary elections in December 1995, both houses of the Russian Parliament spent most of their time focused on domestic issues.

Views of Russian Organizations Involved in the CTR Program

The key "centers of power" in Russia for decision-making on CTR implementation are Minatom, the President's Office, and the National Security Council. The two agencies most involved in the day-to-day operation of the CTR Program are Minatom and the Ministry of Defense, both of which have signed umbrella agreements with the U.S. Department of Defense. Each of these bureaucracies has its own particular strengths and weaknesses. Minatom's greatest weakness bureaucratically is its poor relationship with powerful oil and gas interests in the government, headed by Prime Minister Viktor Chernomyrdin and Oil and Gas Minister Igor Shafranik. The President's Office is hampered by a lack of experience in the practical implementation of negotiated agreements, including the CTR Program. The National Security Council is encumbered by internal dissension and its constant organizational restructurings.

These offices also differ in terms of their concerns about and support for CTR implementation. Moreover, many other offices and individuals within Russia's vast bureaucracy are involved in CTR Program implementation and hold sometimes strong opinions on its success or failure thus far. Table 5-1 summarizes, in general terms, attitudes toward the program within Russian ministries and other key bodies involved in CTR decision-making and implementation, both in the government and the parliament.

It is significant that in contrast to Minatom's apparent support for the program when it was initiated, some of the strongest skepticism toward CTR now is found at this agency. On the one hand, Minatom Minister Mikhailov has recognized that his ministry has an urgent need to improve MPC&A systems, railcar security, nuclear emergency

Table 5-1. Key Russian Organizations and Individuals and Their Views on CTR.

Organization and key individuals	Attitude and comments
Minatom Viktor Mikhailov, Evgenii Mikerin, Mikhail Ryzhov	Mainly negative Mikhailov: "If I had been asked, not as Minister but as a scientist, whether it was worth signing the agreements with the Americans, my response would have been 'no'." [a]
Ministry of Defense Gen. Evgenii Maslin	Very positive Maslin: "The U.S. offered us aid, free of charge. We have no money in our budget to solve the disarmament problems ourselves. Why should we say 'no'? The CTR helps us at the MOD a lot." [b]
Ministry of Foreign Affairs Sergei Kislyak	Mixed Deputy Foreign Minister Georgii Mamedov: "Agreements concluded with the United States on the Nunn-Lugar fund fully reflect Russia's national interests and meet Russia's concerns.... At the same time, we would expect U.S. assistance to be given more actively to Russian enterprises and not converted into a subsidy to U.S. companies. We cannot be satisfied by the fact that 50 to 90 percent of assistance is spent for U.S. companies, not for Russia. We cannot be satisfied either by the proportion between promised and disbursed funding." [c]
Committee on Convention-Related Issues of CW and BW Pavel Siutkin, chairman	Generally positive Siutkin: "There is no doubt we need this assistance, especially in areas related to chemical weapons destruction.... However, as yet we've gotten no more than $20 million from the promised $55 million." [d]

[a] Interview with Viktor Mikhailov, *Yadernyi Kontrol*, No. 2 (1995), pp. 9–11.
[b] Author's interview with General Maslin, July 1995.
[c] Author's interview with Sergei Kislyak, July 1995.
[d] Author's interview with Pavel Siutkin.

response capabilities, and fissile material controls, and that he lacks domestic sources of funding for these projects. On the other hand, he has also argued that:

we would be able to improve MPC&A ourselves.... I am personally satisfied by the implementation of only two agreements: on containers and on the storage facility design. Frankly speaking, it is the U.S. side that is

Organization and key individuals	Attitude and comments
President's Office Yuri Baturin, president's aide for national security	Generally positive Baturin: "We generally support the idea of the Nunn-Lugar fund, and we expect it to increase, not to diminish in the coming months. The problem of reducing nuclear and proliferation risks is a very complicated and delicate one. We would appreciate any assistance in this context but we would deny any pressure, any linkages and conditions, any dishonest games around this aid." [e]
Gore-Chernomyrdin Commission Viktor Chernomyrdin, Oleg Soskovets	Generally positive Key commission members appear to be supportive of the parts of the CTR Program relating to conversion, export controls, and MPC&A, but are critical of the lack of involvement by Russian enterprises.
National Security Council Valerii Manilov	Positive Valerii Manilov, deputy secretary of the National Security Council: "We welcome the U.S. Nunn-Lugar plan and believe in its fast implementation, with the understanding that the money should be invested in Russia, not outside it."
State Duma Subcommittee on Arms Control Vyacheslav Nikonov	Positive Nikonov remains skeptical of DOD's effectiveness in implementing CTR, and has indicated a preference for the Department of Energy to become general contractor of the program on the U.S. side.
State Duma Committee on Defense Sergei Yushenkov	Positive Generally positive, but disappointed at the lack of progress with the chemical weapons destruction program.

[e] Author's interview with Yuri Baturin, president's aide for national security, December 1994.

responsible for these delays. We've received much less equipment than was promised. Moreover, the assistance we get is mostly assistance to U.S. companies, not to us. The Americans offered us a total of $400 million [in CTR assistance]. But in 1994, we lost $400 million because the Americans did not open for us free, nonprotectionist access to the U.S. uranium market [for sales of surplus Russian enriched uranium]. We could sell uranium and our advanced technologies overseas if there were no protectionist barriers. We could invest the profits—into improvements in Russian MPC&A systems, containers, and so on.[16]

Other sources in Minatom have stressed their dissatisfaction with the way DOD implements the CTR Program. They would prefer to deal with the U.S. Department of Energy (DOE), which, from their experience, appears to produce more concrete results. For example, in the first year of the program, DOD lost spending authority for $218 million of its original $400 million Fiscal Year (FY) 1992 budget authorization due to its failure to obligate the funds in a timely manner. Minatom sources claim that they were fully prepared to spend this money to solve urgent problems. In another example, DOD spent $8 million in CTR funds on heavy equipment, such as bulldozers and road graders, although there is no shortage of these in Russia. These Minatom sources have also said that, based on past experience, lab-to-lab cooperation is much more attractive than cooperation at the government-to-government level.

These tensions notwithstanding, there are several encouraging examples of U.S.-Russian technical cooperation for threat reduction. At the Institute of Physics and Power Engineering (IPPE) in Obninsk, for example, the United States has used CTR assistance funds to create an MPC&A system that is now in use. Scientists at the facility where the system was installed have said that control and accounting of up to 96 percent of the facility's plutonium and highly enriched uranium were less than ideal in the past. Blocks of fissile material differed widely in weight and composition and were practically impossible to track within the facility. Moreover, facility portals lacked an advanced control system. As one of these scientists has observed, "We haven't had any case of nuclear smuggling, ... but theoretically it cannot be excluded. The U.S. system and equipment is what we need."[17]

Despite the apparent enthusiasm among specialists at Minatom facilities for cooperating with the United States to improve MPC&A capabilities, IPPE Director Viktor Murogov is generally skeptical about the role that U.S. aid can play in reducing proliferation risks in Russia:

---

16. "Interview with Viktor Mikhailov," *Yadernyi Kontrol*, No. 2 (1995), pp. 9–11.

17. Author's interview with a research scientist at the Institute of Physics and Power Engineering (IPPE), Obninsk, May 1995.

You should understand that the $250 million allotted by the Americans to Mayak[18] is a small sum. If you investigate the problem, you will see that we have been losing at least that much money supplying Ukraine with fuel to compensate for its transfer of warheads. Minister Mikhailov is constantly criticizing it, and he has a point: the American aid very often doesn't help us. It would be better if we used Mayak as a testing ground for developing new technologies, including technologies from third countries, as well as for the utilization of plutonium from third countries.[19]

By contrast, the Russian MOD has had a very positive view of CTR implementation, particularly as it pertains to strategic offensive arms elimination. Nonetheless, MOD officials privately voice their concern over U.S. attempts to pressure Russia to undertake CTR projects at specific facilities, with close involvement by U.S. personnel. These concerns center around the Mayak facility and the Elektrostal plant, which produces fuel for naval reactors. Sources in the Russian MOD have insisted that for CTR to be a "cooperative" program, it should maximize reciprocity, such as through reciprocal exchanges at U.S. and Russian facilities, such as Mayak and the Hanford facility in Washington state.

A key organization in the Russian MOD is the 12th Main Directorate, which is responsible for nuclear weapons operations and is headed by General Evgenii Maslin. Responding to criticism of U.S. motivations and the use of the CTR Program as a means of supporting U.S. contractors, General Maslin has observed:

Any country would do the same as the U.S. has been doing—helping their own companies first and Russia next.... They allocate funds, but do it for their own manufacturers. Let's take the supercontainers example (we call this type of container "TPD"). Of course, we could build such containers, and we actually have been building them. Such TPDs cost 32 million rubles a month ago. Now it might cost 50 million rubles. The supercontainers the Americans have been delivering to us are absolutely free of charge to the Russian MOD. Why not make use of them? There is a point of view that they want to disarm us. But this is only natural. Americans have been afraid of us for a long time; they still are, and they will be for some time in

18. Mayak, also known as Chelyabinsk-65, is the nuclear complex at which a central storage facility is being built for nuclear materials from disassembled nuclear weapons.

19. Author's interview with IPPE Director Viktor Murogov, May 1995. A version of this interview is reprinted in *Yadernyi Kontrol*, No. 7 (1995), pp. 9–11.

the future. But we try to see that the agreements we conclude are mutually beneficial. As far as the Nunn-Lugar Program is concerned, Americans have been fulfilling their commitments very well. They ask us what we need most. So we asked for another 600 containers. We suggested they design carriages that can be used in emergencies, special railway cars. They could supply computer equipment, which is one of the weakest points of our industries, to establish a reliable accounting and control system. I think that all the proposals by Americans have to take into consideration Russia's national security. The signed agreements fully reflect the demands of national security. If we have money, then we will be able to do that—ourselves. But now what we can do is accept U.S. aid and thank them for it.[20]

Table 5-2 displays, on a simple scale, general attitudes about implementation of current CTR projects by key CTR decision-making bodies in the Russian government and parliament. In sum, Russian officials have cited the following as the main obstacles to CTR implementation: attempts to make CTR assistance conditional and to link the funding to Russian-Iranian nuclear contracts; slow implementation and obligations of funds by the United States; expenditure of the lion's share of CTR funds in the United States on U.S. contractors, rather than giving the money directly to Russian enterprises; extreme bureaucratization of the process by DOD, making government-to-government cooperation much less effective than lab-to-lab cooperation; and the small number of U.S. specialists sent to Russia to assist in CTR implementation.

Russian Bureaucratic Competition

Another key problem for effective implementation of the CTR Program where Russia is concerned is the bureaucratic competition that exists within the Russian executive branch. Ministries and other executive structures compete fiercely for influence in the decision-making process. Related to this is the severe lack of coordination among Russian official institutions on political-military issues. Competing or overlapping agendas can be identified among a number of executive agencies, although on particular issues traditional rivals may become partners.

---

20. "Interview with Evgenii Maslin," *Yadernyi Kontrol*, No. 5 (1995), p. 11.

Table 5-2. Evaluation of the Current Stage of CTR Projects for Russia.

Project	Minatom	MOD	Duma Committee on Defense	President's Office
Int'l Science & Technology Center [a]	Good	Good	Good	Good
Defense Conversion	Very poor	Poor	Poor	Very poor
Nuclear Emergency Response Equipment and Training	Excellent	Excellent	?	?
Export Controls Assistance	Very poor	Very poor	Very poor	Very poor
MPC&A [b]	Very poor	Good	Satisfactory	Satisfactory
Strategic Offensive Arms Elimination	Not applicable	Excellent	Poor	Satisfactory
Chemical Weapons Destruction	Very poor	Poor	Very poor	Very poor
Fissile Material Containers [c]	Excellent	Excellent	Excellent	Excellent
Armored Blankets [d]	Satisfactory	Excellent	Excellent	Excellent
Fissile Material Storage Facility	Satisfactory	Not applicable	Satisfactory	Excellent
Enhanced Rail Car Security	Good	Excellent	Good	Good

[a] The Duma should ratify the agreement.
[b] More active involvement by the U.S. Department of Energy would be welcome, as it appears to have greater technical expertise in this area than the Department of Defense.
[c] Project finished.
[d] Project finished.

Competition among Russian decision-making bodies has been a critical stumbling block to U.S. and Russian partners developing workable implementation plans in a timely fashion. Too often the Russian government appears to speak with multiple, contradictory voices on particular issues relevant to CTR. Moreover, implementation of particular CTR projects has frequently been stalled because of a lack of clear lines of responsibility within the Russian bureaucracy, a condition that has been aggravated by frequent presidential decrees creating new oversight bodies or assigning new bureaucratic responsibilities to particular agencies at the expense of others. Competition between Minatom and the Federal Atomic Inspectorate (Gosatomnadzor, or GAN) for control of CTR programs to improve nuclear facility safety and security and competing mandates between the MOD and the Committee on Convention-Related CBW Issues regarding chemical weapons destruction are both notorious examples of this dynamic at work. Although the problem of bureaucratic competition and miscoordination has been repeatedly discussed at the level of the President's Office, no effective solution has yet been found. One approach, likely to be implemented in the near future, is to establish an interagency coordinating bureau under the Defense Council of the Russian Federation with oversight of military and foreign policy issues.

The Role of the Russian Media and Non-governmental Organizations

Until recently, the Russian media has paid scant attention to the CTR Program. What news or opinions were voiced on the program's implementation in its first few years were generally neither positive nor negative. Beginning in May 1995, however, there was more coverage than usual about the CTR Program in the Russian media; most was devoted to attempts by the U.S. Congress to reduce or even freeze financial assistance to Russia.[21] *Izvestia* was very critical of the decision of the U.S. House of Representatives to cut CTR funding. It referred to the $171 million in assistance that was first confirmed and then frozen by the House as a "stump of aid."[22] *Kommersant Daily* was even more critical, especially of the suggestion to link nuclear threat reduction assistance to ambiguous "biological suspicions."[23]

After months of barely acknowledging CTR activities, the Russian media started to paint a very negative image of the CTR Program. Through mid-1996 there were few if any positive comments on CTR

---

21. *Izvestia,* June 17, 1995, p. 3; and *Kommersant Daily,* June 15, 1995, pp. 1, 3.

22. *Izvestia,* June 17, 1995, p. 3.

23. *Kommersant Daily,* June 15, 1995, pp. 1, 3.

implementation in the nation's media. This suggests that the Russian government and its ministries have failed to work with the media to portray the CTR Program in a more positive light for Russian public opinion. In fact, no press release on the CTR Program has ever been published and distributed to the central media by Russian authorities. The only place in Moscow where interested journalists can find adequate information about CTR Program implementation is the U.S. Embassy, and only one newspaper, *Kommersant Daily*, provides more or less regular information about CTR developments. Skepticism on the part of some Russian government officials regarding the effectiveness of the CTR Program affects their comments to the press or results in the absence of any comments at all.

With a few exceptions, including the Center for Political Research in Russia (PIR Center), Russian nongovernmental organizations (NGOs) and research centers generally have paid little attention in their research programs to CTR implementation in Russia. Thus they have not played any role in influencing distribution of CTR funds in Russia or in recommending better uses for these funds. The experience of the PIR Center demonstrates, however, that decision-makers, on the whole, are interested in involving NGOs in the dialogue on the CTR Program. Governmental officials who wish to make their comments and recommendations on CTR implementation known to the United States have sometimes preferred to use NGOs as an indirect and nongovernmental way to disseminate such comments.

The role of NGOs in assisting Russian officials to improve the CTR Program is very limited but nonetheless can be very useful. It is limited because of the lack of a tradition of government-NGO dialogue in Russia. However, the situation has slowly started to change for the better. Russian government officials and especially legislators increasingly are seeking more descriptive information and analytical materials about future Russian involvement in the CTR Program, about the difficulties and obstacles of that involvement, about the position of U.S. officials, and about relevant discussions at international seminars and workshops. Increasingly, NGOs are being asked to supply decision-makers with information and analysis about the CTR Program. By meeting these information dissemination needs, NGOs in Russia are beginning to have an influence, albeit indirectly, on the CTR process. Organizing seminars and workshops on Nunn-Lugar implementation, stressing such issues as conversion, MPC&A, and strategic offensive arms elimination, would be a second way that Russian NGOs could influence this process. However, as yet there is no practice of Russian NGOs organizing such seminars. A key factor in this regard is the financial dependence of the seminar organizers on the Russian government and its ministries.

Conclusions

In its early months, the CTR Program faced considerable opposition in Russia from Russian parliamentarians and the public at large. Suspicion of U.S. motives in offering to assist Russian nuclear disarmament and nonproliferation goals was a natural consequence of more than 40 years of distrust and fear of the West. Eventual approval and broader support for cooperative threat reduction in these critical early months were due in large part to the strong voices of support emanating from the Russian Ministry of Defense, Minatom, and other Russian bureaucracies, who argued that cooperation with the United States was critical to meeting the complex military-technical demands of Russia's arms control and nuclear security requirements. The support of these organizations, in turn, was the direct result of the enthusiastic offers of assistance from key legislators and policymakers in the United States.

This bureaucratic consensus in Russia in favor of cooperation with the West has eroded considerably, and many of the individuals who once provided key support to the CTR Program have become outspoken critics of its delays and mismanagement. Implementation problems, including administrative delays and complex auditing requirements on the part of the United States and the underutilization of local Russian enterprises to perform CTR tasks, have soured key bureaucratic players on U.S.-Russian cooperation. Moreover, the CTR Program has been caught up in the larger political mood, manifest in the December 1995 electoral gains of Russian Communists and ultranationalists, that has turned against cooperation with the West and has come to see such cooperation as a means for the United States to further weaken Russian national capabilities. Aggravating this tension is the increasingly vocal chorus of criticism from legislators and opinionmakers in the United States who have come to regard assistance to Russia as a means of influencing or forcing Russian policy on a number of unrelated political or military issues.

Rebuilding the bureaucratic consensus that once existed for U.S.-Russian cooperation will require a number of steps. At a minimum, current and future assistance projects must be implemented in a way that does not waste CTR funds and makes better use of indigenous Russian personnel and technical resources for cooperative projects. The administrative waste and delays that have slowed critical assistance programs have only encouraged cynicism on the part of Russian bureaucratic players and the public at large. Winning back the support of these individuals, who are crucial to the overall demilitarization process, will require a number of administrative changes, some of which are already under way and some of which have been suggested by Russian officials themselves. Granting the U.S. Department of Energy greater oversight of MPC&A activities with Russia, for example, may be the best way to reduce the burdensome administrative delays that have hamstrung DOD activities in this area. Given the preference of Minatom officials for working with DOE, this simple measure may be enough to rebuild a strong working relationship between the United States and Minatom.

U.S. officials should also recognize that there are many voices within the Russian bureaucracy involved in CTR implementation who remain generally or strongly supportive of the program but have been discouraged by recent problems. A greater degree of flexibility on the part of the United States, such as providing more of the contracts for CTR activities to local Russian enterprises, is likely to help reduce program costs and delays even as it promotes greater goodwill on the part of Russian participants. In this vein, U.S. legislators may want to reconsider their linkage of CTR assistance to a variety of problems in U.S.-Russian bilateral relations.

For its part, the current government in Moscow must redouble its efforts to resolve the bureaucratic disputes that have delayed implementation of time-urgent demilitarization and risk-reduction activities. It also must try to do a much better job with its own public diplomacy in support of the CTR program. At a minimum, the Russian government must make a greater effort to keep the Russian public and interested opinion-makers informed of the status and successes of U.S.-Russian cooperation. In the absence of any official support for the CTR Program, bureaucratic inertia and criticism have been allowed to erode the special relationship that might have evolved with the United States from joint demilitarization efforts. Russian NGOs have begun to play a role, albeit tentatively, in building such channels of communication. Similarly, these organizations and their equivalents abroad could play a role in reinvigorating the dialogue between key Russian decision-makers, legislators, and opinion-makers with their American counterparts. Achieving this would be a first step in rebuilding a groundswell of support for the CTR Program and U.S.-Russian cooperation in general. It could demonstrate to Russians the tangible benefits of CTR assistance and demonstrate to U.S. decision-makers the urgent need for and real self-interest of this venture.

Chapter 6

The CTR Program and Russia

Is a New Start Possible?
A Russian View

Alexander A. Pikayev

More than four years have passed since the United States initiated the Nunn-Lugar Cooperative Threat Reduction (CTR) Program to assist former Soviet states with their weapons dismantlement and nonproliferation agenda, and it is now possible to render an initial assessment of the successes and failures of this critical program. Several hundred million dollars have been spent under the CTR Program to help Soviet successor states dismantle the nuclear legacy of the Cold War and put in place safeguards against the theft or diversion of weapons materials and technologies. The momentum created by the CTR Program has, in turn, generated a number of complementary assistance efforts by the United States and other Western nations, both bilaterally and multilaterally. This chapter reviews some of the achievements and shortfalls of the first four years of the Nunn-Lugar Program and related efforts as they have been implemented in the Russian Federation, which is by far the largest recipient of U.S. threat reduction and nonproliferation assistance.

By mid-1995, although more than $612 million in spending had been proposed by the U.S. Department of Defense (DOD), only three-fifths of this amount, $348 million, had been obligated through signed contracts for specific projects. Moreover, of these obligated amounts, only $119 million—less than 20 percent of total DOD proposed spending for Russia—had actually been disbursed as real goods and services.[1] In

---

1. See *Nuclear Successor States of the Soviet Union: Nuclear Weapon and Sensitive Export Status Report* [hereafter CEIP/MIIS Status Report], No. 3 (July 1995), published by the Monterey Institute of International Studies and the Carnegie Endowment for

---

This chapter was written in August 1995 and reflects progress in the CTR program and related efforts up to that date.

average annual terms, the amount of CTR funds actually spent over the first four years of the program has been estimated at $34 million, which constitutes less than eight percent of Russia's Fiscal Year (FY) 1995 weapons dismantlement budget.[2]

Although these figures suggest that, in dollar terms, CTR implementation has been less than successful, in fact a number of improvements in CTR implementation have been made since FY 1994. One measure of this steady improvement is the rate at which proposed funds have been actually set aside or "obligated" for specific demilitarization and nuclear security projects in Russia. According to DOD estimates, the rate of obligation for proposed CTR funds in FY 1994 proposed under the CTR Program increased fourfold over FY 1993, while the FY 1995 rate was estimated to be more than six times greater than FY 1993.[3]

Unfortunately, these improvements may have come too late. Growing criticism in the Republican-led U.S. Congress of the CTR Program and of Russian political and military "misbehavior" has led to threats of substantial cuts in CTR spending authority as well as numerous conditions on future assistance. In Russia, inflated expectations of U.S. assistance have been replaced by growing disappointment in the program's inefficiency and underfunding. This gloomier outlook on the program has coincided with a more general cooling in U.S.-Russian relations.

Despite the early promise of bilateral relations at the end of the Cold War, the new uneasiness between Russia and the United States has led to a negative reinterpretation of all that was accomplished during the post–Cold War honeymoon. As the program which underwrote the most visible and profound achievement of this period—nuclear disarmament—the CTR Program is especially vulnerable to criticism. This fact makes it imperative to look beyond the CTR Program's evident faults and suggest possible improvements that could reinvigorate the program in coming years. Visible proof of the program's effectiveness, even in an unfavorable political climate, can underscore the necessity and feasibility of continuing the U.S.-Russian

---

International Peace, Table I-F, pp. 39–41.

2. Federal Budget of the Russian Federation for FY 1995, March 1995.

3. U.S. Department of Defense, *Cooperative Threat Reduction*, April 1995.

dialogue on nuclear issues, regardless of what administration occupies Moscow or Washington.

This assessment begins by reviewing the status of several CTR projects in Russia, paying particular attention to how levels of assistance proposed by the United States for individual projects have compared to actual disbursements of goods and technical services to carry out CTR activities. More important, this analysis compares the amounts of assistance provided by the United States to Russia's own expenditures for weapons dismantlement, improvements to nuclear safeguards, and other activities. Such an analysis reveals that U.S. and Russian efforts in some instances have not been complementary: in certain project areas, U.S. assistance makes only a marginal contribution and is far outpaced by Russia's own spending; however, in other areas of concern, CTR funds have not been used to fill gaps in areas where indigenous Russian efforts have been weak or ineffective. While U.S. CTR assistance has provided tremendous added value to several urgent demilitarization and nonproliferation tasks in Russia, in some cases where Russian officials have devoted insufficient resources to these problems, the CTR Program's potential remains largely unfulfilled.

The middle third of this review of the CTR effort considers the difficulties that face the program and U.S.-Russian cooperation generally from the instability within Russia's decision-making bureaucracy. Frequent and unpredictable personnel and organizational changes have become the hallmark of government in the Russian Federation and have, in several instances, pitted agency against agency in a competition for influence and foreign assistance dollars. This assessment attempts to review some of the key organizational players and bureaucratic developments in Russia, in part to assist CTR Program managers and other U.S. decision-makers to navigate these problems more effectively.

Finally, this chapter concludes by assessing Russian perspectives on the program and suggesting ways in which the CTR Program and similar efforts might be improved. By reviewing how well CTR projects have been implemented, how effectively they address their nominal threat reduction and nonproliferation goals, the degree to which they have contributed to Russia's indigenous efforts in these areas, and how well these projects have navigated and survived in Russia's bureaucratic environment, this assessment makes several concrete recommendations for sustaining the CTR effort and carrying it forward to accomplish its agenda.

CTR Program Implementation in Russia

Progress achieved in various CTR projects varies considerably (see Table 6-1). In some CTR projects—such as for design of a fissile material storage facility, railcar security, and providing emergency response equipment—more than four-fifths of proposed funds had been spent as of mid-1995. By contrast, in the areas of storage facility equipment; fissile material protection, control, and accounting (MPC&A); and export controls, only a small percentage of proposed funds had been disbursed. Other successfully implemented projects include the International Science and Technology Center (ISTC), supply of armored blankets for nuclear weapon transport, and military-to-military contacts. However, by mid-1995, only six of the 14 CTR projects listed in Table 6-1 had more than one-third of proposed funds disbursed.

Safe, secure transportation of nuclear warheads from locations in non-Russian republics back to Russia was one of the most urgent military-technical tasks facing Russia in the immediate post-Soviet era. According to the Russian military, transportation represents the most vulnerable component of the nuclear weapons life cycle. This risk was especially high between 1992 and 1995, when approximately 3,200 strategic warheads[4] were transported from decommissioned delivery vehicles deployed in Russia, Ukraine, Kazakstan, and Belarus to dismantlement facilities and storage sites in Russia. The United States provided CTR assistance for weapons security, transportation, and storage, and this aid has been of great help to the overall Russian effort.[5]

---

4. According to a 1994 U.S. estimate, Russia has been dismantling 2,000–3,000 nuclear warheads annually. See Testimony of Ashton B. Carter, Assistant Secretary of Defense, Before the Senate Armed Services Committee, April 28, 1994. Moreover, thousands of tactical nuclear warheads were transported to alternative storage sites in an effort to reduce the number of nuclear storage facilities and dismantlement plants. According to the chief of the 12th Main Directorate, Colonel-General Evgenii Maslin, the Russian military closed a number of nuclear storage facilities in Ukraine, Belarus, and Kazakstan, as well as near Nal'chik, Republic of Kabardino-Balkaria, and in the Russian Far East.

5. In April 1995, Russian Defense Minister Pavel Grachev and U.S. Secretary of Defense William Perry signed two new agreements under which the United States would provide $20 million to improve the security and accounting of nuclear weapons. Of this amount, $17 million was to be used for transportation security and

Table 6-1. Implementation of CTR Projects.

Project	Main Russian Recipient(s)	Amount proposed ($M)	Amount disbursed as of 6/95, in $M, as percentage of amount proposed	
Storage Facility Design	Minatom	15.00	12.87	85.8%
Railcar Security	Ministry of Defense (MOD)	21.50	17.65	82.1%
ISTC	Russian scientists	35.00	22.85	59.7%
Armored Blankets	MOD	5.00	2.91	58.1%
Military-to-Military Contacts	MOD	11.55	3.84	33.3%
Fissile Material Containers	Minatom	50.00	10.09	20.2%
Arctic Nuclear Waste	No umbrella recipient	30.00	5.44	18.1%
Chemical Weapons Destruction	MOD/CCB	55.00	7.72	14.0%
Strategic Offensive Arms Elimination	State Committee for Defense Industries (GKOP)	162.00	19.74	12.1%
Defense Conversion	GKOP enterprises	40.00	3.89	9.7%
Storage Facility Equipment	Minatom	75.00	2.52	3.4%
Emergency Response Equipment	MOD	15.00	11.19	74.6%
MPC&A	Minatom	30.00	0.57	1.9%
Export Controls	Not determined	2.26	0.01	0.4%
Russian Total		21.8% disbursed of total proposed		

$3 million for facility security. See "Perry Adds $50 million to Support Dismantlement of Russian Weapons," *Post-Soviet Nuclear & Defense Monitor,* Vol. 2, No. 16 (April 25, 1995), p. 3. In June 1995, an additional $12 million in U.S. aid was pledged during the Gore-Chernomyrdin meeting in Moscow: $10 million for transportation and $2 million for storage of nuclear weapons and fissile materials. The grants were to be used to buy "supercontainers" to store weapons prior to dismantlement and to acquire computers to improve the accuracy and efficiency of accounting for Russia's nuclear stockpiles. Some funds will also be spent on training of nuclear weapons custodial forces. See "Defense Ministry Receives $24 Million for Weapons Dismantlement," *Post-Soviet Nuclear & Defense Monitor,* Vol. 2, No. 20 (July 12, 1995), p. 2.

CTR projects to prevent proliferation of nuclear expertise from Russia have also achieved considerable success. At a time when Russian military science faces extreme budgetary shortfalls,[6] the risk of Russian nuclear talent emigrating to potential proliferating countries is quite high. Using CTR funding, the United States, in cooperation with the European Union and Japan, established the International Scientific and Technological Center in Moscow in March 1994. As of August 1995, more than 10,000 former Soviet scientists (of which the majority are Russian) were employed in more than 180 ISTC-funded projects.[7] The ISTC budget was increased from $2 million in FY 1994 to $17 million in FY 1995, and all these funds were obligated.

Progress has also been made in building U.S.-Russian military-to-military contacts. Although no CTR funds were obligated for these activities in FY 1993, in FYs 1994 and 1995, one-third of the proposed budget had already been spent, and this amount is likely to increase steadily in the future. This program is growing in political importance and is likely to be the main conduit for Russian military dialogues with the West since the Russian military appears reluctant to participate in a similar NATO Partnership for Peace program.

Despite these successes, significant implementation problems have emerged in three critical areas: elimination of strategic offensive arms, destruction of chemical weapons (CW), and improving fissile material protection, control, and accounting. Elimination of strategic and chemical weapons together accounts for more than one-third of total CTR resources; slow progress in these areas has hampered overall CTR disbursements. Slow U.S.-Russian agreement on technical and organizational aspects of CW destruction is the major reason for delays in disbursing CTR funds for CW destruction. The project was begun in earnest only in 1994.[8]

---

6. In many Russian military research institutes, the monthly salary does not exceed $50. Even this less-than-adequate sum is paid irregularly and, very often, salaries are not paid for several months.

7. For a detailed case study on the history, status, and future prospects of the ISTC, see Chapter 13 by Adam Moody in this volume.

8. Almost $8 million has been disbursed for the U.S.-Russian evaluation of CW neutralization technology by the CW Destruction Analytical Lab. The project is coordinated by the U.S. Army Chemical Material Agency, which opened a chemical weapons support office in Moscow in June 1993. In May 1994, DOD awarded a

No such explanations can account for delays in strategic arms elimination, where CTR assistance has been extraordinarily slow despite Russia's record of decommissioning its strategic delivery vehicles.[9] CTR assistance supported ICBM silo elimination in four Russian Strategic Rocket Forces (SRF) bases.[10] Eighteen million dollars in CTR-funded equipment for destroying ballistic missile submarine (SSBN) hulls and ballistic missile launch tubes was delivered in 1994 to three SSBN elimination facilities: Zvezda (in Bolshoi Kamen, near Vladivostok), Zvyozdochka (in Severodvinsk, Arkhangelsk oblast), and Nerpa (Murmansk). CTR-funded equipment for heavy bomber elimination valued at $5.5 million has also been delivered to Engels Air Force Base near Saratov.

A series of U.S.-Russian agreements in 1995 attempted to improve this situation by committing additional resources to strategic arms elimination.[11] However, these additional funds are unlikely to improve

---

contract to draft an operational plan for destroying Russian chemical weapons to Bechtel International. See U.S. General Accounting Office (GAO), *Weapons of Mass Destruction: Reducing the Threat from the Former Soviet Union*, GAO-NSIAD-95-7 (October 1994), p. 23. DOD expects to provide funds in the near future for design and construction of a prototype chemical munitions destruction facility capable of destroying 500 metric tons of nerve-agent-filled artillery munitions per year. See U.S. Department of Defense, *Cooperative Threat Reduction*, April 1995, p. 16.

9. By the fall of 1995, Russia had decommissioned approximately 430 land-based strategic missiles, including heavy SS-18 intercontinental ballistic missiles (ICBMs). Twenty strategic nuclear submarines with almost 300 submarine-launched ballistic missiles (SLBMs) were made non-operational by having their launch tubes cut off in accordance with START I procedures. Three dozen heavy bombers were decommissioned, and 64 were destroyed. These decommissioned weapons were capable of delivering more than 1,000 warheads, primarily to targets in the United States. These figures were calculated by the author, based on conversations with top Russian military officials in August and September 1995.

10. SS-18s were deployed at one of these bases, Uzhur.

11. During his April 1995 visit to Moscow, U.S. Defense Secretary William Perry amended an earlier agreement with the Russian State Committee for Defense Industries (GKOP) to give GKOP an additional $20 million for equipment, training, and technical support to dismantle and eliminate strategic submarines, liquid missile propellant, solid rocket motors, heavy bombers, ICBMs, SLBMs, and ICBM silos. However, additional "technical discussions" were necessary to determine specific services and equipment to be procured. Similarly, in the June 1995 meeting of the Gore-Chernomyrdin Commission, U.S. Vice President Al Gore committed

project implementation. Management of previous assistance was already inadequate; increasing funding levels will only aggravate the management problem rather than solve it. New funds may only create new areas of activity rather than improve existing projects.

Progress under the CTR Program to improve fissile material control and accounting in Russia—the second central task of the program—has been scandalous, given the threat posed by diversions of fissile materials from Russia. Less than six percent of a proposed $10 million had been disbursed by May 1995. Some changes beginning in 1995 are encouraging, however. Although MPC&A discussions between DOD and Minatom stalled repeatedly, there has been rapid progress in the laboratory-to-laboratory program, managed by the U.S. Department of Energy (DOE). Decentralized management over MPC&A activities in the lab-to-lab program gave more freedom of action to the program's participants—Russian nuclear labs and their U.S. counterparts. Authority for MPC&A activities was transferred from DOD to DOE, which proved to be a more flexible player, and $15 million in FY 1995 funding was transferred from DOD to DOE to implement the lab-to-lab program. One of the reasons for this change was the greater attention being given to MPC&A issues by White House officials.

Lab-to-lab MPC&A improvements have been made at several key nuclear facilities in Russia. Besides installing U.S.-made equipment in Russian facilities, the lab-to-lab program also sponsors joint development and production of such equipment with Russian enterprises. The success of the lab-to-lab approach has provided needed momentum in the area of MPC&A, encouraging Russia's Ministry of Atomic Energy (Minatom) to open up more facilities for cooperation. This momentum was not merely a question of the amount of assistance offered by the United States. Increased assistance was accompanied by measures designed to ensure project implementation. Working relationships were established not only with responsible Russian agencies, but with the final recipients of aid. Moreover, U.S. and Russian coordinators approached the issue on an equal footing. As a result, the general political situation surrounding MPC&A is beginning to improve, and more high-level attention is being paid to MPC&A issues, as illustrated

---

new CTR funds for dismantling nuclear weapons. The GKOP received $12 million for dismantling strategic nuclear missiles and launchers, as required by the START I Treaty, and for disposal of solid and liquid missile propellant.

by the organization of a G7+1 summit[12] devoted to nuclear safety in April 1996.

Work on designing and equipping a fissile material storage facility at Mayak (Chelyabinsk-65) has been far from satisfactory. The first stage of this $90 million project was a rapid and early success, but its second stage, expected to cost $75 million, remains deadlocked. Only three percent of proposed funds had been disbursed by mid-1995. Although Minatom initiated construction of the Mayak facility in the fall of 1994 and the first sets of CTR-funded equipment were delivered to the construction site, Minatom was obligated to pay the lion's share of construction expenses, for which it had no budget. This stumbling block was overcome when the United States agreed to provide additional aid to partially fund construction activity. If completed, the facility would be an important, tangible symbol for the CTR Program and, more broadly, for the U.S.-Russian partnership. For the U.S. public, it would provide evidence that their government's effort to reduce the threat of illegal fissile material trafficking from Russia is making real headway. For the Russian public and decision-makers, such an ambitious construction project would demonstrate that the CTR Program is not devoted solely to destruction of Russian weapons systems and other national assets. This would have a subtle but nevertheless powerful impact on Russian perceptions of the CTR Program.

Another CTR task that has been poorly implemented is the conversion to civilian purposes of Russian military-industrial facilities, for which less than ten percent of proposed funds have been disbursed. Only four demonstration conversion projects have been concluded, and only three of these have been successful.[13] In another defense conver-

---

12. As an observer at the June 1995 G7 summit in Halifax, Russian President Boris Yeltsin proposed that a G7 summit convene in the spring of 1996 in Moscow, in commemoration of the tenth anniversary of the Chernobyl accident. The characterization "G7+1" was used by Russia prior to the April 1996 summit to strengthen its position as an up-and-coming partner of equal status with the G7 states.

13. The four joint stock projects were: (1) between Double Cola and NPO Mashino-stroenia to bottle and distribute soft drinks; (2) between Hearing Aid and ISTOK to design and manufacture hearing aids; (3) between International American Products and NPO Leninets to manufacture dental chairs; and (4) between Rockwell International and GosNIIAS to manufacture air traffic control equipment. See Dunbar Lockwood, "The CTR Program: No Time To Pull the Plug," *Arms Control*

sion effort, the U.S. DOD signed a contract with American Housing Technologies (AHT) to convert three Russian defense plants to manufacturing prefabricated housing for demobilized military personnel. The DOD provided $20 million and AHT provided $5 million for the project. However, converting sophisticated, high-tech factories to the production of simple housing materials is sure to face criticism in Russia. Moreover, the converted enterprises will face strong competition from existing Russian construction plants.[14] Mistakes such as these can be explained in part by the DOD's lack of experience with conversion problems. To its credit, the DOD recognized this problem and, in March 1994, established the Defense Enterprises Fund (DEF), an independent body charged with underwriting promising U.S.-Russian joint business ventures. The DEF is managed by civilian representatives from the private sector with experience in conversion. Unfortunately, in 1995 this promising initiative was left unfunded due to congressional opposition.

Implementation of the Arctic Nuclear Waste Assessment project has had modest results, and in the context of the overall CTR Program, is of relatively marginal importance. The project was initiated in 1993 and is managed by the U.S. Office of Naval Research. During the June 1995 meeting of the Gore-Chernomyrdin Commission, the United States and Russia agreed to assess radionuclide contamination flows from the Mayak and Krasnoyarsk nuclear facilities into the Arctic basin. However, this is only a peripheral issue in the context of overall Arctic nuclear contamination: the Arctic basin faces a much more immediate threat of radioactive contamination from nuclear submarine dismantlement in Severodvinsk and Murmansk. Refocusing the project and spending as yet unobligated funds toward resolving this second problem would be more in line with core CTR goals.

Very little progress has been made in the CTR Program's projects to improve export controls. This lack of progress is reflected in the fact that by mid-1995, only $10,000 had been disbursed for export control enhancements out of the $2.26 million originally proposed. However,

---

Today, June 1995, p. 10.

14. The main problem facing Russia's housing construction industry is not lack of production capability, but lack of orders. Thus this project may only exacerbate problems in the industry as a whole, and at these converted plants in particular. As newcomers, they will hardly be able to compete in the current market.

unlike other former Soviet republics, Russia inherited a sophisticated export control system from the Soviet Union. Although this system must be adapted to new economic realities, such a task does not merit assistance under the CTR Program. The lack of Russian interest in receiving CTR funds for export control confirms that Russia is likely to be able to maintain effective export controls relying primarily on its own resources.

Nor is it is clear what the goals of the export control project are. The main threat of weapons proliferation from Russia is posed by the potential diversion of fissile materials and nuclear warheads. This threat requires improving storage and transport of nuclear materials and reducing the opportunities for illegal export. This could be achieved by strengthening protection of Russia's borders and customs controls, yet neither Russian agency responsible for these issues—the Federal Border Service (FPS) or the Customs Committee (GTK)— were involved in project negotiations. Export control negotiations took place with Minatom, the MOD, and even with the Federal Service for Hard Currency and Export Control (FSVEK), which controls dual-use technology exports. Although important, such controls have little in common with the CTR Program's focus on illicit exports of nuclear materials.[15]

In sum, critical CTR projects supporting safe transport, storage and destruction of nuclear weapons and secondary tasks such as preventing a Russian "brain drain" through the ISTC and expanding military contacts have been the most successfully implemented to date.

---

15. The CTR Program's lack of progress on export controls contrasts sharply with highly effective European efforts to assist former Warsaw Pact and some post-Soviet states, such as by equipping their customs officials with radiation detectors. This is especially curious given the DOD's apparent understanding of the problem in its response to a 1994 GAO report. In that response, a DOD official wrote: "Our export control assistance program involves training specialists, helping the governments draft laws and regulations, and assisting in developing border posts." As the first two tasks do not apply to Russia, which possesses an effective export control system, presumably limited CTR resources would concentrate on "developing border posts" along the lengthy Russian borders with other states of the former Soviet Union. See U.S. GAO, *Weapons of Mass Destruction*, GAO-NSIAD-95-7 (October 1994), p. 38. The border problem was partially resolved when a customs union was established among Russia, Belarus, Kazakstan, and Kyrgyzstan. Unlike Russia, Belarus and Kazakstan received CTR assistance to improve their border controls.

However, other projects, such as eliminating strategic weapons, destroying CW stockpiles, and improving fissile material safeguards, have been poorly executed. Projects to demilitarize Russian defense industries have lacked seriousness and suffered from an incomplete understanding of Russian industrial planning. The export controls project has been the most poorly executed program to date and has not even stayed within the scope of the CTR project, whose focus is weapons of mass destruction. Happily for the program's future, some promising changes have been made, particularly in fissile material controls. Funding obligations have also been increased for destroying strategic delivery vehicles and chemical weapons, although this may not necessarily lead to qualitative improvements in the execution of these projects.

Achievement of the CTR Program's Core Goals

The previous section assessed how well CTR projects have been implemented in terms of the degree to which obligated CTR funds have been disbursed. A more important question is whether the composition of the CTR Program and the funding allocated to individual projects has been appropriate to achieve the stated goals of the program. One way to measure the value added by the CTR Program is to compare CTR funding for particular projects to funding allocations for the same activities in Russia's federal budget. These comparisons are illustrated in Table 6-2.

Russian authorities appear to have underestimated the financial requirements of some demilitarization and nuclear security activities. U.S. CTR assistance had the potential to play a major role in addressing such shortfalls in areas such as fissile material security (MPC&A), strategic offensive arms elimination, CW destruction, and defense conversion. However, this potential has remained largely unrealized because of the program's slow implementation.

Between 1992 and 1995, average annual proposed CTR assistance for MPC&A activities ($64.2 million) was almost one-third of what was allocated by the FY 1995 Russian federal budget for Minatom, which oversees all fissile material management activities. CTR funds thus could have made a significant contribution to improving fissile material security in Russia, particularly when one considers that most of Minatom's budget is devoted to warhead elimination and only a portion to fissile material security. This opportunity went largely

Table 6-2. Russian and U.S. Financing of Demilitarization Activities.

FY 95 Russian Federal Budget Activity	FY95 RF Budget ($M)	Related CTR Assistance, FY 1992–95 ($M)			
		Amount Proposed		Amount Disbursed (5/95)	
		FY92–95	Annually	FY92–95	Annually [a]
Nuclear weapons dismantlement	306	139.5	72.6	51.4 [b]	20.4 [b]
Nuclear-powered weapons destruction (SSNs, SSBNs)	90	20.6	10.3	NA	NA
CW destruction	20	55.0	23.3	7.7	2.6
Special fuels & ammunition destruction	22	31.4	15.7	–	–
Subtotal	438	246.5	121.9	59.1	23.0
Military R&D	949	35.0	17.5	22.9	10.4
Fundamental research	341	35.0	17.5	22.9	10.4
Minatom expenses (MPC&A, etc.)	195	150.0	64.2	26.1	9.2
Defense conversion	176	40.0	26.7	3.9	2.6
Environmental protection	254	30.0	10.0	5.4	1.8
Housing construction	673	20.0	20.0	–	–

[a] Annual average figures are calculated taking into account dates of signing relevant agreements.
[b] Includes disbursements for SSBN elimination. Projects agreed to in late 1995 are not included.

unrealized, however. Actual CTR disbursements, on an annual basis, did not reach even five percent of Minatom's FY 1995 budget authority. In all areas of strategic offensive arms elimination, proposed annual CTR contributions were about one-quarter of what Russian authorities were able to spend. In reality, the disbursed CTR amount of $20 million has only slightly exceeded five percent of Russian expenditures in this area. Assistance to SSBN destruction—arguably the most acute of Russia's weapons elimination problems—was particularly underbudgeted by both Russian and U.S. planners. Russia's extensive requirements for SSBN dismantlement resulted in CTR funds being obligated much more rapidly than expected. By October 1994 almost 90 percent of funds proposed for submarine dismantlement were obligated, compared to about 50 percent for eliminating all strategic offensive arms. CTR assistance might also have made a major contribution to transportation and disposition of liquid propellants from ballistic missiles if actual disbursements had matched proposed funding levels. In annual terms, proposed CTR funds in this area are similar to amounts in the FY 1995 Russian budget. Moreover, since the relevant Russian budget item also covers elimination of other types of fuel and ammunition, proposed CTR activities in this area could have had a major impact on this important environmental problem.

The most serious missed opportunity for the CTR Program in Russia is in the area of chemical weapons destruction. The Russian budget allocated very modest sums for CW elimination—just $20 million for FY 1995. If the $55 million proposed under the CTR Program had been disbursed, the pace of Russia's chemical disarmament could have been doubled.

CTR assistance, at even modest levels, could have also played a very visible role in accelerating conversion of the Russian military-industrial complex to civilian and commercial purposes. The Russian federal government allocated insufficient funds for this purpose (only $176 million in FY 1995 and no more than $280 million in government credits for conversion projects). Full implementation of CTR conversion projects could cover up to one-eighth of Russian conversion activities. Instead, CTR defense conversion activities have emphasized housing construction, which seems counterproductive. The proposed $20 million to convert military plants into factories producing housing construction equipment is a very small portion of what is spent annually by the Russian government and local authorities for housing construction. In the FY 1995 federal budget almost $700 million is planned for the activity; another $550 million is allocated for military housing construction in the defense budget. In this context, CTR assistance is not sufficient to visibly improve the situation.

A more promising conversion strategy is to finance joint stock companies between Russian and U.S. enterprises. This would help liberate Russian defense plants from control by government agencies, especially the State Committee for Defense Industries (GKOP). Decentralizing the defense industry would also boost current economic reforms and reduce the responsibility of the Moscow bureaucracy. Missteps in defense conversion are especially disappointing since they are likely to be the most important factor in reducing the future threat from the Russian military-industrial complex. An increase of CTR funding to about $100 million annually could significantly accelerate the process.

The $22.85 million in annual CTR funding for the ISTC in 1994–95 represents only about two percent of Russia's $1 billion FY 1995 expenditure on military research and development (R&D). The relative amounts suggest that the ISTC cannot hope to compete with the Russian government in providing attractive jobs to military scientists and preventing their emigration to potential proliferators. The ISTC has not been a failure, however. U.S. multilateral efforts to establish a large new research center in Moscow, the average annual funding of which exceeds federal expenditures for several regional branches of the Russian Academy of Sciences, is an important symbol for the future of Russian civilian research. This is particularly true at a time when Russian basic science is on the verge of collapse.

In FY 1995 the Russian government was able to spend only $254 million for environmental protection and did not have a nationwide program devoted to Arctic problems. In this context, the average of $55 million allocated annually by the CTR Arctic Nuclear Waste Assessment in 1992–95 represents an important contribution. However, it remains unclear what relevance this project has to the core CTR goal of threat reduction.

Thus, although CTR funds played an important supporting role, in most cases Russia has allocated much greater resources to demilitarization and nuclear security projects. In critical areas such as strategic weapons elimination, fissile MPC&A, and CW destruction, the CTR Program's contribution could have been significant, but slow disbursements of aid have prevented it from achieving this potential. More important for strategic weapons elimination is the fact that, from the beginning, the CTR Program, like similar Russian spending, has paid inadequate attention to dismantling nuclear submarines. Given the modest financing of some of these projects in Russia's federal budget, proposed levels of CTR assistance could have provided the United States with important leverage to shape developments in these areas.

These appear to be the major failings of the CTR Program to date. Nonetheless, a window of opportunity remains. Unobligated or potential future CTR funds could be concentrated in the most promising CTR project areas, including safe transport and storage of nuclear warheads, nuclear submarine destruction, storage and disposal of missile and submarine fuel, CW destruction, construction of a fissile materials storage facility, and defense conversion.

The Challenge to CTR Implementation from Bureaucratic Instability

Russia's bureaucracy has traditionally been characterized by its huge scale, inefficiency and considerable overlap in responsibilities among various agencies. These deficiencies came into sharp focus during Russia's transition from a centrally planned, totalitarian system to a more open society oriented toward market economics. Transitional strains were intensified by the collapse of the Soviet Union and the radical changes in defense and foreign policies. Between 1992 and 1993, the bureaucratic system was further destabilized by a confrontation between the Russian president and the Supreme Soviet, and Russian society remains in transition.

In addition to poor program management by the United States, bureaucratic instability in Russia has been a key reason for delays in delivering CTR assistance, especially for submarine dismantlement, CW destruction, export controls, and defense conversion. Table 6-3 presents the major Russian negotiators and recipients for these and other CTR projects as of 1995.

The importance of bureaucratic stability for CTR implementation can be seen in the evolution of the Russian military command—one of the main CTR recipients and one of the most stable institutions throughout the post-Soviet period. In December 1991, the Soviet Ministry of Defense was reorganized into the CIS Supreme Command (Glavkomat), which, through its 12th Main Directorate, retained control over nuclear weapons. The 12th Main Directorate oversaw the withdrawal of tactical nuclear weapons from non-Russian republics, which was successfully completed by June 1992. The formal establishment of the Russian Defense Ministry (MOD) in April 1992 initiated the transfer of nuclear responsibilities from the CIS Glavkomat to the Russian MOD.[16] Throughout these changes—from the Soviet Defense

---

16. Reportedly these responsibilities, including control over the 12th Main Directorate, were tacitly transferred as early as summer 1992. Nevertheless, by law, the chief of the CIS Joint Armed Forces possessed control over nuclear weapons until the formal abolition of his position in the spring of 1993.

Table 6-3. Negotiating and Recipient Organizations in Russia.

CTR Project	Main Negotiator	Main Recipients	Potential Recipients
1992 Framework Agreement	Ministry of Foreign Affairs (MID)		
Armored blankets	Ministry of Defense (MOD)	MOD (12th Main Directorate)	
Railcar security	MOD	MOD (12th Main Directorate)	Ministry of Transportation (MPS)
Emergency response	MOD	MOD	Ministry for Civil Defense and Emergency Situations (MChS), Minatom
Strategic offensive arms elimination	GKOP	MOD (RVSN,[a] DA[b]), GKOP enterprises	
CW destruction	CCB/MOD	MOD (chemical defense personnel), GKOP enterprises	Local authorities, Ministry of Environmental & Natural Resources Protection, Academy of Sciences
Defense conversion	GKOP	GKOP enterprises, NPO Mashinostroenia, GosNIIAS, ISTOK, Leninets	Russian Space Agency (RKA), NGOs, enterprises
MPC&A	Minatom, GAN, Kurchatov Institute, Minatom labs	Minatom enterprises, Kurchatov Institute, Minatom labs, GAN	
Fissile material containers	Minatom	Minatom enterprises	Federal Atomic Inspectorate (GAN)
Storage facility design	Minatom	Minatom enterprises	GAN, MP[c]
Storage facility equipment	Minatom	Minatom enterprises	GAN, MP
Military-to-military contacts	MOD	MOD	
Export controls	Minatom, MOD, FSVEK		Minatom, Ministry for Foreign Economic Relations (MVES), MID, MOD, Federal Security Service (FSB), Foreign Intelligence Service (FSK), Customs, NGOs, Federal Border Control Service (FPS)
Arctic pollution	No umbrella Russian recipient	U.S. contractors	MP, Minatom, Ministry for Ethnic & Regional Policy (MN), RAN[d], GAN, Navy, GKOP enterprises

[a] RSVN = Strategic Rocket Forces   [b] DA = Long Range Aviation
[c] MP = Ministry of Natural Resources   [d] RAN = Russian Academy of Sciences

Ministry, to the CIS Glavkomat, and finally to the Russian MOD — the 12th Main Directorate remained responsible for nuclear weapons transportation and storage. It remained a well-known and stable institution for negotiating all aspects of CTR assistance for nuclear weapons transport and storage on Russia's territory. This is one of the reasons why CTR projects in this area were unaffected by bureaucratic changes. At the same time, as described more fully below, changes in other parts of the MOD bureaucracy significantly hampered development of a chemical weapons disarmament policy.

Another important CTR negotiator and recipient, the State Committee for Defense Industries, was established in 1992 from the merger of several Soviet ministries that previously controlled all defense industry.[17] Despite the new realities of transitioning to a market economy, GKOP failed to establish a strong relationship with industrial enterprises nominally under its control as had existed during the Soviet era. Nor was GKOP the sole source of income for these enterprises as were its Soviet-era predecessors such as the Ministry of Shipbuilding. GKOP's role was diminished further in 1993–94 when control over several of Russia's most successful aerospace plants was given to the Russian Space Agency (RKA). GKOP also failed to establish control over arms exports, which was given to a special state monopoly, Rosvooruzhenie, created by presidential decree. Moreover, some defense factories, including the powerful, MiG-producing Moscow Aviation Industrial Association (MAPO), found their own way to world markets without GKOP's assistance or oversight. GKOP was further undermined in December 1994 by the establishment of the State Committee on Military and Technology Policy (GKVTP), which was given similar responsibilities, including weapons dismantlement. The result was an intense competition between GKOP and GKVTP.

An unfavorable bureaucratic environment makes GKOP more committed to maintaining its access to CTR negotiations and distribution. This remains an important source of leverage against other agencies, especially RKA and GKVTP. Nonetheless, the committee's bureaucratic weakness has led to delays in CTR projects for which it is responsible. Although it has been relatively successful in negotiating

---

17. The best known of these ministries were the Ministry of General Machine-Building (Minobschemash) and the Ministry of Shipbuilding. The latter dealt with construction and dismantlement of naval arms, including attack submarines (SSNs) and ballistic missile submarines (SSBNs).

CTR assistance from the Pentagon, GKOP's poor relations with Russian industrial enterprises have resulted in a wide gap between obligated and disbursed funds for CTR projects, particularly strategic offensive arms elimination.

Bureaucratically, the Ministry of Atomic Energy has been least affected by recent political and economic turmoil. It is an empire controlling dozens of enterprises, many of which are situated in closed cities such as Arzamas-16. As with CTR's nuclear weapons projects negotiated and executed by MOD, Minatom's institutional stability has aided progress in most of the projects for which it is responsible. Problems in implementing some projects, such as equipping a fissile materials storage facility, are partially due to such uncontrollable factors as an explosion at Tomsk-7 in April 1993. Some project delays can also be attributed to the extreme sensitivity of the issues they address, or to "old thinking" by some Minatom officials who are suspicious that the United States has ulterior motives for providing assistance.

Difficulties in realizing MPC&A improvements are partly due to the fact that Minatom's international and domestic credibility in this area has been eroded by reports of nuclear thefts and smuggling from Minatom enterprises. Under U.S. and German pressure, the Yeltsin administration issued a decree in September 1994 that established an intergovernmental commission to improve security and accounting for nuclear materials, implying that the existing system was inadequate. This was a significant blow to Minatom, which had repeatedly affirmed the reliability of its control and accounting system. Moreover, a competing agency, the Federal Atomic Inspectorate (Gosatomnadzor, or GAN), was chosen to chair the commission. Although GAN's oversight role was defined in presidential decrees as early as June 1992, the September 1994 decree confirmed its legal power to regulate nuclear safety in all Minatom and MOD facilities. However, GAN evidently preferred not to antagonize Minatom with its newfound authority. Although GAN had ordered the closure in 1994 of a Minatom facility, the Bochvar Institute, on grounds of inadequate safety measures, no known confrontations between GAN and Minatom occurred after the September decree.

Unconfirmed evidence suggests that GAN maintained a low profile after the Bochvar case in exchange for Minatom's agreement not to compete with it for MPC&A assistance from the U.S. Department of Energy. Another explanation may be the tense relations that existed between GAN and the Russian Navy. Relations deteriorated after April 1993, when a presidential decree opened MOD facilities to GAN inspectors for the first time. In the fall of 1994, GAN began to use its new authority to inspect Russian naval nuclear facilities. However, the commander of the White Sea naval base at Severodvinsk refused to allow GAN inspectors onto the facility, in clear defiance of at least two of President Yeltsin's decrees. GAN was forced to formally appeal to the General Prosecutor's Office to order the Navy to change its position.[18] In July 1995, MOD facilities were removed from GAN responsibility. This example illustrates GAN's bureaucratic weakness, which prevents it from challenging influential agencies like MOD and Minatom.

In 1994 Minatom faced a much more powerful opponent, the Russian Ministry of Internal Affairs (MVD), which openly accused it of inadequate material control and accounting.[19] By the spring of 1995, however, the poor performance of MVD-controlled internal troops in Chechnya undermined the MVD's bureaucratic position. Moreover, the general deterioration of U.S.-Russian relations in late 1994, due to the Chechnya campaign and other issues, made the Yeltsin administration less vulnerable to U.S. pressure. In this environment, the poorly orchestrated U.S. campaign against Minatom's nuclear reactor sale to Iran only increased the ministry's domestic leverage. In the eyes of many Russian decision-makers, Minatom's firm position contrasted favorably with the weak Kremlin policy of unilateral concessions to the West, which failed to buy even Western neutrality over Chechnya.[20]

---

18. "Priznaniye komissara politsii prokuroru respubliki" (Confession of the police commissioner before the public prosecutor), *Severnyi rabochii* (Northern worker), December 8, 1995.

19. In February 1994, Minatom Minister Viktor Mikhailov made an unprecedented démarche, asking MVD Minister Viktor Yerin to stop commenting on Minatom's "poor" safety situation, saying that view was "based purely on fantasies and fabrications." CEIP/MIIS *Status Report* (Russian language version), No. 2 (March 1995), p. 74.

20. Immediately after Viktor Yerin's resignation as Minister of Internal Affairs, Minatom Minister Mikhailov, now a hero of anti-American resistance, was nominated as a full member of the Security Council, an unprecedented privilege for Minatom. As a result, in the spring and summer of 1995 Minatom's domestic position consolidated considerably.

Although early CTR projects with Minatom, such as the design of a fissile storage facility, represent some of the rare successes of the program, more problematic negotiations with Minatom in 1995 suggest that its interest in receiving CTR funds had declined considerably. Between 1992 and 1993, with Minatom's funding and future up in the air, CTR assistance was considered a key factor in the ministry's survival, and Minatom chief Mikhailov made several speeches in support of the program. Since that time, the ministry's financial footing has become more secure. It was among the ten largest funding recipients in the FY 1995 Russian federal budget.[21] In addition, Minatom has been able to control the extremely lucrative nuclear export market. In 1994, its nuclear exports exceeded $1 billion, a 20 percent increase over 1993. Exports have thus brought funds to Minatom that are an order of magnitude greater than what it could expect from the CTR Program.

At the same time, Minatom's uranium exports to the United States and Western Europe have been subject to severe quotas and restrictions. According to one Minatom estimate, the ministry has lost $100 million each year due to U.S. Department of Commerce restrictions on Russian uranium imports. This naturally has increased Minatom's interest in alternative markets in the developing world and has led to growing dissatisfaction with the idea of cooperating with the West. Failure to carry out an agreement to purchase surplus Russian highly enriched uranium further deprived the United States of important leverage in its relations with Minatom.

Improvements in export controls have been complicated by the confusing bureaucratic situation of another CTR partner agency, the Federal Service for Hard Currency and Export Control. In 1994, FSVEK emerged from the Department of Export Control, which was part of the powerful State Planning Committee (Gosplan) in the Soviet era.[22]

---

21. This may not have been sufficient to maintain Minatom's entire archipelago of closed cities, but it at least guaranteed the survival of the ministry's Moscow headquarters.

22. In late 1991, Gosplan was reorganized into the Ministry of Economy and Finance, which was subsequently split into two ministries in 1992. The Export Control Department remained in the Ministry of Economy. In 1993–94, it reported to both Economic Minister Aleksandr Shokhin and First Vice Prime Minister Oleg Soskovets, who chaired the Interagency Export Control Commission. In 1994, the department was merged into the newly established FSVEK. Although the transition

FSVEK's control over hard currency was poorly defined, and there was competition from other powerful hard currency controllers such as the Central Bank and the Ministry of Finance. The establishment of the State Committee on Military and Technology Policy also posed a challenge to FSVEK. GKVTP was a potential channel for exporters of dual-use technology to circumvent FSVEK controls. FSVEK's new vulnerability coincided with its increased interest in receiving CTR funds.

Plans for chemical weapons destruction in Russia have been similarly held hostage to bureaucratic politics. In early 1992, the scale of U.S. CW demilitarization assistance was overestimated considerably, and access to it was considered an important source of institutional leverage within Russia's emerging bureaucratic system. The Committee on Convention-Related Problems of Chemical and Biological Weapons (CCB) was established in that year as an umbrella agency to coordinate all chemical and biological disarmament activities. By the summer of 1992, the CCB had prepared a chemical weapons destruction program that was approved by presidential decree in June 1992 and sent to the Supreme Soviet in the fall. It was rejected in early 1993 by the Russian Parliament, however, due to the protests of local authorities in areas designated for CW destruction.[23] In August 1993, President Yeltsin established an interagency commission chaired by First Vice Prime Minister Oleg Soskovets to search for alternative CW destruction sites.

In 1993 and 1994, the increasing domestic role of the military undermined the CCB's bureaucratic position. The MOD, through its Troops for Radioactive, Biological and Chemical Protection (TRBCP), began to take the lead in developing CW destruction plans. Tacit support by the Soskovets Commission and a December 1994 government directive approving the MOD's leading role strengthened its

---

resulted in a higher status for the department, its bureaucratic position remained weak.

23. For an excellent discussion of the role of local Russian authorities in the CW dismantlement process, see Igor Khripunov, "The Human Element in Russia's Chemical Weapons Disposal Efforts," *Arms Control Today*, July–August 1995, pp. 16–21.

position considerably.[24] Interagency competition between the CCB and the TRBCP in 1993–94 not only paralyzed new CW destruction programs, but prevented both agencies from receiving the limited funds provided by the Russian federal budget. In FY 1994, less than half of approximately $40 million allocated for CW destruction was actually disbursed by the Russian Ministry of Finance. Moreover, failure to notify the U.S. side of the location for a chemical analysis laboratory caused delays in disbursing CTR funds.

By early 1995, Russia's poor military performance in Chechnya the previous year had weakened the MOD's domestic position, encouraging nonmilitary institutions such as the CCB to regain lost turf. In March 1995, President Yeltsin established a new interagency commission that reported directly to the president and was chaired by Presidential National Security Advisor Yuri Baturin. The CCB was made into a working group within the commission. The Russian Parliament also played a role in this bureaucratic competition by cutting the FY 1995 budget for CW destruction in half, to $20 million, on the grounds that only half of the FY 1994 authorized funds had been spent. Although the FY 1995 budget resolution did not specify which agency was responsible for CW destruction, it provided the CCB with such a modest budget ($160,000) that it jeopardized the committee's ability to operate.

Not surprisingly, this new round of interagency competition coincided with progress in disbursing CTR assistance for CW destruction. Naturally both CCB and the TRBCP were interested in securing access to additional resources, especially given the minimal CCB budget. In this context, the Pentagon's March 1995 announcement that it would ask Congress for up to $1 billion to help Russia destroy its chemical weapons only intensified this struggle. Adding to this bureaucratic melee in 1995, the GKOP, which had not previously expressed great interest in CW destruction, began to criticize the MOD for the safety of stored CW agents which it was planning to destroy at a later stage. GKOP's participation in this arcane debate was interpreted as its attempt to gain access to additional federal and U.S. CTR funds.

---

24. One indication of the expanded role of the MOD/TRBCP is the fact that, although the 1992 CTR umbrella agreement was signed by the CCB, the follow-on implementation agreement on CW destruction assistance was signed by both the chairman of the CCB and the chief of the TRBCP, General Stanislav Petrov.

These bureaucratic developments illustrate how U.S. assistance (or even the suggestion of aid) has influenced the Russian decision-making and bureaucratic process. In this unstable and irrational milieu, it is impossible to anticipate the consequences of this influence. Although the behavior of agencies such as MOD and Minatom is more or less predictable, U.S. attempts to promote certain agencies or particular CTR projects can have unforeseen and undesirable results.

THE BUREAUCRATIC IMPACT ON CTR IMPLEMENTATION

U.S. policymakers should also note that more influential agencies within Russia's bureaucracy, measured by their ability to win internal budget fights, have tended to have more success with obligations and disbursements of CTR assistance. Table 6-4 illustrates the strong correlation between the amount of funding an agency receives from the Russian federal budget and the rate at which its CTR projects are implemented. For example, MOD (which, among CTR recipient agencies, enjoys the most funding from the Russian budget) had the most success in implementing CTR projects. For MOD-managed projects, more than 40 percent of proposed funds have been disbursed (if CW destruction is exempted, the amount rises to two-thirds).

It is significant that Minatom, which has been heavily criticized for its lack of cooperation in the CTR Program, has the second highest success rate where CTR disbursements are concerned. Seventeen percent of funds originally proposed for Minatom-led projects have already been disbursed. Considering the delays in the construction of the fissile materials storage facility caused by the explosion at Tomsk-7 and problems with containers delivered by a U.S. contractor, this figure could have been significantly higher.

The State Committee for Defense Industries, despite its urgent bureaucratic and financial interest in receiving CTR assistance, has been less successful than Minatom, with only 12 percent of proposed assistance disbursed to its projects. Potential CTR resources available to GKOP are twice the size of its annual budget. Unlike Minatom, GKOP cannot supplement its federal budget with export revenues. Similarly, FSVEK is probably even more anxious to receive CTR funding, which would be three times its modest annual budget. In reality, however, FSVEK's core concern, export control improvements, remains the least successful area of CTR implementation.

Thus, successful implementation of CTR projects is not a function of institutional interest in obtaining access to CTR funds. The reality is

Table 6-4. Budgets of Selected Russian Agencies Pertinent to CTR Negotiations and Distribution.

Agency	FY95 Budget ($M)	CTR Assistance Projects, FY 1992–95 ($M)			
		Amount Proposed		Amount Disbursed	
		FY 92–95	Annually	FY 92–95	Annually
MOD	9,150	108	47.1	43.31	16.36
Minatom	203	150	64.2	26.05	9.20
GKOP	37	190	85.0	23.53	11.77
GAN	2	10	NA	NA	NA
FSVEK	1	2.3	0.8	0.01	0.00
CCB	0.2	55	23.3	NA	NA

SOURCE: FY 1995 Russian federal budget, March 1995. MIIS/CEIP Status Report, July 1995.

that modest budgets equate to limited influence in Russia's bureaucratic system. Despite their interest in doing so, weak agencies cannot compete with more influential institutional players to secure access to CTR aid. In other cases, weak agencies do not have sufficient resources to implement their CTR projects. For example, even if CCB consolidates its role as the main distributor of CTR assistance for CW destruction, it will inevitably have to involve MOD and perhaps also GKOP.

Events to date demonstrate the importance of continuing to deal with stable, traditional institutions in Russia. Improving CTR implementation will not be possible without taking bureaucratic issues into account. Where appropriate, oversight of key CTR projects should be redirected to more stable agencies and recipients.

This is especially true of Minatom. U.S. attempts to deal directly with Minatom's subsidiary organizations or with competing agencies such as GAN are useful only insofar as they improve Minatom's negotiating position. Some Russian officials have complained of U.S. attempts to label Russian agencies as either "bad" or "good," and to support institutions considered good. During the June 1994 meeting of the Gore-Chernomyrdin Commission, for example, top U.S. officials pressured the Minatom leadership to transfer greater inspection authority to GAN. In fact, U.S. lobbying for GAN undermined rather than improved its leverage with Minatom. U.S. CTR assistance to GAN was already twice the agency's annual budget, and to avoid the appearance of being an agency working for U.S. interests, GAN was forced to adopt a low profile and demonstrate its loyalty to Minatom. U.S. officials should not fool themselves by believing that multiple points of contact can be used to undermine Minatom's bureaucratic position and make it more amenable to U.S. views on particular issues. If Minatom is weakened significantly, this could lead to an interagency power struggle to divide up its legacy. In that bureaucratic chaos, it would be difficult to find a recipient responsible enough to manage as ambitious a project as the fissile material storage facility. Multiplying the number of MPC&A programs and points of contact would only be counterproductive.

THE ROLE OF THE MINISTRY OF FINANCE

Another idiosyncrasy of Russian bureaucratic politics is that neither MOD, Minatom, nor GKOP is directly authorized to spend budget funds for weapons dismantlement. According to the FY 1995 budget act, dismantlement expenditures are not to come from national defense accounts, but from funds for fulfilling Russia's international obligations. In FY 1995, more than $4 billion was authorized. The lion's share of these funds belongs to the Ministry of Finance, which is among the most powerful of Russian ministries and whose FY 1995 budget of $17.3 billion was almost twice Russia's annual expenditure for national defense.[25]

The Ministry of Finance transfers budgetary authority to agencies directly involved in the dismantlement process. Often this is done in monthly installments, the size of which is reevaluated each month prior to release. Under this month-by-month procedure, recipient agencies are unable to make long-term funding plans for their disarmament activities. Uncertainty over domestic funds increases their interest in using CTR assistance, which carries with it certain conditions, including ones favoring the use of U.S.-supplied equipment and technology. In turn, this raises objections from domestic industries, which claim that they could produce the same equipment at a lower price. These

---

25. Act of the FY 1995 Federal Budget of the Russian Federation, March 1995.

controversies taint the overall program in the eyes of many Russian decision-makers.

The unusual role of the Ministry of Finance is a precaution against bureaucratic instability and rapid inflation. As long as Russian government agencies remain responsible for disarmament activities (at least through 1996), the Ministry of Finance will need to play its watchdog role. That is why it is so important to involve the Ministry of Finance in CTR planning. The ministry plays a leading role in completing draft annual federal budgets, and as a principal source of weapons dismantlement funds, it has a broad, integrated picture of financial shortages and poor performance by responsible agencies. Coordinating plans with the United States would help better allocate funds and improve the efficiency of both Russian budgetary expenditures and CTR assistance.

Shortfalls in the CTR Program

Russian complaints about the CTR effort include the following observations:

- its scale is insufficient, and it is being implemented too slowly;

- in almost all cases, U.S. rather than Russian organizations are the primary contractors;

- CTR deliveries reduce the market for Russian military industry;

- CTR assistance is aimed at undermining the high-tech capabilities of Russian military industry;

- CTR assistance often addresses secondary problems;

- CTR assistance is often conditioned on overly intrusive transparency measures;

- CTR is used as a tool to interfere in Russian domestic policy; and

- the United States is attempting to link aid to Russia's position on unrelated political-military issues.

Problems with the CTR program only provide ammunition for opponents of Russia's rapprochement with the West. Statements by Presidents Mikhail Gorbachev and Boris Yeltsin since 1991 have created the impression among the Russian public that Moscow's profound unilateral foreign policy concessions made in the late 1980s and early 1990s would be offset by massive Western aid to revive Russia's collapsing economy and assist its disarmament efforts. The illusion was supported by Western statements that the West would provide Russia with up to $40 billion in aid. Russian critics of CTR now argue that these promises were empty. One Russian official has remarked caustically that under the CTR Program, "the United States has done nothing real except send endless delegations, discuss issues, and sign all sorts of small and big agreements."[26] This impression is shared by some decision-makers from other former Soviet states. One official from the Kravchuk administration in Ukraine has privately characterized U.S. assistance as "nuclear tourism."

Critics stress that the United States failed to assist Russia even in an area vitally important to Washington itself—eliminating Russian nuclear and chemical weapons. Very modest funds were allocated for these purposes, compared to the gains the West achieved from Russia's disarmament. Even in a project for secure transport and storage of Russian nuclear warheads, which has been touted as a relative success by both DOD and MOD officials, a U.S.-Russian umbrella agreement on this activity was signed only after Russia withdrew, on its own, thousands of tactical nuclear weapons from the former Warsaw Pact states and non-Russian newly independent states of the former Soviet Union. From the outset, proposed CTR assistance was clearly insufficient for dismantling Russia's military machine. Moreover, only a very small portion of these funds has actually been delivered and only after repeated delays. A growing part of the Russian public believes that Moscow was deceived by the West and has been abandoned with an enormous disarmament burden.

These criticisms are reinforced by the fact that most CTR funds have been provided to U.S. contractors. The Pentagon's CTR literature mentions that "DOD occasionally buys goods or services directly in the

---

26. "Russia's Nuclear Reactor Sale to Iran, Ukrainian Relations: Interview with Evgenii Mikerin, Head of Directorate, Minatom," *Post-Soviet Nuclear & Defense Monitor*, June 12, 1995, p. 15.

NIS."[27] Nonetheless, in a list published by the Pentagon in 1994 of more than 100 companies and organizations awarded CTR contracts, only three non-U.S. companies appear: one Russian (Energomashexport); one Ukrainian (Yuzhnoe Design Bureau); and one German (Kirow Leipzig). Moreover, the $5.9 million awarded to the German company for two contracts exceeded the combined amount awarded to the Russian and Ukrainian companies.

One Russian official described the storage facility design project (which, based on DOD statistics, could be interpreted as the most successfully implemented project) in the following way: "The Pentagon says it has allocated about $14 million for the structure design.... The United States did give a design institute in St. Petersburg $1 million for general design work. Another $280,000 came to Russia in the form of equipment and machinery." Replying to an interviewer's question on the status of the remaining $13 million, the official stated: "This is in the United States. Nobody knows what has happened to this money, but a lot of it most likely has been spent on multiple business trips by U.S. officials."[28] The U.S. policy of not buying Russian goods and services for CTR projects appears to be based on protectionist considerations, not on cost effectiveness. Undoubtedly it would be much cheaper to purchase equipment in Russia; substantial savings would result from transportation costs alone.

In many cases, U.S.-supplied equipment and services have Russian analogs of equal or greater quality. After long negotiations, for example, the Russian design for a fissile material storage facility was recognized as more sophisticated and was ultimately chosen over a U.S. design. In another similar case, U.S.-made cutting tools supplied to destroy Russian submarine hulls did not meet Russian specifications.[29]

---

27. U.S. Department of Defense, *Cooperative Threat Reduction*, April 1995.

28. "On the Reactor Sale to Iran, CTR, Other U.S.-Russian Nuclear Matters" (interview with Valery Bogdan, general manager of Minatom), *Post-Soviet Nuclear & Defense Monitor*, May 16, 1995, p. 6.

29. The shears supplied by the United States, Harris Guillotine Automatic Baler Shears, model BSN-30-220A, were of insufficient capacity; they could only handle materials with a resistance two to five times lower than what was required. The Harris shears could be used only for cutting the light inner hull of some Russian subs. They will likely be used only for cutting scrap. See *NIPTB Onega Study upon Request of Defense Committee of the State Duma*, February 3, 1995, p. 3.

Table 6-5. U.S. Equipment Delivered to Zvyozdochka Dismantlement Facility Compared to Potential Russian Analogs.

U.S.-Delivered Equipment	Status of Russian Analog
MSD-160 and MPS-150 mobile excavator shears	No Russian analog
Triple dynamic cable shredder	Russian analog under development
Oxyacetylene torches	Russian analog of equal quality
Plasma cutter	Russian analog of equal quality
Portable filter and ventilator	Russian analog of equal quality
Welder's air-fed hoods	Russian analog of equal quality
Welder's protective clothing	Russian analog of equal quality
Harris automatic guillotine baler shears	More advanced Russian analog (Tyazhstankogidro-press HBO340 hydraulic scrap shears) [a]

SOURCE: NIPTB Onega Study upon Request of Defense Committee of the State Duma, February 1995, pp. 2–3, 5–6.

[a] The Harris shear procurement accounted for half of all submarine dismantlement assistance ($10.7 million). Moreover, it is in this case, where Russian requirements were not met, that a superior Russian analog exists. While Harris shears are capable of cutting hulls of a thickness of no greater than 16–20 millimeters, the Tyazhstankogidropress Hydraulic Shears, produced in Novosibirsk, are able to cut hulls up to 80 millimeters thick (with the same metal resistance).

According to a study by the Severodvinsk-based Onega Research and Development Bureau conducted for the Russian Duma's Defense Committee, out of eight types of U.S.-made equipment shipped to the Zvyozdochka naval dismantlement facility, five had Russian analogs that were of equal quality, two exceeded the performance of their Russian analogs, and, in one case, equivalent Russian equipment actually performed better (see Table 6-5).

By contrast, in the ISTC project, a large portion of CTR funding has reached Russian recipients directly ($20 million in 1994–95). According to an estimate by the Moscow-based Committee for Critical Technologies and Nonproliferation, direct ISTC contracts to Russian participants were worth more than contracts awarded directly to Russian recipients in all other CTR projects.[30] Some progress is also being made in the strategic arms elimination project. In September 1994, the Russian company Energomashexport was awarded a $3.9 million contract (one-fifth of project funds disbursed to date) to produce flatbed railcars. By contrast, in the lab-to-lab program, which operates outside the formal CTR framework, 25 percent of funding is used to purchase Russian-made fissile material control equipment.

Besides its political ramifications, the requirement that U.S. personnel carry out all technical support—design, production, transportation, and assembly—also increases delays and expenses since these personnel must also be transported from the United States. In 1994, there was a particularly long waiting period between delivery of submarine dismantlement equipment to Russia and the arrival of the U.S. assembling team. For several months, unassembled machinery was stored in the open at Murmansk and Severodvinsk.[31] In the absence of competition, U.S. contractors lose interest in their equipment after it is delivered. U.S. technicians assemble the equipment in Russia but provide little support thereafter. Nor do U.S. officials appear to maintain close oversight of projects, how well the equipment works, or what improvements could be made, which creates a favorable atmosphere for delivering obsolete or inferior equipment. The shipment of inadequate U.S.-made fissile material containers is a prime example of how poor U.S. quality control can cause delays in CTR projects.

This situation is the result not only of U.S. reluctance to "buy Russian," but also, as mentioned above, of the Ministry of Finance's financial policy, which forces other Russian ministries to choose CTR deliveries over equivalent or better Russian-made equipment. Progress is urgently needed in the area of using Russian equipment as well as in improving coordination between responsible U.S. and Russian agencies.

---

30. However, U.S. delays in disbursing funds for the ISTC were so lengthy that, out of 36 ISTC awards made in March 1995, 20 were funded by non-U.S. sources, 15 by combined U.S., European Union, and Japanese funds, and only one by U.S. funds alone.

31. Irina Stalinskaia, "Amerika Rossii podarila 'Akulyu past'" (America gave Russia a shark's jaw), *Ekonomika i zhizn'* (Economy and life), No. 28, December 17, 1994.

Using mainly U.S.-made equipment also means that Russian industry is being squeezed out of the weapons dismantlement market. A related problem cited by CTR critics is that the program is undermining the high-tech capabilities of Russia's defense industry. Regrettably, the results of even some successful conversion projects support this claim. For example, according to one CTR project, the Reutov-based NPO Mashinostroenia, which designs and builds sophisticated ICBM and cruise missile technologies and developed the Almaz-1 imagery satellite, will be reoriented to bottling soft drinks. A St. Petersburg enterprise, Leninets, which develops and produces avionics for fighter and bomber aircraft, as well as missile electronics and computer systems, will produce dental chairs in a CTR-funded joint venture with International American Products. In a third project, the Russian enterprise ISTOK will manufacture hearing aids. In only one project, between GosNIIAS and Rockwell, will the high-tech potential of a Russian enterprise be fully realized, in this case to manufacture air traffic control systems.

Significant delays are also caused by intrusive transparency and audit requirements to guarantee the proper use of CTR assistance. Since many projects deal with sensitive nuclear security issues, U.S. auditing and inspection demands met with understandable resistance from Russian negotiators. U.S. requirements gave some credence to opposition views that CTR assistance was nothing more than a cover for stealing or, at best, buying Russia's nuclear secrets. Delays caused by transparency requirements were particularly severe in MPC&A and export control projects. However, by 1995 some progress had been made to resolve this issue. Minatom's concerns as to U.S. intentions were neutralized when DOE opened its own fissile material sites at Hanford and Oak Ridge to Minatom delegations. This demonstration of reciprocity improved DOE-Minatom relations and helped break Minatom's stalemate in MPC&A. Another important innovation was to establish a joint training center at Obninsk to train Russian personnel to oversee MPC&A upgrades at Russian facilities rather than using intrusive bilateral transparency measures. Not all U.S. agencies have shared DOE's flexibility, however. The U.S. Navy, which is responsible for the Arctic Nuclear Waste Assessment, showed considerable resistance to Russian requests to visit Puget Sound to learn how the U.S. Navy deals with submarine reactor compartments before transporting them to Hanford.

Finally, it should be noted that U.S. attempts to use CTR funding to force foreign policy concessions from Russia are likely to backfire. CTR assistance is not large enough to leverage Russia's positions on unrelated foreign policy issues. Nor is any Russian agency so dependent on CTR assistance that it will risk lobbying the government to accept such U.S. linkages.

Improving the CTR Program

One possible strategy for improving the CTR Program is to tinker with particular program elements to fix implementation problems. However, such a mechanistic or piecemeal approach is unlikely to yield meaningful results and may cause additional, unanticipated problems. Alternatively, assistance resources could be redirected and concentrated on the most successful projects while less successful ones are scaled back or eliminated. But U.S. and Russian planners cannot simply concentrate on developing CTR projects that have already proved successful at the expense of projects that have failed but are cornerstones of the CTR mandate, such as eliminating weapons of mass destruction and improving fissile material storage. The success of these core missions is a key criterion for assessing the entire program.

Achieving a real breakthrough in CTR implementation will require radical program improvements. Special emphasis should be placed on improving projects to eliminate weapons of mass destruction and protect fissile materials from unauthorized access and use. Some promising qualitative changes are already taking place in the area of MPC&A, providing grounds for optimism. This strategy requires a number of urgent measures to be undertaken.

Greater purchases of Russian equipment and services to implement CTR projects is absolutely critical. This could reduce Russian objections to the CTR Program while establishing a network of Russian enterprises that support both the program and continued cooperation with the United States in general. It could also accelerate CTR implementation by giving Russian institutions an interest in timely delivery, assembly, and quality of demilitarization equipment and services. Russian industry involvement in dismantlement would also tie its interests to further arms reductions in the future. The Russian defense industry has been the biggest loser from the end of the Cold War, making it a pillar of Russia's Communist and ultranationalist political movements.

Promoting U.S.-Russian joint-stock companies to produce goods and services for CTR tasks may be an effective compromise to buying Russian-made equipment. Precedents have already been established in the defense conversion project. A similar initiative is under way in Ukraine, where a joint-stock company has been established to destroy ballistic missiles. Joint-stock companies will also be able to solve equipment production and delivery problems on their own, without long bilateral government negotiations. Joint-stock companies could also help create long-term industrial ties between Russian and U.S. enterprises. This would improve demilitarization results and also create a bilateral economic network. Participating enterprises would be naturally committed to close political relations between the two countries.

The joint-stock approach could help overcome a particularly important bureaucratic obstacle to eliminating strategic nuclear weapons. Recent problems in this area have been the result of the weaknesses of Russia's implementing agency, the State Committee for Defense Industries, and its inability to work with Russian industrial enterprises. Funding joint-stock enterprises directly, while keeping the GKOP in an oversight role, could accelerate strategic arms elimination and help decentralize the Russian economy. The defense sector remains largely centralized and subordinated to bureaucrats in Moscow. Decentralizing the defense industry and helping some enterprises profit from CTR-funded nonmilitary production through joint-stock companies could significantly facilitate demilitarization. Thus a joint-stock strategy could fulfill two CTR missions—dismantling weapons stockpiles and promoting the demilitarization of the Russian economy.

Another set of measures should be aimed at creating a competitive environment among CTR donor and recipient agencies. The MPC&A project, for example, is significant because progress was achieved as soon as DOD's role was complemented by DOE involvement. On the recipient side, direct contacts with Russian enterprises and labs would help decentralize and demilitarize the Russian economy. However, a competitive environment should not be created at the risk of jeopardizing relations with Russia's main bureaucratic organizations. Cooperation with these institutions is necessary in some areas where decentralization is unattainable or undesirable. Only a large, centralized organization like Minatom, for example, could manage such an ambitious project as the fissile material storage facility. In this respect, rhetoric that blames "bad" or "old thinking" ministries will not ease negotiations with them and will only provoke retaliation. At the same time, praising "good guys" within Russia's bureaucracy will only undermine their bureaucratic position. The focus should be on continued cooperation with the most stable and influential institutions, such as the Ministry of Defense and Minatom. These institutions are powerful and stable enough to guarantee CTR project implementation despite the potential bureaucratic turmoil and challenges they may face. Their positive attitude toward the CTR Program is vitally important in gaining the cooperation of Russian decision-makers.

Coordinating CTR assistance with Russia's own efforts requires involving the Russian Ministry of Finance in both the negotiating process and informal consultations. The ministry is responsible for distributing budgetary funds for weapons elimination and is one of the most powerful of Russian government agencies. Closer cooperation with it might create a more favorable bureaucratic atmosphere for CTR implementation.

Transparency agreements might be possible if they are accompanied by reciprocity measures. In this respect, reciprocity should not be limited to visits by Minatom delegations to Hanford and Oak Ridge. Other U.S. facilities should be also opened for visits by representatives of other interested Russian institutions.

Decentralization of CTR assistance must be accompanied by stricter audit control. Nevertheless, it is hardly possible to send U.S. auditors to all recipient Russian organizations. A solution might be to mimic the strategy used for MPC&A at Obninsk—training Russian personnel to oversee and audit other Russians. Such a cooperative initiative could be launched through contacts between the U.S. Congress and the Russian Federal Assembly, which is equally interested in preventing illegal diversions of foreign aid. Other institutions, such as the Ministry of Finance and the presidential administration, could participate in such an audit initiative. A new role for GKOP could be to audit joint-stock companies formed by defense enterprises.

Current weapons dismantlement plans under the CTR Program should focus greater attention and resources on eliminating nuclear submarines. This is the most acute problem in the strategic arms reduction area and is a growing source of public concern in Russia. Submarine dismantlement could be accomplished more effectively with greater involvement by Russian enterprises and joint-stock companies to develop and manufacture advanced cutting technologies and provide other support. This would accelerate the program since it would encourage a groundswell of bureaucratic support. Russia's inability to safely dismantle decommissioned nuclear submarines creates risks of radioactive contamination not only in areas near dismantling facilities but also in the Arctic basin, which directly affects the United States. This risk requires diverting misguided funds for the Arctic Nuclear Waste Assessment project to an environmental impact assessment of submarine dismantlement in the White Sea and Barents Sea basins. Current projects to dismantle nuclear subs should be similarly refocused on improving safety and physical protection of spent naval reactor fuel. Storage and transportation facilities for such fuel deserve CTR support. Russia also lacks technologies for eliminating solid fuel submarine-launched ballistic missiles (SLBMs), which could be another CTR area.

Another weapons elimination activity requiring more attention is disposal of missile fuel. Inadequate Russian financing of this potentially dangerous activity provides the CTR Program with an unusual opportunity to be proactive. Since considerable progress was made by involving Russian organizations in producing railcars for liquid missile fuel transportation, this subproject could be an example of successful U.S.-Russian CTR cooperation in which Russian enterprises play an important role.

On a more general level, the CTR Program should pay more attention to constructive projects in order to demonstrate that it is not intended purely for the destruction of Russia's national assets. Allocating additional funds to finish storage facility construction could help transform the project into a positive symbol of CTR activity. The CTR Program could also be elevated in the eyes of the Russian public and political opinion by tackling problems that are of acute public concern. A project to rehabilitate CW destruction sites, for example, could encourage Russian ratification of the Chemical Weapons Convention, which is paralyzed by concerns over the grave environmental consequences of CW destruction.

Similarly, a new large-scale assistance initiative, perhaps a CTR II, could encourage ongoing ratification of START II. According to many members of the Russian Parliament, a new Russian commitment to disarmament will require not only increased U.S. assistance to implement old arms treaties, but the allocation of sizable new resources as well. There is a strong possibility that a Russian ratification resolution will make START II implementation conditional on, among other things, a new U.S. disarmament assistance program. Such a CTR II might include the following initiatives:

- reuse of SS-18 ICBMs withdrawn under START II as commercial space launch vehicles;

- alternatively, other measures to increase Russian access to the international commercial space launch markets could be defined;

- removal of U.S. restrictions on Russian uranium imports, perhaps by compensating U.S. producers for losses incurred;

- involvement of Russian enterprises in cooperative R&D on state-of-the-art military technologies;

- conversion of missile-producing enterprises to develop and produce disarmament equipment;

- increased aid for ICBM silo elimination and for transport, storage, and disposal of missile propellants;

- SSBN dismantlement and secure transport and storage of naval reactors and fuel;

- new funds for construction of a fissile materials storage facility;

- initiation of a program of contacts between U.S. and Russian defense industrialists;

- environmental restoration of weapons destruction sites;

- a trilateral U.S.-Russian-Kazakstani initiative to purchase and dismantle seven Bear-G heavy bombers that remain in Semi-palatinsk; and

- increased assistance to Ukraine to accelerate dismantlement of ICBMs and silos on Ukrainian territory.

Chapter 7

Russian-U.S. Cooperation on Nuclear Weapons Safety

Evgenii P. Maslin

Events of recent years have demonstrated profound changes in the security relationships among the nations of the world. The end of forty years of Cold War between the United States and Russia has resulted in far-reaching geopolitical transformations worldwide. The bipolar state of affairs that characterized Cold War international security affairs—dominated by the rivalry, arms race, and mutual deterrence of two nuclear superpowers—has withered away. As a result of the disappearance of the bipolar system, meaningful nuclear threat reduction is now achievable.

As the presidents of Russia and the United States have stated on several occasions over the past five years, considerable progress has been achieved toward strengthening global strategic stability and nuclear security. This progress has been based, in large part, on the steady, judicious reductions in levels of weapons systems deployed by the United States and Russia and the timely dismantlement of nuclear weapons and their delivery vehicles pursuant to arms control agreements. Both countries have reduced their nuclear arsenals considerably and are now adopting measures to improve the transparency of the arms reduction process and strengthen confidence in its irreversibility.

Despite these achievements, the progress made in Cold War–era problems of superpower arms control have, unfortunately, been eclipsed by the increasing challenge of nuclear weapons proliferation around the globe. Moreover, U.S.-Russian weapons reduction and nuclear security efforts have been greatly complicated by this proliferation trend. Addressing the proliferation challenge will require steadfast and coordinated political, diplomatic, and economic efforts by many states and multinational organizations. The global problem of proliferation requires a global response; it is a concern not only for the United

States and Russia, but for the entire world community. It will be impossible for any one nation to act unilaterally to meet this challenge. However, the threat of weapons proliferation is nonetheless a special challenge and responsibility for Russia, which is the caretaker of an enormous stockpile of weapons materials and is the home to tens of thousands of individuals with nuclear weapons expertise. The danger that nuclear weapons, technologies, or know-how may proliferate to countries seeking to develop a weapon capability is a particularly vexing problem for Russian planners, who are attempting to implement arms reduction agreements and undertake a massive restructuring of Russian nuclear forces and other defense assets. Arms reduction, nuclear security, and nonproliferation efforts are, by their nature, closely linked in the minds of these planners.

The interplay of these issues is illustrated in the time-urgent measures Russia has had to implement since the dissolution of the Soviet Union in 1991. The immediate result of the Soviet Union's disintegration was to place thousands of tactical and strategic nuclear weapons in the hands of suddenly independent states. Russia immediately undertook urgent measures to ensure the operational control over formerly Soviet tactical nuclear warheads in these states by transporting the weapons back to Russian territory. The return to Russia of several thousand tactical nuclear weapons was a critical measure to prevent their possible theft and proliferation and was completed by May 1992.

Russia and the United States undertook considerable additional efforts to achieve agreements on deactivation of strategic nuclear weapons and the assignation of such weapons to Russia for further dismantlement. Russia assumed primary responsibility for ensuring nuclear security on the territories of Ukraine, Kazakstan, and Belarus, and the results of Moscow's efforts have been dramatic. As of early 1996, all nuclear warheads—more than 1400 in total—were withdrawn from Kazakstan to Russia.[1] In Belarus, 63 SS-25 road-mobile ICBMs and their warheads were transported back to Russia by the summer of 1996, and Russia and Belarus have reached agreement on transferring 18 SS-25s and warheads remaining on Belarusan territory by the end of 1996.

---

1. One undetonated nuclear device, with a yield of less than one kiloton, remained buried in Degelen Mountain at Kazakstan's Semipalatinsk nuclear test site. It was destroyed with conventional explosives on May 31, 1995, leaving Kazakstan free of nuclear weapons.

By late March 1996, Ukraine had transferred to Russia about 1,500 nuclear warheads, including SS-19, SS-24, and ALCM warheads. If the past rate of transfer continues, the transfer of all warheads remaining in Ukraine (about 300 as of early 1996) is expected to be completed by the end of 1996. At Russian facilities overseen by the Ministry of Atomic Energy (Minatom), more than 900 of the nuclear weapons removed from Ukraine have been destroyed under Ukrainian supervision.

Some critics in the West have, of late, begun to raise questions as to Russia's security objectives and its long-term commitment to arms control and nuclear nonproliferation. In light of these criticisms, it is important to note Russia's dramatic effort to secure the thousands of tactical nuclear weapons on former Soviet territory and its concrete steps toward practical implementation of the START I accords. The speed with which Russia transported these weapons from outlying republics to secure storage in Russia and began the weapon dismantlement process obscures the fact that Russian operational planners were forced to overcome a daunting array of technical and organizational challenges. Serious difficulties emerged, for example, in ensuring adequate security in the transport of these weapons.

The Russian Defense Ministry and Minatom have become adept at transporting and dismantling nuclear weapons, and have taken the necessary protective measures to ensure the safety of this process. Several overriding issues will continue to complicate Russia's denuclearization efforts, however, and future U.S.-Russian efforts in this area must focus on certain key problems. First, at the technical level, there continues to be a shortage in Russia of special-purpose transport trains and warhead "supercontainers." Transport and storage containers for fissile materials are also in critically short supply at Minatom. The deteriorating technical state of equipment and railway transportation has forced Russia to consider the possibility of an incident involving nuclear weapons transport. Continued improvements to the transport process—various technologies, equipment, and facilities developed and manufactured in Russia and elsewhere—will be required throughout the arms control process to ensure damage control in case of nuclear accidents.

A second overriding concern is the worsening criminal situation in some regions of the former Soviet republics, as well as in Russia itself. Increasing lawlessness is a foreseeable but unfortunate consequence of the tremendous political and economic upheavals that have taken place in Russia and the former republics since 1991. The rise of a criminal element in certain regions has made the theft of nuclear weapons and components, as well as nuclear terrorism, a real possibility. These conditions have forced Russia to reexamine the whole system of nuclear weapons protection and to strengthen accounting and control procedures over fissile materials.

Finally, the problem of declining living conditions for Russian military specialists and civilian personnel working in the Russian nuclear weapons complex has become particularly urgent. This problem concerns both personnel within the Ministry of Defense and Minatom. A weak social security system, a severe housing shortage, and drastic job cuts in the nuclear industry and the military contribute to the threat that nuclear specialists and technologies may proliferate into other countries. The most effective means to stem this potential flow of expertise would be to ease the housing and unemployment burdens that these specialists face every day. Finding an ultimate solution to the economic and social problems of downsizing the Russian nuclear complex will be a formidable challenge for the long term. Russia has overcome adversity of a similar or greater magnitude throughout its history, however, and it will undoubtedly find a solution to its present dilemmas. Nonetheless, the immediate proliferation consequences of these social-economic problems give the United States and the world community at large a compelling reason to join Russia in finding a solution to them.

Russian leaders and operational planners greatly appreciate the cooperation that the United States has extended through the Nunn-Lugar Cooperative Threat Reduction Program, overseen for most of its duration by the U.S. Department of Defense. U.S. cooperative assistance in the areas of nuclear weapons storage, transportation, dismantlement, and destruction have helped Russia manage a battery of complex military-technical tasks at a time when the country faces great social, economic, and political difficulties. The Nunn-Lugar Program can rightly claim to have accelerated Russia's reduction in military expenditures and to have increased the safety and security of Russia's nuclear weapons withdrawals and reductions. Russian concerns about possible disruptions in the strategic balance, meanwhile, are alleviated by ongoing U.S. nuclear reductions.

However, it is important to state definitively that the result of U.S.-Russian cooperation in these areas is not only to provide Russia with the means to help itself. The program also greatly furthers U.S. interests. In the estimation of U.S. officials and experts, the provision of a relatively small amount of funding under the Nunn-Lugar Program will provide an enormous return in eliminating direct threats to U.S. security and contributing to global nonproliferation and nuclear security goals as well. Moreover, because the program utilizes many U.S. contractors to provide Russia with equipment and technical assistance, the program provides firms and personnel at home in the United States a direct economic benefit as well.

U.S.-Russian cooperation on the Nunn-Lugar Program speeds the disarmament process, enhances confidence and transparency in this effort, and provides a unique milieu for building understanding and trust between the two states. The entire international community also benefits from greater confidence in the future and expanded cooperation in other fields. This is why it is logical and correct that other states are providing assistance to Russia for nuclear weapons dismantlement and destruction. The United Kingdom, France, and Italy all contribute (in varying degrees) to this assistance.

For its part, the United States has already completed or is in the process of fulfilling several Nunn-Lugar Program threat reduction obligations. Areas of U.S.-Russian cooperation that have been particularly important in the Russian Defense Ministry's efforts to demobilize and transport former Soviet nuclear weapons for dismantlement include the following:

- The United States provided 250 six-panel sets of nylon ballistic blankets and 252 ten-panel sets of kevlar "soft-armor" blankets to enhance the protective capability of nuclear weapon containers and vehicles in transport. The Russian military has actively used these items to protect warheads from fire and other consequences of possible accidents as well as from small-arms fire from potential terrorist attacks as the weapons are transported from deployment sites in former Soviet republics to dismantlement facilities in Russia.

- Russia has received 100 retrofit kits to improve the safety and security of nuclear weapons transport railcars. Conversion kits provided since 1993 have increased intrusion detection and thermal protection on Russian railway freight cars used for weapons transport. U.S. Nunn-Lugar funds were also used to provide 15 kits to upgrade observation/control cars for Russian military personnel guarding weapons transport trains. This equipment has greatly enhanced physical security and fire protection for weapons in transit to dismantlement facilities.

- The United States has provided considerable "emergency response" equipment and training to help Russian personnel respond to potential accidents or other incidents involving nuclear weapons, particularly when they are in transit. More than 1,400 items have been delivered to Russian personnel under this Nunn-Lugar project, including communications equipment, radiological and chemical protective clothing, personnel dosimetry and radiological sampling equipment, emergency access equipment (e.g., cutting tools), and personal computers with dispersal model software. This equipment outfits specialists from nuclear emergency units of both the Ministry of Defense and Minatom. In 1994, a series of complex training exercises was undertaken, involving nuclear emergency techniques and methods using U.S. equipment. Such training has allowed Russian specialists to improve their practical skills, and it has confirmed the high reliability and effectiveness of these methods.

- The Department of Defense—with technical support from the Department of Energy—has allocated $50 million to provide Russia with several thousand special containers to provide safe transport and storage of fissile material obtained from the dismantlement of Russian nuclear weapons. Resembling large, stainless steel barrels, these "supercontainers" will greatly improve the safety, security and accountability of thousands of tons of fissile material from dismantled warheads.

As weapons transport and dismantlement efforts have progressed, officials and technical experts on the U.S. and Russian sides—particularly MOD officials and their counterparts in the Pentagon—have conducted regular meetings to discuss progress to date as well as additional problems and requirements that have emerged. Since the initial outlays of assistance under the program, the U.S. DOD and the Russian MOD have signed additional agreements or amended ongoing agreements to meet emerging requirements. Two agreements were signed in April 1995, for example, that supplemented ongoing cooperation for safe transport and storage of nuclear weapons and materials. Under these agreements, the United States agreed to supply additional transport containers for dismantled nuclear weapons, additional railway units for nuclear warhead control and protection, and computer hardware and software to assist Russian control and accounting of its nuclear inventories.

In addition to agreements signed with the Ministry of Defense, the United States has signed several other cooperation agreements with Minatom and other Russian agencies with oversight over particular demilitarization activities. Nunn-Lugar projects to be carried out under the direction of Minatom include: the delivery of transport and storage containers for fissile materials; the installation of material control and accounting equipment for nuclear materials at Minatom facilities; and hardware and software assistance in the design and construction of protective and ecologically sound storage facilities for dismantled nuclear materials.

Over the life of the Nunn-Lugar Program, U.S. and Russian personnel have made tremendous strides up the "learning curve" as they have implemented a complex set of military-technical tasks. One important dividend of this cooperation has been the development of close personal contacts between various Russian and American officials and experts. The program has given each side a unique opportunity to understand the other side's concerns and requirements. The interaction at the operational level, between U.S. and Russian personnel with direct responsibility over nuclear operations, has been particularly valuable. Cold War–era distrust, strained relations, and suspicions have been set aside as both sides have joined to solve a common set of problems. Negotiations have been conducted in an atmosphere of goodwill and are aimed at achieving optimum, mutually beneficial outcomes.

While working together in the nuclear sphere, Russian and U.S. personnel have also discovered additional avenues for cooperation, including data exchange in the sphere of safety and security of nuclear weapons. The Russian side (and probably also the American side) believes that current assistance serves the interests of both sides, and thus supports continued cooperation.

Unfortunately, to fully meet the demands of its dismantlement and nuclear security agenda, Russia will require further assistance. A key challenge to which more attention and resources must be devoted is the problem of nuclear terrorism. Russia and the United States must combine forces to move actively and energetically against nuclear terrorism. The two must work more closely than ever jointly to monitor, track, protect against, and possibly interdict unlawful nuclear activities around the globe that threaten the security of either state. Such an effort can begin at home, by providing Russia with the technical means to protect and account for nuclear weapons and materials in its inventory at facilities that remain vulnerable to terrorist theft. U.S. cooperation with the Russian MOD has been marked by technical successes as well as improved understanding, and the United States now must build and maintain a similar relationship with Minatom, which will be the caretaker of the Russian nuclear materials stockpile over the long term and the first line of defense against nuclear terrorism.

Nor should future assistance be limited to addressing strictly technical or operational problems. Overshadowing the current technical shortfalls in Russian capabilities to transport, store, protect, and dismantle its nuclear weapons is a much more fundamental problem: the security and stability of the personnel and technical experts charged with overseeing this process. The deteriorating social and living conditions of the Russian military's nuclear specialists, who are rapidly being discharged from service due to Russia's financial constraints, is an urgent priority. The social-economic insecurity of these critical personnel is an insidious problem, for it threatens to undermine— indeed, circumvent—all of the technical improvements that the United States and Russia have or plan to put in place to protect Russian nuclear technologies from diversion. Although derided by some in the United States as "social welfare," improving the security of core nuclear expertise in Russia is an issue that goes to the heart of the proliferation problem. It cannot be addressed by Russia alone.

Russian officials have raised this issue repeatedly in meetings with their American counterparts over the course of the Nunn-Lugar effort, and the United States has provided some assistance in this area, such as by constructing housing for Russian military personnel. A much more comprehensive solution to this problem must be found, however. Without a secure means of providing for themselves and their families, it is possible that many of these expert personnel will seek employment elsewhere, with foreign sponsors in other lands, and for their livelihood they may choose to barter the critical weapons knowledge they have gained in the Soviet nuclear complex. The proliferation of scientific and technical knowledge about all weapons, but especially weapons of mass destruction, must be prevented. This was a fundamental premise of the U.S. law that established the Nunn-Lugar Program. Meeting the "social" problems embedded in demilitarization must become a top priority. No less an authority than Senator Sam Nunn, the co-sponsor of this critical legislation, has observed that what is required is a greater degree of "humanism" in the program's activities.

In sum, the Nunn-Lugar Cooperative Threat Reduction Program has, to date, achieved several critical technical milestones that have helped Russia meet the immediate nuclear security problems that emerged with the dissolution of the Soviet Union. Nunn-Lugar projects have provided direct assistance to the Russian Defense Ministry at a time of unparalleled political and economic difficulties, and thus have helped Russia find its way "out of the woods" in the nuclear sphere. As important as the accomplishments of the program, however, has been the manner in which it has been executed. The Nunn-Lugar process, particularly as it has evolved between the Russian Ministry of Defense and the U.S. Department of Defense, has consistently respected the interests, concerns, and sovereignty of both sides. The parties to this effort have approached its tasks in a spirit of professionalism, mutual respect, and "jointness" that has improved trust and greatly accelerated work on these time-urgent problems.

U.S.-Russian cooperation has provided practical material benefits to each side, deepened mutual understanding, and formed the basis for long-term relations that will build confidence and trust between the United States and Russia. As U.S.-Russian demilitarization matures, and moves to the next phase, the two sides must build upon this promising foundation. Complex military-technical problems will continue to be a key focus of U.S.-Russian efforts, as each side carries out its obligations under strategic arms agreements as well as the Chemical Weapons Convention. However, future cooperation must move beyond strictly technical problems. What is required now is a fuller assessment of what is needed to lock in the improvements made so far and strengthen safeguards against proliferation. Developing bilateral and multilateral approaches to easing the social and economic fallout of Russia's demilitarization must surely be at the top of this agenda. The extreme urgency of these issues, for nonproliferation and for global security, cannot be emphasized too strongly.

Chapter 8

Reducing the Nuclear Threat through Joint Efforts

The View from Ukraine

Kostyantyn Hryshchenko

After more than four years, it is now an appropriate time to analyze the achievements and shortcomings of the Cooperative Threat Reduction (CTR) Program in order to define the next steps and elaborate plans for future nuclear threat reduction. The following discussion offers several observations on how the CTR Program has been implemented in Ukraine and how well it has addressed Ukraine's demilitarization, denuclearization, and other goals. A particular focus of this discussion is the evolution of Ukraine's landmark decision to renounce its claim to the nuclear arsenal left on its territory by the Soviet Union and the role that U.S. cooperative assistance played in this decision. It also assesses the role that CTR and other U.S. assistance has had, particularly in the immediate aftermath of the Soviet breakup, in building a strong framework for the bilateral relationship between the two countries. This chapter concludes by offering some suggestions for advancing and strengthening U.S.-Ukrainian cooperative assistance in ways that will help Ukraine achieve not only the military-technical goals of the post-Soviet era but its economic and social objectives as well.

Preconditions for the CTR Program in Ukraine

As a consequence of the dissolution of the former Soviet Union, Ukraine inherited an enormous nuclear missile capability. Ukraine became the owner of 212 strategic delivery systems, including 130 SS-19 intercontinental ballistic missiles (ICBMs), 46 of the most advanced SS-24 ICBMs, and 36 heavy bombers equipped with long-range air-to-surface nuclear cruise missiles. According to the provisions of the START I Treaty, these systems accounted for a total of 1,512 nuclear warheads, making Ukraine the *de facto* owner of the third largest nuclear arsenal in the world.

Ukraine had nothing to do with the decisions that led to the deployment on its territory of this vast nuclear force. At the same time the Ukrainian people were forced against their will to finance an exhausting nuclear arms race during the Cold War at the expense of Ukraine's well-being and economic development. In declaring its ownership of nuclear weapons deployed on its territory, Ukraine considered these arms only a material asset and irrelevant to Ukraine's security as a traditional deterrent. This basic assumption was the foundation for the proclamation by the Ukrainian Rada in the Declaration on State Sovereignty of July 1990 that Ukraine would neither acquire nor produce nuclear weapons. This decision was confirmed in a number of subsequent political documents and practical actions taken by Ukraine. Some of the landmark political decisions by Ukraine on its way to becoming a non-nuclear state include:

- October 1991: Statement by the Ukrainian Rada "On the Non-Nuclear Status of Ukraine";

- December 1991: Reaffirmation of the Declaration on the State Sovereignty of Ukraine;

- May 1992: Completion of the withdrawal of tactical nuclear weapons to the Russian Federation for destruction;

- May 1992: Signing of the Lisbon Protocol, whereby Ukraine committed itself to adhere to the Nuclear Non-Proliferation Treaty (NPT) as a non–nuclear weapon state;

- November 1993: Ratification by the Rada of the START I Treaty, with reservations;

- January 1994: Trilateral Statement by the presidents of Ukraine, the United States, and the Russian Federation;

- February 1994: Removal by the Rada of its reservations to Article V of the Lisbon Protocol and decision to accede to the NPT;

- November 1994: Accession by Ukraine to the NPT as a non-nuclear state; and

- May 1995: Support by Ukraine for indefinite extension of the NPT at the NPT Review Conference.

The process that led to these decisions was difficult and filled with contradictions. Ukrainian parliamentarians and the Ukrainian people as a whole faced several novel problems of state-building as well as new political, economic, and military realities. Among the major issues confronting Ukraine were the need for adequate security guarantees and the necessity to secure financial and technical assistance to eliminate its nuclear arsenal. The CTR initiative played a key role in resolving the latter issue and helping Ukraine decide to adhere to the NPT as a non–nuclear weapon state. Ukraine will have to bear most of the financial and other costs of its decision to forgo the nuclear option. However, the United States and other Western countries have the moral responsibility to aid Ukraine's efforts to reduce the reliance of the world's nations on nuclear weapons for their security.

From the outset, Ukrainian officials stressed that assistance should be aimed not only at the physical elimination of ICBMs, but also at the critical environmental and nuclear safety issues involved in this process. Another key problem involved in weapon destruction concerns those individuals—mostly military personnel—who were responsible for the combat readiness of strategic nuclear forces deployed in Ukraine and who are now tasked with destroying the same weapons that previously provided for their livelihood. The issue here for the United States and the CTR Program is not simply providing social assistance to foreign nationals, but ensuring that reductions in nuclear forces are expedited with minimal risk to safety and the environment.

Evolution of U.S. and Ukrainian Positions in the CTR Negotiations

The urgency of the disarmament and nuclear security challenges facing Ukraine required innovative and rapid solutions. Technical cooperation between the United States and Ukraine under the CTR Program has proved to be a creative response to these challenges.

U.S.-Ukrainian consultations in Kiev in 1992 were the first step in bilateral cooperation to provide assistance to Ukraine for its nuclear disarmament needs. By this time the United States had declared its readiness to allocate up to $90 million to Ukraine for transportation, storage, and eventual dismantlement of nuclear arms as well as for developing safeguards against proliferation of nuclear weapons. A number of obligatory preconditions were presented to Ukraine for this assistance, including:

• allocating a considerable amount of Ukraine's own resources for the weapons dismantlement process;

• refraining from military modernization programs exceeding reasonable defense requirements;

• not using fissile materials from dismantled weapons for military purposes;

• assisting the United States in verifying the arms elimination process;

• abiding by all valid arms control agreements; and

• upholding human rights.

In addition to these general conditions, the United States also stipulated that assistance would only be rendered once Ukraine had ratified the START I Treaty and acceded to the NPT.

In the summer of 1992, the United States proposed an umbrella agreement and several implementation agreements as a legally binding framework to provide material and technical assistance to eliminate strategic offensive arms deployed in Ukraine. At this time Ukraine had not yet begun the process of deactivating missile complexes. However, Ukraine was actively seeking ways to fulfill its disarmament obligations under the Lisbon Protocol to the START I Treaty, which it had signed on May 23, 1992. Hence, the U.S. proposal to provide such assistance was accepted enthusiastically in Kiev.

In the bilateral consultations that ensued, the Ukrainian Ministry of Foreign Affairs was charged with playing the role of coordinator. Ukraine's Ministry of Defense (MOD); its Ministry of Machine-building, Military-Industrial Complex and Conversion; the State Committee on Nuclear and Radiation Safety (part of the Ministry for Environmental Protection and Nuclear Safety); and the Expert and Technical Committee of the Cabinet of Ministers were all participants in the negotiating process. These ministries and committees were empowered to negotiate and conclude the relevant implementation agreements over which they had executive control.

By October 1992, following bilateral consultations at the delegation level, a draft umbrella agreement was agreed to on a preliminary basis. Ukraine insisted on a series of amendments to the draft texts proposed by the United States, calling for larger amounts of assistance and extending assistance for the social welfare of Strategic Nuclear Forces servicemen retiring as a result of weapons dismantlement. The Ukrainian side was adamant in its refusal to allow the United States to place conditions on this assistance.

Ukraine's position was understandable considering the economic crisis gripping the country and the realization that its disarmament obligations could only be met with considerable financial, material, and technical assistance. The amount of assistance offered had to be proportionate to the scope and expense of Ukraine's proposed weapons destruction projects, which, in financial terms, nearly equaled the costs of producing nuclear weapons during the Cold War. In this context Ukraine believed that it could not carry out nuclear disarmament without taking into account state interests in environmental protection, the social welfare of decommissioned servicemen, and conversion of military-industrial enterprises.

It is also important to acknowledge that Ukraine had to undertake an ambitious disarmament program at a time of deep economic recession and social instability, interethnic conflicts in neighboring countries, and direct threats to its territorial integrity. Bearing this in mind, it becomes clear that Ukraine's effort to rid itself of nuclear weapons was not an attempt to enrich itself by "bargaining" with its non-nuclear status, as was repeatedly alleged, but only an attempt to address an unprecedented burden that it still mostly bears by itself.

The United States, for its part, demonstrated considerable flexibility. In December 1992, Washington announced an increase in assistance to Ukraine of $175 million, and in the summer of 1993, it announced that it would no longer consider Ukraine's ratification of START I or its accession to the NPT as necessary preconditions for U.S. assistance. This latter decision was particularly important: it gave a considerable boost to the CTR negotiation process and prompted additional discussions on a number of levels. An umbrella agreement on eliminating strategic nuclear weapons and preventing the proliferation of weapons of mass destruction was subsequently signed between the United States and Ukraine on October 23, 1993. Shortly thereafter, five CTR implementation agreements were also signed. Moreover, it was announced that the total amount of CTR assistance to Ukraine would be increased to $350 million by 1995.

To reach this point, the U.S. government had to overcome considerable opposition. The lack of understanding on the part of those who opposed assistance to Ukraine was vividly demonstrated in a speech by the president of the American Association for the Advancement of Science, who declared during an international seminar in November 1993 that Ukraine's demands for aid sounded a lot like blackmail and that $175 million granted to Ukraine under the CTR Program was the most that the American taxpayers could possibly afford. At the same time, he suggested that if Ukraine did not accept these terms, the United States and Russia should force Ukraine to hand over all its nuclear weapons by other means. Suggestions such as these were common at the time.

Moreover, Ukraine's nuclear policy was repeatedly compared with that of Iraq and North Korea. Kiev's attempts to give due consideration to START I ratification were interpreted by the West as shameless bargaining. Instead of support, Ukraine felt political and economic pressure and was accused of nearly derailing the nuclear disarmament process. The same allegations could be heard from some of Ukraine's immediate neighbors.

Under these conditions it was extremely difficult for the Ukrainian Rada to reach a decision concerning START I ratification. However, Ukrainian parliamentarians were strongly influenced by the U.S. decision to provide aid for nuclear disarmament, and on November 18, 1993, the treaty was ratified. The Rada voted to fulfill Ukraine's obligations under the terms of the treaty with respect to its legal, technical, financial, organizational, and other provisions, but bearing in mind the situation at that time, the Rada also delineated certain conditions for Ukraine's accession to the treaty, including assurances for its nuclear security and environmental protection. These reservations were perceived in different ways by the international community. Again, certain voices accused Ukraine of any number of sins. Nevertheless, Ukraine continued to direct its efforts toward the goal of eliminating nuclear weapons.

The signing on January 14, 1994, of the Trilateral Statement by the presidents of the United States, the Russian Federation, and Ukraine was a real breakthrough. It removed a number of key stumbling blocks from the negotiation process since the United States, Russia, and other nuclear states provided Ukraine with security assurances, appropriate financial and technical assistance to eliminate nuclear weapons, and compensation for the cost of the highly enriched uranium contained in these weapons.

The signing of the Trilateral Statement and additional steps taken by the president and the government of Ukraine in response to the Rada's reservations about ratifying the START I Treaty prompted the Rada to vote on February 3, 1994, to remove its reservations to Article V of the Lisbon Protocol and accede to the NPT. Again, the aid provided to Ukraine played an important role in this decision. The Rada's legislation stressed that these reservations were lifted in particular because the United States had "assured Ukraine that it would render technical and financial assistance for the reliable and safe dismantlement of nuclear weapons and the storage of fissionable materials and that it would pursue rapid implementation of the relevant agreements for such assistance."

This is all part of the historical record now. Ukraine's actions were critical to initiating the START I implementation process. Since these early negotiations on CTR, Ukraine has steadily pursued its policy of nuclear disarmament. All offensive missile systems have been deactivated, and all warheads have been transferred back to Russia.

However, the status of the Trilateral Statement is a matter of serious concern. There have been ongoing difficulties and delays in the delivery of nuclear fuel from Russia, in violation of Russia's commitments pursuant to the statement. As a result, Ukraine has been unable to accumulate assemblies for its organic stock reserve at its nuclear power plants, thus affecting the level of nuclear safety.

CTR Implementation

In assessing CTR implementation it should first be noted that, overall, the program has become a stable and rather effective tool for nuclear threat reduction. The CTR process, by engaging the participants in a wide range of problem-solving, became a unique experience in bilateral cooperation. More important, it helped give the process of nuclear disarmament a dynamic pace and helped the citizens of Ukraine understand that they were not alone in facing these challenges. Similarly, the dialogue fostered by the CTR Program helped U.S. political and governmental circles understand that disarmament is a multilateral process with not only military and political dimensions but economic, social, and ecological ones as well. The U.S. view of Ukraine has changed over the course of CTR negotiations from suspicion of Ukraine as a source of nuclear instability to a much more businesslike partnership.

In addition to its basic framework agreement, the CTR Program consists of ten implementation agreements totaling more than $349 million in U.S. assistance. Thus, at least materially, the results of the program have been generally positive. As of December 1995, the total value of obligated funds (contracts signed between the United States and Ukraine) amounted to $271 million. Actual disbursed funds amounted to more than $97.3 million, of which more than $40 million was in the form of contracts with Ukrainian facilities and companies. The greatest progress has been achieved in the area of eliminating strategic nuclear arms[1] which was the major priority for the United States. For this purpose, about $162 million in material and technical assistance had been obligated to Ukraine as of December 1995, of which Ukraine had received $59.4 million in disbursed funds.[2]

A CTR project to establish a government-to-government communications link with the United States,[3] worth $2.4 million, is nearly complete. The first communication line was commissioned in January 1995 and is now being used to transmit messages pertaining to the START I and Intermediate-Range Nuclear Forces (INF) treaties.

A key priority of Ukraine has been to carry out projects for converting defense industrial facilities to commercial and civilian purposes.[4] Defense conversion projects under the CTR Program were the result of persistent lobbying by the Ukrainian government. Defense conversion has opened new avenues for bilateral cooperation on the urgent "social" aspects of nuclear disarmament by converting MOD

---

1. The "Agreement on the Provision of Material, Services and Related Training in Connection with the Elimination of Strategic Nuclear Arms" was signed by the U.S. and Ukrainian governments on December 5, 1993.

2. U.S. Department of Defense, CTR Program Office, *CTR Funding by Country,* December 18, 1995, pp. 1–2.

3. The "Agreement on the Provision to Ukraine of Material and Services for the Establishment of a Government-to-Government Communications Link" was signed by the U.S. and Ukrainian governments on December 18, 1993.

4. The "Agreement on Conversion of Enterprises of the Military-Industrial Complex" was signed by the U.S. and Ukrainian governments on March 25, 1994.

engineering facilities to plants for building housing for retired Strategic Nuclear Forces personnel. Of the $50 million committed by the United States to defense conversion under the Industrial Partnering Program (IPP),[5] $20 million was designated for housing construction. Yet this assistance only begins to address the "social" aspects of demilitarization. According to MOD data, the total amount needed to provide retired nuclear personnel with housing, medical care, and new employment is about $700 million. By late 1995, the MOD had constructed 1,820 dwellings for these personnel, but resources to meet the bulk of these estimated costs are not available.

Ukraine cannot simply leave retiring servicemen to the mercy of fate and will do its best to satisfy, as a priority, at least the basic needs of Strategic Nuclear Forces personnel being retired. During the 40 years that nuclear missile forces existed in Ukraine, these troops acquired a unique expertise. If Ukraine is unable to secure adequate social and housing conditions for them, it cannot exclude the possibility that some countries, seeking nuclear weapons at any cost, will attempt to hire highly qualified experts from this service. For this reason, Ukraine views these social issues as an integral part of the nuclear disarmament process. Delays in CTR assistance for defense conversion and housing programs will have a negative impact on the larger disarmament process and may delay implementation of plans to eliminate nuclear weapons. Other defense conversion projects are no less important. However, although there has been some progress in converting defense plants for housing construction, other widely publicized programs, such as the joint venture between Westinghouse Electric and NPO Khartron to manufacture instrumentation and control devices for nuclear plants, have had few substantial results. By late 1995, housing contracts and rendered services according to this agreement amounted to about $32 million.

---

5. In late spring 1996, the Industrial Partnering Program was renamed Initiatives for Proliferation Prevention. The change was made because many in the U.S. Congress erroneously assumed that the program's objectives revolved around the transfer of U.S. technology to NIS institutes. While industrial interactions are important, the program's primary focus is to contribute directly or indirectly to U.S. nonproliferation objectives.

There has been progress in the development of an export control system in Ukraine.[6] Following a long series of consultations and technical reviews, export control equipment has started to arrive in Ukraine and will be used to construct an export control infrastructure. U.S. commitments in this area amount to $13.26 million. However, only $6.9 million of this had been utilized by July 1996. Regrettably, there has been very little progress in two critical CTR project areas: improving Ukrainian fissile material protection, control, and accounting (MPC&A) systems, and improving Ukrainian nuclear emergency response capabilities in connection with warhead transport to Russia.[7] The United States has committed itself to providing $22.5 million for MPC&A and $5 million for emergency response training and equipment. However, only some $10 million in computer hardware has been sent to Ukraine thus far, although there have been numerous visits by American technical experts to Ukrainian nuclear facilities.

The practical return from another project, the Science and Technology Center in Ukraine (STCU) established by Ukraine, Canada, the United States, and Sweden, has not been substantial. U.S. commitments to the STCU amount to $15 million, which was designated in part for direct grants to Ukrainian scientists formerly employed in the military sector. By mid-1996, only about $2.4 million in U.S. assistance had been disbursed to the center's account.

Judging by this brief overview, one can see that CTR implementation is characterized by both clear successes as well as significant shortfalls. The United States, emphasizing the importance of the CTR Program and widely publicizing its participation in it, has characterized program implementation as wholly successful. But the U.S.

---

6. The "Agreement between the Expert and Technical Committee of the Cabinet of Ministers of Ukraine and DOD of United States on the Provisions of Assistance to Ukraine Related to the Establishment of an Export Control System to Prevent the Proliferation of Weapons of Mass Destruction from Ukraine" was signed on December 5, 1993.

7. The "Agreement on the Development of the State System of Monitoring, Accounting and Physical Protection of Nuclear Materials to Prevent Nuclear Arms Proliferation from Ukraine" and the "Agreement on the Provision of Ukraine with Equipment and Related Training of the Personnel to Control Probable Emergency Situations in Connection with the Export of Nuclear Charges from Ukraine for their Destruction in the Process of Strategic Nuclear Weapons Liquidation" were both signed by the United States and Ukraine on December 18, 1993.

assessment is based on such criteria as declared commitments, financial obligations by the U.S. government, and the number of contracts signed in the United States. Ukrainian officials, however, measure program implementation by the amount of material and technical assistance actually received by Ukraine, the number of contracts signed with Ukrainian firms and agencies, and whether formal notification of these deliveries has been made. This difference in approach has caused substantial misunderstanding in the past. Such was the case in August 1994 when U.S. Undersecretary of State Lynn Davis announced that $277 million in assistance had been sent to Ukraine, whereas Ukrainian officials calculated a figure of only about $4 million. Developing a common approach to assessing the progress of CTR assistance is one of the many problems that still remain in implementing the CTR Program. Without such a common understanding, it will be difficult to assess what work has been done and what additional steps are required.

Directions for Future Efforts

In general, CTR projects to assist Ukraine with eliminating nuclear arms are progressing in accordance with established schedules. There have been several tangible benefits to the CTR Program thus far.

First, politically, the program is helping the United States and Ukraine overcome stereotypes and view each other as partners rather than enemies. This change substantially influenced Ukraine's decision to adopt a non-nuclear status.

Economically, the CTR Program is helping to alleviate the financial burden of Ukraine's nuclear disarmament at a time of deep economic crisis. It is also aiding the conversion of Ukrainian military-industrial enterprises and developing and implementing new joint technologies that will help Ukraine's development of a market economy.

Socially, the CTR Program has given former Strategic Nuclear Forces personnel and defense industrial employees reasonable hope for a better future. Jobs are being created, preventing an exodus of highly qualified military and scientific personnel from Ukraine. These steps have significantly defused social tensions in areas of Ukraine where nuclear weapons were deployed.

Militarily, the CTR Program has meant that the United States and Ukraine no longer aim nuclear weapons at each other's territory. Military contacts have dramatically intensified, and greatly simplified channels of communication have facilitated implementation of nuclear disarmament treaties. Ukraine's decision to become a non–nuclear weapon state has actually made the proliferation of nuclear weapons from Ukraine an impossibility.

Ecologically, the CTR Program will, step-by-step, help reduce the threat posed by unauthorized, unsafe, or criminal nuclear actions. For the first time in 40 years the Ukrainian people, who have been subjected to the grave effects of the Chernobyl disaster, have the opportunity to ecologically rehabilitate the former nuclear weapons sites on their territory.

Despite these benefits, the CTR Program's powerful potential clearly has not been fully realized. Several implementation problems must be addressed if the program is to be revitalized. First, program implementation and utilization of CTR funds have been hampered by a lack of coordination between government agencies and firms in both Ukraine and the United States. Second, the material and technical services that have actually been delivered to Ukraine do not, by any means, cover all the costs that Ukraine bears in the nuclear disarmament process. The amount of assistance must correspond to the extent of the tasks to be performed. Third, with respect to the relationship between political-military and economic issues, U.S. assistance cannot be regarded as charity, and must correspond at least to the amount of money that the United States is saving because of the end of the arms race. Suffice it to say that the entire program of assistance to Ukraine for nuclear disarmament will cost American taxpayers half the price of one B-2 aircraft acquired by the U.S. Air Force. Fourth, the United States must be active in all areas of assistance, not merely those that directly affect it, such as eliminating nuclear warheads and strategic delivery vehicles. Ukraine's priority is the social aspects of the nuclear disarmament process, and these issues urgently need to be resolved.

To conclude, it is worth considering some potential measures to improve the efficiency of CTR implementation. A key measure to improve the program would be to revise the cost estimates of aid to Ukraine. Current CTR legislation authorizes a certain amount of funding for disarmament and nonproliferation assistance to Ukraine but also mandates that much of this assistance be provided by or through U.S. firms with a number of procedural requirements. However, if the costs of the tenders, consultations, contracts, and transportation to Ukraine of equipment and material (most of which, incidentally, can be produced in Ukraine) and the additional costs of related technical services and support were added up, it would be clear that the actual value of assistance is less than half the cost. This is why Ukrainian officials would prefer to place CTR Program orders directly with Ukrainian factories, sharply reducing expenses for transport and service. Ukraine already has had some practical experience in this regard: a rocket fuel interim storage facility that was constructed by a Ukrainian firm received a positive evaluation by U.S. experts.

A second improvement would be to rationalize the financing and reporting procedures established under the CTR legislation. Funds for specific CTR projects are transferred from U.S. Department of Defense (DOD) accounts, and these transactions are periodically reported to the DOD General Inspector of Finance and to the Congress. There is a significant delay between the notification of Congress about proposed obligations and the granting of real funds for actual obligations. This causes needless delays in payments for CTR activities and results in the loss of authorized funds.

Another way to increase the efficiency of the program is to apply innovative approaches to its fulfillment. The implementation agreement concluded on June 24, 1995, allows for financing of Ukrainian firms and enterprises to take part in special CTR projects, integrated by a U.S. subcontractor. Such a strategy will enable Ukraine to use its own resources to find solutions to the social problems of former servicemen. Ukraine has welcomed this document and considers it an example of the U.S. government's growing understanding of the need to find new approaches to assisting Ukraine. Such new approaches must be comprehensive and touch on the full range of nuclear disarmament problems.

With this need to find new approaches in mind, Ukraine considers the conversion of military resources to civilian ones with the aim of building a market economy and creating jobs for former military personnel to be the most creative form of assistance for the future. Nongovernmental organizations have a special role to play in this regard, such as training and retraining Ukrainian specialists and studying the experiences of converting decommissioned U.S. military facilities to civilian uses and applying these lessons to Ukraine.

Another problem, not strictly part of the CTR Program but closely related to it, is the potential for additional disarmament assistance from 14 developed Western nations, the European Union, and the United States. These countries are prepared to provide financial, material, and technical support to facilitate the elimination of nuclear arms in Ukraine. Projects are being implemented now in cooperation with

Germany, the Netherlands, Japan, Norway, Canada, Sweden, and Denmark. Although the amount of assistance rendered by these countries cannot be compared to the U.S. CTR Program, Ukraine welcomes the aid of these countries. It is yet another sign that the world community has a growing appreciation of the problems Ukraine is facing. Ukraine is doing all that it can to facilitate this process and it would welcome similar steps in this direction by the United States.

Ukraine regrets the lack of official U.S. information regarding CTR assistance beyond 1996. Of special concern in this regard is the fact that U.S. financial commitments appear to be declining even as the costs of nuclear weapons elimination continue to rise. Although the U.S. government allocated $100 million in assistance to Ukraine in Fiscal Year (FY) 1994, only $73 million was allocated in FY 1995.

Moreover, the total budget request for the CTR Program in FY 1996 for all four recipient countries reportedly was nearly cut from $370 million to $171 million. The United States has linked these cuts to alleged Russian biological weapons activities. Whether these allegations are true or not, however, alleged Russian "misbehavior" should not be used as an excuse to cut assistance to other CTR recipient states. This action by the U.S. Congress is of serious concern to Ukrainian officials and has prompted fears that the CTR Program has entered a period of steady decline.

As weapons destruction programs continue into the future, the costs of these activities will grow substantially as peripheral issues related to weapons destruction increasingly come into play. For example, environmental safety and cleanup measures, which will have to be implemented only after weapons elimination is complete, will require approximately $95 million. However, the need to allocate resources for these activities is not taken into consideration in current program documentation. Ukrainian decision-makers must know today whether such assistance will be provided and in what amounts, and thus whether there will be a need to adjust current schedules for nuclear arms elimination appropriately.

There may be serious consequences of further CTR Program reductions after 1995. First, there is the possibility of suspensions in the nuclear weapons elimination process as well as an increasing risk of nuclear accidents or other incidents connected with nuclear weapons transport and dismantlement. The possibility exists that Ukraine may have to look for other sources of financial support for this process. The impact of the factors mentioned above may provoke substantial political difficulties and may even reverse the progress in U.S.-Ukrainian bilateral relations.

However, the Ukrainian side hopes that the United States also understands the necessity of developing and further implementing its nuclear disarmament assistance program and will objectively evaluate its future steps in this direction. Finding the answers to these questions, which are of mutual interest, will not only enhance the effectiveness of CTR implementation but will further the larger interests of humanity.

Chapter 9

Nunn-Lugar Program Assessment

The Case of Belarus

Vyachaslau E. Paznyak

In June 1992, the first contacts were made between Belarus and the United States regarding U.S. denuclearization and demilitarization assistance under the Cooperative Threat Reduction (CTR) Program. These discussions occurred at a time of radical change in Belarus, which had only officially emerged as an independent state through the dissolution of the Soviet Union in late 1991.[1] In 1992, the new republic was in the early stages of forming a decision-making apparatus to tackle a host of hitherto unfamiliar problems. It was only in mid-1992, for example, that an independent Belarusan Defense Ministry was established and began to assume responsibility from Moscow for military affairs in the country.[2] Of particular importance at this time,

---

1. On August 25, 1991, shortly after the failed coup in Moscow by Russian hard-liners, Belarus officially adopted a Declaration of State Sovereignty into its constitution, which had been passed by the Belarusan Parliament on July 27, 1990. On September 19, 1991, Belarus changed its name from the Byelorussian Soviet Socialist Republic (its official name since 1919) to the Republic of Belarus and reestablished the centuries-old state symbols, the white-red-white flag and the Pahonia (Chase) coat of arms. On December 8, 1991, Belarus concluded agreements with Russia, Ukraine, and Kazakstan to establish the Commonwealth of Independent States (CIS). On December 10, 1991, the Belarusan Parliament ratified the commonwealth agreement and denounced the "Treaty on the Formation of the Union of Soviet Republics" that had brought Belarus into the Soviet Union. At the time the CIS agreement was ratified, 69 percent of those polled in the republic approved the commonwealth agreement. Shortly afterward, on December 25, 1991, the United States recognized the independence of Belarus, as well as that of Russia, Ukraine, Armenia, and Kazakstan.

2. On May 6, 1992, the Belarusan Council of Ministers abolished the Belarusan Military District of the former Soviet Union and all of its units except for those that made up the Strategic Forces of the new CIS, which were subordinated to the Belarusan Republic's Defense Ministry.

from the U.S. perspective, was the condition and operational control of formerly Soviet nuclear forces stationed on Belarusan territory. The status of these forces was being clarified in a series of multilateral agreements among the nuclear successor states of the Soviet Union, and in bilateral negotiations and treaties between Belarus and Russia.[3] Moreover, Belarus's declared aim of becoming a non-nuclear state was being codified in a series of international arrangements.

Since 1992, U.S.-Belarusan cooperation under the CTR Program has been marked by a number of remarkable achievements as well as some important setbacks and shortfalls. Moreover, differing assumptions about the purpose and scope of this cooperation on the part of Belarusan and U.S. officials have, since the program's inception, resulted in growing tensions in the bilateral relationship. This chapter attempts to assess the status and future progress of the CTR Program in Belarus and the value added by U.S. assistance to Belarusan efforts to dismantle and redress the military, environmental, and economic legacy of the Soviet era. This chapter also attempts to identify some of the key factors that have affected implementation of CTR projects to date and to consider potential measures that may improve implementation.

Belarus occupies a critical and, in many ways, unique position in the political, economic, and security relationships that have developed among former Soviet republics since the collapse of the Soviet Union. A particular focus of this assessment, therefore, will be to identify the key issues and problems on the Belarusan side that have complicated CTR implementation and to suggest ways in which the United States, in its bilateral relationships with Belarus, Russia, and other former Soviet states, may help ameliorate these problems.

Domestic Political Attitudes Toward Cooperation

Attitudes toward the CTR Program in Belarus have varied considerably, not only over the life of the program but also across different sectors of Belarusan public opinion. In the upper echelons of the Belarusan government, there has been a range of views regarding

---

3. On July 20, 1992, Belarus and Russia concluded the first of several military, political, and economic agreements: an "Agreement on Strategic Forces Temporarily Stationed on the Territory of Belarus," and an "Agreement on Coordinating Activities in the Military Sphere."

cooperation with the United States.[4] On one end of this spectrum, the former Chairman of the Supreme Council, Stanislau Shushkevich, was quite optimistic about U.S. assistance in general and the CTR Program in particular, believing that the program would help consolidate Belarus's independence and further its political objectives as an emerging independent state. In contrast, the Ministry of Defense (MOD) was initially reluctant to become the main point of contact for negotiating and implementing CTR agreements with the United States, not only because it lacked the necessary expertise and was over- whelmed by other problems, but also because it was suspicious of cooperation with its erstwhile adversary on sensitive national security issues. A similar level of distrust initially pervaded thinking in the Ministry of Foreign Economic Relations, which was not enthusiastic about becoming a key player on improving export controls.

Despite these early suspicions, the CTR Program has generally enjoyed a healthy level of support from key government bureaucracies due to their strong institutional interest in seeing it succeed. The government is keenly aware of the political and economic importance of the program's contribution to the denuclearization and demilitariza- tion of Belarus. Politically, the program justifies the choice for demili- tarization that the country made in 1992 and codified in its new constitution, and it weakens the position of those who have criticized this choice for its alleged shortsightedness. Economically, the program also provides critical technical assistance at a time when financial resources are too scarce to meet all of the demilitarization obligations that Belarus has taken on.

A significant base of support also exists for U.S.-Belarusan threat reduction cooperation among several bureaucratic players at the ministerial and subministerial levels. Cooperation with the United States provides one of the few means at the disposal of these working- level bureaucracies to accomplish the complex military-technical tasks for which they are now responsible, such as creation of an export controls system, conversion of defense industrial enterprises, environ- mental restoration of weapons sites, and providing housing, retraining, and employment for demobilized Belarusan troops. At the same time, it is natural that some bureaucrats charged with implementing CTR

---

4. It is significant, however, that the Nunn-Lugar Program has never been discussed in the Belarusan Parliament, even in reference to other issues.

activities have at times tried to pursue their narrower departmental interests at the expense of the program's goals.

Such bureaucratic competition is to be expected and is a relatively minor complication compared to the more systemic problems that have begun to emerge in the U.S.-Belarusan cooperative relationship. Despite the generally strong base of political support that still exists, the optimism in Minsk that greeted the CTR Program and other Western cooperation has clearly yielded to growing skepticism over the real purpose and benefit of cooperation with the United States. Several problems in implementing CTR projects have intensified criticism of the program among government bureaucracies. Particularly troubling to Belarusan officials have been the slow pace of deliveries of U.S. assistance and the requirement that only U.S. enterprises serve as contractors for CTR-related tasks, rather than providing funds directly to Belarusan governmental agencies.

Complicating this loss of official support is the lack of any broader public support for cooperation with the United States and other Western states, particularly on security issues. In general, the public at large in Belarus has had little opportunity to understand the CTR Program's objectives and content. It is common knowledge that Western countries, particularly the United States, are providing Belarus with financial and technical assistance, including aid for nuclear and conventional demilitarization. However, with the exception of one or two key projects, the program's visibility and impact have not been high enough to generate strong public opinion, either positive or negative. In Belarus, as in other former Soviet states, public and official expectations of large-scale economic and social welfare assistance from the West were very high in the first years of independence. Such expectations have now been muted: the conventional wisdom in Belarus is that the country was persuaded by the West to take actions that met the pragmatic security interests of the West, but that Belarus cannot otherwise expect charity from abroad.

CTR Decision-Making and Implementation in Belarus

The sometimes turbulent political history of Belarus since 1992, when the CTR Program first began to make headway, has featured presidential and parliamentary elections, replacement and resignation of key government players, and periodic reshuffling of government bureaucracies.[5] These changes have brought about several lengthy periods of indecision and bureaucratic gridlock and have introduced a number of new appointees throughout the bureaucracy who have needed time to master their positions. A vivid illustration of such inertia was the period following the presidential elections of August 1994, when more than four months passed before a new administration was formed.

Nonetheless, the importance of the CTR Program for implementing Belarus's denuclearization goals has kept it largely outside the fray of domestic political change. Economically, the CTR Program has been close to self-sufficient and, as an assistance program, it has been providing aid rather than taking money from other budget items. Widespread economic difficulties, however, have led to calls for more assistance across a wider number of areas, underscoring the program's limitations. Both the political and economic situation in Belarus has influenced the CTR Program in another roundabout way. The slow pace of economic reforms and problems with organizing free parliamentary elections in 1993–94 contradict a basic precondition for CTR assistance, which is the institution of economic and democratic reforms.

Belarusan decision-making on CTR demilitarization projects has followed essentially the same pattern since 1992. High-level decisions are made by the president, in consultation with the Cabinet of

---

5. For example, on January 26, 1994, Stanislau Shushkevich was deposed as chairman of the Supreme Council and *de facto* head of state. He was replaced for an interim period by his deputy, Vyacheslav Kuznetsov. Two days later, Mecheslav Grib was elected chairman of the Supreme Council. The first presidential elections in Belarus were held in June/July of the same year, and elected Alexander Lukashenka as president of the republic. A year later, in May 1995, Belarusan parliamentary elections and referendums took place. However, a quorum was not elected to parliament and additional elections were scheduled for the fall of 1995. The outgoing parliament attempted to continue its work but was declared illegitimate by President Lukashenka. On June 6, 1995, U.S.-Belarusan cooperation under the CTR Program and other efforts were further complicated by the resignation of Belarusan Defense Minister Colonel General Anatoly Kostenko. First Deputy Defense Minister Lieutenant General Leonid Maltsev was named acting defense minister. See Table 9-1 for a complete list of Belarusan agencies responsible for CTR implementation. For a more general discussion of the foreign policy decision-making process in Belarus, see Vyachaslau Paznyak, "Belarus's Foreign Policy Priorities and the Decision-Making Process" in Adeed Dawisha and Karen Dawisha, eds., *The Making of Foreign Policy in Russia and the New States of Eurasia* (New York: M.E. Sharpe, 1995), pp. 141–156.

Ministers[6] and the National Security Council. These are then debated and voted on by the parliament.[7] The Ministry of Foreign Affairs (MFA) then prepares the preliminary texts for negotiations on cooperation with the United States.[8] More detailed agreements are then concluded between the Belarusan Ministry of Defense[9] and the U.S. Department of Defense (DOD), and oversight of specific projects is later delegated to the appropriate governmental agency.

Table 9-1 displays the principal Belarusan government organizations and key individuals that have been involved in the negotiation and implementation of the CTR Program. One of the most important organizations within the MOD that has been charged with implementing several CTR agreements, including projects on a continuous communication link and on the destruction and environmental restoration of missile launch facilities, is the National Agency for Arms Control and Inspections (NAKI).[10] Defense industry conversion issues,

---

6. After the first Belarusan president, Alexander Lukashenka, was elected in the summer of 1994, the Council of Ministers was reorganized into the Cabinet of Ministers, and the functions of the abolished directorates and secretariats were inherited by the National Security Council. In the Cabinet of Ministers an assistant to the prime minister on defense affairs serves as liaison between the MOD and the Cabinet and other government agencies on some questions of CTR implementation. Since July 1994, the Cabinet of Ministers has been headed by Prime Minister Mikhail Chigir, who replaced Vyacheslav Kebich.

7. Mecheslav Grib currently chairs the Belarusan parliament. He replaced Stanislau Shushkevich on January 28, 1994.

8. Key players in the Belarusan MFA involved in CTR assistance negotiations include Deputy Foreign Minister Andrei Sannikov; Head of the Department of International Treaties Ivan Naidovich (formerly Valentin Fisenko); and, more recently, Head of the Directorate of International Security and Disarmament Alexander Baichorov.

9. The Belarusan MOD is currently headed by Pavel Kozlovsky. Key current and former subordinates involved in CTR negotiations include former MOD Deputy Chief of Staff Major General Alexander Yegorov; First Deputy Defense Minister Alexander Tushinsky; and Adviser for Military Policy Affairs to the Minister of Defense Major General Yuri Portnov. The MOD's Directorate for Negotiations and Agreements has traditionally assisted in negotiations and preparation of agreements.

10. NAKI was created in June 1992 to replace the MOD's Department for the Implementation of Treaties.

Table 9-1. Belarusan Agencies and Individuals Responsible for CTR Projects.

Project	Responsible Organizations	Key Individuals
Emergency Response	•Civil Defense Headquarters •Ministry for Emergency Situations & Cherno- byl Affairs [a]	Anatoli Liplyansky Ivan Kenik
Export Controls	•Ministry of Foreign Economic Relations •State Customs Committee •Belarusan Frontier Forces	Victor Pas'ko [b]
Continuous Communication Link	National Agency for Arms Control & Inspec- tions (NAKI) [c]	Maj. Gen. Yevgeni Nikulin
Environmental Restoration ("Project Peace")	•NAKI •Topographic Service of the Armed Forces of Belarus •Republican Scientific and Technological Cen- ter (ECOMIR) •Ministry for Natural Resources & Environ- mental Protection	Yevgeni Nikulin Grigory Kobelev Alexander Kovalev
Industrial Partnerships *Housing* *Training Centers*	•KRAS Corp/Integral •Byelocorp Scientific/BelOMO •FSG/Minsk Computer Amalgamation •Planning & Production Unit for Construction & Quartering of Troops (MOD) •Belarusan Center for Retraining & Employ- ment of Demobilized Servicemen	Victor Yemelyanov; Eduard Kaloshkin Vyacheslav Bursky Anatoly Harlap Col. Vladimir Novikov Mikhail Pankov
Military-to-Military Contacts	MOD	
International Science and Tech- nology Center (ISTC) Branch Office	Belarusan Academy of Sciences [d]	Dr. Sergei E. Chigrinov
Strategic Offensive Arms Elim- ination (SS-25 Launch Facility Destruction)	•NAKI •Ministry of Natural Resources & Environmen- tal Protection	Yevgeni Nikulin
Nuclear Infrastructure Elimination [e]	NAKI	Yevgeni Nikulin
Materials Protection, Control & Accounting (MPC&A)	Ministry for Emergency Situations and Cherno- byl Affairs[f]	

[a] The Ministry for Emergency Situations and Chernobyl Affairs was created in 1994 by merging three state committees: the State Committee for Nuclear and Industrial Supervision (Gospromatomnadzor), the State Committee for Chernobyl Affairs, and the State Committee for Hydrometeorology.
[b] Chief, Non-Tariff Regulation Directorate.
[c] NAKI is under the direction of the Belarusan MOD.
[d] Projects will be overseen by an ISTC branch office established at the Belarusan Academy of Sciences Science and Technology Center at Sosny (near Minsk).
[e] Dismantlement of nuclear infrastructure to provide opportunities for the civilian use of former strategic missile bases.
[f] Formerly overseen by the State Committee for Nuclear and Industrial Supervision, chaired by Alexander Zuev, prior to this committee's merger into the Ministry for Emergency Situations and Chernobyl Affairs.

which have largely been the purview of the MOD, were initially managed by First Deputy Defense Minister Alexander Tushinsky. Other key organizations in this area have included the MOD's Science and Technical Committee and, more recently, the Ministry of Economy's Committee on the Economic Issues of Defense and the Ministry of Industry's Department of Defense Industries and Conversion.

Supervision of the entire CTR negotiation and implementation process was originally delegated to the Council of Ministers' Department of Citizens' Rights, Public Security and Defense Matters, which was subsequently reorganized into the State Secretariat for Combating Crime and National Security, and later into the Directorate for Coordinating the Activities of the Administrative Bodies. To coordinate and control the implementation of CTR agreements, the Council of Ministers issued Enactment No. 969 on October 28, 1993, which established an Interdepartmental Coordinating Council and attempted to designate specific ministries, departments, and organizations to implement particular CTR projects. Although the council held several working sessions, little coordination has been undertaken besides ad hoc interagency meetings and close cooperation between the Foreign and Defense Ministries.

Belarusan nongovernmental organizations (NGOs) unfortunately have played little direct or supporting role in implementing the CTR Program. Indirectly, seminars and conferences with U.S. counterparts[11] have highlighted the importance of Belarusan membership in nonproliferation and export control regimes, thereby helping to fulfill some of the preconditions for Nunn-Lugar assistance. Otherwise, however, there traditionally has been little NGO participation in resolving Belarusan security issues.

---

11. For example, in April 1992, an international conference on nonproliferation was hosted by the Monterey Institute of International Studies and attended by U.S. and CIS officials and representatives of nongovernmental organizations. On October 8–9, 1992, Belarus's first international conference on international security and nonproliferation of nuclear weapons was held in Minsk, organized by U.S. and Belarusan nongovernmental organizations: the Belarusan Peace Committee, the Institute for Foreign Languages, the Monterey Institute of International Studies, New York University, and the Department of Journalism of the Belarusan State University. Additional NGO workshops on nonproliferation and export controls were held in June and October 1994.

Progress of the CTR Program in Belarus

In their joint statement on the results of President Clinton's January 1994 trip to Belarus, former Chairman of the Belarusan Supreme Council Stanislau Shushkevich and President Clinton noted, "In its clear commitment to nonproliferation and to a strong regime of export controls, Belarus is well-placed to play a leading role in developing the policy framework and expertise that would benefit not only Belarus but also the other newly independent states and the world." Unfortunately this remains mostly rhetoric, but it has the potential to be much more than this.

A number of factors, on both the U.S. and Belarusan sides, have contributed to delays in assisting Belarus achieve its lofty denuclearization and demilitarization goals. Key problems that had to be resolved at the outset of U.S.-Belarusan cooperation included Belarus's need to inventory all military facilities and assets on its territory[12] and to develop the necessary level of expertise to implement potential U.S. assistance. For its part, the United States did not appear prepared to immediately offer an assistance package once Belarus became an independent republic. The U.S. stance reflected both a cumbersome bureaucratic process for distributing aid and a desire to be reassured that Belarus would in fact meet the preconditions for assistance, i.e., a commitment to denuclearize, demilitarize, and institute democratic and economic reforms.[13]

Other initial differences between Belarus and the United States that delayed CTR implementation concerned not only the total amounts of

---

12. The inventory of armaments, equipment, and property of the Belarusan armed forces was completed in January 1994.

13. U.S. assistance for weapons dismantlement was predicated upon presidential certification that the Soviet Union or its successor states were: (1) making substantial investments of their resources in the dismantlement or destruction of the weapons; (2) forgoing military modernization programs exceeding legitimate defense requirements; (3) forgoing the use in new weapons of fissionable components from dismantled weapons; (4) facilitating U.S. verification of weapons destruction; (5) complying with all relevant arms control agreements; and (6) observing internationally recognized norms of human rights. See Theodor Galdi, *The Nunn-Lugar Cooperative Threat Reduction Program for Soviet Weapons Dismantlement: Background and Implementation*, U.S. Congress, Congressional Research Service, December 29, 1993, p. CRS-3.

assistance required but, more fundamentally, the purpose and scope of such aid. Belarusan officials came to see U.S. assistance as a reward for their efforts to dismantle the nuclear and military legacy of the Soviet era, and they fully expected that the United States would help to mitigate the social and economic impact of demilitarization. However, the United States had a much narrower objective—ensuring the denuclearization of Belarus and other newly independent states. These differences have grown into permanent, existential tensions in the program, and have permeated the history of U.S.-Belarusan negotiations and implementation of the CTR Program.

At first glance, it would appear that CTR project implementation has been relatively successful in Belarus, but the process has not been without problems. The CTR umbrella agreement between the United States and Belarus was signed on October 22, 1992, and remains in force for five years. Two of the ten existing implementing agreements, one on emergency response equipment and training and one on export controls, were signed in 1992 along with the umbrella agreement.

Three major changes in U.S. Nunn-Lugar legislation contained in the Fiscal Year (FY) 1993 DOD Authorization (PL 102-484, October 23, 1992) allowed the use of CTR funds to support (1) the demilitarization and conversion to civilian purposes of former Soviet defense industries; (2) the establishment of science and technology centers in CIS states to engage former Soviet scientists and engineers in nonmilitary research; and (3) the expansion of contacts between U.S. military personnel and those of the newly independent states.[14] This legislation opened the way for additional U.S.-Belarusan agreements, four of which were signed in 1993: on a continuous communication link, the environmental restoration of former strategic rocket facilities, industrial partnerships, and expanded defense and military contacts.

In 1994, fewer implementing agreements were concluded, but not for lack of funding. Not only was $6 million in undesignated funds left over from 1993, but President Clinton also promised an additional $25 million in CTR assistance during his visit to Minsk in January 1994.[15]

---

14. Ibid., p. CRS-3.

15. On January 15, 1994, President Clinton made an official visit to Belarus during which he commended the republic's foreign policies and pledged continued U.S. support for the implementation of its denuclearization program. Clinton announced that the United States would provide an additional $25 million under the Nunn-

The likely reason for the delay in implementing further assistance agreements was the aura of political uncertainty caused by a number of Belarusan political developments that year: the forced resignation of Stanislau Shushkevich (an advocate of U.S.-Belarusan cooperation) as chairman of the Supreme Council in January; a reshuffling and consolidation of the government bureaucracy; and the Belarusan presidential elections, with subsequent delays in forming a cabinet and developing domestic and foreign policies. In the midst of this confusion, delays in the negotiations on CTR implementation negotiations created a flurry of shuttle diplomacy between Washington and Minsk, but with little real progress in 1994.

In 1995, bilateral CTR activity was revitalized. Two agreements covering three projects were signed in 1995: on strategic offensive armaments elimination (covering SS-25 launch facility destruction and propellant elimination) and on fissile material protection, control, and accounting.[16]

Several of the agreements signed by the United States and Belarus to dismantle the Soviet arsenal left behind in Belarus and enhance weapons proliferation safeguards have been amended since they were first signed; other, relatively less complex projects have remained unchanged, and some of these have been completed. The value of many of these projects has increased over the past four years as the CTR Program has evolved. The value and status of funding obligations and disbursements for CTR projects in Belarus, as of July 1996, are displayed in Table 9-2. U.S.-Belarusan cooperation has achieved several

---

Lugar legislation for the safe and secure dismantlement (SSD) of nuclear weapons. The assistance raised to $100 million total SSD funds committed by the United States to projects in Belarus.

16. In January 1995, a U.S. delegation headed by Dr. Gloria Duffy, Deputy Assistant Secretary of Defense and Special Coordinator for the CTR Program, visited Minsk to discuss CTR implementation with representatives of the Belarusan Foreign Ministry, Defense Ministry, Ministry of Foreign Economic Relations, and Ministry for Environmental Protection. In June 1994, Dr. Duffy headed a second U.S. delegation to meet with the Belarusan MOD and NAKI officials. At the June meeting, an agreement totaling $19 million in U.S. assistance was finalized and signed that covered elimination of fixed launch structures and liquid propellant from SS-25 missiles, dismantlement of Belarus's nuclear infrastructure, and development of civilian uses of former strategic missile bases in Belarus. An additional agreement provided $3 million for improvements to fissile material protection, control, and accounting in Belarus.

important goals. Nonetheless, as Table 9-2 illustrates, obligation and disbursement of CTR funds have been slowed by technical and organizational difficulties. In some cases, however, the low level of disbursements are far out of proportion to the problems that have been encountered.

STRATEGIC OFFENSIVE ARMAMENTS ELIMINATION

At peak deployment in the mid-1990s, 81 single-warhead SS-25 Topol intercontinental ballistic missiles (ICBMs) were based in Belarus. All of these SS-25s are road-mobile, and remain under formal Russian jurisdiction and control. In December 1995, Russia and Belarus reached an agreement to transfer the remaining missiles and warheads back to Russia, and as of mid-1996, 63 SS-25s had been transferred to Russia with their warheads.

Although the SS-25s are road-mobile and are in the process of being physically removed from Belarusan territory, Belarus is obligated under the terms of the START I Treaty to eliminate fixed-site launch facilities for SS-25s. CTR assistance is helping Belarus meet its START I obligations and is helping Belarusan officials safely dispose of highly toxic SS-25 liquid propellant which is stored at its launch facilities. On June 23, 1995, a CTR implementation agreement was signed by the U.S. Defense Department and the Belarusan MOD to assist in the elimination of strategic offensive arms remaining in Belarus. Specifically, $8 million was designated for elimination of SS-25 launch pads, and an additional $8 million was designated for safe, environmentally sound elimination of SS-25 liquid propellant. In June 1996, the United States supplemented this amount with an additional $12.9 million, raising the total CTR sum allocated to Belarus for strategic offensive arms elimination to $28.9 million.[17]

Progress in these efforts has been complicated by the evolving security relationship between Belarus and Russia and the fact that Russia retained formal responsibility for much of the strategic weapons infrastructure in Belarus after 1991. In July 1993, the United States offered to assist Belarus in eliminating SS-25 fixed structures and their foundations on its territory in accordance with START destruction

---

17. "More Nuclear Disarmament Funds Promised for Belarus," *OMRI Daily Digest*, June 10, 1996.

Table 9-2. Value of CTR Projects in Belarus (U.S. $M).

Project (Year of Agreement)	Notified 7/96	Obligated				Dis- bursed 7/96
		6/93	9/94	7/95	7/96	
Strategic Offensive Arms Elimination ('95)	33.90	–	–	–	2.39	0.08
Site Restoration (Project Peace) ('94)	25.00	–	6.00	16.66	19.43	10.75
Industrial Partnerships ('93)	20.00	–	9.80	19.60	19.70	12.10
Export Controls ('92)	16.26	0.30	1.60	4.26	9.98	6.38
Emergency Response ('92)	5.00	3.30	4.29	4.30	4.98	4.09
Defense Enterprise Fund ('94)	5.00	–	–	5.00	5.00	5.00
Science & Technology Center ('95)	5.00	–	–	–	4.95	0.49
Defense & Military Contacts ('93)	3.52	–	0.20	0.43	0.74	0.36
Material Protection, Control & Accounting ('95)	3.00	–	–	–	2.89	0.49
Continuous Communications Link ('93)	2.30	0.20	0.69	1.00	1.06	0.79
TOTAL	118.98				71.12	40.53

SOURCE: Based on reports generated by CTR Program Office, U.S. Department of Defense, July 1, 1996, and previous months.

requirements, but the offer remained on the table for some time.[18] The START agreement stipulated that SS-25 fixed structures were to be eliminated by Russia. However, Belarus objected to the Russian method of eliminating these structures because of the unacceptable level of environmental damage. Moreover, Russia was not eager to take on the

18. Ibid.

high costs of eliminating these launch pads. The United States, Russia, and Belarus agreed to employ U.S. technical assistance to find a more environmentally sound means of destroying SS-25 launch facilities. The United States is currently finalizing its proposals, which will specify the destruction method to be used and nominate an appropriate contractor to perform the operation.

Efforts to dispose of toxic and volatile SS-25 liquid propellant have also had a complicated history. The United States sent a technical team to Belarus in August 1994 to identify potential projects for $6 million in CTR funds that were left undesignated in 1993.[19] The Belarusan side expressed an interest in assistance to convert liquid rocket fuel from tactical weapons. However, when U.S. technical experts met with their Belarusan counterparts, they were told that Belarus could not provide information about the chemical composition of the liquid rocket fuel or the proposed conversion process until after a pilot plant became operational in October 1994. The United States reiterated its willingness to work with the government of Belarus to identify a program of assistance in the area of liquid fuel conversion.[20] The propellant elimination agreement became possible only after Russia shared the propellant's chemical formula with the United States.

---

19. In March 1993, U.S. Secretary of State Warren Christopher pledged an additional $65 million to facilitate Minsk's denuclearization efforts. On July 21–23, then Chairman Shushkevich visited Washington, where he deposited Belarus's instruments of accession to the Nuclear Non-Proliferation Treaty. During this visit, on July 22, Defense Secretary Les Aspin and Belarus Minister of Defense Pavel Kozlovsky signed three agreements to help ensure the safety, security, and dismantlement of former Soviet nuclear weapons in Belarus. The agreements provided $59 million in additional direct U.S. assistance to Belarus, bringing total U.S. assistance to approximately $75 million. The funds were to be used in three areas: up to $25 million for environmental restoration of former Soviet Strategic Rocket Forces sites; up to $20 million for defense conversion activities under the Industrial Partnering Program, and to help provide military housing and retraining programs for decommissioned Strategic Rocket Forces officers; and up to $14 million for export control assistance to prevent the proliferation of technology and material for weapons of mass destruction. Six million dollars remained uncommitted after the March announcement because Washington and Minsk could not reach agreement on how this money should be spent.

20. See Cooperative Threat Reduction Program Description attachment to the letter of U.S. Ambassador Kenneth S. Yalowitz to Chairman of the Supreme Council of the Republic of Belarus Mecheslav Grib, December 16, 1994, p. 8.

ENVIRONMENTAL RESTORATION (PROJECT PEACE)

One of the more urgent environmental requirements of the post-Soviet era is the rehabilitation of contaminated former Strategic Rocket Forces (SRF) facilities in Belarus. The purpose of this CTR project, funded through a Congressional initiative called "Project Peace," is to provide the necessary equipment and expertise to the MOD, the Ministry of Natural Resources and Environmental Protection, and other responsible Belarusan agencies to facilitate the environmental restoration of these facilities. A CTR implementation agreement for this project was signed on July 22, 1993, with an effective period of four years, and the United States has pledged a total of $25 million to this effort, making it the second largest CTR project in Belarus.

In addition to being one of the largest CTR projects in dollar terms, the environmental site restoration project has also been one of the more successfully implemented. To date, all relevant equipment has been purchased, and an analytical chemistry lab has been established to support cleanup efforts at former SRF facilities. In April 1995, a CTR contract for remediation planning, training, and technical assistance was awarded to Arthur D. Little, Inc. Additional procurements, completed in October 1995, will equip a multifunctional photo laboratory and a geoinformation system, and will support environmental remediation activities at former missile sites.

INDUSTRIAL PARTNERING PROGRAM

A critical goal of Belarusan officials has been to mitigate the impact of demilitarization on economic, industrial, and social welfare. The Industrial Partnering Program (IPP) supports this goal by helping to convert and privatize excess military-industrial capacity in Belarus by underwriting joint ventures between Belarus and Western industrial partners. Other related CTR projects provide a small amount of additional funds to establish vocational retraining centers and construct housing for demobilized SRF officers.

Belarus's CTR defense conversion program was the earliest to be implemented and is one of the more advanced CTR projects in this area. A four-year implementing agreement was initialed on July 22, 1993, and the project has a total value of $20 million. A U.S.-Belarusan Joint Commission on Defense Conversion was established in March 1994, and, as of July 1996, $9.15 million in financial support had been disbursed to several joint ventures. These include:

- KRAS Corp.-Integral, to manufacture integrated circuits. Production began in early 1995. In June of that year, Minsk requested $2.6 million to complete work on this joint venture, and in July 1995 the project was completed.

- Byelokorp Scientific-BelOMO, to jointly manufacture laser pointers. Production began in early 1995, and the project was completed in July 1995.

- FSG-Minsk Computer Amalgamation (MCA), to manufacture radio frequency computer modems and battery chargers. The venture began production early in 1995, and the project was completed in September 1995.[21]

IPP defense conversion activities in Belarus have not been without problems. One complication that remains unresolved concerns property rights for U.S. contractors who have provided equipment for joint ventures with Belarusan counterparts. Another point of contention is that, as a prerequisite for promoting conversion projects, the United States has stipulated that identified production facilities in Belarus must be privatized. Specifically, these enterprises either must be capitalized with no less than 50 percent private investment, or there must be active development plans under way to privatize them. The stated purpose of the IPP is "to assist in the conversion and privatization of excess military-industrial capacity through financial assistance." However, the requirements of this program and of the Defense Enterprise Fund (DEF), a private nonprofit organization, are difficult to reconcile with the realities of privatization. Private capital has been very hesitant to invest in these enterprises, and privatization is just beginning in earnest now. Moreover, these firms are likely to wish to retain some capability for military production to pursue the market for defense products. In any case, even if, for political and economic reasons, conversion and privatization in Belarus could find some common ground, they still require a legal framework to provide firm guarantees to foreign investors. The legal basis for the protection of

---

21. Integral formerly manufactured nuclear-hardened integrated circuits for the Soviet military. BelOMO previously manufactured satellite systems, night vision devices, and range finders for the Soviet military. Minsk Computer formerly designed and developed mainframe computers for the MOD.

private capital in Belarus is in its formative stages.[22] Truly successful defense industrial conversion will require a climate that is more conducive to private investment, which will necessarily have to await broader economic and legal reforms.

CTR assistance under the Industrial Partnering Program is also supporting construction of housing for demobilized Strategic Rocket Forces officers. It has been estimated that more than 9,300 Belarusan servicemen have been left without any means of housing themselves and their families.[23] A total of $10 million has been devoted to this project, and as of July 1995, $7.4 million had been awarded. A Bulgarian company, ABB SUSA, received a contract for the construction of 150–200 apartments at Folush. The project commenced in September 1995 after some initial site-clearing delays and was scheduled to be completed by November 7, 1996.

Through a similar agreement, CTR funds are supporting the development of training centers for decommissioned SRF personnel. Five million dollars of the funds available for expanded U.S.-Belarusan defense and military contacts was designated to create a training center in Kolodischi (near Minsk), with branches in Lida and Brest, and to provide them with automotive, woodworking, and sewing equipment, as well as computer and English-as-a-second-language labs. Equipment for a computer training center and an automotive training center has been delivered, and additional lists of equipment to be delivered are being finalized.

EXPORT CONTROLS

Assisting Belarus's Frontier Forces, State Customs Committee, and other responsible agencies to develop effective export control institutions and mechanisms is a critical task in preventing the proliferation of weapons of mass destruction, fissile material, and associated technologies across national borders. Controls over the movement of strategic commodities were complicated in January 1995 when Belarus,

---

22. Decrees by the Belarusan Council of Ministers that are relevant to the republic's defense conversion efforts include: On the Inventory of Armaments, Military Hardware, and Property of the Armed Forces of the Republic of Belarus; On Granting Tax Privileges to Enterprises that Undergo Conversion; and On Preservation and Rational Utilization of the Equipment of Military Bases Abandoned by the CIS Strategic Forces Due to Their Relocation to other Regions.

23. See *Zvjazda*, June 16, 1995.

Kazakstan, and Russia signed a customs union that harmonized their foreign economic policies, removed tariffs and duties on trade among the three, and lifted customs controls along their common borders.[24] As a result of the union, customs checks along the Belarusan-Russian border have been eliminated, leaving the Belarusan-Polish border as the only well-guarded Belarusan border. There are periodic checkpoints on the Belarusan border with Ukraine and with the Baltic states, but these checkpoints can be easily circumvented. The movement of goods and personnel between Belarus and Russia was made even easier in April 1996, when the two countries signed a treaty creating a new union that merged many of their economic and legal policies. Although the full implications of the Russo-Belarusan union treaty are difficult to foresee, the two sides have committed to joint protection of their common external border.[25]

In order to improve Belarus' export control system and capabilities, a CTR agreement was signed in October 1992 and amended in April and July 1993. Total assistance promised by the United States under this project, as of mid-1996, amounts to more than $16 million. U.S. assistance has included joint development of improved customs control procedures, training of Belarusan personnel, and equipping export control officials with appropriate technologies to monitor and enforce cross-border transit restrictions. Before appropriate equipment was procured, the project featured working group meetings between Belarusan officials and officials of the U.S. Commerce Department and

---

24. The customs union was formally signed by representatives of the three republics on January 28, 1995. See "Russia, Belarus, Kazakstan Sign Customs Union Agreement," *Rossiiskaia Gazeta*, January 28, 1995, in FBIS-SOV-95-0227-S, February 9, 1995. The union was only a coordinating agreement, however, and implementation of its measures required bilateral arrangements between each of the three nations.

25. The union treaty, officially titled the "Agreement on the Formation of a Community," was signed by Russian President Boris Yeltsin and Belarusan President Lukashenka in a formal ceremony on April 2, 1996. Lukashenka termed the agreement the "highest form of community within the CIS," and Yeltsin noted that it "opens a qualitatively new phase in relations between Russia and Belarus." See Peter Rutland, "Text of Russo-Belarusan Union Treaty Revealed," *OMRI Daily Digest*, March 29, 1996; and Scott Parrish, "Yeltsin, Lukashenka Sign Integration Agreement," *OMRI Daily Digest*, April 2, 1996. See also David Hoffman, "Russia, Belarus Announce Agreement on Plan to Form New Union," *Washington Post*, March 24, 1996, p. A32.

the U.S. Customs Service to assess Belarusan equipment needs and to provide training and information seminars on nonproliferation policies, international technology control regimes,[26] and the drafting of export control legislation.[27]

As of January 1995, slightly more than $1 million had been spent on procuring export control support equipment. On September 16, 1994, the first contract was awarded for procurement of a local area network (LAN) system and other computer peripherals to support a centralized, automated export license administration in Minsk. Delays in installing this equipment stemmed from the failure of Belarusan officials to promptly identify where the LAN was to be located. The equipment was kept in storage in Germany until the summer of 1995, when the Ministry of Foreign Economic Relations, the end-user of the computer equipment, moved into a new building. Automatic data processing and radiation monitoring equipment for detecting nuclear materials was also provided to officials of the Belarusan Customs Committee,[28] and further procurements are planned.

Although this was one of the first areas of U.S.-Belarusan cooperation, improvements in export control have been marked by delays. The first procurement was completed in September 1994, yet two years later, in July 1996, only slightly more than $6 million (39 percent) of the total of $16 million set aside by the United States for export control assistance had actually been disbursed for equipment, training and technical assistance, and logistics support.

---

26. For example, on January 14, 1994, Belarus and the United States exchanged diplomatic notes bringing into effect a mutual assistance agreement between their customs services.

27. Preparation of export control legislation went on for more than a year before a final document was submitted to the Cabinet of Ministers for approval in July 1995. Since the Customs Union between Belarus and Russia was created, export control regulations in Belarus have been unified and harmonized with those of Russia.

28. In June 1995, President Lukashenka signed a decree abolishing customs controls on Belarus's borders with Russia. Two months later, Belarusan Customs Committee officials and their U.S. counterparts began work on introducing a new system of export controls.

EMERGENCY RESPONSE

This project, the total value of which is $5 million, provides emergency response equipment and related training and materials to enhance Belarus's capability to respond to nuclear weapons accidents or incidents. The U.S.-Belarusan implementation agreement was signed in October 1992, with an amendment to extend implementation for an additional two years signed in October 1994. As one of the two oldest CTR projects, its implementation has been rather smooth, and most deliveries were completed by November 1995.

DEFENSE ENTERPRISE FUND

The Defense Enterprise Fund was established in March 1994 by the U.S. Defense Department as a private, nonprofit organization to assist in the conversion and privatization of former Soviet military-industrial enterprises by providing loans to industrial joint ventures between U.S. and former Soviet enterprises. Five million dollars has been earmarked for this endeavor, all of which has been obligated. A $1–2 million investment in a joint venture between the U.S. KRAS Corporation and Planar to manufacture integrated circuit equipment has been approved, and about a dozen other prospective projects are under review.

ISTC BRANCH OFFICE

The purpose of the International Science and Technology Center (ISTC) is to provide research opportunities and thus gainful employment for scientists and engineers formerly involved in nuclear and chemical weapons development. The total funds earmarked for Belarusan ISTC activities is $5 million. No formal agreement has been signed, but on October 17, 1994, the Supreme Council of the Republic of Belarus passed legislation to join the ISTC agreement.[29] The organizational details to enable Belarusan scientific and technical personnel to participate in ISTC-sponsored projects have been settled, and as of early 1996, one project had been funded. An ISTC branch office has been established at the Science and Technology Center of the Belarusan Academy of Sciences at Sosny, near Minsk.[30] Incorporation documents

---

29. The original ISTC charter was signed on November 27, 1992.

30. The Sosny branch is headed by Director General Dr. Sergei E. Chigrinov.

for the branch office are awaiting adoption by the Belarusan Cabinet of Ministers.[31]

EXPANDED DEFENSE AND MILITARY CONTACTS

A memorandum of understanding and cooperation was signed in October 1993 for $7.5 million in CTR obligations to support a project to promote improved military-to-military relations between Belarus and the United States. By July 1996, $740,000 had been obligated to support orientation visits and more than 30 military-to-military contacts. Planning continues for future exchanges which include professional development seminars and training.

FISSILE MATERIAL PROTECTION, CONTROL, AND ACCOUNTING (MPC&A)

The MPC&A project in Belarus will assist the creation of a national system for the control, accounting, and physical protection of nuclear material used for peaceful purposes.[32] Belarus has completed regulations and a work plan for an MPC&A system that will be in accordance with International Atomic Energy Agency (IAEA) standards, and these are now being implemented by the Committee for the Supervision of Safety in Industry and Nuclear Power Engineering (Promatomnadzor).[33]

MPC&A discussions between the U.S. government and Belarus began in September 1992. However, an MPC&A implementation

---

31. On November 27, 1992, the United States, Japan, the European Community, and Russia signed an agreement in Moscow establishing an International Science and Technology Center to help redirect former Soviet scientists and engineers to peaceful purposes. Observers from Belarus and Kazakstan attended the March 1995 ISTC board meeting, and an ISTC branch office was subsequently established in Belarus to support Belarusan scientists. For a complete history of the ISTC, see Chapter 13 by Adam Moody in this volume.

32. The "Agreement Between the Defense Ministry of Belarus and the U.S. Department of Defense on Control, Accounting, and Physical Protection of Nuclear Material to Assist in the Prevention of Nuclear Weapons Proliferation" was signed on June 23, 1995.

33. Promatomnadzor is a component of the Ministry for Emergency Situations and Chernobyl Affairs. See John Shields and Greg Webb, eds., *Nuclear Successor States of the Soviet Union: Nuclear Weapon and Sensitive Export Status Report*, No. 4 (May 1996) (published jointly by the Monterey Institute of International Studies and the Carnegie Endowment for International Peace), Table I-E, p. 31.

agreement was signed by the two countries only in June 1995. Work which began prior to this agreement is proceeding at the Institute for Power Engineering Problems at Sosny. The United States will fund improvements at the central alarm station, MPC&A upgrades, training in physical protection, nondestructive assay, tamper-indicating devices, and other MPC&A equipment. U.S. teams visited Sosny in August and November 1995, and work at the site is expected to be completed by the end of 1996.[34]

Japan and Sweden are also providing MPC&A assistance to Belarus. The United States has formed a committee with Japan and Sweden to coordinate MPC&A aid to Belarus,[35] and the three governments are cooperating to carry out immediate physical protection upgrades at Sosny. U.S. and Swedish experts cooperated on a site survey in April 1994 and provided recommendations for physical protection upgrades to the IAEA. Japan has provided a computerized information system to monitor and control storage and movement of nuclear material as well as technology to manufacture measuring instruments and telecommunications upgrades to facilitate data exchange between Japan, Belarus, and the IAEA.[36] Belarus was scheduled to receive additional MPC&A equipment and technical assistance from Sweden in early 1996.[37]

CONTINUOUS COMMUNICATION LINK

A CTR agreement was signed in January 1993 to provide a continuous communication link between Belarus and the United States to help Belarus meet its communications and reporting obligations under the terms of the START and Intermediate-Range Nuclear Forces (INF) treaties. U.S. and Belarusan negotiators agreed on a modern system configuration, equipment delivery schedule, and logistics support plan. An amendment to extend implementation for an additional two years was signed in October 1994, and the United States made a total

---

34. For details on U.S. and multilateral MPC&A activities in Belarus, see Chapter 15 by Jessica Stern in this volume.

35. Shields and Webb, *Nuclear Successor States of the Soviet Union*, p. 31.

36. *Nihon Keizai Shimbun*, November 1, 1994, as reported in "Tokyo to Give Technical Aid on Nuclear Materials to Belarus," JPRS-TND-94-020, November 17, 1994, pp. 6–7.

37. Shields and Webb, *Nuclear Successor States of the Soviet Union*, p. 31.

commitment of $2.3 million for these upgrades. An interim equipment configuration was installed in August 1993 at NAKI, although equipment for a permanent system was not delivered to NAKI until October 1995. Considering the small amount of resources devoted to this project compared to others, implementation has been excessively long. As of July 1996, only $790,000 (about one-third) of the agreed amount of $2.3 million had been disbursed as actual goods and services to provide this link.

Sustaining and Improving the CTR Effort

As the preceding description has demonstrated, important progress has been made in some CTR projects in terms of actual obligations and disbursements of funds. Moreover, despite the sluggishness of early efforts to assist Belarus with its demilitarization goals, there has also been progress in establishing additional CTR projects to meet Belarus's complex technical needs. This is especially true of the relatively recent projects to eliminate SS-25 launch structures and propellants, progress on which was only possible once several political and bureaucratic bottlenecks were overcome.

In most cases, despite the rapid and often unpredictable political changes in Belarus since the CTR Program began, U.S.-Belarusan cooperation has not become a hostage of political battles. However, it has not been immune to delays. These delays have been observed on a number of levels at different stages of project development and have been the result of both bureaucratic and structural factors.

In many cases, there have been protracted periods of inaction when unanticipated problems required further study to be resolved.[38] Organizational and bureaucratic factors have also slowed CTR implementation, including a lack of coordination among bureaucratic players in both Belarus and the United States. In some cases, important information has been compartmentalized among bureaucracies with competing interests. On the Belarusan side, for example, project implementation has been hampered in many cases because some senior-level bureaucrats have not shared critical information provided by the United States with the lower-level officials who are actually

---

38. For example, it took more than six months to prepare and sign the CTR implementation agreement on strategic offensive arms elimination.

responsible for implementing CTR projects and meeting agreed program milestones. The frequent reshuffling of ministry posts, departmental reorganizations, and the introduction of new faces into ongoing CTR projects has also played havoc with agreed CTR time-tables.

Most of the CTR Program's resources and efforts are focused on the status and disposition of former Soviet—now Russian—weapons of mass destruction. There is thus a special requirement in carrying out CTR projects in Belarus that deal with the legacy of these weapons to better coordinate procedural and technical activities with Russia. Implementation of a withdrawal schedule of the Russian SRF set the time frame for some activities, regardless of U.S. or Belarusan actions. However, the CTR experience with SS-25 site destruction and remediation projects has demonstrated the benefits of early and regular discussions with Russian demilitarization planners.

An examination of CTR implementation also reveals several structural factors that have hampered completion of these projects. Abrupt changes in the Belarusan political, legal, and economic system have generated a great deal of turbulence that U.S. planners, like their Belarusan counterparts, must learn to navigate. Likewise, the lack of appropriate laws or imperfections in recent legislation have either discouraged or created unintended complications for some demilitar-ization activities. In the midst of this change and disorder, the United States and the CTR Program have created a certain measure of stability to carry out critical denuclearization and demilitarization goals. Nonetheless, achieving some of the CTR Program's core objectives, particularly conversion of former defense industrial enterprises to commercial purposes, will depend on Belarus's successful completion of key economic, legal, and political reforms. Such reforms have been the *sine qua non* for continued U.S. assistance under the CTR Program; more importantly, they will be essential if Belarus is to create an environment that will attract foreign enterprises and stable investment for the long term.

The achievements of Belarus's denuclearization and demilitariza-tion activities under the CTR Program far outweigh the problems that have been encountered. However, current CTR funds only begin to touch on the larger issues with which Belarus must grapple in the coming years. Helping Belarus overcome the economic, industrial, and other burdens of the past several decades will require assistance of a different, longer-term nature. It is clear that termination of the CTR

Program in Belarus would have the most profound impact on the republic's commitment to carry out its demilitarization agenda and become a strong supporter of global nonproliferation efforts. It would also have dire consequences for the well-being of the citizens of Belarus, who continue to struggle with the environmental and social legacies of the Soviet era. At a minimum, such a development would stall implementation of a wide range of vital projects, including creation of a national export controls system, which is of tremendous international importance; environmental restoration, delays in which would further undermine the health of a nation polluted by the Chernobyl disaster and decades of lax industrial conditions; conversion of defense enterprises, which is impossible for Belarus without outside assistance; and housing construction and retraining for demobilized SRF officers, which remains among the most serious obstacles to eliminating strategic missile bases.

These last two areas of unfinished business are particularly urgent from a social welfare standpoint. The economic upheaval and social dislocation that have come with demilitarization, if allowed to persist, will cause deep frustrations in Belarus. Curtailment or cancellation of CTR assistance will only aggravate this state of affairs, and, as is clear from events since 1991, there are political forces that would be inclined to use such cutbacks as a means to heighten anti-Western feelings and set back the cause of reform. Reductions in such assistance will also almost certainly slow the pace of demilitarization in Belarus and will encourage the country to continue to rely on military industry and the arms trade for its economic survival. Moreover, such reductions will make it extremely difficult for Belarus to carry out its obligations under bilateral and multilateral arms control agreements.

Key priorities for future demilitarization assistance to Belarus include more aggressive conversion of defense industrial enterprises, the elimination of conventional armaments, and the establishment of a robust system of export controls. Nor should the CTR Program abandon the promising and essential work it has done in the areas of environmental restoration and officer housing and retraining. In terms of program management and execution, future assistance might be expedited and both time and money might be saved for other useful activities by abandoning the restrictions on engaging Belarusan contractors, materials, and equipment in CTR projects.

Opposition in the U.S. Congress to the CTR Program and other efforts to assist former Soviet states appears to be motivated in part by suspicions that Russia may be unwilling to carry out its arms control obligations. Although Russia remains the largest former Soviet recipient of U.S. aid, problems in the bilateral U.S.-Russian relationship should not be allowed to pollute cooperative efforts with other newly independent states. If these congressional attitudes prevail, then an approach that differentiates between CIS states would be useful to avoid needlessly tarnishing one CTR partner state with the behavior of another.

Nongovernmental organizations, in both Belarus and the United States, which have so far played only a marginal role in the CTR implementation process could play an important part in instituting some of the improvements to the CTR Program suggested here. NGOs are a natural mechanism for improving communication and coordination between officials, legislators, and working staffs in the United States and Belarus and for disseminating information about cooperative efforts to the public at large. Specifically, NGOs could provide a critical "push" to ongoing and future CTR efforts by monitoring implementation of CTR projects and evaluating the program's performance; providing cooperative liaisons among the governmental agencies involved, as well as among national and foreign nongovernmental actors; and familiarizing the Belarusan public with the CTR Program's objectives, status, and bottlenecks through the mass media, thus inviting constructive feedback.

These suggestions for improving the management and implementation of the CTR Program could be of help politically, economically, and organizationally, but the more important issue for the future of U.S.-Belarusan cooperation is one of scope. It is vital for the CTR Program's integrity to maintain its comprehensive approach, one that does not focus myopically on denuclearization, but embraces a variety of demilitarization and nonproliferation problems, and pays particular attention to the social and ecological impacts of demilitarization. The program should not be viewed in isolation as serving only U.S. interests; in fact, it is no less significant for the national security of Belarus and other former Soviet states. From this perspective, it is not a concession on the part of either the donor or the recipient country, but rather a common cause of enhancing international security. Now that the CTR Program is nearing completion, it is essential to build upon its achievements and experiences by finding other vehicles to carry on its critical but as yet unfinished work.

Chapter 10

Implementing the CTR Program in Kazakstan

Oumirserik T. Kasenov, Dastan Eleukenov
& Murat Laumulin

Kazakstan played a critical role in the Soviet nuclear weapons program and in the Soviet Union's overall nuclear strategy during the Cold War. Uranium, beryllium, and other strategic materials were mined and processed for use in Soviet reactors and in the Soviet weapons complex in Kazakstan. Nuclear research was carried out in Kazakstani facilities that supported Soviet reactor design and development. Hundreds of nuclear weapons tests were carried out at Semipalatinsk, in eastern Kazakstan, and hundreds of heavy intercontinental ballistic missiles (ICBMs), armed with nuclear warheads, were deployed at missile fields in various parts of the republic.

Kazakstan is now laboring to dismantle the weapons legacy left behind by the Soviet Union and redirect the country's strategic resources and talents to peaceful purposes. Although Kazakstan has received assistance in this effort from a number of sources, the U.S. Nunn-Lugar Cooperative Threat Reduction (CTR) Program remains the most serious effort to date to address these problems. The program is viewed as an extremely important initiative in Kazakstan. However, there is a growing sense of skepticism regarding its effectiveness, and attempts by legislators in the U.S. Congress in Fiscal Year (FY) 1995 to reduce the program's funding by nearly half met with great concern in Almaty. It is worth emphasizing that since the CTR Program was first introduced, its purpose and implementation mechanisms were well understood in Kazakstan, and officials there never viewed it as a means of reaping financial reward.

Kazakstan shares the U.S. goals of nonproliferation and nuclear risk reduction, and it was in the spirit of these goals that Kazakstan actively joined the CTR Program and is successfully implementing its main tasks, removal of nuclear weapons from Kazakstan's territory and dismantlement of the infrastructure that supported development of nuclear weapons and other weapons of mass destruction. Criticism of the program in the United States and periodic calls for reducing or eliminating it have perhaps been inspired by the illusion that the denuclearization process is simple and virtually cost-free. However, reduction or elimination of this vital program would have several negative consequences. Besides its direct impact on Kazakstan's denuclearization plans, reductions in CTR funding at this critical juncture would reduce Kazakstan's basic trust in the policies of the United States.

The Status of CTR Projects in Kazakstan

According to assessments by Kazakstani government officials and technical experts, prior to 1996, the CTR Program was implemented slowly in almost every area, with the exception of its most basic projects, such as establishing a government-to-government communication link between Washington and Almaty to facilitate data reporting for arms control agreements. Although the CTR Program has been in effect for more than four years, the rate at which specific projects have been implemented has been quite slow. In fact, several CTR projects only began implementation in 1994. However, since the spring of 1995, some promising changes have been instituted in the program to improve its implementation in significant ways.

In April 1995, Kazakstan fulfilled its main obligation under the START I agreement when the last of Russia's nuclear warheads—more than 1,400 in total—were removed from Kazakstani territory and transferred to Russia.[1] Among the CTR projects being implemented in

---

1. This was officially confirmed by the Kazakstani Foreign Ministry on May 24, 1995. See Doug Clarke, "Kazakstan Free of Nuclear Weapons," *OMRI Daily Digest*, April 26, 1995, p. 2–3; Doug Clarke, "Kazakstan Confirms It Is Nuclear Free," *OMRI Daily Digest*, May 25, 1995, p. 3. At the time that the last of these warheads were transferred back to Russia, one undetonated nuclear device with a yield of approximately 0.4 kilotons remained buried in Degelen Mountain at Kazakstan's Semipalatinsk nuclear test site. The device, which was to be used in a 1991 physical irradiation experiment, had been buried in a 592-meter-long tunnel approximately 130 meters from the surface. In August 1991, the test range was closed, the test was never conducted, and the undetonated bomb was left buried. A joint Russian-Kazakstani commission had considered dismantling the device and shipping it to the Chelyabinsk-70 nuclear center for further disassembly. Concern over a possible accident, however, led the commission to recommend that the device be destroyed by conventional explosives. The device was subsequently destroyed in this manner

Kazakstan, four are of particular importance: destruction of strategic delivery systems; creation of an export control system; improvement of management and control of nuclear materials; and conversion of the Kazakstani defense industry.

Several governmental organizations in Kazakstan participate in the negotiation and implementation of these CTR projects. Destruction of missile systems and missile silos involves the Ministry of Defense, the Committee for Defense Industry, the Kazakstan State Corporation for Nuclear Energy (KATEP), and a number of other state bodies. A governmental commission coordinates this work. Several ministries and agencies are involved in developing a national system of export controls, including the Ministries of Internal Affairs, Defense, Industry and Trade, and Economics, the Committee for Defense Industry, the Atomic Energy Agency, and the Customs Committee. Moreover, a Government Commission for Export Control has been established that eventually will be the main agent setting policy in the export control area.

Defense conversion projects are overseen by the Committee for Defense Industry and the Ministry of Economics, in consultation with other experts, particularly members of the International Executive Service Corps (IESC), an association of retired U.S. industry officials. Joint U.S.-Kazakstani organizations, working with the IESC and others, also play a role in CTR defense conversion projects. Details of ongoing work in each of these areas and the success with which CTR projects are being implemented are outlined below.[2]

---

on May 31, 1995, at 13:16 Almaty time. See Douglas Busvine, "Kazakstan to Blow Up Four-Year-Old Nuclear Device," Reuters, May 25, 1995; Bruce Pannier, "Kazakstan to Explode Nuclear Device," OMRI Daily Digest, May 24, 1995, p. 2.

2. In addition to the projects outlined below, which are of greater long-term interest to Kazakstan and for which work has been proceeding for some time, the United States and Kazakstan have reached agreement on a multiyear cooperative effort to permanently seal the Degelen Mountain nuclear test tunnel complex at the Semipalatinsk site. The cooperative project, signed in October 1995, will demilitarize the complex using environmentally sound methods to close and seal its tunnels. The complex was the site of Soviet nuclear tests from 1961 to 1969. The project, to be executed by the Defense Nuclear Agency and the National Nuclear Center of Kazakstan, is targeted for completion in 1999, with a minimum of 60 tunnels sealed each year. Six million dollars were designated to cover the project's first phase, a geological and radiological survey of the complex, to determine the most appropriate means of sealing the tunnels there.

MISSILE SILO DESTRUCTION

Strategic offensive arms elimination represents the largest share of Nunn-Lugar obligations in Kazakstan, but until very recently, it has been one of the slowest projects to be implemented, measured in terms of dollars disbursed compared to dollars obligated to this project. The major task under this Nunn-Lugar project is to provide assistance in destroying SS-18 ballistic missile silos in Kazakstan, in accordance with START requirements.[3]

This project began in the summer of 1994. However, it was only in February 1996 that the U.S. Department of Defense (DOD) awarded a contract for destroying the silos to a joint-venture team composed of the Swedish-Swiss industrial group ABB and the Houston-based construction company Brown and Ruth. Under the terms of the $31 million contract, these companies are to destroy 148 missile silos located in four different missile fields in Kazakstan. Kazakstan has taken upon itself the responsibility for destroying the command and control apparatus for these ICBMs under the terms of a previous agreement with the United States.[4]

A key factor that has slowed implementation of this project is the need to coordinate work plans with Russia, which is understandably concerned with preserving sensitive or secret information about the unique construction of its silos in Kazakstan. These security concerns have been resolved, but they delayed the project by several months. Some delays in work schedules also arose because of unfavorable winter weather conditions at these sites.

A more fundamental problem that has affected progress on silo destruction is the lack of enthusiasm for the project in Kazakstan, a result of the CTR Program's requirement that most technical work in this area be conducted by U.S. and other foreign companies and non-Kazakstani personnel. Use of mostly American labor is unjustified considering its relatively high cost. Enterprises in Kazakstan are

---

3. According to the January 1996 START Memorandum of Understanding, 22 SS-18 ICBMs and 24 associated silos remain deployed in Kazakstan. Under START rules, ICBMs remain accountable until they are removed from their silos and their bases, and silos remain accountable until they are destroyed. See U.S. Arms Control and Disarmament Agency, *START Treaty Memorandum of Understanding Data for Republic of Kazakstan*, January 1, 1996, Annex A, p. 7.

4. Francis Williams, "Foreign Companies Will Help Kazakstan Dismantle Missile Silos," *Finansovye izvestia*, No. 20, February 23, 1996, p. 1.

particularly interested in working with American firms in significant stages of the project, which would give them desperately needed work as well as opportunities to develop contacts with U.S. technical experts and industrial managers. Instead, Kazakstani specialists have been limited to participating in only the low-technology and low-skill aspects of silo destruction.

EXPORT CONTROLS

As with other aspects of its economic and security policies, Kazakstan began work on establishing a viable system of export and border controls almost from the moment of its independence from Moscow in December 1991. One of its first actions in the area of nuclear export controls, for example, was to sign the Minsk Accord of June 1992, whereby Kazakstan, along with other former Soviet signatories, agreed to abide by Nuclear Suppliers Group guidelines in controlling exports of nuclear materials and nuclear-related dual-use materials.[5]

Almaty has made a high-level commitment to controlling the flow of technology, personnel, and strategic commodities across its borders. Kazakstan's interest in rigorous supervision of exports is a component of its wider and long-standing concern for strengthening controls along its borders as a defense against the free movement of criminal or subversive elements into its territory. Kazakstani officials have repeatedly stressed that illegal exports and technological or economic espionage are among the country's most crucial domestic problems. A January 1996 presidential edict confirmed Almaty's commitment to this issue by outlining a menu of organizational and technical improvements that should be achieved by the year 2000. Crucial factors cited in this edict for developing stronger border controls include the implementation of more advanced technologies for detecting intruders and the development of a clearer, more organized and efficient Kazakstani infrastructure for its border control forces.[6]

---

5. Under the terms of the Minsk Accord, whose formal title is the "Agreement on the Basic Principles of Cooperation in the Field of Peaceful Use of Nuclear Energy," Commonwealth of Independent States (CIS) member signatories agree to follow the requirements of INFCIRC/209 (Zangger Committee) and INFCIRC/225 (NSG trigger list), Articles 1 and 5.

6. Oleg Khe, "Concept and Program of the Strengthening and Development of the Border Forces Drafted," *Panorama*, No. 3 (January 26, 1996), p. 15; this article is translated and reproduced in FBIS-UMA-96-040-S, January 26, 1996.

Kazakstan's export control system is still evolving, but the government has made significant progress building safeguards against technology proliferation. Enforcing controls over exports of strategic commodities and technologies is a formidable challenge for the republic, given its size and terrain and its common border with many Asian states. Moreover, following its independence from Moscow, Kazakstan lacked the legal framework for a national export control system as well as the robust administrative and technical infrastructure needed to maintain and enforce these controls.

The first step in this process was to develop the legal framework for controls over exports. For the first four years of Kazakstan's independence, export controls were based on executive decrees rather than national legislation.[7] However, an export control law has now been developed that will put such controls on a much firmer legal basis and provide emerging Kazakstani enterprises with clearer, more stable procedures for exporting dual-use or other sensitive items. Nunn-Lugar assistance played an important role in supporting this legislative process. In the spring of 1995, Kazakstani officials conferred with U.S. legal and technical experts in a monthlong series of meetings in Washington, D.C., funded in part by the Nunn-Lugar Program. U.S. experts assisted these Kazakstani officials in developing early drafts of an export control law, using similar legislation already developed in Russia as a legal point of departure.

U.S.-Kazakstani collaboration helped to develop comprehensive legislation that established a system of export controls, limited export destinations, and designated government agencies responsible for monitoring and enforcement. A great deal of effort was devoted to coordinating emerging Kazakstani export control legislation with

---

7. Prior to the adoption of formal export control legislation in the spring of 1996, two presidential decrees formed the legal basis for export controls in Kazakstan: Decree No. 2021 (January 11, 1995) On Liberalization of Foreign Trade Activities, and Decree No. 66 (January 19, 1995) On the Order of Export and Import of Goods (Works, Services) on the Territory of the Republic of Kazakstan. These decrees stated that all goods except "goods of national importance" could be exported by any economic entity in Kazakstan. "Goods of national importance" included weapons, nuclear materials, production technology, and expertise, other military technologies, and certain dual-use commodities (e.g., radioactive isotopes), and could be exported only with the authorization of the Cabinet of Ministers. Cabinet of Ministers' Decree No. 183 (March 9, 1993) has also been a key component of Kazakstan's export control system.

similar laws in Belarus and Russia.[8] The new law, On Export Control of Weapons, Military Equipment, and the Production of Dual-Use Materials[9] was subsequently passed by the Mazhilis and the Senate (the lower and upper chambers of the Kazakstani Parliament) on May 3 and June 3, 1996, respectively. Nunn-Lugar funds have thus directly helped to lay a legislative foundation for export controls.

The second major task on the export agenda is to establish the organizational basis for monitoring and enforcing controls. On March 24, 1995, Resolution No. 338 of the Cabinet of Ministers, "On Measures for Further Development of the System of Export Control in the Republic of Kazakstan," created the Governmental Commission on Export Control (GCEC). The commission was given top-level status and is headed by First Vice Prime Minister Garry Shtoik. Supervising agencies will be created within the commission to oversee particular categories of controlled commodities and products.

A final component of improved export controls is to train the personnel who will actually monitor and enforce these restrictions and to equip them with the technology appropriate to their tasks. It is in this aspect of export control development that the Nunn-Lugar Program has perhaps made the greatest contribution. Efforts to train export control personnel are continuing, with significant Nunn-Lugar assistance. Under one such project, U.S. technical experts participated in an export control training seminar held in July 1995 at the Kazakstan Institute of Strategic Studies.

---

8. Oleg Khe, "Law Prepared on Exports Controls of Military Products," *Panorama*, No. 7 (February 23, 1996), p. 3.

9. The law, which consists of 13 articles, specifies the export control responsibilities of the Cabinet of Ministers and the executive. It identifies items subject to export controls: weapons, including conventional weapons; materials used in weapons production; nuclear materials; dual-use materials, technology, and equipment; chemical materials and technology that can be used to produce chemical weapons; and disease agents that can be used to produce biological weapons. The law forbids the re-export of such items by recipient states to third countries once they are exported from Kazakstan. The law supports Kazakstan's participation in economic sanctions against states that violate international export control agreements. See "Mazhilis odobril zakonoproyekt ob exportnom kontrole vooruzheniy, voennoy tekhniki, i produktsii dvoinogo naznachenia" (Parliament adopts bill on export control of weapons, military technology, and dual-use items), *Panorama*, No. 17 (May 3, 1996), p. 2.

The United States and other foreign governments have pledged several million dollars to assist Kazakstan with the technical aspects of export controls, particularly in the nuclear sphere. For example, the U.S. Department of Defense (in coordination with the Commerce Department and other agencies) has obligated more than $7 million as of mid-1996 under the CTR Program for export control training, technical assistance, and equipment. Officials and experts of the U.S. Customs Service have helped Kazakstani specialists complete an assessment of Kazakstani export control procedures, automation efforts, and technical requirements, and have assisted development of a marine patrol program for the Caspian littoral. Some Nunn-Lugar funds have gone toward the purchase of six new coastal patrol boats on the Caspian Sea. The U.S. Energy and Commerce Departments have provided similar assistance.

Although export control legislation has been adopted, more work will be required before an effective system of export control is fully in place in Kazakstan. The most important thing now is to train export control specialists in every ministry and government agency involved in this area. The difficulty here is to ensure that the financial incentives for lax oversight of exports from Kazakstan—particularly of sensitive nuclear materials and technology—do not outweigh the goals of nonproliferation.

Another important issue that will affect future U.S.-Kazakstani cooperation in this area will be the evolving economic and political relationship between Kazakstan and other newly independent states (NIS) of the former Soviet Union. In January 1995, Kazakstan reached an agreement with Belarus and Russia to establish a customs union whereby customs controls along their common borders would be abolished.[10] Russia and Kazakstan have eliminated tariffs and trade

---

10. Kazakstani Resolution No. 367 and Resolution No. 381, passed on September 6, 1995, and September 19, 1995, respectively, established the legislative basis in Kazakstan for the customs union. In turn, a December 1995 Moscow meeting between Kazakstani First Deputy Prime Minister Nigmatzhan Isingarin and Russian Under-Secretary Aleksei Bolshakov defined formal mechanisms to implement a customs union and strengthen bilateral economic collaboration. See "On the Affirmation of the Protocol of the Meeting of the Government Delegations from the Russian Federation and the Republic of Kazakstan About the Conclusion of the First Stage in the Realization of the Agreement on a Customs Union," signed by the Republic of Belarus and the Russian Federation with the Republic of Kazakstan in Moscow on January 20, 1995, from August 19, 1995, *Sobranie aktov*

volume restrictions and no longer operate most major customs checkpoints along their common border.[11] This is a quite natural outgrowth of the growing need to forge economic ties and develop economic opportunities with Kazakstan's neighboring states. Measures such as these will be essential if the republic is to fulfill its economic and industrial potential and carry out its fledgling economic reforms. Russia was slow to formally ratify the customs union, which caused some concern in Kazakstan's business community.[12] Nationalist political forces in Kazakstan have also assailed the treaty, creating additional obstacles to its implementation.[13] Nonetheless, the long-term trend is likely to be one of closer economic integration and cooperation among the NIS.

That such cooperation is increasing should not obscure the fact that Kazakstan has made a strong, high-level commitment to controlling the illegal flow of technology and materiel, particularly in the nuclear sphere, across its frontiers. The United States should not let fears of economic collaboration among former Soviet states erode its support for Kazakstan's export control improvements and other reforms. Nor should U.S. officials or lawmakers allow problems in the U.S. bilateral relationship with Russia to pollute the spirit of cooperation that has been built up with Kazakstan since its independence.

---

presidenta Respubliki Kazakstan i pravitelstva Respubliki Kazakstan, November 30, 1995, pp. 53–55; and "On the Abolishment of Customs Control Along the Border of the Republic of Kazakstan and the Russian Federation," *Sobranie aktov presidenta Respubliki Kazakstan.*

11. "Derbisov on Customs Affairs, Security," *Kazakstanskaia pravda,* August 30, 1995, in FBIS-SOV-95-173, August 30, 1995.

12. According to Moukhtar Ablyazov, president of the company Astana-Kholding, delayed ratification reflected Moscow's attitude that the agreement was not established between "equal partners." See "They Do Not Give the 'OK' to the Customs House," *Pravda,* January 14, 1996, p. 1.

13. For example, upon returning from a February 1995 meeting in Moscow that included discussion of the union, Kazakstani Prime Minister Akezhan Kazhegeldin was assailed by nationalists for "betrayal of national interests." See "A New Trend In CIS Integration?" *The Monitor,* Vol. 1, No. 2 (Spring 1995).

FISSILE MATERIAL PROTECTION, CONTROL, AND ACCOUNTING
An important aspect of the growing problem of economic and technological espionage in Kazakstan is the fact that much of the attempted
illegal exports reported to date have involved nuclear-related commodities.[14] A natural corollary to improvements in export and border
controls, therefore, are enhancements to safeguards of fissile material
at Kazakstani nuclear facilities, such as the BN-350 breeder reactor at
Aktau and the research reactors at Almaty and Semipalatinsk. Kazakstan is acutely aware of the implications of fissile material security for
global efforts to control the proliferation of nuclear weapons. The
republic has a strong economic interest in maintaining its nuclear
industries and participation in worldwide commercial nuclear markets.
It has thus taken a number of steps to be a responsible nuclear supplier
and be in complete conformance with international nuclear safeguards
and guidelines. Although as of mid-1996, Kazakstan has not yet been
accepted as a member of the Nuclear Suppliers Group, it has embraced,
in a series government decrees, the NSG guidelines for controlling
exports of fissile and dual-use nuclear materials. Adoption by the
parliament in June 1996 of export control legislation that includes the
NSG control list represents another step toward formal compliance
with all international norms of nuclear commerce.

Kazakstan acceded to the Nuclear Non-Proliferation Treaty in
February 1994; IAEA inspections are being implemented at all relevant
Kazakstani nuclear facilities. However, the most important effort to
secure Kazakstan's fissile material is the on-going technical cooperation
with the United States and other countries to improve material
protection, control, and accounting (MPC&A). The United States and
the Republic of Kazakstan signed an MPC&A implementing agreement
in December 1993. However, in 1994 and early 1995, while these
activities remained under DOD stewardship, work on improving
MPC&A at Kazakstani facilities proceeded at an exceedingly slow pace.
The pace of activity accelerated considerably in 1995 when manage-

---

14. In a January 1995 interview, for example, Kazakstan's State Security Committee
Chairman Jenisbek Jumanbekov lamented the problem of economic espionage and
outright theft, particularly of nuclear technology. Jumanbekov reported 406 cases
of attempted illegal exports of raw materials for the year and said that his bureau
was attempting to halt such thefts. See "Corrupt Business Rampant in Kazakstan,"
Post-Soviet Nuclear & Defense Monitor, January 31, 1995, p. 11.

ment of these improvements was transferred, on the U.S. side, to the Department of Energy (DOE).

Thus far, the bulk of CTR MPC&A assistance has been in the form of training Kazakstani nuclear personnel in the principles of physical protection and material control and accounting. Representatives from the Almaty research reactor, the Kazakstani Atomic Energy Agency (KAEA), the Institute of Atomic Energy at Semipalatinsk, and the Aktau BN-350 reactor received MPC&A training from DOE specialists over a period of several months in late 1995 and early 1996. This, fortunately, has set the stage for more significant technological improvements to these facilities. DOE technical experts conducted site surveys at both Aktau and Almaty in early 1996 to lay the basis for designing potential MPC&A measures. DOE plans to install a spent fuel gate monitor at Aktau, and the Japanese government is cooperating with DOE in this effort. DOE has also provided MPC&A training and equipment (including a computer system) to personnel at the nuclear fuel fabrication plant overseen by the Ulba State Holding Company. Nuclear material security upgrades are also under discussion with officials at Semipalatinsk.

The Kazakstani government and specialists at Kazakstani nuclear facilities have welcomed MPC&A cooperation with the United States, particularly once this cooperation moved to a series of concrete, practical measures after 1995. Personnel on both sides have developed a solid rapport, and it appears likely that nuclear cooperation will continue to bear fruit. However, as in other areas of Nunn-Lugar cooperation, this program in the future must begin to make greater use of local expertise and locally available materials and supplies. Greater use of local resources may help to alleviate the financial burden facing the CTR Program, particularly in the nuclear field. Compared to Russia, the number of nuclear facilities in Kazakstan is small, but this obscures the enormity of the MPC&A problem facing Kazakstan. The full cost of bringing Kazakstani nuclear facilities up to date in terms of MPC&A should not be underestimated. The effort is likely to require resources that are well beyond those currently obligated under the program.

DEFENSE INDUSTRY CONVERSION

Conversion to civilian and commercial purposes of industrial enterprises devoted to military production under the Soviet system is of paramount importance to Almaty. Millions of dollars of CTR funding have been disbursed under the Defense Enterprise Fund toward defense industry conversion in Kazakstan. A nonprofit joint U.S.-Kazakstani Committee on Conversion has been established and is supported in its work by several entrepreneurial and nongovernmental organizations. Moreover, there has been an abiding interest in such conversion programs on the part of counterpart Kazakstani organizations. Yet, despite all of these positive forces at work and despite months of preliminary work, there are few successful examples of conversion.

The principal Kazakstani agency coordinating defense conversion work, the Committee for the Defense Industry under the Cabinet of Ministers, was created at the end of 1995. The Ministry of Science Academy of Sciences represents the Kazakstani side on the joint conversion committee with the United States. Considerable effort in implementing CTR projects for defense industry conversion has also been made by the International Executive Service Corps.

There have been several opportunities for U.S. officials and industry representatives to familiarize themselves with defense conversion opportunities in Kazakstan. In 1994, for example, a Kazakstani delegation that included representatives from several of Kazakstan's defense organizations visited the United States seeking American partners interested in joint defense conversion projects. In the spring of 1995, another seminar organized by the IESC for managers at Kazakstani defense industrial enterprises took place in Houston. The program was largely limited to the organizational aspects of conversion, that is, the allocation of resources for the establishment of industrial partnerships between Kazakstani and U.S. organizations. Occasions such as these have led Kazakstani officials to surmise that the United States is actively interested in conversion projects and that several such projects might be pending. However, fierce opposition in the U.S. Congress to NIS defense conversion initiatives and budget cuts in these programs have instead raised serious doubts in Kazakstan as to the U.S. government's true intentions in this area.

Besides the erratic support of these efforts in the Congress, several factors can be identified that explain the lack of tangible progress on defense conversion in Kazakstan. First, the economic crisis in Kazakstan has prevented quick resolution of problems in the country's transportation, communication, and financial infrastructure, which is crucial to creating a stable environment for foreign investment and economic activity. Second, very little information has been provided to U.S. businesses and entrepreneurs about the possibilities of capital investment in Kazakstan's economy. Nor is sufficient attention devoted to defense conversion issues in the Kazakstani media. Management of CTR defense conversion activities by the U.S. Department of Defense has also hampered progress. For example, DOD has engaged in the unfortunate practice of shifting from direct contracts signed with the Defense Special Weapons Agency to investments through the Defense Enterprise Fund (DEF), a private nonprofit corporation that underwrites U.S.-CIS joint business ventures. This has had critical impact in FY 1996, when the U.S. Congress chose to stop funding the DEF.

The decline in the volume of state-sponsored defense production has become a powerful stimulus for Kazakstani industrial enterprises to implement conversion plans. There are more than 130 organizations in Kazakstan that were previously involved in defense programs of the Soviet Union and are now united under the aegis of the Committee on the Defense Industry. These organizations are structured as shareholder societies, government holding companies, and government shareholder companies, and they have at their disposal state-of-the-art equipment, technologies, and intellectual potential.

In order to revitalize Kazakstan's defense conversion effort, U.S. and Kazakstani planners need to differentiate among the various types of industrial enterprises that exist in Kazakstan from the Soviet era and to more carefully identify those that are the most promising candidates for conversion. This is especially true given the current mood regarding NIS defense conversion in the United States. Conversion programs must make better use of ever scarcer resources, and they must be able to demonstrate some key "successes" if momentum is to be built behind this effort.

There are several candidates for conversion in Kazakstan's defense industrial complex. Facilities that produced conventional arms are the most stable and most mobile assets with the best chance of survival, and they are already in an active phase of conversion. One of the conversion projects involves a $5 million contract with AT&T to jointly develop communication lines. After an initial period of delays, experts believe the project is now being carried out effectively. Probably the most successful project underway is the conversion of the former Gidromash plant in Almaty. As a result of the project, the joint venture Byelkamit has been created. The facility will produce high tech cryogenic tanks for export. There are also a number of candidate firms that were formerly associated with the production of strategic weapons. These tend to be more unwieldy organizations, although the majority of investments will be directed to them. The future of these facilities will depend greatly on how well the CTR Program is implemented.

A third category of defense industrial enterprises include high-technology nuclear facilities. Their survival as scientific and economic complexes will in large measure depend on cooperation with Russia. Defense conversion work at the Kazakstan nuclear test site at Semipalatinsk, for example, is being implemented within the guidelines of the CTR Program, and is coordinated by the Kazakstani Ministry of Science Academy of Sciences. A U.S.-Kazakstani joint enterprise, Semtek, was also created at the Institute of Atomic Energy in Kurchatov for the further conversion and use of the experimental complex there.

The fourth category of potential conversion activity concerns Kazakstan's "uranium empire," the diminishing but still significant network of mining and processing industries. Out of an original 12 Kazakstani ore mining companies, only five remain. This last category does not lend itself easily to structural and technological reform and conversion. The future of other, related industries and facilities in Kazakstan, such as the reactor fuel fabrication facility at Ulba, will in many ways depend upon the fate of the uranium industry as a whole. This industry could become a source of new financial opportunities for Kazakstan, but it could also become a source of concern in the area of nonproliferation.

Problems of Financing

The fundamental question in CTR implementation is financial. Neither the public at large nor specialists in the field have a clear understanding of the finances required for disarmament, conversion, and nuclear security in Kazakstan or the role of the resources allocated from the CTR Program. This is further complicated by the fact that there are often conflicting reports on the U.S. and Kazakstani sides of the levels of funding being allocated. Contributing to this uncertainty is the ever-changing policy of the United States, a consequence of the volatile situation in Congress. Moreover, even when they are accurate, financial figures do not by themselves give a clear indication of the processes involved in CTR implementation. For example, CTR resources initially promised to Kazakstan and allocated for disarmament activities were estimated at between $70 and $150 million. However, in 1994, Russian experts testified that a sum of $99.96 million would be required for denuclearization activities alone in Kazakstan, including $5 million for management and control of nuclear materials.

In addition to direct assistance from the United States, Kazakstan will likely continue to receive help through other channels. A number of foreign governments and international organizations contribute to projects on conversion, disarmament, nuclear security, export controls, and addressing the "brain drain" of Kazakstani scientific expertise. The International Science and Technology Center (ISTC) has allocated $11 million to support Kazakstani nuclear scientists and technicians formerly employed in Soviet weapons programs. Russia provides considerable direct assistance to demilitarization and nuclear security efforts. Ties with Russia in the nuclear field are understandably strong, and cooperation in this area will likely continue into the future. The International Atomic Energy Agency has obligated $800,000 to the development of export controls. Japan has made direct contributions to material protection, control and accounting projects and to the dismantlement of certain strategic military capabilities in Kazakstan. Discussions are also under way with foreign governments and industry on joint enterprises directed at converting Kazakstani defense industries.

Despite this promising potential, however, the linchpin of Kazakstan's demilitarization plans, in both the near and long term, is successful implementation of the CTR Program. In light of this fact, doubts have arisen over how quickly and successfully and to what degree CTR projects in Kazakstan can fulfill their purpose. Past implementation problems and funding uncertainties have raised serious concerns in Almaty. Given the promising preliminary work that has been accomplished in areas of critical interest to Kazakstan, the voting record of the U.S. Congress and its suggestions of curtailing or eliminating the CTR Program have heightened Kazakstani concerns for the future.

Case Studies of CTR Projects

Chapter 11

Minatom and Nuclear Threat Reduction Activities

Oleg Bukharin

The Russian Ministry of Atomic Energy (Minatom) is a gigantic organization whose research institutes and production facilities design, manufacture, and provide life-cycle support to nuclear warheads. Minatom also operates an array of nuclear fuel-cycle facilities and research centers that support the warhead production complex, as well as naval propulsion and civilian nuclear power programs. These functions and capabilities make Minatom the key Russian agency in achieving the several interrelated nonproliferation objectives: safe and secure dismantlement of nuclear warheads; prevention of proliferation of nuclear weapons design expertise, and stabilization of the nuclear weapons infrastructure; and security of weapons-usable nuclear materials. Several U.S.-Russian cooperative threat reduction (CTR) initiatives are designed to achieve these objectives and involve Minatom as a central actor.

Safe and secure dismantlement of nuclear warheads has been facilitated by agreements on the design and construction of a fissile material storage facility at the Chelyabinsk-65 site, provision of containers for fissile materials from weapons, and safe and secure transportation of nuclear warheads (which includes agreements on emergency response equipment, railcar security, and armored blankets). Only the projects on safe and secure transportation of nuclear warheads have been relatively trouble-free. The fissile material container agreement, although called successful by Minatom's Minister Viktor Mikhailov[1] was delayed until 1996. The storage facility project also has a troubled history of delays and the actual construction did not begin until 1995–96.

---

1. Interview with Viktor Mikhailov, *Yadernyi Kontrol*, February 1995, p. 11.

Approaches to stabilizing vital weapons institutes and preventing proliferation of weapons design expertise from Russia include activities of the International Science and Technology Center (ISTC) and the Industrial Partnering Program (IPP). The programs have provided support to Russian scientists and facilitated their conversion to peaceful work. These initiatives, however, are just beginning to address the problem of converting Minatom's production facilities.

The issue of nuclear safeguards has been actively discussed by the United States and Minatom since the spring of 1992. However, aside from safeguards-related cooperation between nuclear laboratories, few practical results were achieved before 1995. By the end of 1994, a comprehensive strategy to deal with fissile materials emerged within the U.S. government. In addition to improvements in the security of fissile materials, the principal goals of the strategy included: transparency of fissile material operations, prevention of accumulation of fissile materials, and safe and secure disposition of fissile materials from weapons. In 1994, the United States and Russia agreed to cease production of weapons-grade plutonium, shut down plutonium-producing reactors, exchange data regarding national inventories of fissile materials and nuclear weapons, develop procedures to verify inventories of highly enriched uranium (HEU) and plutonium removed from warheads, and develop commercial arrangements for the U.S.-Russian HEU sales agreement. With the exception of the HEU agreement, implementation of these important initiatives, however, has been delayed or halted.

Inside Minatom

There is a high degree of centralization and compartmentalization in Minatom with respect to CTR activities. Minatom Minister Mikhailov participates in political meetings with top-level U.S. officials and is personally involved in the negotiations with the United States on many important issues. His direct access to Russian Prime Minister Viktor Chernomyrdin provides for strong representation of Minatom's interests, both at home and at high-level political meetings with U.S. leaders, such as presidential summits and sessions of the Gore-Chernomyrdin Commission. Minatom Deputy Minister Nikolai Yegorov has been identified as a counterpart to James Goodby, the principal negotiator of many CTR agreements in the United States. At the level of senior joint implementation groups (SJIGs), negotiations are carried out by senior experts from Minatom's central offices and heads of its main directorates and committees (e.g., Vladislav Balamutov, Evgenii Mikerin, et al.). Presumably officials at this level and higher participate in shaping Minatom's policy on cooperation with the United States. Technical group discussions (the level below the SJIGs) involve technical experts and managers from Minatom's relevant directorates and production and research facilities.

Several of Minatom's administrative units are directly involved in the day-to-day work on CTR projects. The Committee for International Relations, under Mikhail Ryzhov, provides support to negotiations and coordination, and is also responsible for working with other agencies of the Russian government. The Legal Department of Minatom reviews all pertinent papers to assure that cooperative activities and agreements are consistent with domestic and international laws, and to prevent unauthorized transfer of know-how and intellectual property.

Cooperative activities are screened by Minatom's 2nd Main Directorate, the Directorate for Physical Protection of Nuclear Materials and Facilities, under Vladimir Bogdanov. Formerly a Minatom-assigned KGB unit, the 2nd Main Directorate is responsible for the protection of classified information and can veto any cooperative activity that could potentially compromise secrecy and security. The directorate interfaces with the Federal Service of Counterintelligence and other Russian security agencies.

A number of individual research centers and production facilities participate in the lab-to-lab and government-to-government safeguards activities. This participation is cleared by the supervising directorate, the Legal Department, the 2nd Main Directorate, and the Committee for International Relations. Until recently, cooperative safeguards activities and domestic programs were coordinated by the Committee for Emergency Situations under Victor Gubanov.[2] In June 1995, the overall responsibility for the federal nuclear safeguards program was transferred to the 2nd Main Directorate; the Committee for International Relations was designated a coordinator of international safeguards activities.

Many major CTR agreements are implemented with the participation of Minatom's 4th and 5th Main Directorates. The 5th Main Directorate, the Main Directorate for Nuclear Weapons Research and

---

2. Gubanov reports directly to Deputy Minister Yegorov.

Development, headed by Georgy Tsyrkov, and its weapons design laboratories have an important role in the CTR projects on safe and secure transportation of nuclear warheads and design of a fissile material storage facility, as well as in the lab-to-lab activities on scientific cooperation, conversion, and nuclear safeguards. The directorate works closely with the Ministry of Defense's 12th Main Directorate (the Main Directorate for Nuclear Weapons, directed by General Evgenii Maslin), and 6th Main Directorate (the Main Directorate for Warhead Production, headed by Evgenii Dudochkin). The Ministry of Defense's 12th Main Directorate is responsible for negotiating most of the warheads-related agreements.[3]

Minatom's 4th Main Directorate for the Fuel Cycle, directed by Evgenii Mikerin, and its principal facilities (Chelyabinsk-65, Tomsk-7, Krasnoyarsk-26, Yekaterinburg-44, Krasnoyarsk-45) are directly involved in agreements on shutting down plutonium production reactors, verifying plutonium stockpiles, constructing a fissile materials storage facility, and selling HEU to the United States.[4] The directorate is responsible for all projects involving production facilities of the uranium enrichment and plutonium production complex (e.g., the ISTC's Project 40 on safeguards at the Tomsk-7 reprocessing plant and the material protection, control, and accounting [MPC&A] project at the civilian plutonium storage facility at Chelyabinsk-65). In some cases, however, the production facilities report directly to Minatom's leadership.

The CTR track records of the 4th and 5th Main Directorates have differed widely. The agreements and programs of the 5th Main Directorate (e.g., safe and secure railcars, armored blankets, emergency response, and lab-to-lab projects) have been relatively trouble-free and successful. This contrasts with the difficulties that have besieged the 4th Main Directorate's principal projects, such as construction of a fissile material storage facility, plutonium production shutdown, transparency, and HEU sales.

In part, the difference is due to the different nature of the directorates themselves. The 5th Main Directorate is composed of research institutes which are less dependent on Minatom's administrative and

---

3. Some agreements were negotiated by Deputy Minister Yegorov.

4. The design of the fissile material storage facility was developed by the St. Petersburg-based Institute of Energy Technologies (VNIPIET).

production structures, and which have diverse technical and intellectual capabilities. The projects stabilize the directorate and its institutes, help carry out their strategic mission (safety and security of the nuclear arsenal and warhead dismantlement), and expand work to new areas (e.g., safeguards and commercial activities). Moreover, the institutes of the 5th Main Directorate, as part of the infrastructure providing direct support to nuclear weapons (for transportation, arsenal maintenance, and dismantlement), are believed to be better organized and in better shape financially than the rest of the nuclear complex. This facilitates prompt and complete implementation of CTR agreements. By contrast, the 4th Main Directorate and its giant production facilities are under much greater economic stress and are highly dependent on Minatom's political leadership and industrial infrastructure. Managers of the production facilities are less interested in CTR projects because they interfere with day-to-day operations and do not bring tangible benefits.

The difference in performance between the two directorates also stems from the different nature of the CTR projects under their purview and approaches to their implementation. The projects of the 5th Main Directorate are relatively small and involve simple transfers of equipment and expertise or cooperative technical work. Most interactions take place between technical experts who have a strong professional affinity for each other. The lab-to-lab program is in an even better situation because it minimizes the political and bureaucratic problems inherent in government-to-government negotiations.

The projects of the 4th Main Directorate, such as U.S.-Russian HEU sales and plutonium reactor shutdown agreements, are very large and have a considerable impact on production facility operations and on the social and economic situation in associated closed cities. These CTR projects are often connected to issues of nuclear commerce and thus are extremely sensitive for the directorate and its major facilities. These connections also touch upon the interests of many powerful groups, in both Russia (e.g., local authorities, the Ministry of Finance, the Ministry of Economics, production facilities) and the United States (e.g., uranium producers, utility companies, USEC),[5] making negotiations inherently complex and difficult.

---

5. The U.S. Enrichment Corporation (USEC) is a quasi-governmental corporation which is to be privatized. USEC is a major producer of commercial uranium enrichment services.

Cooperative Projects With Minatom

U.S. cooperation with Minatom has evolved in the following three inter-related areas: (1) safe and secure dismantlement of nuclear warheads; (2) prevention of proliferation of weapons design expertise; and (3) nuclear safeguards and fissile material management. Cooperative projects in each of these areas are briefly reviewed below.

DISMANTLEMENT OF NUCLEAR WARHEADS
The process of warhead dismantlement in Russia retraces the steps involved in their production. The Ministry of Defense's 12th Main Directorate delivers nuclear warheads for disassembly to the dismantlement plants of Minatom's 6th Main Directorate. The individual nuclear components of the dismantled warheads are packaged into containers and, after a period of storage at the dismantlement plants, are shipped for storage. Plutonium and HEU components are sent to Chelyabinsk-65 and Tomsk-7; tritium is sent for storage and recycling to Chelyabinsk-65; and thermonuclear fuel (lithium-6 deuteride) is sent to Novosibirsk.[6]

The large-scale dismantlement of Soviet nuclear weapons began in the late 1980s and has continued at a rate of 1,500-2,000 warheads per year. The high rate of dismantlement has caused a shortage of storage capacity for warhead components. High volumes of nuclear warheads and fissile materials being shipped and inadequate safety in the railway system have increased the risk of an accident involving nuclear warheads or materials. Under these circumstances, Minatom's leadership has identified the following priorities for cooperation with the United States: (1) design and construction of a fissile materials storage facility; (2) production of fissile material containers; and (3) safety and security of warheads and materials in transit.

WEAPONS MATERIAL STORAGE FACILITY. According to Minatom, the lack of a secure storage facility for fissile materials from weapons is the principal bottleneck in the dismantlement operation. The existing facilities often do not meet modern requirements of safety and security

---

6. Because of the chemical instability of plutonium components and the possibility of plutonium contamination, Minatom stores plutonium components only at those sites with plutonium processing capabilities. These are Tomsk-7 and Chelyabinsk-65.

and are close to capacity. A request for assistance to construct a modern facility was made in the fall of 1991 and the agreement on the storage facility project was signed in September 1993.

The history of the project has been convoluted and troubled.[7] Minatom's original plan to build a 110,000-container facility in Tomsk-7 failed due to local opposition.[8] A new plan envisaged construction of two facilities at Chelyabinsk-65 and Tomsk-7. In the spring of 1995, Minatom decided to drop Tomsk-7. Changes in planning, construction schedules, and design have brought confusion and caused massive delays in the implementation of the project. Another serious problem emerged when Minatom requested funding for the actual construction of the facility. Minatom successfully persuaded the United States to dedicate some funds to construction of the facility, and the construction of facility walls and floors began in 1995–96.

FISSILE MATERIAL CONTAINERS. The agreement to provide 50,000 containers for fissile materials from nuclear weapons is a tangible contribution to the security of nuclear materials in Russia and the continuation of its warhead dismantlement. According to Minatom's Minister Viktor Mikhailov, Russia will need more than 100,000 containers to accommodate fissile materials recovered from weapons. Domestic production is not sufficient to meet these requirements. However, implementation of this agreement was delayed due to manufacturing problems experienced by DNA's contractor for the project, Scientific Ecology Inc. of Oak Ridge, Tennessee. Deliveries of

---

7. Agreements on design and construction of a storage facility were signed by Minatom and the U.S. Department of Defense (DOD) on September 2, 1993. Minatom has agreed to make the storage arrangements transparent so that the United States can verify the adequacy of safeguards at the facility. The parties agreed on the General Safety Criteria for the Russian Fissile Material Storage Facility, and VNIPIET, Minatom's design institute in St. Petersburg, completed design work in the spring of 1994. The U.S. Defense Nuclear Agency (DNA) began procuring construction equipment for Chelyabinsk-65 in the summer of 1994. Construction operations broke ground at Chelyabinsk-65 in July 1994, and the first phase of the facility (with a capacity of 25,000 containers) is planned for operation in 1999.

8. Local resistance to the storage facility was reinforced by the April 1994 explosion at the radiochemical plant at Tomsk-7.

containers began in 1996 and continue at a rate of 1,000 containers per month.

EMERGENCY RESPONSE EQUIPMENT AND TRAINING. Like the U.S. Department of Energy (DOE), Minatom operates technical groups to respond to accidents involving nuclear weapons. This capability was enhanced by the provision of equipment and training under the emergency response agreement. This U.S.-Russian agreement also involved training of weapons experts from Arzamas-16 and other Minatom units at the Los Alamos National Laboratory. Implementation was largely completed by the fall of 1994. The work was useful and helped to build trust between the two nuclear weapons establishments.

PREVENTING PROLIFERATION OF WEAPONS DESIGN EXPERTISE
Technical expertise is a crucial element in a nuclear weapons program. According to classified research conducted in Arzamas-16, expert know-how and assistance can reduce development time in a hypothetical weapons program to less than a year and can significantly improve the design parameters of an explosive device. Such expert assistance would be of great value for a subnational terrorist group.

Minatom has a unique pool of an estimated 2,000–12,000 experts that have expertise in nuclear weapons design and production. In addition, some 3,000–5,000 work on HEU/plutonium production and processing. Most of these people work in research institutes and production facilities of Minatom's 4th, 5th, and 6th Main Directorates. Providing reasonable living standards and job security for weapons experts, and defense conversion of the warhead production complex, are the principal means to prevent proliferation of weapons expertise from Russia. The Russian government has taken steps to stabilize the warhead production complex, but inadequate funding has made these efforts difficult. Two U.S. initiatives designed to prevent diffusion of weapons expertise from Russia are the International Science and Technology Center (ISTC) and the Industrial Partnering Program (IPP).

INTERNATIONAL SCIENCE AND TECHNOLOGY CENTER. The principal objective of the ISTC is to keep Russian weapons experts at home, working on nonmilitary research. The center was established in November 1992 by an agreement among Russia, the United States, Japan, and the European Union and began its work in Moscow in the winter of 1994. The ISTC Governing Board has already approved dozens of projects related to reactor safety, waste management, nuclear safeguards, basic physics, and biotechnology. By mid-1996 the center supported about 12,500 scientists, engineers, and technicians for a period of up to three years. Although the ISTC operates out of Minatom's Institute of Impulse Technologies, it works with many institutes outside of Minatom as well.

INDUSTRIAL PARTNERING PROGRAM. Cooperation between U.S. and Russian nuclear weapons laboratories was initiated in 1992 to "provide useful work and facilitate technical exchange." In June 1994, this cooperative effort evolved into the NIS Industrial Partnering Program, administered by the U.S. Department of Energy. The program's goals include preventing a "brain drain" from the weapons design institutes, stabilizing the technology base at key institutes in the newly independent states (NIS) of the former Soviet Union, and helping to develop cooperative ventures with U.S. industry. IPP projects are designed to have three principal phases. During the first phase, DOE's national laboratories work with their counterparts in Russia (as well as in Ukraine, Kazakstan, and Belarus) to identify and validate marketable technologies. During the second phase, U.S. industry, which is involved in the program through a consortium known as the United States Industry Coalition, participates in these projects through cost-sharing contracts. During the third phase, U.S. industry takes over the projects to make these technologies available to the market. The IPP has been very successful. As of the fall of 1995, more than 2,000 weapons experts from 77 institutes of the former Soviet Union were engaged in non-military work.

SECURING RUSSIA'S FISSILE MATERIALS

Minatom controls most of Russia's fissile materials that reside outside nuclear weapons. Minatom's facilities are protected by an industrial security system which unfortunately is plagued by a number of serious deficiencies. In 1992–93, having recognized this problem, Minatom began to develop a technical program to improve accounting, control, and physical protection of fissile materials in its inventory. However, inadequate funding has stalled progress in this area. Meanwhile, the economic and social crisis in the Russian nuclear industry and in the country at large has further eroded the security of nuclear materials.

The U.S. government began exploring possibilities to assist the Soviet Union in securing fissile materials in the fall of 1991, immediately after Congress enacted the Soviet Threat Reduction Act. Formal talks with Russian authorities began in March 1992, and in September 1993, Minatom and the U.S. Department of Defense signed a formal agreement on material protection, control, and accounting.[9] The initial effort focused on building a model MPC&A system at the low-enrichment fuel fabrication plant at Elektrostal. By the spring of 1994, however, it became obvious that the effectiveness of the Nunn-Lugar MPC&A agreement remained limited. To correct the problem, the U.S. government proposed a number of new safeguards initiatives that have become a part of a more general strategy to control fissile materials.

GOVERNMENT-TO-GOVERNMENT PROGRAM. The program was designed to achieve near-term security of fissile materials at selected high-risk facilities by providing equipment to meet urgent security needs (portal monitors, intrusion detection sensors, video systems, etc.). The program originally focused on a plutonium storage facility in Chelyabinsk-65. As of summer 1996, the parties agreed to extend the program to an additional 11 high-risk research centers and production facilities and to work on security of fissile materials in transit.[10]

LABORATORY-TO-LABORATORY MPC&A PROGRAM. The lab-to-lab MPC&A program was established in June 1994 to complement the government-to-government program. The lab-to-lab program has been very successful. In addition to direct nuclear security upgrades in Arzamas-16, Chelyabinsk-70, Obninsk and other Russian facilities, the lab-to-lab program has helped to expand Minatom's safeguards community by redirecting former nuclear weapon designers towards safeguards-related work. The program also has provided examples of successful

---

9. The scope of the initial MPC&A agreement included work in the following areas: (1) regulatory oversight; (2) a model MPC&A system at the low-enriched uranium fuel fabrication plant at Elektrostal; and (3) definition of requirements for a training center in Obninsk.

10. As of summer 1996, the list of facilities for MPC&A cooperation included the following: HEU fuel fabrication line at Elektrostal, civilian plutonium storage facility in Chelyabinsk-65, Institute of Physics and Power Engineering in Obninsk, Institute of Atomic Reactors in Dimitrovgrad, Production Association "Luch" at Podolsk, Novosibirsk Chemical Concentrates Plant, Beloyarsk nuclear power plant, Sverdlovsk branch of the Institute of Power Technology in Beloyarsk, Khlopin Radium Institute in St. Petersburg, Krasnoyarsk-26, and Yekaterinburg-44.

cooperative projects, and encouraged advocates of international cooperation in both the U.S. and Russia. Since the spring of 1994, the participation in the lab-to-lab program has considerably increased and now includes six U.S. national laboratories and over ten Russian facilities (including Russia's nuclear weapons laboratories and warhead assembly/disassembly plants).

TRANSPARENCY AND IRREVERSIBILITY OF DISARMAMENT. The issue of transparency was addressed in two initiatives. In March 1994, the United States and Russia agreed to develop a mechanism to confirm inventories of HEU and plutonium that have been released from dismantled weapons. In September 1994, the parties decided to discuss the possibility of exchanging data related to aggregate stockpiles of fissile materials and warheads. U.S. and Russian experts have explored potential techniques and the scope of fissile material measurements to verify the presence of a warhead component inside a container. Progress toward a mutual reciprocal experiment and exchange of stockpile information, however, has been stalled by the lack of a cooperation agreement allowing the two countries to exchange restricted data.

PREVENTING ACCUMULATION OF FISSILE MATERIALS. The initiative to prevent accumulation of weapon-usable fissile materials is based on the agreement signed by U.S. Vice President Al Gore and Russian Prime Minister Viktor Chernomyrdin in June 1994. The two parties agreed to shut down the plutonium production reactors that continue to operate at Tomsk-7 and Krasnoyarsk-26 by the year 2000; to identify technically and financially viable options to replace those reactors as regional sources of energy; and to develop a compliance regime to assure that no freshly separated plutonium is used in weapons. Implementation of this agreement was essentially stalled, however. Minatom declared that Russia stopped producing plutonium for weapons in October 1994, and thus had fulfilled its obligations. Minatom explicitly links progress in verifying plutonium stocks and reactors with progress in developing alternative sources of energy. (The reactors produce heat for nearby cities and cannot be shut down without replacement.) Future U.S. assistance will probably be limited to conversion of the reactors to a fuel cycle that does not require reprocessing.

DISPOSITION OF FISSILE MATERIALS FROM WEAPONS. Disposition of plutonium is addressed by a joint U.S.-Russian working group on plutonium disposition options that was formed in January 1995. The progress of the working group has been modest, mainly because of differences of views on the value of plutonium. Minatom treats plutonium as an asset, continues to reprocess spent reactor fuel, and plans to pursue a large-scale plutonium economy. This contradicts U.S. policy, which seeks to minimize the use and accumulation of plutonium.

The disposition of HEU from weapons is addressed in a U.S.-Russian agreement, according to which the United States will purchase at least 500 tons of HEU from Russian nuclear weapons in the form of low-enriched uranium (LEU) for use in nuclear reactors. Although the agreement was signed in February 1992, political problems and technical difficulties delayed initial deliveries of uranium to the United States until the spring of 1995.

Problems Affecting Cooperation

Thus far, the CTR process has had only limited success in reducing the nuclear threat from Russia. The difficulties encountered stem from the political and economic situation in Russia as well as from the way cooperation has been organized. Specific CTR problems are described below.

THE LACK OF HIGH-LEVEL POLITICAL LEADERSHIP
From the very beginning the issue of fissile materials lacked focused and comprehensive political leadership in both the United States and Russia. As a result, the negotiations process was managed on a working level, through an interagency process. This approach has two inherent weaknesses: the slow pace of exchanges between U.S. and Russian counterparts, and confusion due to the lack of communication between technical experts. From the U.S. perspective, this situation was described well by Frank von Hippel, former Deputy Director of the White House's Office of Science and Technology Policy:

In order to assure that the Government is speaking with one voice, most U.S. government communications to other governments are channeled through a few State Department or Embassy officials working from "talking points" prepared by interagency committees. This limits the rate of communication to one significant round every few months. In between both bureaucracies ponder the response of the other side and prepare the next round of proposals and associated talking points. The process is so ponderous that most people involved lose track of the forest for the trees.

Sometimes the State Department was busy and delivered the message so cursorily, or at such a low level, that there was no response. Sometimes the response was "no", but we didn't understand why so we would reiterate the proposal, hoping for a different response, just to be rebuffed again. We went through such an exercise in frustration in connection with the Nunn-Lugar Agreement for Cooperation on fissile-material security. At one point we became convinced that Russia considered virtually all facilities containing weapons-usable materials "military" facilities. Vice President Gore therefore proposed and Prime Minister Chernomyrdin agreed, in their September 1993 meeting, that U.S.-Russian cooperation on fissile-material security would extend to "military" as well as civilian fissile material. This agreement was reiterated in somewhat watered-down form in the January 1994 Clinton-Yeltsin summit statement. Yeltsin's and Chernomyrdin's agreement however, had no effect on Minatom, which absolutely refused, in meeting after meeting, to expand the Nunn-Lugar agreement on cooperation on fissile-material security to cover military materials.

After a year of fruitless dialogue [on fissile material security], we learned by accident that we [the United States and Minatom] had been talking past each other. A negotiator from Minatom came to Washington to discuss this issue among others. Since the State Department's negotiator was out of town, I volunteered to fill the gap. We exchanged the Russian and U.S. proposed language for the amendment and found that we were as far apart as ever. I then invited the Russian official to lunch and tried to explore what was behind the Russian version. Much to my surprise, I learned that Minatom was willing to expand the cooperative effort to cover a broad range of weapons-usable fissile materials. Its objection was to extending this cooperation to materials in classified forms such as weapons components and naval-reactor fuel. I reported this back to the interagency group and it was decided that Minatom's offer, while not everything we wanted, provided plenty of important opportunities to use the resources for a cooperative program.[11]

11. Frank von Hippel, "Working in the White House on Nuclear Nonproliferation and Arms Control: A Personal Report," *FAS Public Interest Report*, Vol. 48, No. 2 (March/April 1995).

The lack of political leadership and fragmentation of policy are even more serious in Russia. There is often a disconnect between Minatom and other governmental agencies and between Minatom and the national political leadership. This is explained in part by Minatom's institutional tradition of secrecy and power. Inadequate coordination also stems from the lack of a formal interagency process. In the past, inputs from individual agencies were assimilated and molded in a coherent policy by the Central Committee of the Communist Party. This mechanism was destroyed in 1991, and nothing has been created since to fill the vacuum. At present, the Foreign Ministry organizes interagency meetings to discuss CTR problems, but this is not enough to develop a sound and consistent national policy.

Nor is everything well within Minatom itself. Arcane bureaucracy, disorganization and turf battles are exemplified by the following: In the spring of 1995, there was intense competition among several of Minatom's units for control of safeguards cooperation. According to Minatom staff, preparing and sending even a trivial piece of correspondence requires authorization from several directorates and departments of the central headquarters and may take weeks. Policymaking is restricted to a narrow circle of Minatom's top managers and is isolated from Minatom's broader technical community.

It is also important to note that the Russian government has very few resources with which to work. For example, only a handful of people work on Minatom-related CTR projects in the Foreign Ministry. There is also a language problem: very few people in the government speak or read English, and a qualified linguistic service is not always available and is expensive for impoverished governmental agencies. Thus, as one Russian diplomat has put it, "a 20-page document in English received two days before the scheduled meeting may represent an insurmountable problem." These human resource and logistical problems limit the capability of Russia to deal with CTR issues effectively and in a timely fashion.

THE ECONOMIC CRISIS IN THE RUSSIAN NUCLEAR INDUSTRY
In 1992–93 the nuclear industry plunged into an acute economic crisis. State orders dropped several-fold. For example, state orders for Tomsk-7, a fissile material processing and warhead components manufacturing facility, dropped by a factor of six compared to 1987. And even for this work the federal government did not pay in full: only 68 percent of production was paid for in 1994. These production difficulties result in

unemployment and social dislocation.[12] Moreover, virtually no funding is allocated to modernize the technical and industrial infrastructure. Minatom's facilities also face the enormous task of decontamination and decommissioning.

This economic crisis within the Russian nuclear industry affects CTR activities in several ways:

AGGRAVATION OF THE FISSILE MATERIALS PROBLEM. The problem has become more acute because of the general deterioration of Minatom's infrastructure (storage facilities, transportation systems, etc.), loss of qualified personnel, and decreased morale and discipline at nuclear facilities. Minatom's infrastructure is also stretched by the influx of fissile materials from dismantled weapons.

LOW PRIORITY FOR COOPERATIVE ACTIVITIES. Minatom managers and facility operators are preoccupied with the economic crisis and associated social and economic problems. CTR goals and activities are viewed as a secondary priority and, often, as an inconvenience. The practice of spending CTR funding on U.S. contractors or to support exchange visits has created a highly cynical attitude toward CTR cooperation.

LIMITATIONS ON THE IMPLEMENTATION BASE IN RUSSIA. The crisis in Russian society has disrupted the network of centralized controls and links between production facilities and research institutes, and resulted in personnel losses and eroded capabilities to resolve even simple technical and logistical problems. Inadequate funding has also slowed Minatom's internal programs, such as the federal safeguards program. In addition, Russian budget allocations are often insufficient to fund the Russian part of CTR projects.[13]

---

12. Up to one-third of the working-age population of Tomsk-7 may be unemployed by the year 2000. Moreover, many facilities operate only a few days per week and thus suffer from hidden unemployment. For example, the Novosibirsk chemical concentrates plant and the Glazov mechanical plant operated only three days per week for most of 1994.

13. This has a direct bearing on CTR negotiations. For example, Minatom has been a strong advocate of less costly and less intrusive techniques to verify that no newly produced plutonium is used for weapons.

LINKAGE BETWEEN CTR PROGRESS AND NUCLEAR TRADE ISSUES. Minatom's leaders have frequently voiced their dissatisfaction with what they describe as U.S. attempts to oust Russia from the world market for nuclear technologies. Specific problems they cite include constraints imposed on imports of uranium products to the United States and Europe, U.S. opposition to the Russian-Iranian reactor deal, and Russia's inability to participate meaningfully in the agreement with North Korea to build new power reactors in that country. Commercial disputes have caused bitter resentment on the part of Russian industry.

SENSITIVITY OF NUCLEAR FACILITIES AND OPERATIONS
The secrecy that surrounds virtually any issue related to nuclear weapons and fissile materials in Russia has been a major obstacle to cooperation. There are elements in the nuclear and security establishments and in the legislative branches of both the United States and Russia that continue to view the other country with suspicion and the U.S.-Russian relationship as adversarial. For example, some in Minatom and in the Russian Duma believe that the true motive of the United States is to gain access to those few secrets that remain.[14]

Russian production facilities have been especially difficult to work with. Even those facilities primarily involved in commercial nuclear fuel-cycle activities have been difficult to gain access to because of the collocation and integration of civilian and military production activities. Some progress has been achieved on the basis of reciprocity (e.g., exchanges of visits to plutonium storage facilities at Hanford and Chelyabinsk-65). This approach, however, has limitations because of the asymmetry of production activities in the United States and Russia, particularly with respect to plutonium production. Moreover, the lack of funds has made it difficult for facility managers and security personnel to arrange visits by foreigners. (Typically, such visits entail expenses such as masking of secret information and equipment, provision of trained escorts, safety and medical arrangements, and others measures.)

Data exchange and cooperative activities have been hampered by Russian laws regarding state secrets. According to Russian law, release of classified information to a foreign state requires a governmental

---

14. Minatom Director Mikhailov, for example, was accused by the former Russian Parliament of selling secrets.

resolution that must be approved by the Parliament.[15] In the fall of 1994, the United States and Russia began negotiations on a cooperative agreement that would authorize exchanges of restricted and classified information. It is expected that the agreement will clear the way for many important initiatives, including stockpile data exchange and confirmation of inventories of fissile materials released from weapons.

Conclusions

U.S.-Russian cooperation to reduce nuclear dangers has already yielded a number of positive results. In some important areas (e.g., nuclear safeguards) joint efforts with the United States have been vital in implementing Russian domestic programs. U.S. planners have learned from the early years of CTR cooperation and are now more understanding of Russia's needs and problems. Use of Russian labor and equipment, reciprocal arrangements in visiting nuclear sites, and other cooperative measures are now more acceptable to the U.S. side.

However, many achievements that were anticipated in the early stages of the CTR process have not materialized. Cumbersome bureaucracies in both countries have made progress painful and slow. It has also become apparent that building trust between two former Cold War enemies requires time and that ups and downs in the U.S.-Russian relationship are inevitable.

Under these circumstances, the U.S. policy in dealing with Minatom should be guided by a few long-term strategic goals. These should include:

COOPERATION BETWEEN U.S. AND RUSSIAN NUCLEAR COMPLEXES. U.S. and Russian nuclear laboratories and research institutes have been developing successful scientific cooperation and joint efforts on safeguards. This cooperation should be extended to include production facilities as well. Direct involvement of Minatom's production facilities in the cooperative activities is critical for achieving practical results in the areas of fissile material management, nuclear safeguards, and

---

15. In order to sign an agreement on the exchange of classified information, the State Technical Committee (a governmental body that reports directly to the president) must submit a special request to the government.

defense conversion. The ISTC, MPC&A, lab-to-lab, and IPP programs should form the basis of such cooperative activities.

CONVERSION AND RECONFIGURATION OF THE RUSSIAN NUCLEAR COMPLEX. The Soviet nuclear complex was designed to support a nuclear arsenal of 45,000 warheads and a nuclear power-generating capacity of 200 GWe. These targets contrast starkly with the projected START II level of 3,500-5000 warheads and the existing nuclear power program of approximately 20 GWe. The Russian nuclear complex is oversized and unsustainable, and this problem will continue to dominate the behavior of Minatom's leadership. The complex needs time, determination, and skills to become a viable organization. It appears, however, that Minatom does not have any consistent policy on restructuring the complex.

Several ongoing cooperative projects have the potential to create long-term non-weapons-related missions for Minatom's facilities and thus have significant conversion value. These include the HEU sales agreement, the power replacement initiative for Tomsk-7 and Krasnoyarsk-26, the agreement on a fissile material storage facility at Chelyabinsk-65, and the plutonium disposition study. The U.S. contribution to the conversion effort could also include educating a new generation of Minatom managers, suggesting viable non-nuclear conversion strategies, and helping to integrate Russia into the world nuclear infrastructure.

TRANSPARENCY OF FISSILE MATERIAL OPERATIONS AND DISMANTLEMENT. Increased bilateral transparency regarding fissile material operations, safeguards, and dismantlement could be a cornerstone of Russia's involvement in international nonproliferation activities, including a global fissile material cutoff regime, limitations on the use and stockpiling of weapon-usable fissile materials, international safeguards, and other efforts.

STRONG REGULATORY AUTHORITY IN RUSSIA. Minatom continues to operate as a largely unaccountable and closed organization. This monopoly is counterproductive for the nuclear complex and for CTR cooperation. The monopoly could be dissolved gradually by strengthening the political clout, competence, and technical capabilities of the Russian regulatory agency, Gosatomnadzor. Support for the Kurchatov Institute, an independent research center, would also be beneficial.

The Russian government also has an important role in speeding up Minatom's CTR projects. Specific areas of improvement include: (1) streamlining the bureaucratic process within Minatom and organizing a comprehensive interagency process; (2) increasing the priority of warhead dismantlement and nonproliferation activities and decoupling these activities from nuclear commerce; and (3) developing and implementing a viable conversion and reconfiguration strategy for the Russian nuclear complex.

Chapter 12

Sustaining Nuclear Threat Reduction Programs

The "Bottom-Up" Approach

Katherine E. Johnson

In recent years, a number of foreign policy disputes have contributed to a widening rift between Moscow and Washington; Russia's handling of the Chechen conflict and NATO's plans for expansion have been two of the most visible irritants in the U.S.-Russian relationship. The U.S. "honeymoon" with Boris Yeltsin's government, so evident in the immediate post–Cold War period, is clearly over. Worsening bilateral relations with Russia have prompted increased congressional scrutiny and criticism of all types of U.S. assistance to Russia,[1] including the

---

1. As of September 1996, the Department of Defense has notified Congress of over $1.4 billion in assistance to Russia, Ukraine, Kazakstan, and Belarus. Over $1 billion of this amount has been obligated. Funds for additional nuclear threat reduction initiatives have come from a number of other appropriations or from individual agency budgets. Some examples include: (1) Freedom Support Act–funded assistance projects for, *inter alia*, Russian officer resettlement and the Industrial Partnering Program (IPP); (2) the Nonproliferation Fund; (3) DOD's military-to-military training program; (4) the Department of Energy (DOE) lab-to-lab programs; (5) the Department of Commerce defense conversion initiatives; and (6) the Arms Control and Disarmament Agency (ACDA) entrepreneurial workshops on defense technology conversion (funded by ACDA's special projects budget and DOE sources). In Fiscal Year (FY) 1996, the nuclear threat reduction budget was "balkanized" even further when several Nunn-Lugar programs were transferred to other agencies. Funding and responsibility for material protection, control, and accounting (MPC&A) was moved to DOE; the International Science and Technology Center (ISTC) is now funded through Department of State general appropriations; and Commerce's FY 1996 budget request included funding for export control

---

This chapter is excerpted from a larger study by the author entitled U.S.-FSU Nuclear Threat Reduction Programs: Effectiveness of Current Efforts and Prospects for Future Cooperation, *published by the Center for International Security Affairs, Los Alamos National Laboratory, August 1995.*

Cooperative Threat Reduction (CTR) Program and other nuclear threat reduction assistance efforts. Russian attitudes toward U.S. assistance have also become increasingly negative.

However, the nonproliferation and national security objectives of threat reduction programs, i.e., securing the nuclear arsenal of the former Soviet Union and preventing the spread of nuclear weapons and related materials, remain valid and should continue to be pursued. How can this best be ensured? One key variable in the survival of threat reduction programs will be the administration's ability to identify those programs that have been most successful in achieving their goals and the reasons for their success, and then to apply these lessons to future assistance efforts. Identifying "what works" in the former Soviet Union (FSU) and structuring future programs accordingly will be essential for managing future congressional criticism; a demonstrably effective threat reduction program is more likely to win congressional support. Lastly, "what works" in Russia and other Soviet successor states is largely a function of attitudes, needs, and desires in these countries. The United States must make a greater effort to factor the perceptions of recipient states into the equation when developing future or implementing current threat reduction programs.

Maintaining Congressional Support

Members of the 104th Congress were less inclined than their predecessors to support Nunn-Lugar and other FSU threat reduction ventures. It is likely that the souring of U.S.-Russian relations would have diminished enthusiasm for aid to the FSU regardless of the political composition of Congress. Nonetheless, the political sea change that occurred with the November 1994 elections has had a profound impact on U.S.-FSU cooperative endeavors. Republican commitment to slash federal spending in all areas, including foreign aid, indicate that FSU assistance programs will, in the coming years, continue to be carefully scrutinized, frequently criticized, and probably scaled back.

In analyzing congressional attitudes toward Russian assistance programs, it is helpful to distinguish between the several "camps" of

---

activities in the former Soviet Union (FSU). For the most comprehensive listing of all U.S. assistance programs to the FSU, see the Department of State's report, *Government Assistance to and Cooperative Activities with the Newly Independent States of the Former Soviet Union*, released April 1996.

congressional critics of Nunn-Lugar and similar programs. At one end of the spectrum are those who believe, to varying degrees, that it is a geostrategic mistake to assist Russia financially. Russia, it is claimed, is incapable of breaking with its antidemocratic, imperialistic past, and Western assistance to Moscow only frees up resources for the Russian military, the Federal Security Service, and other forces of repression, both internal and external. This camp of "intractables" includes those who believe that most, if not all, foreign aid should be cut in the post–Cold War world.[2]

While the administration and congressional supporters of continued assistance to the FSU have urged that aid be "delinked" from issues such as the war in Chechnya, nuclear sales to Iran, and other irritants in the U.S.-Russian relationship, a second group of assistance critics increasingly view aid to Russia as a vehicle for modifying Russian behavior. Supporters of continued assistance believe that a "pragmatic relationship," "cooperat[ing] when we can and deal[ing] with differences as they arise without letting any one problem damage the relationship,"[3] is the best way to keep Russia and other FSU states on the road to reform. Opponents of this approach, however, believe that the West should in no way give the impression that it is acquiescing to Russian "misbehavior." They fear that continued assistance will only encourage the continuation of unacceptable policies and behavior by Moscow, and they believe that aid should be used as leverage. For this group, diminished support for threat reduction programs in the Republican-controlled Congress is less a function of a lack of support for the goals of Nunn-Lugar and other programs *per se* than a reflection of differing views of the best means to achieve those goals. The larger objectives of these programs—safe and secure dismantlement of former Soviet nuclear weapons, proliferation prevention, and continued reductions in the former Soviet defense and nuclear complexes—are not questioned.

---

2. Senate Foreign Relations Committee Chairman Jesse Helms may be the most prominent proponent of this view. See, for example, his remarks in a report of the Senate Budget Committee accompanying Senate Congressional Resolution 13 (No. 104-82), wherein he asserts that he has "never supported foreign aid spending and believe[s] we must make sharp cuts in this area over the next several years as part of the overall effort to achieve a balanced budget."

3. Lee H. Hamilton,"U.S. Aid to Russia Serves Our Interests," *The Christian Science Monitor*, April 24, 1995, p. 19.

A third group questions the efficacy of discrete elements of the larger threat reduction program and/or the implementation of the program itself. For example, these critics note the slowness of program implementation and the failure to quickly transfer funds to the FSU, the failure to develop a long-term planning process, and funding requests based both on future needs and the effectiveness of current programs. They have expressed concern that money is being spent on "nonpriority" programs that do not directly pertain to weapons dismantlement or safety.

These criticisms are, to varying extents, legitimate. There are, however, valid reasons why the objectives of the Nunn-Lugar Program and others often have not been fully met or only belatedly met. Moreover, in several cases, there are signs that early obstacles are being overcome. The administration has emphasized the difficulties it encountered in concluding initial agreements with recipient countries in the early years of the Nunn-Lugar Program and has noted that, with the exception of a few amendments to existing agreements, all negotiations with recipient states have been concluded and the U.S. government can now focus on program implementation. Other factors that have slowed program implementation in the past, such as cumbersome restrictions preventing Nunn-Lugar dollars from being spent on local contractors in recipient states, have now been loosened. Furthermore, a greater effort at long-term planning and oversight is being made. For example, in May 1994, DOD established a CTR Program Office and tasked it with developing multiyear program plans and expediting the audit and examination (A&E) process of various Nunn-Lugar Programs. The first multiyear plan was finalized in mid-1995 and provides an objectives-oriented plan for providing assistance through FY 2001. Lastly, the administration notes that, although they may be "nonpriority," programs to provide housing for former Soviet Strategic Rocket Forces officers and to convert FSU defense production facilities to civilian uses are indirectly but crucially linked to the "priority" objective of weapons elimination. By law, Strategic Rocket Forces officers in Belarus, Ukraine, and Kazakstan cannot be demobilized until housing is provided for them, a stipulation that would delay weapons dismantlement and base closings.

Despite these improvements, scrutiny of the Nunn-Lugar Program continues. While candid assessments of the program's shortcomings and the obstacles it has encountered may be adequate to convince many congressional critics, a larger strategy of improved program coordination and "congressional diplomacy" may be required if threat reduction efforts are to survive the foreign aid budgetary ax.

There are currently 19 federal agencies charged with administering assistance to the FSU; at least five agencies (the Departments of Defense, Energy, State, and Commerce, and the Arms Control and Disarmament Agency) oversee implementation of threat reduction programs. The Clinton administration has made several efforts to establish oversight over individual agency programs, such as by appointing a State Department coordinator for assistance to the newly independent states of the FSU and by forming an interagency working group to coordinate all former CTR Programs. Nonetheless, a February 1995 U.S. General Accounting Office (GAO) report stated that, to date, the coordinator had focused on technical assistance alone and had not developed "a clearly articulated strategy for achieving the overarching goals [necessary] for helping the countries of the FSU achieve their reform objectives.[4]

While DOD's CTR Program office has in large part addressed this criticism by developing its objectives-oriented program plan, all five agencies involved in threat reduction efforts should work together to establish new milestones for success in order to assist Congress in judging progress and to justify continued funding; congressional attitudes are likely to turn heavily on the administration's ability to demonstrate results. Moreover, any milestones developed should be realistic if they are to avoid raising false expectations of success. One example that meets these criteria is the DOD CTR plan to complete the denuclearization of Ukraine, Belarus, and Kazakstan by the end of 1996.[5] Similar milestones and goal-oriented program plans should be developed in other areas. For example, substantial progress toward

---

4. U.S. General Accounting Office, "Former Soviet Union: U.S. Bilateral Program Lacks Effective Coordination," GAO/NSIAD-95-10 (February 1995), p. 3.

5. EDITORS' NOTE: This goal was realized in November 1996, when the last nuclear warhead was removed from Belarus.

accounting of fissile material—a goal whose prospects are increasing[6]—is an objective likely to win favorable congressional sanction.

In addition to clearly articulated goals and program plans to achieve them, the basic logic of threat reduction efforts should continue to be stressed to key members of Congress.[7] According to one congressional expert:

the many committees and individual members need to be reminded periodically of why a bipartisan consensus in Congress has consistently supported the Nunn-Lugar Program. The reasons for aiding Russia ... are not always self-evident, especially against the backdrop of Russian behavior. What would be different if the programs ended? To paraphrase Senator Nunn: Given what we have spent over the past decade to counter the threat posed by Soviet nuclear weapons, how much is it worth to destroy thousands of missiles and take apart the warheads.[8]

The clearer a program's link to vital U.S. national security interests, the more likely it is to win congressional support. The nonproliferation goals of the Nunn-Lugar Program—preventing the nuclear assets of the FSU from falling into hostile national or subnational hands—should be continually stressed, and successes, such as Project Sapphire, should be underscored. As the link to vital national interests becomes weaker or less immediate, congressional support is likely to wane. It is important

---

6. A June 1995 GAO report asserts that, "while [MPC&A] projects have had little direct impact in improving material protection, control and accounting over weapons-usable civilian material at FSU nuclear facilities, the prognosis for doing so is improving as a result of recent agreements with Russia to upgrade controls at some facilities." See U.S. General Accounting Office, *Weapons of Mass Destruction: Reducing the Threat from the Former Soviet Union: An Update*, GAO/NSIAD-95-165 (June 1995), p. 20.

7. There are numerous congressional committees with purview over threat reduction programs. In addition to the House International Relations and Senate Foreign Relations Committees, several other committees control the purse strings of threat reduction programs. The House National Security and Senate Armed Services Committees control the Nunn-Lugar budget and the Senate Energy and Natural Resources and the House Science Committees control the DOE budget, through which the MPC&A program will now be funded.

8. Zachary S. Davis, excerpt from a study prepared for Los Alamos National Laboratory, "Congressional Perspectives on CTR Programs: Can Support Be Sustained?" (April 1995).

that Nunn-Lugar and similar programs are viewed as distinct from other aid efforts. Threat reduction efforts have a near-term impact on U.S. security interests; efforts aimed at promoting democracy are focused on ensuring long-term good relations between the FSU and the West.

Although many NATO and G7 nations are already providing threat reduction assistance to former Soviet states, increased funding from Japan and others would be of great importance. "Burden-sharing" has always been a popular notion on Capitol Hill. Similarly, further developing U.S. industry involvement in threat reduction programs will reduce the financial burden on the U.S. taxpayer. The Industrial Partnering Program (IPP) and, to a lesser extent, the International Science and Technology Center (ISTC) both rely on involvement by and financial resources from U.S. industry. Greater involvement of industry in promoting other denuclearization and nonproliferation efforts in the FSU should be encouraged.

One member of Congress has suggested that the Clinton administration prioritize its foreign aid commitments. Is assistance to Russia relatively more or less important than aid to, for example, Egypt and Israel? With foreign aid to all countries being cut, it has been suggested that the administration clearly articulate where it can and cannot stomach large reductions in its budget requests.[9] Articulating which threat reduction programs are of greater and lesser priority has also been suggested as a way to ensure that the administration, rather than Congress, decides where cuts will be taken.

Lastly, it is important to convince those members of Congress who espouse the "linkage" theory that threats to cut off assistance are unlikely to make the Russians more amenable to the American way of thinking. The cooperative approach, for all its faults, has fostered a great deal of trust and goodwill between the two sides; a strategy of retaliation or punishment is unlikely to have the same result.

---

9. Sonny Callahan, House Appropriations Foreign Operations Subcommittee Chairman, remarks at a March 9, 1995, subcommittee hearing, as reported in *Post-Soviet Nuclear and Defense Monitor*, March 14, 1995, p. 3.

Maintaining the Support of Russia and Other Former Soviet States

The success or failure of nuclear threat reduction efforts in the FSU will depend largely on the behavior and attitudes of Russia and other successor states—for example, their commitment and ability to sustain reform and their willingness to support U.S. nonproliferation and disarmament objectives. However, there is much that the U.S. government can do to alleviate the suspicions and tensions that have developed in the course of implementing threat reduction programs. Despite the growing catalogue of larger foreign policy disputes, there remains a striking compatibility of interests in threat reduction ventures, especially if U.S. programs can be restructured in a way that takes into account Russian perceptions, sensitivities, and needs.

First, the United States must recognize that Russia's great power status, however reduced, and its resulting pride dictate the need for special care. Russia must perceive all programs as being in the interest of both parties. Any suspicion that the United States is imposing its will upon the recipient state, engendering unilateral Russian disarmament, or taking advantage of temporary weakness and/or chaos to conduct military or economic espionage could doom an individual program to failure. The emphasis on the cooperative nature of threat reduction efforts should be stressed in all phases of program planning and implementation.

Second, the United States should only make promises it can keep; it should propose only those programs for which it is reasonably confident that funding, interest, and commitment can be sustained. This will, of course, be increasingly difficult for the Clinton administration, given the uncertain budgetary climate in the Congress. However, with proper planning and congressional consultation, the administration should be able to develop a reasonable sense of which programs are politically unpopular and therefore at risk for future cuts. As in its relations with Congress, the administration should also avoid raising expectations in the FSU too high. Providing recipient states with realistic assessments of the number of jobs involved and the amount of money to be transferred could help prevent the dashed hopes and resulting disillusionment that occurred in the early years of Nunn-Lugar and other programs.

Third, although efforts have been made both to increase the pace of aid delivery and decrease the number of conditions, or "strings," attached to aid disbursement (e.g., by streamlining contracting procedures and eliminating, where possible, prohibitions against procuring equipment from FSU sources), greater effort should be made to utilize the resources of recipient states. Not only will this provide employment opportunities in FSU states, it will also help foster the notion that these programs are truly joint ones.

The aforementioned points are not in any way meant to suggest that Russia and other Soviet successor states are simply "misunderstood" or that U.S. insensitivity is solely to blame for problems in implementing these threat reduction programs. Recent Russian behavior raises some serious questions about that country's long-term intentions in the fields of nonproliferation and disarmament. A number of irritants in the U.S.-Russian relationship mentioned previously—nuclear sales to Iran, the war in Chechnya, and the possibility that START II will not be ratified—are coupled with U.S. allegations that Russia is now (or may soon be) in violation of a number of arms control accords. A June 1995 GAO report states that "despite several recent promising developments, it seems unlikely that Russia will be able to destroy its total chemical weapons stockpile in accordance with time frames stated in the Chemical Weapons Convention."[10] More ominously, a recent ACDA report concluded that "some Russian facilities may be maintaining the capability to produce biological warfare agents" in possible violation of the Biological Weapons Convention.[11] Because continued Nunn-Lugar funding is contingent upon presidential certification that recipient states are complying with "all relevant arms controls agreements," the U.S. side must work quickly to resolve these disputes, keeping in mind Russian security considerations, logistical problems, and institutional competition.

In sum, threat reduction programs of the future must be based on clear national security interests that both the Russians and the Congress can understand. There are many areas in which Russian and American interests are compatible and in which cooperation is working and can continue to work. The challenge for U.S. policy will be to identify those areas and to implement resulting programs in a way that garners the support of a significant majority of the players in the Russian aid game.

---

10. U. S. GAO, *Weapons of Mass Destruction*, p. 16.

11. Reuters, "U.S. Renews Concerns about Germ Warfare Programs," July 19, 1995.

The Lab-to-Lab and "Bottom-Up" Approach

The DOE's lab-to-lab program has often been cited as an example of a relatively cost-effective and successful threat reduction effort. The remainder of this chapter will attempt to explore why this has been the case and how the "bottom-up" approach inherent in the lab-to-lab program might be applied to other, less technical areas of cooperation.

HISTORY AND CURRENT STATUS

Direct contact between scientists from U.S. weapons laboratories and their Soviet counterparts began in the waning days of the Cold War. During negotiations on the verification protocols to the Threshold Test Ban Treaty, scientists from both the Soviet and U.S. sides were brought together to provide their respective delegations with technical advice. As a result of these and other interactions throughout the mid to late 1980s (such as joint experiments in space and astrophysics), U.S. and Soviet weapons scientists came into frequent contact and, based on their parallel technical expertise and shared scientific interest, began to build extensive personal and institutional relationships.

As the Cold War drew to a close, many in the U.S. national laboratory and government policy communities came to realize that these contacts could be used to support the larger foreign policy goal of stabilizing FSU weapons institutes in order to prevent a "brain drain" of weapons scientists,[12] as well as to further common nonproliferation and disarmament objectives.

After much internal U.S. government debate and planning (and a year-long delay in National Security Council authorization, owing primarily to preoccupation with the Gulf War), invitations were issued to the directors of Arzamas-16 and Chelyabinsk-70 to visit Los Alamos National Laboratory and Lawrence Livermore National Laboratory in early February 1992. Reciprocal visits by U.S. laboratory directors occurred later that month. Discussions which occurred during these and later visits established the basis for future scientific collaborations; in May 1992, agreement was reached to pursue collaboration on a number of topics, including basic science, environmental and computer

---

12. The situation of scientists at many Russian institutes by the early 1990s was grim: salaries were not being paid, and the resulting economic hardships endured by many institute employees raised concerns that scientists would be tempted to emigrate and seek lucrative weapons development work in other countries.

science, advanced materials, and nonproliferation. It was agreed that expert exchanges would take place in the ensuing months to identify specific projects that could be undertaken in these subject areas.

Also in May 1992, DOE and the State Department agreed upon a set of principles for lab-to-lab cooperation. Work would proceed in the categories agreed upon with the Russians, but any work pertaining to weapons would be prohibited. All interactions would be coordinated through the State Department, and the lab-to-lab program would work closely with federal agencies to help ensure the success of the newly formed International Science and Technology Center. These principles were intended to ensure that the lab-to-lab effort would be consistent with and supportive of larger U.S. government endeavors.

By 1994, the first "umbrella contract" between Los Alamos and Arzamas-16 had been signed. Similar agreements were subsequently concluded between Lawrence Livermore and Chelyabinsk-70 and between Sandia National Laboratories and both Russian weapons labs. These flexible agreements laid out the administrative, financial, and legal arrangements necessary to expedite the implementation of subsequent, programmatically oriented contracts.

The first lab-to-lab programs were in the area of "scientific conversion" and included technical meetings, symposia, joint experimental work, and commissioned studies in a number of areas of mutual scientific interest.[13] The purpose of these interactions was threefold: to promote peaceful science at the Russian institutes; to learn from one another (the Russian side has much to offer the U.S. scientific community); and, most important from a threat reduction perspective, to stabilize former Soviet weapons institutes by providing interesting and challenging non-weapons-related work for FSU scientists who, without alternative sources of employment, might otherwise feel compelled to leave their institutes.

Other lab-to-lab programs with similar goals include the Industrial Partnering Program (recently renamed the Initiatives for Proliferation Prevention program) and laboratory involvement in ISTC projects. Although the ISTC is managed by the Department of State, the laboratories are extensively involved in program development and

---

13. Joint projects have been undertaken in a number of areas, including computational science, environmental remediation, accelerator transmutation of waste, and technology commercialization, as well as a broad selection of topics in fundamental science, including collaboration in pulsed power and high energy-density physics.

implementation for both the IPP and ISTC. With appropriate administration guidance and oversight, scientists from U.S. laboratories work with their Russian counterparts to develop ISTC proposals and projects that are of real value both to U.S. laboratories and to the overall scientific community.[14] Los Alamos alone is a counterpart to eight ISTC projects.[15]

The U.S. laboratories are working with the State Department to develop a more collaborative, "programmatic" approach to ISTC projects. In the early days of the ISTC, proposals on unsolicited topics were accepted from the Russian side. The U.S. labs are now making an effort to discuss and decide upon research topics of mutual interest and benefit prior to their actual submission to the ISTC Governing Board, which approves funding. In this way, it is hoped that future projects will be truly collaborative and of scientific value to both the Russian and U.S. sides.

The IPP was established in 1994, and $35 million was allocated for cooperative ventures between DOE laboratories, FSU institutes, and U.S. industry.[16] These partnerships are designed to provide FSU weapons scientists with the opportunity to develop civilian technologies that have commercial potential. Although policy oversight responsibilities are performed by the Departments of State and Energy, day-to-day management of the IPP rests with the labs and the U.S. Industrial Coalition, which was formed to coordinate industry involvement in the IPP. Over 60 FSU institutes and ten DOE laboratories are involved in the program. More than 200 IPP projects have been approved, approximately 10 percent of which are industry cost-shared, and according to laboratory figures, more than 2,000 FSU scientists have been employed by the IPP thus far. Phase II of the project is just

---

14. There will be similar laboratory involvement in the Ukrainian science and technology center.

15. These projects are in the following areas: accelerator transmutation of waste, numerical simulation of nuclear reactor accidents, nuclear material control at Tomsk-7, atmospheric pollutant modeling, groundwater modeling, lidar for detecting hydrocarbons, ultrahigh-magnetic-field generators, and development of a book on shock-wave physics.

16. It was estimated that as much as much as $20 million would be available for IPP projects in FY 1995 and FY 1996. The Office of Management and Budget request for FY 1997 is $55 million.

getting under way. During this phase, as industry begins to take a leading role in proposal development and project implementation, program leadership will shift from government to industry.[17]

In addition to their scientific conversion efforts and involvement in the ISTC and IPP, the U.S. nuclear weapons laboratories are extensively involved in efforts to improve fissile material protection, control, and accounting (MPC&A) measures at FSU facilities to prevent the theft or diversion of weapons-usable nuclear materials. Although the U.S. national labs have provided support to larger U.S. government MPC&A efforts since their inception, in mid-1994 six DOE labs (Los Alamos, Sandia, Lawrence Livermore, Oak Ridge, Pacific Northwest, and Brookhaven) established a complementary program to deal with fissile material control issues, from the "bottom up," at nuclear research facilities overseen by the Russian Ministry of Atomic Energy (Minatom). In one of the best examples of the efficiency of the lab-to-lab approach, representatives from U.S. labs and Russian institutes negotiated and concluded contracts within a six-week period.[18] Since that time, an MPC&A demonstration facility has been constructed at Arzamas-16 and will certify equipment for installation throughout the entire Russian nuclear weapons complex. The demonstration facility will be used to introduce the technology to Russian nuclear facility operators and to instruct them on its operating philosophy. These facility operators will then incorporate the equipment and ideas into their own plants. The lab-to-lab MPC&A program has also been responsible for the installation of a physical protection system and computerized nuclear material accounting system in a key building at Moscow's Kurchatov Institute that is involved in experiments with highly enriched uranium (HEU). Most Minatom nuclear research

---

17. John R. Deni and Anne M. Harrington, "Beyond Brain Drain: The Future of 'Non-proliferation Through Science Cooperation' Programs," paper presented at the Conference on New Frontiers in Arms Control, University of Maryland, March 1995, pp. 16–17.

18. This should be contrasted with the larger U.S. government MPC&A effort, the implementation of which was repeatedly stalled. As of March 1995, three years after the program first came into existence, only $2 million out of the $45 million earmarked for this purpose had actually been obligated.

facilities are now involved in the lab-to-lab program, and a number of additional projects are under way at these locations.[19]

The lab-to-lab MPC&A program is managed by a multilab steering group consisting of the six previously mentioned U.S. laboratories and eight Russian technical institutes. A budget of $40 million was requested for the program in FY 1996, an increase of $25 million over the previous year's budget.

The U.S. nuclear weapons laboratories are also involved in a number of other areas related to nuclear safety and nuclear disarmament. These include a series of expert exchanges on safe and secure handling of hazardous materials and technical support for government-to-government initiatives on nuclear weapons disarmament and safety (e.g., support to International Atomic Energy Agency safeguards for excess weapons material, implementation of a proposed global fissile material cut-off regime, and unclassified technical exchanges on warhead safety and security). The laboratories have also provided technical support, equipment, and training for several Nunn-Lugar Programs. These include design assistance for the Russian fissile material storage facility and emergency response equipment and training for all four nuclear successor states. Los Alamos, Lawrence Livermore, Sandia, and Oak Ridge are also involved in planning for ACDA/DOE entrepreneurial workshops.

EFFECTIVENESS OF THE LAB-TO-LAB APPROACH

To a significant extent, the lab-to-lab program has not been subject to many of the criticisms of aid to the FSU that have been heard so frequently from members of Congress[20] and from aid recipients

---

19. These projects include design of MPC&A systems at the Institute of Technical Physics, Chelyabinsk-70, and the Institute of Physics and Power Engineering, Obninsk, as well as at the bulk-handling facility at the Institute of Inorganic Materials near Moscow. A portal monitoring system is being certified for use at the Institute of Automatics in Moscow, and discussions are under way on developing MPC&A systems for Tomsk-7, Sverdlovsk-45, and Chelyabinsk-65.

20. It should be noted, however, that two of the programs in which the laboratories are involved, the ISTC and the IPP, face an uncertain funding future on Capitol Hill. Many in Congress have expressed concerns about spending U.S. funds to stabilize or subsidize institutes that continue to engage in weapons-related work. The FY 1996 Senate Defense Authorization bill, for example, included a provision prohibiting spending on "any program established to assist nuclear weapons

themselves. A number of factors which have hampered the larger U.S. threat reduction effort—slowness of program implementation and aid disbursement, FSU suspicions of U.S. motives, and incongruity of U.S.-Russian interests—are much less pronounced in the lab-to-lab case.

Many of the administrative obstacles to Nunn-Lugar Program implementation have not been encountered by the lab-to-lab effort. The time-consuming processes of concluding agreements and disbursing money have been simplified by the lab-to-lab's streamlined contracting procedures and lack of cumbersome, congressionally imposed restrictions. As a result, the lab-to-lab program has been able to demonstrate tangible results quickly, especially in the MPC&A area. The lab-to-lab programs are also extensively coordinated. Coordination occurs among the relevant U.S. laboratories themselves, between the U.S. labs and the U.S. government,[21] and perhaps most important, between the U.S. labs and the aid recipients.

The lab-to-lab ventures, from the beginning, have been conceptualized, planned, and implemented in a truly collaborative manner. Because the lab-to-lab program involves individuals with shared interests and similar backgrounds, common goals are easier both to identify and to implement. No project was or is undertaken that is not a priority objective for both the U.S. and Russian sides. This has precluded much of the FSU stonewalling common to several of the Nunn-Lugar Programs, in which FSU enthusiasm did not match that of the United States. As mentioned earlier, the labs are working closely with the Department of State to apply such a collaborative, or programmatic, approach to the ISTC, which is the one program in which they are extensively involved but do not have managerial responsibility. Another factor which may help facilitate program approval and

---

scientists in the states of the FSU until 30 days after the date on which the Secretary of Defense certifies in writing to Congress that the funds to be obligated will not be used to contribute to the research, development or production of weapons of mass destruction." In response to these concerns, Viktor Mikhailov, Russian Minister for Atomic Energy, has asserted that, while Minatom has two directions—disarmament and maintenance of the scientific quality of the institutes—the American side should realize that "the second is essential [for implementing] the first." (Remarks at International Pugwash Conference, February 1995.)

21. This coordination process is in part the result of Washington's desire to maintain a degree of control over unruly laboratory "cowboys" and to prevent lab "freelancing."

implementation is the fact that, once conceptualized at the lower levels, lab-to-lab programs are then "sold" by each side's scientists to their respective governments. Instead of a U.S. official advocating a program to the Russian government, the recommendation comes from a Russian scientist or Minatom official. Scientific and technical interactions are also relatively nonpoliticized.

The collaborative approach has also helped reinforce trust between program participants, the foundation for which was established over the course of many scientific collaborations that took place both before and after the collapse of the Soviet Union. Recipients of U.S. cooperative assistance have had a significant say in deciding which projects will be undertaken. This has helped to mollify the suspicions of Russian and other former Soviet officials that the United States is taking advantage of Russian weakness in order to steal secrets and technology or to contract out work to "cheap" FSU labor.

Lastly, many of the lab-to-lab programs provide employment opportunities and salaries to former Soviet weapons scientists for non-weapons-related work.[22] Providing income directly to FSU personnel has helped to deflect FSU criticism that U.S. assistance is merely an excuse to subsidize U.S. industry. Lab-to-lab scientific ventures also help to sustain and convert the research and development (R&D) base of the FSU, a key to future technological and economic development in these countries.[23]

Russian scientists have on many occasions expressed their satisfaction with and appreciation of the lab-to-lab program, crediting it with helping both to sustain the future of the Russian labs and to prevent a "brain drain" of weapons scientists. Even the intractable Russian Minister of Atomic Energy, Viktor Mikhailov, who has been so critical of threat reduction programs, has been generally pleased with the overall lab-to-lab effort.

This said, however, the lab-to-lab program is not without its defects. Although the coordination process among U.S. labs is extensive, some Minatom officials have complained that no U.S. laboratory has been given the lead on MPC&A, and that although "lots of people

---

22. For example, approximately one-third of lab-to-lab MPC&A funds and approximately 50–70 percent of ISTC funds go directly to payment of FSU scientists' salaries.

23. Deni and Harrington, "Beyond Brain Drain," p. 17.

come to discuss MPC&A, there [is] a lot of repetition, and clarification [is] needed."[24] On a larger scale, comparing the successes of the lab-to-lab program with those of the overall U.S. government threat reduction effort is perhaps a bit unfair. Because it is relatively small, the lab-to-lab effort is likely to encounter fewer obstacles to success than the larger U.S. effort. The lab-to-lab focus is also extremely narrow, and although it can be credited with helping to stem the flow of weapons scientists and nuclear materials from the FSU, it is merely supportive of larger U.S. government efforts.

HOW WELL DOES THE "BOTTOM-UP" APPROACH WORK AND CAN IT WORK IN OTHER AREAS?

The "bottom-up" approach in the FSU is being successfully applied in a number of other areas. Building relationships among people with shared interests and similar backgrounds, while at the same time promoting U.S. foreign policy objectives, is a method employed by several current U.S. threat reduction and nonproliferation programs.

DOD's military-to-military program in the four nuclear successor states of the FSU was established in 1993, and in its first year, $15 million was authorized under the Nunn-Lugar Program for expanded defense and military contacts with Russia, Ukraine, Belarus, and Kazakstan.[25] The program has several objectives: (1) to promote larger denuclearization and nonproliferation efforts; (2) to enhance stability by regular exchanges on defense strategy and to enhance transparency in budgets and programs; (3) to encourage and assist the restructuring and downsizing of the FSU defense establishment; (4) to build support for democratic reforms; (5) to help FSU militaries better understand democratic societies, especially civil-military relations, and defuse "enemy" images of the West; (6) to develop long-term institutional relationships for substantive professional dialogue and cooperation; (7) to increase U.S. understanding of what is happening within defense establishments in the FSU, as a hedge against a reversal of reforms; and

---

24. Minatom Minister Mikhailov to Ambassador Goodby, remarks cited in unclassified U.S. government reporting cable 220742Z, July 1995. It should be noted, however, that Mikhailov subsequently praised the demonstration MPC&A system built by the United States at Arzamas-16.

25. The military-to-military program was allocated $13.6 million and $5 million in FY 1994 and FY 1995, respectively. The FY 1996 budget request was for $10 million.

(8) to encourage participation in the NATO Partnership for Peace program.

As with the lab-to-lab program, DOD's military-to-military contacts are designed to promote larger national security objectives through bottom-up interactions. As of June 1995, over 110 high-level exchanges, exercises, sister base/unit exchanges, and exchanges of experts on specific defense and military issues had been concluded. Although initial military-to-military contacts were at the senior level and were highly formalized, more recent contacts at the rank of lieutenant colonel and colonel have taken place and, according to the DOD official charged with program implementation, "are now beginning to get something accomplished."[26] The first joint U.S.-Russian peacekeeping exercise has been undertaken in Russia, and a joint peacekeeping doctrine manual is being drafted. Joint U.S.-Russian search and rescue exercises have also been conducted in Alaska. Ukrainian and Belarusan forces have visited several U.S. facilities, and U.S. Coast Guard officials have visited Kazakstan to help local officials develop a Caspian Sea patrol.[27]

Another similarity has been the relative ease with which military-to-military contacts have been implemented and sustained. Unlike other Nunn-Lugar Programs, complex contracting and procurement procedures do not apply, and because the individuals involved have shared interests and come from similar backgrounds, programs of mutual interest are relatively easy to identify and pursue. Many of the activities now being pursued, such as theater missile defense discussions with the Russians, the joint peacekeeping exercise and manual, and disaster relief exercises, were initiated at the suggestion of Russian participants.

Because the goal of DOD's military-to-military program—reducing the military threat through increased dialogue and cooperation—is less tangible than the lab-to-lab's objectives of stemming the flow of weapons and scientists from the FSU, it is difficult to assess its ultimate impact. It is unclear whether greater understanding between mid-level

---

26. Author's interview with Bill Harris, Director, Plans and Programs, Office of the Deputy Assistant Secretary of Defense (International Security Policy) (Russia, Ukraine, and Eurasia), June 1995.

27. Office of the Secretary of Defense, "Information Paper on CTR Program—Expanded Defense and Military Contacts," June 1995.

or even senior-level military officers will influence the decisions of high-level FSU officials, or if the military-to-military contacts can remain as nonpoliticized as scientific interactions. In any event, the military-to-military program is opening up the former Soviet defense establishment to the United States in ways that would have been unthinkable several years ago. Insight into the military strategy and national security perspectives of FSU countries can, at the very least, be a useful confidence-building measure.[28]

A number of Freedom Support Act programs are also working at the grass-roots level in the FSU. These initiatives are aimed at fostering support for democracy and economic reform. Educational exchange and training programs have been developed for bankers, farmers, business people, journalists, educators, and students. In 1994, approximately 10,000 people in the FSU participated in these programs and, according to a State Department report, gained "new skills and insights into a democratic, market-oriented society, and opportunities for networking with counterparts both in the United States and Russia."[29]

The Freedom Support Act also provides funding for training and exchange programs for FSU parliamentarians and other government officials. For example, the Congressional Research Service is working with Russian and Ukrainian parliamentarians to improve their access to information and analytical services in the hopes that the Russian Duma and Ukrainian Rada will develop a more authoritative and better-informed voice in the policy process in their respective governments. A number of commentators, both in the Congress and in Russia, have stressed the importance of these exchange and training programs.[30] They note that these interactions are relatively cost-effective, allow both sides to learn from one another, and build the

---

28. Some, however, have expressed concern that by opening up the U.S. defense establishment, U.S.-FSU military-to-military cooperation could increase the combat capability of what are still potentially hostile states or could serve to decrease the military-technological lead of U.S. forces.

29. U.S. Department of State, *Annual Report to Congress on the New Independent States,* released January 31, 1995.

30. See, for example, Deborah Kalb, "Arbatov: 'U.S. Aid Alone Can't Solve Russia's Problems'," *The Hill,* June 7, 1995; and Lee H. Hamilton, "U.S. Aid to Russia Serves Our Interests," *Christian Science Monitor,* April 24, 1995, p. 18.

cadre of experts needed in so many areas if the Soviet system is to be effectively replaced.

The grass-roots approach to building successful, market-oriented democracies is also being used to support the development of indigenous nongovernmental organizations (NGOs) in a number of subject areas. For example, a number of U.S. NGOs, including the Monterey Institute for International Studies and the Carnegie Endowment for International Peace, are working to develop a cadre of nonproliferation experts in former Soviet states in the hope that they will perform the roles of advocate and "watchdog" that their counterparts in the United States play with respect to the U.S. government on nonproliferation issues. By promoting more public dialogue and interest in nonproliferation and arms control issues, these groups hope to promote greater openness in the relevant government decision-making processes and thus help develop policies more consistent with U.S. foreign policy goals.

In the final analysis, U.S. government assistance efforts, and the goals they are designed to promote, will succeed or fail based on the will and capacity of the governments and the citizens of the FSU. While larger government-to-government initiatives can and have furthered U.S. national security objectives, DOE's lab-to-lab program and similar grass-roots efforts have demonstrated that complementary efforts of a lower-level "cadre" will greatly enhance the prospects for Soviet successor states that are stable, prosperous, and nonconfrontational.

Chapter 13

The International Science Center Initiative

R. Adam Moody

The International Science and Technology Center (ISTC) and the Science and Technology Center in Ukraine (STCU) are a multilateral response to the proliferation dangers created by the dissolution of the Soviet Union. Since the early 1990s, increasing international concern has focused on the potential impact of deteriorating economic, political, and social conditions in Russia, Belarus, Kazakstan, and Ukraine on the disposition of the former Soviet Union's weapons of mass destruction (WMD) and the military, industrial, and scientific infrastructure that supported these weapons. The goal of the U.S. Cooperative Threat Reduction (CTR, or "Nunn-Lugar") Program, is to minimize the potential danger that former Soviet WMD and related technologies and materials could be stolen, sold, or otherwise diverted to unauthorized, possibly hostile, countries or groups. As part of this effort, the United States, in cooperation with key allies and Soviet successor republics, initiated a program to redirect former Soviet weapons scientists, engineers, and technicians to peaceful scientific research activities, reducing the possibility that these personnel would seek weapons development work elsewhere. The ISTC and the STCU represent a multilateral effort to "minimize incentives [for WMD scientists and engineers] to engage in activities that could result in ... the proliferation of technologies and expertise related to weapons of mass destruction."[1]

---

1. See the Preamble to the "Agreement Establishing an International Science and Technology Center" (hereafter ISTC Agreement).

The author is grateful to science center staff, U.S. government officials, and others who contributed to this case study. The contributions of two U.S. State Department officials who corresponded with and were interviewed by the author over an 18-month period were particularly helpful.

The science center initiative was guided in its conceptual development by national security and nonproliferation concerns. Nunn-Lugar legislation as well as the Freedom Support Act of 1992 authorized the U.S. Secretary of Defense "to provide support, technical cooperation, and in-kind assistance for activities between U.S. scientists, engineers, and entrepreneurs and their counterparts in the former Soviet Union" in a number of areas, including research opportunities "within the states of the former Soviet Union that would offer scientists there alternatives to emigration and the proliferation of weapons technology."[2] Although initial Nunn-Lugar Program spending was slow, the science center initiative has demonstrated steady progress in response to the danger of expertise diffusion from the former Soviet Union.

The science center initiative has one primary objective and four secondary objectives.[3] The initiative's overall goal is to give weapons scientists and engineers with knowledge and skills related to weapons of mass destruction or missile delivery systems in the states of the Commonwealth of Independent States (CIS) and Georgia[4] opportunities to redirect their expertise to peaceful activities. Additional objectives of the initiative are: (1) to contribute to the solution of national and international technical problems; (2) to reinforce the transition of former Soviet states to market-based economies responsive to civilian needs; (3) to support basic and applied research and technology development, inter alia, in the fields of environmental protection, energy production, and nuclear safety; and (4) to promote the further integration of former Soviet scientists into the international scientific community. Compared to other Nunn-Lugar programs, most of which are bilateral in nature, the science center initiative's multilateral approach to nonproliferation problems is unique. Although it represents only a small fraction of total assistance to the former Soviet Union, the center represents one of the most important efforts in international nonproliferation today.

---

2. Theodor Galdi, *The Nunn-Lugar Cooperative Threat Reduction Program for Soviet Weapons Dismantlement: Background and Implementation,* Congressional Research Service, Report No. 93-1057F, December 29, 1993, p. 4.

3. The following objectives are from the text of the ISTC Agreement, Article II, Paragraph (B). The substance of the STCU agreement is identical to the ISTC agreement and is therefore not given separate treatment in this chapter.

4. Georgia has since joined the CIS.

This chapter presents a case study on the conception, establishment, and operation of the ISTC and the STCU[5] and pays particular attention to the ways in which the science center initiative has been implemented. This study examines the strengths and weaknesses of how funding for the science center initiative was used, especially the domestic constraints on the program in recipient countries. It also considers how the initiative has been affected by the many ups and downs in the Nunn-Lugar Program, which of late has come under increased scrutiny and sometimes outright attack within Congress and in the media.

This assessment begins with a review of the problem that the science center initiative was meant to address. It examines trends in emigration by former Soviet weapons scientists and technical personnel since 1991 and the domestic and international responses to the "brain drain" phenomenon. It then provides an overview of the events surrounding the establishment of the science center. Latter portions of this study provide a critical assessment of the science center's operations, comparing the center's nominal goals to its actual achievements to date. Research questions that have guided this analysis include:

- What factors contributed to delays in establishing the science center?

- How did the bureaucratic-political processes in the United States, Russia, and Ukraine affect decision-making and implementation of the agreements?

- What domestic factors in Russia and Ukraine hampered or facilitated the center's establishment?

- How effective has the center been in accomplishing its declared objectives?

- What factors have contributed to the successes and shortcomings of the science center initiative?

---

5. For the sake of simplicity, the remainder of the study will use the word "center" to refer to both the ISTC and the STCU. Whenever there is a need to distinguish between the two centers, their proper names (or acronyms) will be used.

The chapter concludes by offering policy recommendations for the center's future, as well as for the future of Nunn-Lugar funding as it relates to the science center initiative.

Soviet Brain Drain

As early as May 1991, before the breakup of the Soviet Union but several years after Soviet President Mikhail Gorbachev initiated his *perestroika* policies, reports began to emerge in the Western press about the possibility that economically disgruntled scientists and engineers were emigrating from the USSR to seek employment with clandestine weapons programs in foreign countries. One of these reports quoted Gurii Marchuk, president of the Russian Academy of Sciences, who, in March 1991, observed that "more than 500 scientists from academy institutes alone have gone abroad, either permanently or on long-term contracts."[6] Other accounts at this time illustrated the growing financial hardships and workplace difficulties that were driving Soviet technical personnel to seek employment elsewhere. For example, Alexander Kanoshenko, financial director of Russia's Kurchatov Institute, a leading Russian design institute for reactors for space and naval propulsion, lamented in 1991 that "the Academy of Science's hard currency budget for buying instruments that aren't available in the Soviet Union was slashed by 50 percent" for 1991.[7]

The Soviet Union's military-scientific community was one of the sectors most vulnerable to the economic and political upheavals that ensued from Gorbachev's reformist policies and were compounded by the eventual breakup of the Soviet Union. What had previously been a career track associated with prestige and pampered living was soon undermined by demoralizing financial uncertainties. Arms reduction policies pursued during Gorbachev's tenure, including a halt to production of highly enriched uranium (HEU) for weapons purposes in 1987 and a nuclear weapons testing moratorium in 1991, opened the

---

6. Andrea Rutherford, "Soviet Union Fears Brain Drain as Scientists Take Work Abroad," *Wall Street Journal*, May 3, 1991, p. A8. See also Mark Hibbs, "'Vulnerable' Soviet Nuclear Experts Could Aid Clandestine Weapons Aims," *Nuclear Fuel*, October 28, 1991, pp. 4–5.

7. Rutherford, "Soviet Union Fears Brain Drain as Scientists Take Work Abroad," p. A8.

door for a series of drastic reductions in defense-related science and engineering budgets. Although industrial workers, soldiers, and other segments of society also felt the downward pressure of Russia's foundering economy, the new economic reality was particularly severe for WMD scientists who earlier had enjoyed an especially privileged status. Some of the hardest hit were those personnel living in Russia's closed cities, the protected nucleus of the Soviet Union's sprawling WMD industry. By early 1992, for example, the residents of Chelyabinsk-70, who had been known in earlier years as the "chocolate people" for their ability to supply outside relatives with food and amenities, had been reduced to adhering to a strict ration card and coupon system.[8] The severity of the country's economic strain had found its mark, ironically, among those who were once the country's catalyst to global nuclear power. In early 1992, the chairman of the newly established Union of Designers of Nuclear Warheads reflected on the disparity of past and present:

Because [Chelyabinsk-70] is closed, the local free-market system has not developed enough to provide alternatives to government housing. Also, because travel to [Chelyabinsk-70] is restricted, [its] stores, which used to be better stocked than the average Soviet stores, are now bare in comparison with Moscow and St. Petersburg.[9]

In the years prior to the Soviet Union's economic malaise and eventual dissolution, Soviet leaders had little reason to be concerned about a possible emigration of scientific personnel, in part because of tight controls over travel abroad. Military research and nuclear commerce with foreign governments and firms were under the strictest centralized control. Viktor Mikhailov, head of Russia's Ministry of Atomic Energy (Minatom), reported in January 1992 that of the more than 100,000 people employed in the former Soviet Union's nuclear weapons development sector, 10,000–15,000 were "in possession of really secret information," and 2,000–3,000 were knowledgeable in advanced technologies, knowledge Mikhailov termed "of paramount

---

8. "Nuclear Brain Drain So Far 'Theoretical'," *Rossiia*, February 5–11, 1992, p. 8, as reported in FBIS-SOV-92-028, February 11, 1992, pp. 7–8.

9. Elizabeth Shogren, "Wounded Nuclear 'Heroes'," *Los Angeles Times*, March 24, 1992, pp. A1, A12.

importance."[10] Mikhailov conceded that although these specialists represented "the gold reserve of our science," they could not be prevented from leaving the country "solely by official means."

One of the official means to which Mikhailov referred was the Law on the Procedures of Exit from the USSR and Entry to the USSR for Citizens of the USSR. The measure was designed to allow freer travel abroad for the Soviet Union's citizenry and was passed by the Supreme Soviet on May 30, 1991, and entered into force on January 1, 1993.[11] However, where WMD scientists were concerned, the law placed a five-year restrictive delay (with the possibility of extension) on travel for personnel who had access to state secrets from the time that they last had access to such information. The government saw such legal measures as essential to preserving the scientific and technological resources fundamental to Soviet society. Nonetheless, the implications of the law's state secrets clause had the potential to heighten the disaffected feelings of Soviet scientists.

The Soviet government was not blind to the economic pressures driving scientific and technical personnel to emigrate, however, and its policies in this area were comprised of carrots as well as sticks. Besides placing new restrictions on movement, the government also attempted

---

10. "Nuclear Scientist Refutes Brain Drain Claim," *Komsomolskaia pravda*, January 31, 1992, p. 1, as reported in FBIS-SOV-92-022, February 3, 1992, p. 6. Estimates of the number of key weapons personnel residing in non-Russian former Soviet republics are more difficult to quantify. According to an early 1995 report prepared for the Stimson Center Project on Eliminating Weapons of Mass Destruction, the number of nuclear-trained personnel in Belarus defies accurate estimation. Most nuclear-trained civilian employees are probably associated with the Institute of Power Engineering Problems at Sosny and the Scientific Research Institute of Nuclear Problems at Belarus State University. The report also states that Kazakstan's nuclear-trained work force is primarily ethnic Russian and Ukrainian. A number of factors, including Kazakstan's refusal to allow dual citizenship, have escalated a brain drain from Kazakstan's nuclear industry. Ukraine's nuclear-related infrastructure, including trained workers and scientists, is second in size only to Russia's. See William C. Potter, "The Politics of Nuclear Renunciation: The Cases of Belarus, Kazakstan, and Ukraine," Occasional Paper No. 22, The Henry C. Stimson Center, April 1995.

11. See Sarah Helmstadter, "The Russian Brain Drain in Perspective," *RFE/RL Research Report*, October 23, 1992, p. 58; and William C. Potter, "Nuclear Exports From the Former Soviet Union: What's New What's True," *Arms Control Today*, January/February 1993, p. 8.

to increase incentives for these scientific personnel to stay, raising the salaries of most scientists in late 1990 and continuing to do so in subsequent years. However, the increases were far from commensurate with skyrocketing inflation, and according to a 1994 report from Russia's State Committee for Statistics, only 17 percent of scientists received a wage higher than the official subsistence level.[12] In any case, such salary increases could only be construed by WMD scientists to be temporary measures, given the budgetary cutbacks in scientific research that began as early as the late 1980s.[13] By early 1992, economic reform had caused the cost of scientific research to increase exponentially, and the Russian Academy of Sciences had total debts and liabilities exceeding 400 million rubles.[14]

Amid these worsening economic conditions, a report was published in Russia in mid-1992 by Vsevolod Medvedev, a member of the Presidium of the Russian Academy of Sciences, that identified three ways in which brain drain was occurring within Russia's scientific community.[15] The first trend identified by Medvedev, "the departure of scientists abroad," simply confirmed what had been reported in Russian

---

12. Vladimir Zakharov and Vladimir Fortov, "Science is Already in a Coma," *Izvestia*, November 2, 1994, p. 4, as reported in FBIS-SOV-94-220, November 15, 1994, pp. 30–31. In 1991, the average wage in Russia's science sector was seven percent lower than the average wage for the rest of the economy. By the end of 1992, this gap had widened to 30 percent; and by late 1993, the average Russian science wage was 38 percent lower. See Vyacheslav Tikhonov, *Kuranty*, May 5, 1995, p. 10, as reported in FBIS-UST-95-030, May 5, 1995.

13. Between 1991 and 1993, Russia's total spending on science dropped from 6 percent of gross national product (GNP) to 3 percent of GNP. By late 1994, total spending on science as a percentage of gross domestic product had dropped to 0.5 percent. See Zakharov and Fortov, pp. 30–31. By mid-1995, Russia's national income had dropped by almost one-half from its 1985 level; scientific research and design spending was one-fourth of what it was in 1985. See Tikhonov, in *Kuranty*, in FBIS-UST-95-030, May 5, 1995.

14. On April 27, 1992, Russian President Boris Yeltsin signed Presidential Decree No. 426, On Urgent Measures Related to the Preservation of Russia's Scientific and Technological Potential. This decree established the Russian Foundation for Fundamental Research which was to provide funds for basic scientific research. See Aleksei E. Levin, "The First Steps in Russia's New Science Policy," *RFE/RL Research Report*, October 23, 1992, pp. 52, 54.

15. Helmstadter, "The Russian Brain Drain in Perspective," p. 57.

and Western media accounts. A second trend, "an 'internal brain drain' whereby scientists simply change professions," cast a somewhat different light on the brain drain issue. Scientists who divorced themselves from the weapons complex and joined the civilian economy, while undercutting Russia's military industries, actually contributed to Russia's economic potential by energizing entrepreneurial industries that were outside the circle of state support, and which often brought in much needed hard currency.[16] The third trend identified by Medvedev was "a buying up of labor resources and technology by foreigners." Medvedev also identified three principal reasons for brain drain from Russia: (1) "inability of the scientist to realize his potential"; (2) "poor quality and limited availability of equipment"; and (3) "perceived negative attitude of society toward scientists."

As conditions worsened, there was increasing concern among Western governments as to the potential for a significant exodus of weapons expertise from the former Soviet Union. A 1991 Western press report alleging that 19 "top Soviet nuclear scientists" had emigrated to Israel, together with other international media allegations that Soviet WMD scientists had been recruited by would-be nuclear powers, illustrated the international community's growing awareness of the issue.[17] In December 1991, a classified U.S. Central Intelligence Agency report, one of many on the dissolution of the Soviet Union ordered by CIA Director Robert Gates, reported that, due to the difficulty of controlling the movement of potential nuclear mercenaries, the Bush administration's goal should be to "slow down, not eliminate, the seepage of ... expertise" from the former Soviet Union.[18] That same month U.S. Secretary of State James Baker had reported after returning

---

16. In a late 1994 report, Vladimir Khlebodarov, president of the Russian Academy of Sciences' Trade Union, said that "over 30 percent of Russian scientists have migrated abroad or rushed into private business in the past three years." See Vladimir Yegorov, "Brain Drain Continues, Another Budget Cut Planned," *Itar-Tass*, November 9, 1994, as reported in FBIS-SOV-94-218, November 10, 1994, p. 26.

17. See, for example, William C. Potter, "Would-Be Nuclear States Covet Soviet Engineers," *San Francisco Chronicle*, November 1, 1991, p. A27; Dan Fesperman, "Soviet Nuclear Scientists Ripe For Offers From Highest Bidder," *Baltimore Sun*, November 17, 1991, pp. 1A, 10A; and "Nuclear Scientists Emigrating," *Nucleonics Week*, November 28, 1991, p. 15.

18. Elaine Sciolino, "Soviet Brain Drain Poses Atomic Risk, U.S. Report Warns," *New York Times*, January 1, 1992, p. A1.

from the Soviet Union that authorities there assured him that they would impose stricter export controls on nuclear-related technologies. However, an official who had accompanied him added, "There is no expectation they will have much success in stopping the movement of people."[19] In testimony before the Senate Committee on Governmental Affairs on January 15, 1992, Gates declared that the most pressing concern of the United States was "a subset of this group [the 1,000–2,000 Soviet scientists with weapons design expertise] whose skills have no civilian counterpart."[20]

One of the most revealing Western reports on the brain drain issue at this time, written by Germany's Federal Intelligence Service (BND) and made public well after the science center concept had taken root in Western policy circles, underscored the severity of the issue. The BND report asserted that several countries, including Algeria, India, Iran, Libya, and Israel, either were currently employing nuclear specialists from the former Soviet Union, or had concluded labor agreements with them; in one case, WMD scientists were reported to have offered their services for hire.[21] In mid-1992, the British newspaper the *Guardian* reported that Ukraine had "turned down emigration applications from more than 30 scientists with expert knowledge of weapons technology."[22] Accounts such as these demonstrated not only the reality of scientific emigration from former Soviet republics at this time but also the understanding by these countries that this flow needed to be slowed. Ukraine and Russia, and perhaps other former Soviet republics, were acutely aware of the potential threat that emigration of these specialists posed, not only for weapons proliferation, but to their own economic and scientific health.

---

19. Ibid., p. A6.

20. R. Jeffrey Smith, "Gates Fears Soviet 'Brain Drain'," *Washington Post*, January 16, 1992, p. A22.

21. "Izvestiya Reports German Study of CIS Nuclear Brain Drain," *Izvestia*, October 20, 1992, p. 7, as reported in FBIS-SOV-92-205, October 22, 1992, p. 4.

22. James Meek, "Kiev Bans Atom Brain Drain," *The Guardian*, February 7, 1992, p. 1.

Formation of the ISTC and the STCU

In the face of growing domestic and Western attention to the brain drain issue Russian Foreign Minister Andrei Kozyrev proposed during a visit to Washington in November 1991 that an international fund for scientific research be established for disaffected Soviet scientists who might otherwise be lured away by lucrative offers from developing countries. In a January 1992 meeting with German Foreign Minister Hans-Dietrich Genscher, Kozyrev reiterated his "international fund" proposal, adding that transparency in emigration/immigration information between countries would help to prevent leaks of nuclear expertise from Russia.[23]

The United States had already begun laying the groundwork for a bilateral program between U.S. and Russian nuclear laboratories that would employ 2,000 Soviet nuclear scientists in an effort to keep them on Russian soil.[24] On February 2, 1992, Presidents Bush and Yeltsin met with their staffs at Camp David and discussed the brain drain issue. In the meeting, Bush proposed a joint U.S.-Russian research center that would allow scientists in both countries to cooperate on peaceful projects. Following the meeting, a flurry of activity, including letters between Baker, Genscher, and Kozyrev, and the first multilateral talks in Moscow on establishing a science center, resulted in a joint announcement on February 17 by Baker, Genscher, and Kozyrev on the establishment of the ISTC. On the same day, the 12 foreign ministers of the European Community (EC) approved the proposal and agreed to

---

23. German Foreign Minister Hans-Dietrich Genscher was an active and vocal proponent of the science center initiative and played a crucial role in rallying Japanese, U.S., and European attention to the brain drain problem.

24. "U.S. Prevention Tactics," *Izvestia*, January 27, 1992, p. 4, as reported in FBIS-SOV-92-019, January 29, 1992, p. 4. According to a U.S. government official, U.S. national laboratories had established contacts with Soviet labs even before the demise of the USSR. The early 1992 U.S. effort to employ 2,000 Soviet nuclear specialists was the beginning of U.S. lab-to-lab activities. Under an agreement between the Department of Energy and the Department of State, lab-to-lab activities began as a stopgap measure when it became evident that it would take longer than originally expected to put the ISTC into operation. Because lab-to-lab activities were easier to implement than the ISTC, it was also used as a vehicle to determine whether or not an ISTC-type initiative would be necessary. The ISTC and lab-to-lab activities were designed to be complementary.

contribute up to 20 million ECU (about $22 million) to the initiative. At the end of February, representatives from Canada, the EC, France, Germany, Japan, Russia, the United Kingdom, and the United States met in Brussels for an experts meeting in which the proposed science center's structure and premises for operation were discussed.

By the beginning of March 1992, the United States tabled a draft text of the agreement. Soon thereafter, Japan, the EC, and the United States expressed their willingness to fund the ISTC, and negotiations continued throughout April and May.[25] By May 24, an agreement was initialed in Lisbon that guaranteed about $75 million in funding for the ISTC. Although there were strong hopes that the agreement would be signed soon after it was initialed, six months passed before this occurred. On November 27, 1992, the United States (committing $25 million), the EC (committing 20 million ECU), Japan (committing $17 million), and Russia (committing "in-kind support to include a facility for the center, as well as its maintenance, utilities, security, and related support") signed the "Agreement Establishing an International Science

---

25. According to a U.S. State Department official, "discussions with other funding countries continued, but in the interest of advancing the agreement negotiations, only the United States, the EC, Japan, and Russia participated in the negotiations. Canada and Sweden both wanted to participate at this point, but were asked to withhold their participation pending the completion of agreement negotiations. They agreed, not knowing that internal Russian delays would push back the signing date of the agreement significantly. When the opportunity finally arose for Canada and Sweden to accede to the agreement, the European Union (EU) opposed either country having a seat on the Governing Board, which both had requested. An added complication was that by the time of the first Governing Board meeting in March 1994, Sweden's negotiations to accede to the EU were well-advanced and the EU entered into side negotiations with Sweden about its participation on the ISTC. The EU ultimately allowed Sweden to accede to the ISTC agreement, with the condition that Sweden withdraw from the agreement in favor of representation through the EU as soon as it had committed its $4 million contribution. As a result of the EU's opposition to Canadian representation on the Board, the government of Canada announced in early 1995 that it would not accede to the ISTC agreement, but would pursue cooperative science and technology programs in the former Soviet Union bilaterally." Author's correspondence with a U.S. State Department official, June 2, 1995.

and Technology Center" that officially established the ISTC in Moscow.[26]

Although the ISTC was now legally established, ratification of the ISTC agreement by the Russian Parliament was required before the ISTC could actually begin operations. For a number of technical, political, and bureaucratic reasons, which are discussed in detail below, ratification continues to be delayed. In December 1993, 13 months after the ISTC agreement was signed, the Russian government and its ISTC partners signed a provisional protocol that temporarily circumvented this ratification requirement and allowed the ISTC to begin operating. The reason for the protocol was the interest of the parties in proceeding with center operations without waiting for the Duma to convene, and the attendant delays in ratification. The provisional protocol entered into force on March 2, 1994. Two weeks later the ISTC Governing Board held its first meeting in Moscow, committing $11.6 million to 23 approved projects involving over 600 Russian engineers and scientists, in addition to hundreds of technical support personnel. [27]

Despite these delays, preparations were being made in anticipation of the ISTC beginning operations. During the year that passed between the signing of the ISTC agreement and the entry into force of the provisional protocol, a preparatory committee, whose primary task was to prepare all internal documents necessary for the ISTC's full operation, went busily about its work in Moscow and Kiev. Representatives from all four negotiating parties worked on the second floor of the Institute for Pulse Technology building in Moscow addressing financial, administrative, staffing, and other issues related to the center's operation. Preparatory committee members also spent the year visiting potential recipients of ISTC project funds. According to one U.S. government official, this "proved to be of significant long-term

---

26. "Russian Science and Technology Center Agreement Signed," *U.S. Department of State Dispatch*, December 7, 1992, p. 875. While the agreement committed Russia to in-kind support for the science center, it was a separate informal statement that committed the Western partners to funds.

27. "First Meeting of International Science and Technology Center Governing Board," United States Information Service News Release, March 18, 1994. At the meeting the Governing Board approved the Statute (pursuant to Article IV of the ISTC agreement), which formally established personnel policies, project development, approval, and financing processes, budget procedures, and other necessary arrangements for the implementation of the ISTC agreement.

benefit to the ISTC,"[28] in that it allowed the ISTC staff to become acquainted with potential clients. From a policy implementation perspective, the preparatory committee's full-time attention to working out the center's operational details before the ISTC agreement was ratified was an important measure in light of the smooth operations and collegial working environment it helped to establish at the ISTC. Moreover, early contacts with Russian scientists and other seed work helped overcome the initial skepticism expressed by many Russian scientists about the center's real potential. Citing past U.S. performance, or perceived lack thereof, in following through with its funding promises, many scientists feared that the ISTC would be just another paper tiger. The fears of these scientists were soon dispelled, however, once the first project proposals were approved and scientists were subsequently paid.

While Russia, with the largest number of weapons research personnel, was the focus of much of the ISTC's activities, the science center was never envisioned as an exclusively Russian enterprise. According to the ISTC agreement, "any state desiring to accede to this Agreement ... shall be permitted to accede to [it]" upon completion of all accession procedures and the approval of the Governing Board.[29] By the time the fourth ISTC Governing Board meeting convened in December 1994, Armenia, Belarus, Georgia, Finland, and Sweden had acceded to the ISTC agreement.[30]

---

28. Although there was no preparatory committee in Kiev until 1994, some members of the Moscow committee made trips to Kiev to facilitate the establishment of the Kiev science center. See John R. Deni and Anne M. Harrington, "Beyond Brain Drain: The Future of 'Nonproliferation through Science Applications' Programs," paper presented at the Conference on New Frontiers in Arms Control, Center for International and Security Studies at the School of Public Affairs, University of Maryland at College Park, March 30–31, 1995, p. 14.

29. ISTC Agreement, Article XIII. For states of the CIS that accede to the agreement, compliance with obligations "undertaken by the Government of the Russian Federation in Articles VIII, IX(C), and X-XII" is mandatory. These articles encompass the ISTC's project auditing and monitoring privileges, the ISTC's status as a "legal person" in the Russian Federation, the diplomatic immunities afforded the ISTC and its staff, and tax exemptions.

30. When Armenia and Georgia acceded to the ISTC, they entered into the agreement with the understanding that projects approved for completion on their territories would not be funded by the United States using Nunn-Lugar funds.

In early May 1995, Belarusan officials held their first meeting with ISTC officials to establish an ISTC branch office[31] in Minsk. Belarus agreed to provide a director and office staff for the branch office. The United States committed $5 million in Nunn-Lugar funding to Belarus, and the first U.S.-funded project in Belarus was approved in December 1995. Kazakstan's accession to the ISTC agreement was delayed for more than a year by Almaty's long-standing suspicions of Moscow, by its loss of important documentation, and by other administrative problems such as a reorganization of government ministries. However, Kazakstan completed all accession procedures by the September 1995 meeting of the ISTC Governing Board and was given a seat on the board in December 1995. An ISTC branch office was established in Almaty under the auspices of the Kazakstani Ministry of Science and New Technologies. The United States committed $9 million in Fiscal Year (FY) 1995 Nunn-Lugar funding and an additional $2 million in FY 1996 Freedom Support Act funds to ISTC activities in Kazakstan. Approximately $8 million in projects were approved for Kazakstan by April 1996, including a major seismic monitoring project (K-36) that will be part of the comprehensive test ban treaty (CTBT) monitoring system. By the time of the March 1996 board meeting, Kyrgyzstan had acceded to the ISTC agreement, Turkmenistan had begun accession procedures, and discussions with Norway were well under way.

With the exception of Ukraine, science center activities in former Soviet republics have been overseen either by the ISTC in Moscow or through an ISTC branch or coordination office. In March 1992, Ukrainian officials stated that it would be politically impossible for

---

Nunn-Lugar funding to the former Soviet Union is limited to the four nuclear successor states with which the United States has signed CTR umbrella agreements. As of Fiscal Year (FY) 1996, funding authority in the Freedom Support Act is being used to support ISTC activities in all other former Soviet republics, excluding Azerbaijan. In Georgia, the ISTC Governing Board has approved the purchase of a computer, facsimile machine, and copy machine for Tbilisi State University, which will provide information and advice to Georgian organizations interested in submitting project proposals to the ISTC.

31. A branch office is a formal office pursuant to the ISTC agreement; a coordination office is not. Rather than functioning as independent science centers, branch and coordination offices essentially are extensions of the ISTC Secretariat, and act as project advisors and administrators. All decision-making power rests with the Governing Board.

Ukraine to participate in an agreement that Russia was negotiating, and in a science center that would be headquartered in Moscow. Minsk had been proposed at one point in the negotiations as the ISTC's headquarters in the hope that, as the CIS capital, its selection would provide reassurance to other CIS countries and would encourage their participation. However, due to political considerations and problems associated with communications and logistics, Moscow was chosen as the ISTC's permanent site.

Therefore, following the initialing of the ISTC agreement in Lisbon on May 24, 1992, separate discussions on a Ukrainian science center were continued with Kiev. Negotiations continued for more than a year, and an agreement establishing the Science and Technology Center in Ukraine was signed on October 25, 1993.[32] At the signing, the United States committed $10 million to the STCU, Canada committed $2 million, Sweden committed $1.5 million, and Ukraine agreed to provide the headquarters facility and all equipment and services, including security. As with the Moscow center, the signing of this agreement was delayed by a number of political and logistical factors. Ukraine's circumstances were significantly different from Russia's, however, given the still formative nature of the Ukrainian government and the lack of necessary resources to establish the center. On July 16, 1994, the STCU agreement entered into force, nine months after it was signed. Almost an entire year passed before the first call for proposals was issued on May 6, 1995. However, because of the timely work of the preparatory committee in seeding the administrative and logistical ground of the STCU, more than 200 proposal briefs had already been received by the time the call for proposals was issued.[33]

---

32. The Ukrainian government designated the National Space Agency of Ukraine (NSAU) to implement the STCU agreement; a Ukrainian interagency advisory board was also formed to assist NSAU. See *U.S. Department of Defense Cooperative Threat Reduction Program Semi-Annual Report,* April 1, 1994–September 30, 1994, Appendix.

33. Deni and Harrington, "Beyond Brain Drain," p. 16. The ISTC differs from the STCU in the way in which the call for proposals is administered. The ISTC employs an open-rolling call for proposals, in which quarterly board meetings are held to review as many of the proposals as possible. Often, the ISTC Governing Board is overwhelmed by the number of proposals submitted for review. The STCU uses a semiannual proposal process, in which proposals may be submitted only during a finite period of time. The STCU holds a minimum of two board meeting per year.

Under the science center scheme, Russian, Ukrainian, and other former Soviet research institutes or other interested parties submit research proposals either to the ISTC or the STCU for funding consideration. Scientific research proposals at the respective centers follow a multistage review process. First, before they are ever submitted, project proposals receive considerable attention from science center staff as they work with Russian, Ukrainian, and other CIS institutes and potential non-CIS partners to develop proposals approaching Western standards. Second, in the case of the ISTC, once proposals are formally submitted, copies are forwarded to members of the Scientific Advisory Committee, composed of European Union (EU), Japanese, Russian, and U.S. members, who review the proposals for scientific merit. In Ukraine, the STCU does not have a Scientific Advisory Committee but depends on the technical assessments of its funding parties. Third, the proposals are sent to the parties for technical and policy reviews and funding consideration. The results are consolidated and then reviewed by an interagency panel that makes funding recommendations. It is at this stage that expert reviewers can recommend that a project be rejected, amended, or approved. At the center's next Governing Board meeting, the project is approved for a period of up to three years, placed on hold pending further action, or rejected. Every effort is made prior to the board meeting to work out all details related to a proposed project, including funding commitments from interested funding parties, via a Coordination Committee. This process protects each funding party's sovereignty to support only those projects in which it has an interest and which support its own research priorities. However, many projects approved by the Governing Board are supported by more than one funding party through cosharing. Funds for approved projects are disbursed quarterly to scientists through local banks at the request of the science center's chief financial officer who obtains the funds from an offshore bank.

This difference in proposal administration reflects, in part, the learning curve of science center implementation. The different scheme was also implemented in order to help the STCU run more efficiently. Since the STCU operates with a much smaller staff and budget than the ISTC, it became necessary to institute a system that corresponded to the STCU's operating capacity.

Difficulties Establishing the Science Center

Ironically, the same multilateralism that provided a measure of stability and transparency to the ISTC, and thus widespread acceptance of the center by Russian scientists, also created a number of bottlenecks and delays during the two years between the initialing of the science center agreement and the center's entry into force. Once the ISTC agreement had been initialed by the funding parties, early optimism soon gave way to intergovernmental wrangling.

Of all the problems that delayed the center's activities, technical factors are perhaps the easiest to identify. For example, although the funding parties had negotiated the agreement on the basis of the English text, with the understanding that the final official text would be in English and Russian, France insisted that French be one of the agreement's official languages. This triggered the requirement that all EC languages be included. Japan followed suit. The tedious and time-consuming process of translating, comparing, changing, and ensuring the contextual consistency of all 11 documents[34] occupied three months.

Bureaucratic and political delays also played a very significant role in slowing the pace of ISTC implementation. During the six-month period between initialing and signing of the ISTC agreement, the Russian government was entangled in extensive interagency consultations over the ISTC's establishment. The measure to establish a Western-funded science center required no fewer than 17 ministerial-level signatures in Russia's government bureaucracy.[35]

Once the agreement was signed by all parties on November 27, 1992, it then required ratification by Russia's parliament, the Supreme Soviet. However, the domestic political and economic situation in Russia at this time was not conducive to implementing a major international agreement. For ten months after the ISTC agreement was

---

34. The eleven languages were Danish, Dutch, English, French, German, Greek, Italian, Japanese, Portuguese, Russian, and Spanish. In addition to the translation factor, there was some uncertainty among the funding parties as to who should be responsible for printing the text of the agreement (a task that eventually fell to the EC), as well as where the signing should take place—in the United States, Russia, Japan, or at the EC. Moscow eventually won out. Other factors, such as the fact that the EC curtails its operations for 30 days during the summer, complicated communications among the funding parties.

35. Author's interview with a U.S. State Department official, June 5, 1995.

signed, the Supreme Soviet limited action on ratification of the agreement to the committee and subcommittee levels.[36] The ISTC was understandably a lesser priority compared to the many economic, political, and social reforms under consideration by the Supreme Soviet at this time. Clashes between President Yeltsin's reformist policies and the Communist orientation of some members of the Supreme Soviet undoubtedly also contributed to implementation delays.

A major reason why the ISTC advanced so slowly through Russia's ratification bureaucracy was the general suspicion of cooperation with the West. Although many institutional changes were brought about by the end of the Cold War and the dissolution of the Soviet Union, the attitudes and sentiments toward the United States harbored during many years of suspicion and distrust were slow to thaw. A basis for trust had not yet been established in late 1992, although great strides were being made. Moreover, once the Soviet empire broke apart into independent regional entities, ultranationalist and xenophobic sentiments percolated to the surface and found their way into many policy-related issues in the Supreme Soviet.

Despite the importance of the brain drain problem for Russia's own social and economic future, these anti-Western suspicions continued to complicate ratification of the ISTC agreement by the Russian legislature. The Supreme Soviet repeatedly delayed ratification, citing a number of concerns and criticisms. Debate on these matters continued for nine months. Foremost on the minds of some deputies was the possibility that the West would have access to Russia's nuclear secrets and other sensitive technologies. The ISTC Governing Board, made up of Japanese, U.S., EC, and Russian representatives, had the authority to review all project proposals in detail, and it was likely that many projects approved by the ISTC would be undertaken in cooperation with Western partners.[37] Many deputies feared that such cooperation, even if limited in scope, would be a major opportunity for technology pilferage by the West. There was also concern in the Russian legislature over the level of intrusiveness permitted by the ISTC agreement, which gave the center the right "to examine on-site ... project activities,

---

36. Deni and Harrington, "Beyond Brain Drain," p. 11.

37. Russia, the EU, Japan, and the United States hold permanent seats on the Governing Board. In total, the ISTC staff consists of about 30 Russian personnel and 16 EU, U.S., and Japanese personnel.

materials, supplies, use of funds, and project-related services and use of funds, upon its notification."[38]

A related concern was the status and sovereignty of Russian intellectual property rights. Would Russia's intellectual property rights be compromised through joint projects with Western firms and scientists? Who would own the discoveries resulting from joint projects? Could the integrity of Russia's scientific expertise be sustained in the face of joint projects? Some Supreme Soviet deputies were concerned that Russian scientific potential was being "sold off" too cheaply through the ISTC. Others questioned the validity of the ISTC's research priorities, since these were to be determined by a Governing Board dominated by Western representatives and a U.S. executive director. Skepticism abounded that perhaps the ISTC was another Western plot conceived to undermine Russia's industrial and scientific integrity.

A key criticism raised by the Supreme Soviet concerned the tax exemption of the ISTC's activities.[39] The ISTC was established to be free of the tax liabilities associated with "for-profit" organizations in the Russian Federation. This exemption applied not only to the center and "commodities, supplies, and other property [used] in connection with the center and its projects," but also to center-related imports and exports (which were to be transported duty-free), the center's non-Russian personnel, including the shipment of personal and household goods, "funds received by legal entities, including Russian scientific organizations, in connection with the Center's projects and activities," and salaries received by scientists and specialists working on center-related activities and projects.[40] With the need for hard currency growing to meet skyrocketing inflation and a devalued ruble, the idea of giving a Western-funded organization a free ride was disturbing to some Supreme Soviet deputies.

Another aspect of this criticism was the apparent "privileged status of foreign personnel." Foreigners working in Russia in support of the

---

38. ISTC Agreement, Article VIII. However, Article VI of the agreement stipulates that this right can be exercised only if the state in which the project is to be carried out has provided a "written concurrence," a formal prerequisite to project approval.

39. Author's correspondence with Ildar Akhtamzyan, assistant professor, Moscow State Institute of International Relations, June 1, 1995.

40. ISTC Agreement, Article X, Paragraphs (i)(a)–(g), (ii)(a)–(b), and (iii).

ISTC would not only be free from Russian income taxes and customs duties, but would be free to enter closed cities to inspect, audit, or otherwise monitor ISTC-funded projects, to "move funds [other than Russian currency] related to the Center and its projects or activities ... into or out of the Russian Federation without restriction,"[41] and would have immunity from immigration restrictions, from social security provisions, and from "arrest, detention, and legal process, including criminal, civil, and administrative jurisdiction, with respect to words spoken or written, and all acts performed by them in their official capacity."[42] These privileges stood out in stark contrast to the restrictive measures the Soviet government had instituted in 1991 to discourage, and in many cases prevent, its best scientific minds from leaving the country.

Eventually, as Yeltsin's political and economic reforms continued on a collision course with the Communist fundamentalism of the Supreme Soviet, Yeltsin dismissed the parliament and forcibly evicted the holdouts from the White House in October 1993. The following month, Yeltsin signed a presidential decree authorizing the Ministry of Foreign Affairs to conclude an agreement granting the ISTC provisional status. During the following weeks, the "Protocol on the Provisional Application of the Agreement Establishing an International Science and Technology Center" was drafted to allow the center to begin operations, pending the future ratification of the ISTC agreement. On December 27, 1993, the provisional protocol was signed by the four ISTC negotiating parties. The protocol then went through the same matrix of ministerial approvals in the Russian government as the original agreement had. On March 2, 1994, Russia gave its official notification that it had completed the necessary internal review (the last of the four negotiating parties to do so), and the provisional protocol entered into force, officially beginning ISTC operations.

---

41. This provision applies specifically to entities (i.e., the ISTC) rather than to individuals. The ISTC is not unique among Nunn-Lugar programs for its auditing requirements. All CTR programs are audited in accordance with established U.S. government auditing procedures.

42. ISTC Agreement, Article X, Paragraph (iii) and Article XII, Paragraph (B)(i)-(v). The exemptions are provided for staff at two levels. The executive director and deputy executive directors have the equivalent of diplomatic status under the Vienna Convention; other staff have the equivalent of administrative and technical status under the Convention.

As of September 1996, the ISTC agreement was still under consideration for ratification by the Russian Duma, which was elected in 1996 to replace the legislature evicted by Yeltsin. Once it is ratified, the ISTC agreement will supersede the provisional protocol that entered into force in March 1994. However, the ratification process in the Russian Duma has been fraught with delays. The Ministry of Foreign Affairs, one of the ministries whose approval of the ISTC is required, did not rule in favor of ISTC ratification until late summer 1995. By the time the ministry submitted the agreement to the Duma, a long list of other international accords submitted to the legislature for consideration had taken precedence. Notwithstanding these delays, Russian authorities have reported that there should be "no substantive objections" to ratification.[43] Once the agreement is reviewed by relevant committees— including those on Defense; Science and Technology; International Affairs; and Budget, Taxes, and Finances—the Duma will conduct two readings, following which the ISTC agreement is considered approved if no objections or issues are raised.

Establishment of Ukraine's science center, the STCU, was plagued by many of the same technical, political, and bureaucratic delays that hampered the ISTC. However, there are several significant differences between the establishment of science centers in Ukraine and Russia.

The STCU faced a number of domestic hurdles in Ukraine that were symptoms not of the center itself, but of a country making a painful transition from the status of a Soviet republic to that of an independent state. Lack of experience and logistical resources, more than any other factor, contributed to problems encountered in establishing the STCU.[44] With the breakup of the Soviet Union, Kiev lost much of its governmental bureaucracy to Moscow, and inherited an inadequate and unreliable banking and communications infrastructure. Still in its formative stage, the Ukrainian government took on several critical responsibilities but lacked the means to coordinate negotiation and implementation of a complex intergovernmental agreement. Complicating this problem was

---

43. Author's correspondence with a U.S. State Department official, September 19, 1996.

44. In addition, while the STCU's startup requirements were basically identical to those of the ISTC, the STCU was established with only $18.5 million, compared to $75 million for the ISTC.

the fact that the U.S. Consulate in Ukraine was transitioning to embassy status.

The first significant delay occurred between May 1992, when the negotiated text of the STCU agreement was initialed, and October 25, 1993, when the agreement was signed. In the intervening months, the Ukrainians proceeded to question or disagree with major portions of the agreement, including several provisions that their own negotiators had originally proposed. For example, the issue of the STCU's diplomatic immunity status, including tax and customs duties exemptions, was the source of numerous communiqués between Kiev and the STCU's funding parties. This issue alone took months to resolve. This post-negotiation "negotiating" was largely due to the fact that Ukrainian representatives lacked clearly established negotiating instructions and authority to conduct these negotiations, with the result that the agreed text required extensive review and revision. In retrospect, it is also clear that Ukraine lacked interagency coordination within its own government, a factor that also contributed to the delay. The document that was finally signed on October 25, 1993, was essentially the same as the one that was initialed 18 months earlier. The "renegotiated" text was more or less an exercise which involved bringing the Ukrainian government through the unfamiliar territory of negotiating the establishment of an intergovernmental organization in Ukraine.

Once the STCU agreement was signed, its entry into force, like that of the ISTC, was contingent on ratification by each state party. For Ukraine, this presented another major hurdle. Between October 1993 and July 16, 1994, when the agreement ultimately entered into force, the Ukrainian government continued to debate the issue of whether the STCU agreement required ratification by the Ukrainian Parliament, or Rada. It was eventually decided that the Rada's stamp of approval would not be necessary, and the agreement entered into force by presidential decree. However, in June 1995, Ukrainian President Leonid Kuchma signed a decree that nullified all previous presidential decrees, including the one that had brought the STCU agreement into force. Later, the Ukrainian Council of Ministers also raised questions about the legality of its own action a year earlier bringing the STCU agreement into force by executive decree, rather than by parliamentary ratification. Technically, these actions put the STCU in a legal state of limbo. As a practical matter, although the STCU continues to operate, nullification of the STCU's implementing decree has led to difficulties in obtaining privileges afforded under the STCU agreement.

Between July and December 1994, much effort was given to reaching a consensus with Kiev as to the nature of the agreement it had just brought into force. Initial meetings in August were marked by accusations that the United States had violated its obligations under the agreement by not transferring $10 million it had committed to the STCU initiative. The United States and the other funding parties found it necessary to reiterate the basic objective of the STCU agreement, which was not to supply the Ukrainian government with U.S. funds, but to fund Ukrainian scientists directly through an established intergovernmental organization.[45]

Following the STCU's first call for proposals (May 11 to June 9, 1995), which netted more than 100 project proposals, the Ukrainian Security Service informed the STCU that all project proposals under consideration must be submitted for security review. Although the Security Service promised the STCU that the review process would be concluded by mid-June 1995, it was not until September that the Service had reviewed the minimum number of 30 proposals that justified a meeting of the STCU Governing Board. This postponed the first board meeting, originally scheduled for September, until December 1995. Interestingly, but characteristic of the STCU implementation experience, the Ukrainian government had agreed in the fall of 1994 to allow Ukrainian scientific institutes to seek security clearances for project proposals before they were submitted to the center, and the STCU had been accepting proposals based on this understanding.

Procuring adequate office space became yet another hurdle to overcome. According to the STCU agreement, Ukraine was responsible for providing the headquarters facility and associated services, as well as for assuring the STCU's security. However, it was not until mid-March 1995 that STCU staff began occupying temporary office space. In December 1994, Ukraine provided only a two-room, one-phone-line office at the top of a 20-story building; security procedures in the building made access to the office so problematic for U.S. and Canadian representatives that little administrative progress was made. In February 1995, Ukraine offered the STCU improved office space, with

---

45. In response to a Ukrainian claim that the Governing Board had to be fully constituted prior to continuing work on establishing the science center, a memorandum of understanding was signed that allowed working groups to immediately begin addressing administrative, financial, and project-related issues in Kiev. These working group meetings took place in Kiev in October and December 1994.

the understanding that it would be only temporary. The parties to the STCU agreement decided in March to operate the STCU in its temporary office, but it was not until late 1995 that permanent facilities were renovated and made ready for STCU staff.[46]

Implementation problems within the United States also contributed to delays in setting up the STCU. Efforts to begin the STCU's operations were complicated by a high-level U.S. government decision in December 1994 to transfer responsibility for the science center program from the Department of Defense (DOD) to the Department of State. Some actions by the STCU, such as its initial equipment purchases or fund transfers, were delayed or made more complex because working-level staff at State and DOD had to resolve details on shifting funding and staff responsibilities. From January to mid-March 1995, U.S. funding activity slowed to a crawl, and a number of important purchases and fund transfers were delayed. One long-term practical effect of transferring program authority to the State Department was to delay, for more than six months, hiring of the two permanent U.S. positions for the STCU executive staff, the chief financial officer and the deputy director. Once the State Department assumed responsibility for providing these staff members, a lengthy new contracting process was begun in February 1995, and was only concluded slightly more than a year later.

Continuing Difficulties in Science Center Operations

Although the ISTC and STCU have made significant progress since their entry into force, a number of technical, organizational, and political problems continue to plague science center operations. Russia's lack of a dependable communications infrastructure in areas far removed from major industrial centers is creating some unique challenges to the efficient operation of the ISTC. The unreliability of Russia's postal service and the lack of necessary communications equipment, such as fax machines, in some remote areas has slowed early implementation of approved projects. Some incremental progress is being made in this area: in March 1996, the center tested electronic transmission of full project proposals and reports, and it is proceeding

46. The current staff consists of a Canadian executive director, Ukrainian and Swedish deputy executive directors, temporary/rotating U.S. staff, and locally contracted Ukrainian scientific, financial, and administrative staff. The administrative operating budget is funded by Canada, the United States, and Sweden.

with installation of a communications system that will include, among other things, a World Wide Web site. Communications continue to be a major concern, however, particularly for ISTC branch and coordination offices.

Politically, the fact that the ISTC agreement remains unratified places certain limitations on the ability of the ISTC to operate as it was intended. Although under its agreement the ISTC functions as a tax-exempt entity in Russia, the Federal Tax Inspection Bureau (GNI) took some time to issue the internal directive requiring local bureaucracies to comply. Generally, local tax inspection offices tended to follow federal regulations (as they understood them) rather than comply with requests from the ISTC for exemption. Although major problems in this area have been resolved, similar implementation delays have been experienced concerning the import of equipment for use in ISTC projects. Differences in federal and local interpretation of the ISTC's status have also been a factor where customs duties are concerned, as well as the taxation of income. The only remaining issue to be resolved appears to be obtaining value-added tax (VAT) rebates. According to a U.S. government official, Russia simply does not have a rebate system in place. By the spring of 1996, the ISTC had $40,000 in accounts receivable on its books for unrefunded VAT.[47]

The name "International Science and Technology Center" has also created some confusion on the part of some Russian government agencies. The ISTC's unique and legitimate status as an international organization has been undermined by other, unrelated trade-based organizations that have adopted similar names. This problem is particularly troublesome to local tax and customs offices, which find it difficult to distinguish between the ISTC and other unrelated organizations.[48] This difficulty has the potential to erode the credibility of the ISTC in the eyes of Russian officials unless it is distinguished in some key way from its imitators. The *Two Year Review*, which was adopted at the March 1996 board meeting, noted that "public identification of the ISTC is very important. The Parties will work with the Secretariat to prepare a logo for the Center."[49]

---

47. Author's correspondence with a U.S. State Department official, April 2, 1996.

48. See Ildar Akhtamzyan, "The International Science and Technology Center: Bureaucratic Games," *The Nonproliferation Review*, Fall 1995, pp. 79–83.

49. See ISTC, *Two Year Review*, March 29, 1996, p. 19.

A key problem for the STCU is the uncertain legal status of the center following the nullification of the decree that brought it into force. STCU inquiries on this matter to the Ukrainian government have yielded conflicting and contradictory responses, indicative of a government that has not yet institutionalized its interagency procedures. As with the Russian science center, problems have also emerged over the STCU's exemption from taxes and customs duties. Initially, the STCU was unable to obtain the release of imported scientific and support equipment for STCU-funded projects due to the Ukrainian government's delay in implementing customs duty exemptions pursuant to the STCU agreement. By late October 1995, two years after the signing of the agreement, the STCU and the Ukrainian customs service agreed to procedures that allowed large shipments of essential equipment for the center's new building. Although customs and tax issues appear to have been resolved, STCU staff appear not to be fully aware of problems until they arise at the intergovernmental working level. For example, despite Ukraine's prior assurance that it would not require STCU deposits in Ukrainian banks to be converted into local currency, in June 1995 the Ukrainian Central Bank informed the STCU that 50 percent of its local deposits had to be converted into local currency at the (disadvantageous) official rate. This issue was not resolved until April 1996. According to one U.S. government official, it is unlikely that these problems would have been solved by government-to-government action alone.[50] The presence of the STCU in Kiev helped resolve, at the working level, a number of problems that were the result of an inexperienced government attempting to operate in an unfamiliar free-market system.

A final impediment concerns the Ukrainian Security Service's review of STCU project proposals. Although the pace of review has been steady—sufficient to clear 65 proposals for review at the May 1996 Governing Board meeting—it has also been very slow. It was expected that after the May board meeting, there would be a severe bottleneck. The United States is currently pushing Ukraine to commit sufficient resources to accomplish this security review and ensure that the maximum number of proposals can be considered and funded.

---

50. Author's correspondence with a U.S. State Department official, April 10, 1996.

Fulfillment of the Science Center's Objectives

It may be several more years before a comprehensive evaluation of the science center's objectives will be possible, given the short length of time that the center has been in operation. However, a short-term analysis can provide important indicators of the center's charted course and of its current and future effectiveness. The remainder of this chapter considers whether the science center appears to be achieving its declared objectives and whether the implementation problems described above have significantly affected fulfillment of these objectives.

Although the goals of the science center initiative are ambitious, it is important to note that this initiative cannot address every possible way in which Soviet weapons expertise might assist or might be used to assist clandestine WMD programs around the world. Recent news reports have alleged, for example, that foreign governments are not only recruiting Russia's underpaid WMD experts to emigrate to these countries but are also enlisting these personnel in weapons projects within Russia's own borders. In 1994 it was reported that India, Iran, Iraq, Pakistan, and several other countries had set up "trade offices" in Moscow and were seeking to involve Russian research centers in their domestic nuclear programs. According to the report, it is "easy to bribe anyone in the [Russian] hierarchy to grant approval [for a foreign nuclear project], or to change the name of the project."[51] While the science center initiative is addressing the problem of Soviet scientific personnel emigrating from the successor republics, it cannot prevent the possibility that foreign "businessmen" from proliferative countries will set up operations in Russia and other post-Soviet republics and attempt to employ former Soviet experts in their own countries and home institutes. If true, such a phenomenon would represent a much larger WMD proliferation problem than the science centers were designed to address.

It should also be noted that the science center initiative was designed not to forcibly prevent brain drain but to provide WMD

---

51. Kathleen Hart, "Russian Weapons Scientists Said to be Working on Foreign Nuclear Projects," *Nuclear Fuel*, November 21, 1994, pp. 2–3. See also Mikhail Urusov, "Russia is Arming China," *Moscow News*, October 7–13, 1994, p. 8; and Christopher Hedges, "Iran May Be Able to Build an Atomic Bomb in 5 Years, U.S. and Israeli Officials Fear," *New York Times*, January 5, 1995, p. A5.

scientists with alternatives to applying their expertise to military-related ventures. The center's current challenge, then, is to provide sufficient economic incentive that idle and underpaid WMD scientists will choose to remain at home, engaged in the peaceful application of their expertise. The fact that ISTC-funded scientists are paid five to seven times the average salary of a specialist in the same field, and two to three times the salary of a specialist in one of Minatom's closed cities, is an encouraging comparison.[52] However, one cannot discount the possibility that foreign governments may actively pursue Russia's scientific elite under the cover of legitimate business practices. Media reports have already identified a new brain drain phenomenon—scientists who "moonlight by modem," supplementing their meager government salaries by supporting foreign WMD projects on the margins of their legitimate activities.[53]

There can be little debate that the ISTC has begun to accomplish its primary nonproliferation objective of providing opportunities for WMD scientists to redirect their talents to peaceful activities. By November 1996, there were about 15,400 former Soviet scientists, engineers, and technicians involved in 280 approved projects. Of the 15,400 scientists, engineers, and technicians, more than 60 percent are WMD or missile specialists, and many of the rest are from the defense industry.[54] The STCU is still in the early stages of formal operation. Two

---

52. See Akhtamzyan, "The International Science and Technology Center: Bureaucratic Games," pp. 79–83. According to Akhtamzyan, this disparity has created tensions between ISTC-funded scientists and their non-ISTC colleagues, who in some cases work in the same buildings and offices. Because ISTC grants go directly to scientists and not to their home institutes, institute directors often feel slighted in not having any control over funding allocations for ISTC-supported projects. However, after projects are completed, the ISTC does reimburse the home institutes of ISTC-funded scientists for up to ten percent of project overhead costs, and it also provides equipment and other supplies directly to the institutes. See U.S. General Accounting Office (GAO), *Weapons of Mass Destruction: Reducing the Threat from the Former Soviet Union: An Update*, GAO-NSIAD-95-165 (June 1995), p. 28.

53. Alan Cooperman and Kyrill Belianinov, "Moonlighting By Modem In Russia," *U.S. News & World Report*, April 17, 1995, p. 45.

54. "ISTC Approves $13 Million for 44 New Projects," *Post-Soviet Nuclear & Defense Monitor*, November 25, 1996, pp. 5–9; and author's correspondence with a U.S. State Department official, early 1996. The State Department projected in June 1995 that, by 2003, a total of 225 projects would be funded by the ISTC, supporting a total of

Governing Board meetings (December 1995 and May 1996) have yielded 50 approved projects representing a $6.1 million funding commitment. A third board meeting was scheduled for December 1996. As of June 1996, the STCU employed over 900 Ukrainian scientists and engineers.[55]

The above figures contrast to early media predictions of an impending mass exodus of disgruntled Soviet weapons scientists from the USSR following its breakup. Available evidence suggests that no such mass exodus has occurred.[56] In fact, there is evidence to indicate that many weapons scientists consider their expertise to be transferable to civilian applications, even without being retrained. A recent report from Russia's Institute of National Population Problems indicates that "up to 80 percent of the specialists of even exclusively militarily oriented enterprises feel that their knowledge and skills can be fully used in civilian production even without retraining."[57] Although opinions vary as to the real possibility of such an exodus, it is clear that without science cooperation efforts such as those supported by the Nunn-Lugar Program, the Soviet WMD scientific community might well have succumbed to the economic, social, and political pressures that ensued from the dissolution of the Soviet Union. It is doubtful that any of the Soviet successor states, which are suffering from a scarcity of alternative employment opportunities, could have single-handedly absorbed into comparable civilian activities the thousands of WMD scientists, engineers, and technicians who suddenly found themselves underemployed or unemployed in the early 1990s.

It is important to note that the ISTC and the STCU were established on the basis of intergovernmental agreements rather than international treaties, and have therefore been inherently more transparent than

12,000 scientists. See U.S. GAO, *Weapons of Mass Destruction: An Update* (June 1995), p. 29.

55. Author's interview with a U.S. State Department official, September 18, 1996.

56. See R. Adam Moody, "Reexamining Brain Drain From the Former Soviet Union," *The Nonproliferation Review*, Spring-Summer 1996, pp. 92–97. According to the U.S. GAO's investigation, "there is already anecdotal evidence that the [ISTC's] funding is having an impact on scientists and allowing them to stay in the [former Soviet Union] and pursue non-weapons activities, rather than have to seek employment elsewhere." See U.S. GAO, *Weapons of Mass Destruction: An Update* (June 1995), p. 69.

57. See Tikhonov, in *Kuranty*, in FBIS-UST-95-030, May 5, 1995, p. 10.

other brain drain prevention efforts.[58] This transparency has contributed to widespread acceptance of the center's work. Moreover, more than half of ISTC funds are distributed directly as salaries to former Soviet scientists (most of whom are required by the ISTC to set up foreign currency accounts to prevent their home institutes from misusing the money) rather than to government organizations or unnamed associations. This fact has raised perceptions of the ISTC's trustworthiness as an intergovernmental organization and its credibility for addressing the grass-roots issue of expertise diffusion.[59] The science center also makes direct, competitive offshore procurements of equipment for approved projects, which limits the potential for unauthorized diversions of funds.

Clearly, the many technical, political, and bureaucratic problems outlined above have had a measurable impact on the science center's ability to achieve its primary objective. Nonetheless, these impediments, particularly those affecting current operations, have not been life-threatening. Problems in the center's operations are due primarily to the fact that the ISTC agreement remains unratified. Although several sources who work closely with the ISTC consider the agreement's ratification a virtual certainty for the Russian Duma, the turbulence of election year politics and the agreement's rather low priority among other international initiatives may continue to delay action for some time. Moreover, the tangible benefits of the science center's operations have allayed many of the criticisms and suspicions that surrounded the center's early development. The ISTC has pursued its mandate quite successfully despite initial concerns in Russia over

---

58. For example, a two-year, $100 million grant to support fundamental science in Russia established in 1992 by Hungarian-American financier George Soros elicited a great deal of suspicion and skepticism from Russia's scientific establishment. The grant was used to create the Moscow-based International Science Foundation for the Former Soviet Union (ISFFSU), and was designed to keep "Soviet scientists working in a time of economic crisis." Through the ISFFSU, research scientists could apply directly for research grants, thereby bypassing the academies and institutes that traditionally maintained control over the distribution of research funds. Another significant effort to prevent Soviet brain drain was a temporary association established by the EC in 1992. The association had an initial budget of 4 million ECU. Reuters, October 12, 1992, as cited in *Executive News Service*, October 13, 1992.

59. See Akhtamzyan, "The International Science and Technology Center: Bureaucratic Games," pp. 79–83.

Western access to Russia's nuclear secrets and technologies, intellectual property rights, and intrusive inspections of ISTC-funded projects in closed cities.[60]

The accomplishment of providing employment alternatives to over 16,000 scientists, engineers, and technicians in the former Soviet Union is especially impressive considering that the science center has achieved this with a funding base that is quite small compared to other Nunn-Lugar programs. The science center program represents less than three percent of total FY 1996 Freedom Support Act and Nunn-Lugar funding to the former Soviet Union.[61] Moreover, science cooperation programs with the former Soviet Union, of which the science center initiative is only one element, represent less than one-tenth of one percent of the U.S. annual budget. [62]

Despite its successes for nonproliferation, the science center initiative has come under increasing criticism in the United States. A typical critique, contained in a 1995 report by the U.S. General Accounting Office (GAO), is that former Soviet scientists working on ISTC-funded projects were, in some cases, continuing to work on Russian WMD projects at their home institutes. State Department officials argue, however, that the underlying purpose of the ISTC is to "intentionally fund weapons scientists in the former Soviet Union"[63] in an effort to redirect their expertise to peaceful employment activities.

---

60. In its June 1995 report, the U.S. GAO observed that "science center projects are ... producing technologies which are accessible to U.S., Japanese, and European governments and firms through licensing and intellectual property rights agreements as part of Science Center grants and contracts. A license for one such project has already been obtained by Delco Corporation, a [California-based] company." Additionally, the ISTC has been unable to monitor projects on a quarterly basis, as it had hoped, due to staffing constraints. While this monitoring process is necessary to address dual-use issues, the lack of consistent oversight has, perhaps, given the ISTC time to come into favor with the more skeptical elements of Russia's bureaucracy. See U.S. GAO, *Weapons of Mass Destruction: An Update* (June 1995), p. 53.

61. Author's correspondence with a U.S. State Department official, September 19, 1996. While FY 1995 funding included Nunn-Lugar ($24 million) and Freedom Support Act (FSA) ($0.5 million) monies, FY 1996 funding ($15 million) came only from FSA monies.

62. Deni and Harrington, "Beyond the Brain Drain," p. 19.

63. U.S. GAO, *Weapons of Mass Destruction: An Update* (June 1995), p. 69.

More important, the ISTC agreement specifically forbids the use of its funds for weapons-related research; according to the text of the agreement, "the Center shall develop, approve, finance, and monitor science and technology projects for peaceful purposes."[64] All projects, prior to being approved for funding, are carefully scrutinized to determine whether they have dual-use applications, that is, whether they can be applied to both peaceful and weapons-related activities.

Despite the apparent risk of continuing to fund scientists who maintain ties to Soviet weapons labs, there are sound reasons to maintain the ties between these scientific personnel and their home institutes. Their affiliation with these research centers has important social security dividends that play a critical role in keeping these scientists at home. Severing these links would cut off any future possibility for such social benefits as pensions, as well as subsidized meals, office space, equipment, and communications support. No such benefits are proffered scientists who are paid for involvement on ISTC-funded projects. This link has long been viewed by the funding parties as Russia's financial contribution to the ISTC.

Besides its principal goal of redirecting weapons scientists to non-weapons work, the science centers have also been intended as a means to help find technical solutions to pressing national problems in former Soviet republics, to reinforce market-based economic reforms there, to support broad-based technology development, and to help integrate former Soviet scientists into the international scientific community. The effectiveness of the science center in accomplishing these four secondary objectives is more difficult to measure, given the scope of these goals and the short span of time that the center has been in operation. However, there are many indications that the science center initiative is well on course. The projects that have been approved cover a broad range of fields, and therefore have the potential to address a sizable number of national and international technical problems. The ISTC is

---

64. ISTC Agreement, Article II, Paragraph (A). In its investigation, the U.S. GAO noted its concern that the ISTC Governing Board was approving projects that had dual-use applicability. Of particular concern was an ISTC-funded project to develop a streak camera for use in chemical reaction observations and plasma physics research. Although the technology was related to that used in nuclear weapons testing, the project in question was neither designed for nor capable of being used for that purpose. A streak camera is too fast by several orders of magnitude for nuclear test measurements and would not be able to withstand a nuclear blast.

supporting basic and applied research in the areas of nuclear environmental remediation (which has received 17.7 percent of total funding), development of high precision scientific instruments (13.3 percent), energy production (9.1 percent), controlled fusion (8.9 percent), materials (8.9 percent), electronics and computers (7.7 percent), nuclear safety (7.3 percent), and basic research (7.2 percent). Other fields, including medical technologies, space and aviation, and non-nuclear environmental remediation, make up the remaining 19.9 percent of total funding as of April 1996.[65]

While nuclear institutes and technologies were the first priority of the ISTC, current projects span the full range of nuclear, biological, chemical, and delivery system disciplines. For example, according to ISTC staff, ISTC projects now involve about 70 percent of the personnel at GOSNIIOKhT, one of the USSR's leading chemical weapons development centers. Moreover, only a small portion (eight percent) of approved projects involve basic research. The majority of projects involve development (37 percent), applied research (31 percent), and demonstration (22 percent), and thus contribute directly to the former Soviet Union's economic development. The remaining two percent of projects involve feasibility studies of potential new projects in all areas.[66]

It is significant that the ISTC supports research in nuclear environmental remediation and development of instruments for this and other purposes, as this area is in need of serious attention in the former Soviet Union, as well as in some parts of Eastern Europe. The fact that almost eight percent of ISTC funding is devoted to electronics and computers also demonstrates how project funding is prioritized in accordance with current needs in former Soviet states, in this case the need for a reliable communications infrastructure. Almost 40 percent of total ISTC project funding is devoted to problem areas such as these. This is due not only to the nature of project proposals submitted but also to the direction by the Governing Board, which has sought to fulfill the mandate of the

---

65. See ISTC, *Two Year Review,* March 29, 1996, p. 5.

66. See *International Science and Technology Center Second Annual Report,* January–December 1995, p. 5.

ISTC agreement to contribute to the solution of national and international technical problems.[67]

Most of the projects that are approved and financially supported by one of the ISTC's funding parties include full-fledged participation by Western firms and/or research institutes. As of March 1996, more than 300 non-CIS institutes and organizations were collaborating on ISTC projects at more than 160 CIS institutes. The fact that major Russian weapons institutes are cooperating with these Western organizations supports another of the ISTC's primary aims: promoting the integration of former Soviet scientists into the global scientific community. Noteworthy participants from the West include Los Alamos National Laboratory, Lawrence Livermore National Laboratory, Rockwell International, General Motors, the University of Minnesota, the Observatory of Côte d'Azur (France), and the Japan Atomic Energy Research Institute. From Russia, significant participants include the Research Institute for Experimental Physics (Arzamas-16), the Siberian Chemical Plant (Tomsk-7), the Mining and Chemical Complex (Krasnoyarsk-26), the Research Institute for Technical Physics (Chelyabinsk-70), and many others.[68] Most significant in this cooperative scientific exchange are the small business spin-offs created through interinstitutional project ventures. These cooperative efforts provide mechanisms for former Soviet scientists and engineers not only to learn entrepreneurial skills, but to become adept at proposal writing and project management. These skills are retained by the scientists, thus strengthening the commercial basis of Russia's changing economic structure. No other single element of the ISTC's mission is more supportive of Russia's transition to a market-based economy than the business skills and knowledge gained by Russian scientists through cooperative project involvement.

Moreover, these "exposure exercises" promote Nunn-Lugar nonproliferation objectives by giving WMD scientists and engineers opportunities to become acquainted with peaceful uses of their

---

67. Another factor the board considers in approving or disapproving a particular project is whether it has potential longevity beyond the contracted funding period.

68. The majority of funding for approved projects has gone to Arzamas and Chelyabinsk, closed cities which are the former Soviet Union's primary sites for nuclear weapons research and design. As of September 1996, Arzamas and Chelyabinsk had received about $12 million and $10 million respectively, representing about 20 percent of total ISTC funding.

expertise. Although there seems to be a general reluctance on the part of some former Soviet scientists to venture out of the world of pure science and into the less familiar (and less friendly) business world, colleagues of those working on ISTC-funded projects are becoming aware of the tangible benefits, such as those mentioned above, afforded their compatriots through collaboration with Western organizations.[69]

Conclusion

What of the future of the science center initiative? In its initial stages, the science center was conceived with a view to the immediacy of the problems it addressed, namely, stemming the exodus of weapons expertise from the Soviet Union. This focus was due not only to the urgency of the brain drain problem, but also to the still formative nature of Nunn-Lugar funding implementation.[70] Without a formal structure or clear political mandate for long-term assistance to the former Soviet Union, long-term strategic planning for the science center's future direction and sources of funding were not addressed. According to one U.S. government official, at the time that the ISTC concept was being developed, it would have been unthinkable to presume that the United States would provide, for example, $25 million over an indefinite number of years to the science centers. In these early months of planning, the focus was entirely on addressing the problem at hand, not on sustaining the science center effort over the long term.[71] The result of this shortsightedness is that now, just as it has begun to

---

69. *International Science and Technology Center First Annual Report*, p. 11. In 1995, under the Project Development Program, 340 CIS scientists, all of whom were involved in ISTC projects, traveled to foreign countries where they "[met] with collaborators and [participated] in scientific conferences." See *International Science and Technology Center Second Annual Report*, p. 4.

70. In a late 1994 report, the U.S. GAO concluded that "[Nunn-Lugar] program officials have not established a process to ensure that annual budget requests are driven by a long-range assessment of tasks that need to be accomplished ... ." The GAO recommended that "the Secretary of Defense institute a proactive, long-term CTR planning process to help DOD properly allocate the billions of dollars it hopes to spend over the next several years among many competing—and shifting—demands." See U.S. GAO, *Weapons of Mass Destruction: Reducing the Threat from the Former Soviet Union*, GAO-NSIAD-95-7 (October 1994), pp. 1, 13.

71. Author's interview with a U.S. Department of Energy official, June 7, 1995.

make real headway against the brain drain problem, the science center is threatened by a lack of secure, stable financial support beyond the end of the century.

Reductions in funding by the United States and other science center participants raise serious issues for the center's continued existence and its future effectiveness. In FY 1994, the United States committed $25 million for a two-year period to the ISTC and $10 million to the STCU. For FY 1995, the U.S. commitment increased by $24 million for the ISTC and $5 million for the STCU. However, for FYs 1996–98, the State Department has planned to commit a total of $18 million per year to the science center program (ISTC and STCU) and then plans to cut its allocations significantly after 1998, "with a gradual decline to almost zero in [FY 2003]." [72]

As an intergovernmental agreement, the science center initiative has been supported largely by contributions from participating governments. Nonetheless, at the time the initiative was conceived, the parties to the agreement anticipated that, once the center was established, nongovernmental organizations, particularly industry, would provide increasing financial support to the science center effort. To this end, the science center agreement authorizes the center to "establish appropriate forms of cooperation with governments, inter-governmental organizations, non-governmental organizations ([including] the private sector) and programs," and to "receive funds or donations from governments, inter-governmental organizations, and non-governmental organizations."[73] This provision was intended to form a bridge to industry and other nongovernmental bodies that would not only redirect Soviet weapons science to peaceful, commercial applications but would also assist former Soviet republics in their transitions to market-based economies.

---

72. U.S. GAO, *Weapons of Mass Destruction: An Update* (June 1995), p. 29. As of August 1996, the total U.S. funding commitment of $49 million to the ISTC was allocated as follows: $35 million to Russia ($34.585 million obligated, $31.914 million disbursed); $9 million to Kazakstan ($8.9 million obligated, $0.64 million disbursed); and $5 million to Belarus ($4.95 million obligated, $0.468 million disbursed). Of the $15 million the U.S. had committed to the STCU as of August 1996, $14.932 million had been obligated and $2.374 million had been disbursed. See U.S. GAO, *Weapons of Mass Destruction: Status of the Cooperative Threat Reduction Program*, GAO-NSIAD-96-222 (September 27, 1996), p. 31.

73. ISTC Agreement, Article III, Paragraph (iii)–(iv).

Planned reductions in government funding reflect this projected financial commitment by nongovernmental organizations. But despite this assumption, no concrete plan was put into effect to ensure that industry and other organizations actually adopted responsibility for the science center effort. The science center agreement does not expressly mandate that the center transition from government funding to other-than-government sources. The lack of long-term planning for funding the center reflects not only the haste with which the brain drain issue was initially addressed, but also the inability of the negotiating parties to foresee the science center's future funding requirements (if any) or the capabilities of their respective governments to fund the initiative. The looming gap between the center's continued financial requirements and the eventual termination of government support is especially urgent in light of the U.S. political environment. The political mood in the United States, and particularly on Capitol Hill, is less and less supportive of funding international cooperative efforts, particularly those involving financial assistance to Russia.

This urgency is magnified by the fact that the number of project proposals submitted to the ISTC is increasing from year to year. By the time of the first Governing Board meeting in March 1994, over 150 proposals had been submitted. One year later, over 200 additional project proposals were under consideration at the ISTC. By late March 1996, nearly 300 additional proposals had been submitted for review.[74] The disparity of the center's uncertain financial future *vis-à-vis* the growing interest of former Soviet scientists in employment opportunities provided through the science center initiative has the potential, if not conscientiously addressed, to undermine the science center initiative itself. Redirecting the expertise of underemployed WMD specialists in the former Soviet Union to peaceful civilian applications is too vital to international security and the nonproliferation regime to allow this important initiative to founder.

Since the science center protocol's entry into force, it has become clear that the center's function of redirecting Soviet WMD science can best be served through long-term relationships between industry and WMD scientists, a process one U.S. government official calls the "commercialization of science."[75] This process is most evident where

---

74. See ISTC, *Booklet of Statistics on ISTC Projects*, March 26, 1996, Chart 2.

75. Author's interview with a U.S. Department of Energy official, June 7, 1995.

scientists from former Soviet institutions are developing more of a market orientation as a result of collaboration with Western organizations. Even from its conception, the center's funding burden was envisioned to be transferred from the government's shoulders to industry and other nongovernmental organizations. What was not inherent in the center's conception, however, was a long-term plan to ensure that the transition would be made smoothly and to designate target industries for future long-term employment. In the fall of 1995, progress in these areas was made when the ISTC Governing Board directed a working group of the Coordination Committee to develop procedures to broaden participation in ISTC activities. These procedures—the ISTC Partners Program—were approved at the December 1995 board meeting. At the same time, the board selected the European Center for Nuclear Research (CERN) as the first ISTC intergovernmental partner. CERN contributed about $1 million to two projects at the meeting. Encouraging new partners to join this effort is the major strategic focus of all ISTC parties for FYs 1996–97. Under the Partners Program, the ISTC "seeks to engage partners that can help scientists identify projects with commercial potential that can be pursued once their work under the ISTC is concluded."[76]

Judging from the progress it has made in fulfilling its objectives, the science center initiative appears to be one of the major successes of the Nunn-Lugar Program. This initiative has a number of important short- and long-term implications. In the short term, a potential proliferation danger has been addressed at the source; in the long term, Soviet WMD scientists are experiencing, during a period of economic and political transition, the benefits of applying their weapons expertise to peaceful activities. The skills, knowledge, and economic benefits that result from cooperation with Western institutions in peaceful research contribute in a permanent way to economic stability and the preservation of scientific resources in the Soviet successor states.

This study has attempted to evaluate the successes and shortcomings of the science center and to highlight some of the key problems involved in implementing this critical initiative. Although this analysis has focused on implementation problems in recipient countries rather than those on the U.S. side, the goal of this approach has been to create

---

76. *International Science and Technology Center Second Annual Report*, January–December 1995, p. 21.

a wider understanding among policymakers and the public at large of the implementation dynamics at play in recipient countries. Such issues as government inexperience, lack of necessary resources, and vestiges of Cold War skepticism and animosity are critical but largely underappreciated difficulties which this and other Nunn-Lugar initiatives must face in recipient countries.

The issue now on the table is how to sustain and direct the science center effort. Where U.S. funding is concerned, addressing important nonproliferation concerns in the short term should not overshadow, but should complement, the long-term goal of aiding Russia and the other Soviet successor states in transitioning to market-based economies responsive to civilian needs. The State Department, which assumed U.S. oversight responsibility for the science center program beginning in FY 1996, should develop a long-term plan that includes, at a minimum, identifying target industries, preferably target companies or organizations, that might benefit through cooperation with WMD specialists. The recruitment of additional funding partners from the public and private sectors will ensure that more WMD scientists, engineers, and technicians are given ample opportunities for alternative employment, and that the science center initiative continues to fulfill its mandate well into the next century.

Chapter 14

Export Controls and the CTR Program

Michael H. Newlin

The euphoria in the West over the sudden and unexpected collapse of the Soviet Union in 1991 was tempered by the realization of the growing likelihood that weapons of mass destruction or their constituent technologies in the Soviet inventory could proliferate beyond the borders of Russia and other successor states. In the political, military, economic, and ethnic chaos that arose after the collapse of Soviet Communism, the danger of proliferation was real and immediate. With the disappearance of both Soviet centralized control and ubiquitous Soviet security organizations, the newly independent states (NIS) were faced with a host of emerging challenges, even as they struggled to build their own national institutions.

The immediate focus of this international concern was the status and security of the thousands of nuclear weapons that were on the territory of non-Russian NIS or of former non-Soviet Warsaw Pact members. Immediately after the breakup of the Soviet Union, three of the nuclear successor states—Belarus, Kazakstan, and Ukraine—declared at Lisbon that they would forgo nuclear weapons and accepted the premise that Russia would be the only nuclear weapons successor state. As early as 1991, the United States moved to address the dangers involved in the transfer and storage of these weapons. The initial focus of the Nunn-Lugar initiative, later renamed the Cooperative Threat Reduction (CTR) Program, was the withdrawal of Soviet nuclear weapons to Russia and their safe and secure dismantlement.

Although immediate attention was on nuclear weapons, the Nunn-Lugar Program was intended to prevent the proliferation of all weapons of mass destruction and the means of delivering them. This problem was also of deep concern to U.S. allies; however, since the United States was the principal midwife to the emergence of the NIS, the allies tended to leave the initiative to Washington. The United States recognized at an early stage that the safe and secure dismantlement of weapons of mass destruction should be complemented by the creation of modern and effective export control systems in these emerging republics. However, improvements in export controls were different in kind from many Nunn-Lugar nuclear security initiatives, which could be addressed through technical fixes. Whereas safe transport, storage, and dismantlement of weapons of mass destruction could be achieved by adapting existing technical capabilities, the export control aspect of the Nunn-Lugar Program involved drafting and adopting laws and establishing institutions the likes of which had not existed before in some of these countries.

Although all four nuclear successor states recognized the need for export control regimes, the task of creating them in the NIS, which for 74 years had been part of the Soviet Union, was indeed a daunting exercise. There was no tradition but complete authoritarianism enforced with harsh economic, social, and security measures. Concepts such as an independent legislature, independent judicial system, executive accountability, and individual rights were unknown in practice.

Under the Soviet system, the State Planning Committee (Gosplan) had developed a highly detailed and centralized economic and industrial production plan, incorporating all sectors of the economy, that prescribed the type and quantity of goods, technologies, and commodities that would be produced; identified the industrial enterprises responsible for production; and defined a production schedule. These plans were then vetted by the political authorities, and resources were programmed. Powerful ministries and institutions controlled sensitive areas. For example, the Ministry of Atomic Energy (Minatom) controlled programs to produce highly enriched uranium (HEU) and plutonium that could be used for military or civilian purposes. The Ministry of Defense (MOD) had special internal arrangements to control and protect nuclear warheads, once Minatom had delivered fissile material for these weapons.

Exports were decided upon within the context of Soviet political, military, and economic objectives. Military exports to a client state such as Cuba were heavily subsidized. Military exports to states such as Iraq, Libya, and Algeria, which were in a position to pay with hard currency, were made largely on a commercial basis. However, on the matter of nuclear proliferation, there was a remarkable congruence of interests between the Soviet Union and the West, particularly after Moscow learned a painful lesson from its early nuclear cooperation with China in the 1950s. After this time and throughout the remainder of the Cold War, there was no evidence that either side helped another state acquire nuclear weapons.

Nunn-Lugar Assistance to Export Controls

Implementation of the Nunn-Lugar Program, including its export control component, has been slow, a fact attributable to a number of factors. Since the signature of the Nunn-Lugar agreements, there have been changes of government in Belarus, Kazakstan, and Ukraine as well as in the United States. In Russia, an abortive coup in 1993 caused considerable turmoil domestically as well as in the bilateral relationship with the United States. Belarus, Ukraine, and Russia have experienced bitter disputes between the executive branch and newly formed legislatures eager to assert their authority. In these circumstances, the governments in these countries have resorted to rule by executive decree. This explains in part the fact that, since the breakup of the Soviet Union, most export controls in the NIS have been governed by executive decree rather than by more formal laws adopted by NIS legislatures. In addition to these difficulties, another factor complicating export control improvements has been the changing political and economic relations among the newly independent states, and between each of these countries and the United States.

Procedures for Nunn-Lugar assistance to the individual states were intended to be uniform. First, signature of an umbrella agreement was required between the recipient country and the United States covering general objectives and parameters of the program. For Belarus, Kazakstan, and Ukraine, this first required a commitment to become a non-nuclear weapons state and to ratify the Nuclear Non-Proliferation Treaty (NPT) and the START I Treaty in such a capacity. Second, once the umbrella agreement had been signed, a specific export control agreement was signed laying out the kinds of assistance to be furnished together with certain administrative requirements. Third, a plan of work was negotiated specifying in some detail individual elements of the program and earmarking funds. Although there have been some significant delays in some cases, as of mid-1996, active export control programs were under way in all four nuclear successor states.

Belarus, perhaps because it suffered so severely from the consequences of the Chernobyl disaster, took an early and positive lead under then President Stanislau Shushkevich. Both umbrella and export control agreements under the Nunn-Lugar Program were signed on October 22, 1992. As a reward for its forthcoming attitude, a total of $16.26 million was allocated for Nunn-Lugar export control cooperation.

In Ukraine and Kazakstan, the situation was clouded by the question of disposition of strategic nuclear weapons on their soil. In Ukraine, some voices after independence advocated that Kiev retain some nuclear weapons on Ukrainian territory (a dangerous proposition, since the weapons in question were under the control of the Russian Army). Ukraine did not sign the umbrella and export control agreements until October and December 1993, respectively. These accords took place in the context of trilateral negotiations between Russia, Ukraine, and the United States whereby Ukraine obtained security assurances and economic benefits by agreeing to permit the transfer of the weapons to Russia for dismantlement. A total of $13.26 million was allocated to Ukraine for export control cooperation.

Kazakstan also stalled for time. In spite of diligent efforts by the American ambassador in Almaty and numerous high-level delegations from Washington, progress on Nunn-Lugar remained stalled while Kazakstan watched how the Russian-Ukrainian dispute over nuclear weapons played out. The trilateral agreement between Russia, Ukraine, and the United States encouraged Almaty to move. The umbrella and export control agreements were signed in December 1993 during the visit of President Nursultan Nazarbaev to the United States. Initially, $2.6 million was allocated to Kazakstan for export control cooperation, but in view of the country's size and its critical location, this amount was later increased to $7.26 million.

RUSSIA

Russia, by virtue of the sheer size and variety of its nuclear and other defense and industrial activities, has had the greatest need for technology controls. Quite apart from the ongoing effort to dismantle between 2,000 and 3,000 nuclear warheads each year, Russia has on the order of 100 nuclear operating facilities, including fuel fabrication, reprocessing, and enrichment plants. Russia also has numerous nuclear research institutes where significant quantities of weapons-grade material (i.e., plutonium and/or HEU) are present.

It is ironic that in Russia, which in 1992 was the first to sign the Nunn-Lugar umbrella agreement, difficulties arose over negotiation of the subsidiary agreement covering export control improvements. In

1993, Russia was receptive to early U.S. presentations on export controls, and in anticipation of an agreement, Washington earmarked $2.26 million for this purpose. Problems soon stalled U.S.-Russian momentum in the export control arena, however.

One immediate stumbling block was the fact that, as in other Nunn-Lugar projects, the U.S. Department of Defense (DOD) was the executive agent for export control cooperation (the Nunn-Lugar legislation so designated DOD because the funds came from that agency's appropriations). As a consequence, even though many of the Nunn-Lugar agreements were negotiated by State Department officials, Pentagon lawyers insisted that, on the American side, the agreements be signed by Defense Department personnel. During 1993, efforts were made by both American and Russian teams to reach agreement on an export control accord. When all other issues appeared to be resolved, Russia announced that, for political reasons, it could not sign an export control agreement with the Defense Department.

In order to break the impasse, the United States changed the format to an agreement between the U.S. State Department and the Russian Ministry of Foreign Affairs. At this point, Russia objected, on security grounds, to the standard audit provisions of the draft accord. Finally, in January 1994, in lieu of the usual Nunn-Lugar draft, U.S. Secretary of State Warren Christopher and then Russian Minister of Foreign Affairs Andrei Kozyrev reached agreement on a memorandum of intent that provided for exchanges on export control but eliminated the possibility of furnishing Russia with export control equipment (e.g., computers for managing licensing applications and approvals).

Under an agreed list of activities, export control with Russia consists of seminars and exchanges in areas such as legislation, regulations, organization, operations, multilateral control regimes, dual-use items, and industry outreach. As of mid-1996, approximately $1.6 million had been allocated for export control cooperation. Activities have included seminars in Washington and Moscow on the organization and operation of the two countries' respective export control systems. Other exchanges have dealt with legal and regulatory matters, enforcement, nuclear controls, government-industry relations and customs cooperation.

As in the case of other Nunn-Lugar recipients, export controls in Russia on weapons-related or dual-use commodities have until recently been mandated by executive decree rather than national legislation. Prior to 1995, the Russian export control system with several minor exceptions lacked a firm legislative foundation.[1] This deficiency was remedied in part by the passage in 1995 of two new laws. The first, On State Regulations of Foreign Trade Activity, contained a short section (Article 16) on national export control policy. The second, On the Use of Nuclear Energy, contained provisions related to nuclear export controls.[2]

Another critical domestic factor influencing the effectiveness of Russian export controls and cooperative efforts to improve them is the evolution of Russia's export bureaucracy. In June 1996, Russia provided an outline of its export control system for dual-use and missile technology items, shown in Figure 14-1.

The Export Control Commission of the Russian Federation is headed by a deputy prime minister and reports via the Council of Ministers to Russia's president. Prior to August 1994, the commission's work was supported by the Ministry of Economics with licenses being issued by the Ministry of Foreign Economic Relations. In 1994, a new coordinating body was created by the establishment of the Federal Service for Hard Currency and Export Control (FSVEK).

Transfers of military items and technology were authorized by the Commission for Military and Technology Cooperation until December 1994 when the commission was abolished and replaced by the State Committee for Military Technical Policy. This body is headed by Sergei Svechnikov and reports to President Yeltsin. Until his dismissal in June 1996, former First Deputy Prime Minister Oleg Soskovets exercised oversight of the committee. Some Russian and U.S. analysts have suggested that alterations in the export control structure may help to promote exports of arms and dual-use commodities at the expense of

---

1. These exceptions were a 1992 customs law and Russian Federation Law No. 4902-1, dated April 29, 1993, On Amendments to the Criminal Procedures Code of the RFSFR. The latter law established criminal penalties for unlawful exports of raw materials, equipment, expertise, and services useful for creating arms and military equipment.

2. The latter law, also known as the Atomic Energy Act, initially was passed by the State Duma in July 1995 but was not signed by President Yeltsin. A very similar version was passed on October 20, 1995, and was signed by President Yeltsin on November 21, 1995. The text of the law appears in *Rossiiskaia Gazeta*, November 28, 1995. See also Elina Kirichenko and William Potter, "Nuclear Export Controls in Russia: The Players and the Process," April 1996, unpublished manuscript.

Figure 14-1. Organization of the Russian Federation (RF) Export Control System.

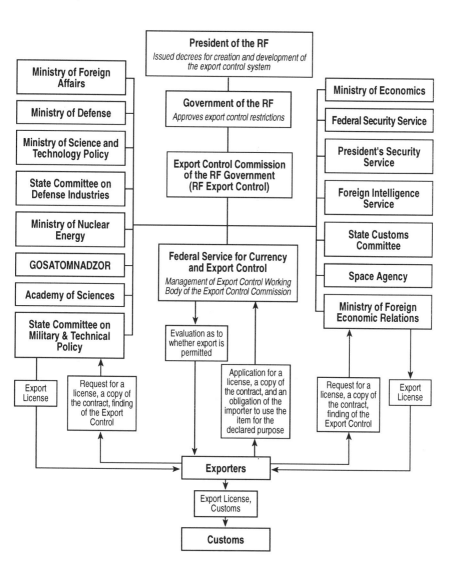

SOURCE: Gary Bertsch and Igor Khripunov, *Restraining the Spread of the Soviet Arsenal: Export Controls as a Long-Term Nonproliferation Tool* (Athens, Georgia: Center for Trade and Security, University of Georgia, March 1996), p. 18.

export controls.[3] This organizational factor further complicates improvements to Russian export controls, which already have been undermined by a lack of secure borders and the evolving nature of export controls in neighboring countries. Moreover, the Russian Customs Service was established only in June 1993. During the subsequent two years, hundreds of new officials were hired, resulting in a relatively high ratio of inexperienced personnel. Exchanges are under way between the U.S. Customs Service and officials at counterpart agencies in Russia to remedy this problem. Despite problems such as these, Russia maintains that it has an experienced and effective export control regime. Russia is a member of the Nuclear Non-Proliferation Treaty which prohibits the transfer of nuclear weapons to non-nuclear weapons states or other assistance in acquiring such weapons. It is also a member of the Nuclear Suppliers Group, the Missile Technology Control Regime (MTCR), and the Australia Group, which works to prevent the spread of chemical and biological weapons through the control of chemical precursors, chemical and biological weapons equipment, and biological warfare agents and organisms.

Alarm has been expressed over the seizure in Western Europe of relatively small amounts of nuclear material believed to have been smuggled out of Russia. There appears to be a consensus among experts and intelligence agencies that most of this illicit material was from research institutes or other nonmilitary facilities. There is no evidence that Russia has violated its nonproliferation commitments or that security of warheads or of stocks of weapons-grade material have been seriously compromised. That being said, there is still room for concern over the ability of Russian authorities, military and civilian, to protect, control, and account for the vast amount of fissile material in the Russian Federation.

---

3. The organizational change occurred as a result of Presidential Decree No. 2251, "On the Russian Federation State Committee for Military-Technical Policy," which was signed by President Yeltsin on December 30, 1994. See *Nuclear Successor States of the Soviet Union: Nuclear Weapon and Sensitive Export Status*, Report No. 4 (Monterey, Calif./Washington, D.C.: Monterey Institute of International Studies and Carnegie Endowment for International Peace, May 1996), pp. 67–68.

UKRAINE

Ukraine is second to Russia in size of population of the Soviet successor states. It possesses not only nuclear facilities but also several industrial enterprises devoted to manufacturing sophisticated defense equipment and dual-use technologies, particularly components and subsystems for ballistic missiles. Even before signature of the Nunn-Lugar umbrella agreement in December 1993, the Ukrainian government gave indications that it was serious about establishing an effective export control system starting from the ground up.

In January 1993, the Ukrainian government created, under the Cabinet of Ministers, the interagency Government Commission on Export Control (GCEC), along with its secretariat, the Expert Technical Committee (ETC). The latter body develops lists of controlled items and issues licenses. Its chairman, Viktor Voschilin, reports to GCEC's chairman, a vice prime minister.[4] The overall structure of Ukraine's export control organization is illustrated in Figure 14-2.

A key issue that complicated U.S.-Ukrainian agreement on threat reduction aid and improvements to Ukraine's export control framework was Ukraine's adherence to certain nonproliferation and technology control agreements. After prolonged negotiations with Russia and the U.S., and the provision of security guarantees and economic assistance in return for withdrawal of nuclear weapons on its territory, Ukraine acceded to the NPT on December 5, 1994, as a non-nuclear weapons state. It is also now a member of the Nuclear Suppliers Group. Ukraine has signed the Chemical Weapons Convention but, as of June 1996, had not yet deposited its notice of ratification. It is also a

---

4. *Nuclear Successor States of the Soviet Union*, p. 70. The GCEC was established by Ukrainian Presidential Decree No. 3 and its specific responsibilities were enumerated in Ukrainian Cabinet of Ministers Resolution No. 160, "On Establishing State Controls over Exports/Imports of Arms, Military Material, and Material Needed for their Production" (March 4, 1993). Resolution No. 160 authorized the GCEC to issue licenses and set quotas on exports and imports of weapons, military and dual-use materials, equipment, and production technologies, including those for nuclear and chemical weapons. It also authorizes the GCEC to conduct assessments of such imports and exports, to create expert committees for this purpose, and to oversee the functions of the ETC. The decree specifies that all decisions by the GCEC on issues within its jurisdiction are binding on all ministries and other government bodies and organizations. Cabinet of Ministers Resolution No. 779 of September 21, 1993, "On the Expert-Technical Committee under the Cabinet of Ministers," specifies the powers and responsibilities of the ETC.

Figure 14-2. Ukraine's Export Control Organization.

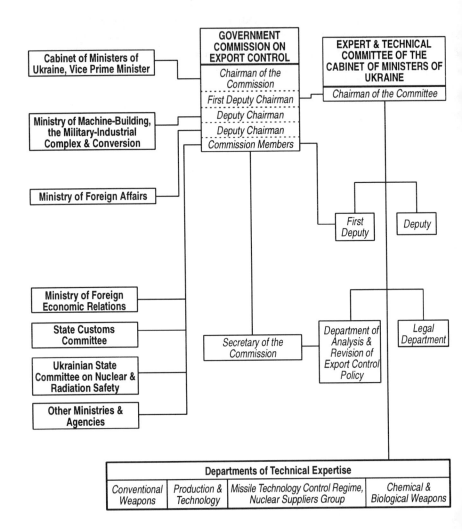

party to the Biological Weapons Convention. Ukraine has not applied for membership in the Australia Group.

The United States has urged Ukraine to join the Missile Technology Control Regime.[5] Ukraine has so far resisted this because it wishes to retain the right to possess MTCR-class missiles, which are not permitted under U.S. criteria for admitting new MTCR members. However, in May 1994, Ukraine signed a memorandum of understanding with the United States undertaking to abide by the guidelines of the MTCR. This development and other indications that Ukraine is seriously supporting international nonproliferation efforts have resulted in a greater willingness by the United States to discuss Ukraine's participation in international commercial satellite launches. The MTCR memorandum of understanding has helped ease international concerns over President Leonid Kuchma's statement that what is good for Yuzhmash (Ukraine's strategic missile industrial complex) is good for Ukraine.[6]

Ukrainian enterprises wishing to export sensitive commodities and technology must first have their status to do so approved by the government. To export controlled items, an exporter applies to the GCEC for a license, and this application is then processed by the ETC. The application is evaluated by the committee's various technical departments and the legal department in consultation with relevant ministries. Decisions take into account political, technical, economic, and military/security issues. For example, the exporter may be required to demonstrate that the commodity will be used only for peaceful purposes, whether adequate physical protection is required and will be provided, and whether international safeguards (such as those of the International Atomic Energy Agency) apply. The vast majority of decisions are based on the technical and legal evaluations of the committee's staff and are approved by its chairman.[7] Although

---

5. The MTCR restricts transfer of missiles, components, and related production technology with respect to missiles able to carry nuclear, chemical, or biological warheads to a distance of 300 kilometers or more.

6. Kuchma is the former director of Yuzhmash, also known as the Southern Machine Building Plant, based at Dnipropetrovsk, Ukraine, which is the largest integrated missile facility in the world.

7. In general the committee recommends either a general license (valid for one year) or an individual license. The GCEC meets monthly to approve or reject the ETC's decisions. Enterprises have the right to appeal a negative decision.

the committee is aware of the desirability of prelicense and end-user verifications in certain cases, such checks are made infrequently due to a lack of expertise and personnel.

In spite of many difficulties, the strong spirit of cooperation between Kiev and Washington has resulted in a viable export control system in Ukraine. All of the $13.26 million in Nunn-Lugar assistance has now been programmed. An early project was for automation equipment to link the Expert Technical Committee with other involved agencies and to create an easily retrievable database. Another project will tie nuclear technical experts into the licensing process. Other projects include x-ray vans, contraband detectors, laboratory equipment, training, and technical exchanges.

Although Nunn-Lugar funds have been fully programmed, other sources of assistance to Ukraine's export control enhancements have been identified. For example, Ukrainian customs will receive $2 million from the U.S. State Department's Nonproliferation and Disarmament Fund. This assistance will focus on designing a system to automate and link 148 border crossing points and eight regional customs centers to customs headquarters. When installed, a customs inspector will be able to verify that the licensing information on a particular item is correct and whether unlicensed goods should have received a license. The system will also be able to provide visual images of what the goods should look like, both packed and unpacked, and it will improve tracking ability.

One delay in these ongoing improvements occurred when Ukraine established an independent committee to report to the president on the effectiveness of all international aid programs to the country. While the report had not been released as of June 1996, the United States had been told that export control assistance was being cited as a model for other assistance programs. Delays in export control assistance to Ukraine were not all one-sided, however. U.S. government budgetary furloughs have also caused a slowdown in improvements.

KAZAKSTAN

Many of the disputes mentioned above between Russia and Ukraine over the control of and compensation for the Soviet Union's strategic assets also involved Kazakstan. Because of this, Nunn-Lugar agreements were not signed between the United States and Kazakstan until December 1993. Reciprocal exchanges of expert delegations began soon after an agreement was reached on a work program that covered all aspects of export control: legal framework, control lists, licensing structure and operations, customs activities including border crossing posts, and training. In the course of these exchanges it became clear that Kazakstan has made a high-level commitment to establishing an export control system. Given the fact that it had to start from scratch and considering the country's size and terrain, its common border with many Asian states, including Iran, and the lack of expertise and infrastructure, the task is a formidable challenge.

Nunn-Lugar equipment delivered to Kazakstan includes hand-held radiation detectors to help customs inspectors detect illicit shipments of fissile and other radioactive materials. Nunn-Lugar funds have also purchased patrol vessels to support a Kazakstani coastal marine patrol program in the Caspian Sea. Agreement has been reached on developing a system to automate export license applications and authorization as well. As of mid-1996, all of the Nunn-Lugar funds for export control had been programmed. A project proposal was submitted for extensive customs automation similar to the one in Ukraine which may also receive funding from the State Department's Nonproliferation and Disarmament Fund.

Kazakstan set October 1996 as the target date to have a functioning export control system. Government officials and legislators in Almaty moved one step closer to this ambitious goal in June 1995, when the Kazakstani parliament adopted comprehensive export control legislation. The new law, On the Export Control of Arms and Military Hardware and Also Natural Resources, Materials, Equipment, and Technology Connected with Their Production, establishes a system of export controls, limits export destinations, and designates government agencies responsible for monitoring and enforcement. Despite this promising development, the October 1996 target date for a fully functional export control system is probably overly optimistic, because of delivery dates of export automation equipment (early 1997) and other factors.

BELARUS

The Belarusan Nunn-Lugar export control program is the oldest, beginning in October 1992. It and the Ukrainian export control program are the most advanced in terms of U.S. intellectual and material assistance.

Belarus acceded to the NPT in July 1993. It is not a member of the Nuclear Suppliers Group but has agreed to adhere to its guidelines.

Belarus is a party to the Minsk Accord of June 1992, the signatories of which agreed to control exports of nuclear and nuclear-related dual-use materials.[8] Moreover, in February 1993, Belarus agreed with Armenia, Kazakstan, Russia, Tajikistan, and Uzbekistan to cooperate in controlling exports of raw materials, equipment, technology, and services used to produce weapons of mass destruction.[9]

As of mid-1996, the lack of formal export control legislation in Belarus was still a problem. However, mirroring recent progress in other NIS, the Belarusan government submitted a draft export control law to its parliament and was hopeful of adoption in 1996. In practice, under current executive decrees, the Ministry of Foreign Economic Relations (MFER) continues to be the lead export control body, and it coordinates its activities with the Foreign and Defense Ministries and the State Security Committee. These agencies develop general export control policies, including identification of restricted countries and participation in international control regimes. The MFER drafts export control laws and regulations, including lists of sensitive items. It issues licenses and maintains a database of issued licenses in coordination with customs and border guards, who are responsible for enforcement. The State Security Committee investigates violations of export controls. Under current government decrees, penalties for violations are few, but officials in Minsk expect to correct this situation with the adoption of comprehensive export control legislation.

Automation has been a key component of the export control assistance program in Belarus. The first major equipment project was for the central export control organization in Minsk. This was followed by a major customs information network valued at $2.3 million which was delivered in 1995. Belarus is a major transshipment route for other regions of the NIS, and the Nunn-Lugar Program is funding construction of model border crossing posts equipped with hand-held radiation detectors and x-ray equipment. The program has also provided some basic equipment, such as vehicles and radios.

---

8. Under the terms of the "Agreement on the Basic Principles of Cooperation in the Field of Peaceful Use of Nuclear Energy," CIS member-states agreed to follow INFCIRC/209 (Zangger Committee) and INFCIRC/225 (Nuclear Suppliers Group Trigger List), Articles 1 and 5, in controlling exports of nuclear materials and nuclear-related dual-use materials.

9. "Six CIS States Join Forces to Enforce Export Control," *Itar-Tass*, February 9, 1993, in FBIS-SOV-93-026, February 10, 1993.

Ongoing Problems and Emerging Trends

The sudden dissolution of the Soviet Union created a dangerous and confused situation that presented multiple political, economic, and security challenges to the United States and its allies and to the leaders and peoples of the NIS. Ukraine, Kazakstan, and Belarus, which suddenly became sovereign and independent states, were burdened with the additional responsibility of creating basic political, legal, and social institutions. Nonetheless, despite these responsibilities, all four nuclear NIS have recognized the need for national export control systems, the basic elements of which include a legal basis for export controls, including lists of controlled items; an organization and procedures for licensing; an effective national customs service; the establishment of immigration and customs frontiers; and an effective enforcement regime.

Whatever one may say about the pace at which the Nunn-Lugar Program and its export control component have been implemented, it is clear that the program has played the critical role in making such a system a reality across all four countries. U.S. assistance is helping these states maintain strong protections against the proliferation of the weapons legacy of the Soviet empire. In the absence of this assistance, political, military, and economic confusion in the vast area from Western Europe to the Sea of Japan after 1991 might have created an ideal environment for the proliferation of weapons of mass destruction.

In Ukraine, Kazakstan, and Belarus in particular, problems were so numerous and resources were so scarce in the aftermath of the Soviet collapse that development of export control regimes in these states would have taken place at a much slower pace had it not been for the Nunn-Lugar Program. Nor has Nunn-Lugar aid comprised only legal and technical assistance. A fundamental but largely unappreciated part of early Nunn-Lugar contacts between the United States and officials in the non-Russian NIS was simply to familiarize these officials with the provisions and procedures of international technology control regimes, such as the Nuclear Suppliers Group and the Australia Group. As newly sovereign states, Belarus, Kazakstan, and Ukraine had quite steep learning curves regarding participation in such international agreements, but their understanding of these provisions was absolutely critical to progress on export controls.

Export control organizations and capabilities in these countries continue to evolve and improve. A number of important technical and legal advances have been made to help stem the flow of weapons-related commodities from former Soviet republics. More important, a culture supportive of the nonproliferation agenda has taken root in these governments, and with it, a recognition of the importance of establishing the legal, organizational, and technical basis for export controls. The Nunn-Lugar Program and other efforts by the United States and its allies have played a powerful role in helping these states make this choice.

Nonetheless, progress has been uneven, reflecting the different political and economic conditions in each of the four nuclear successor states, including the changing dynamics of relations among them and between each of them and the United States. Progress has also been hampered by several systemic factors.

A major element in the situation that has only slowly changed has been the absence of experienced leaders and administrators in the NIS with the desire to undertake radical change. The fact that most of the officials in the NIS are products of the Soviet system has not always made for easy agreement with a former enemy in new and uncertain times, even when objectives were in both parties' interest. Disagreements over the respective roles of the executive and legislative branches of government, especially in Russia and Ukraine, also caused delays.

As noted in several of the cases above, a critical issue with respect to progress on export controls is the fact that NIS governments have tended to rely on rule by decree rather than the rule of law. Significant progress has been made in this area, although this continues to be the case in some of the NIS, where formal export control legislation has been held hostage to other unrelated issues. Nunn-Lugar assistance has aided this transition to the rule of law and several nongovernmental organizations (NGOs) have played a part in this evolution as well. In Ukraine and Belarus, for example, NGOs such as the Monterey Institute of International Studies, the University of Georgia, the Lawyers Alliance for World Security, and the American Association for the Advancement of Science have worked with local officials on draft export control legislation and have sponsored conferences on industry outreach and enforcement.

Political, military, and economic circumstances in each of the Soviet successor states and the evolving relationship among these states will continue to change the context for export control enhancements and other nonproliferation measures. Economic difficulties and the reorganization of security services, for example, not only in Russia but in other NIS, provide fertile ground for the activities of powerful organized crime groups and increase proliferation concerns.

Another factor that has complicated efforts to control the export of sensitive technologies is a series of bilateral and multilateral economic and customs cooperation agreements among NIS governments. In some cases, these coordinating documents appear to have strengthened standards for controlling the flow of strategic materials. All four nuclear successor states, for example, are parties to the June 1992 Minsk Accord that established Nuclear Suppliers Group standards for controlling nuclear exports.

In other cases, however, the implications of this trend toward closer cooperation may be more problematic from the standpoint of nonproliferation. Recent agreements have reduced or eliminated controls along internal former Soviet borders. On January 28, 1995, Belarus, Kazakstan, and Russia signed a customs union intended to harmonize their foreign economic policies, remove tariffs and duties on trade among the three, and abolish customs controls along their common borders.[10] Russia and Kazakstan have eliminated tariffs and trade volume restrictions and no longer operate most major customs checkpoints along their common border.[11] Customs checks along the Belarusan-Russian frontier have been similarly eliminated, leaving the Belarusan-Polish border as the only well-guarded Belarusan border.[12] The movement of goods and personnel between Belarus and Russia was made even easier in April 1996, when the two countries signed a treaty creating a new union that merged many of their economic and

---

10. "Russia, Belarus, Kazakstan Sign Customs Union Agreement," *Rossiiskaia Gazeta*, January 28, 1995, in FBIS-SOV-95-0227-S, February 9, 1995. The union was only a coordinating agreement, however, and implementation of its measures required bilateral arrangements between each of the three nations.

11. Customs controls will be exercised over transit shipments from third countries only. Kazakstani checkpoints, such as the Almaty airport, which formerly were jointly staffed by Russian and Kazakstani customs agents, are now staffed by Kazakstani officials only. Patrols of CIS external borders in Kazakstan (e.g., the border with China) are undertaken jointly by Russian and Kazakstani military forces. See "Derbisov on Customs Affairs, Security," *Kazakstanskaia pravda*, August 30, 1995, in FBIS-SOV-95-173, August 30, 1995. See also "Customs Doesn't Get an Okay," *Pravda*, January 4, 1996, p. 1.

12. There are periodic checkpoints on the Belarusan border with Ukraine and with the Baltic states, but these checkpoints are reportedly easily circumvented.

legal policies. Although the full implications of the Russo-Belarusan union treaty are difficult to foresee, the two sides have committed to joint protection of their common external border. [13]

The Soviet successor governments have made a courageous choice in placing priority on nonproliferation and technology controls in their national security and economic planning. This is particularly true considering the tremendous economic incentives and political pressures that have mitigated against such a choice. U.S. Nunn-Lugar assistance and other bilateral and multilateral aid programs have played a critical role in helping the NIS governments along this path by providing them with the benefit of U.S. legal and organizational experience as well as the technical tools to operationalize this framework. Although the Nunn-Lugar Program has made significant strides, these states will continue to be buffeted by the strains of developing viable economies and establishing stable political and bureaucratic organizations. These strains in turn will have a direct impact on the relationship of the newly independent states with each other and with the United States. As officials and other specialists in the United States continue to work with their counterparts in the NIS to put in place effective legal and technical safeguards against proliferation, they will need to assess how best to reinforce these reforms against these problems.

---

13. The union treaty, officially titled "Agreement on the Formation of a Community," was signed by Russian President Yeltsin and Belarusan President Alexander Lukashenka in an April 2 ceremony. See Peter Rutland, "Text of Russo-Belarusan Union Treaty Revealed," *OMRI Daily Digest*, March 29, 1996; Scott Parrish, "Yeltsin, Lukashenka Sign Integration Agreement," *OMRI Daily Digest*, April 2, 1996; and David Hoffman, "Russia, Belarus Announce Agreement on Plan to Form New Union," *Washington Post*, March 24, 1996, p. A32. The two sides formally signed the treaty on April 2, 1996.

Chapter 15

Cooperative Activities to Improve Fissile Material Protection, Control, and Accounting

Jessica Eve Stern

Ironically, some of the changes that have allowed us to reduce the world's stockpile of nuclear weapons have made our nonproliferation efforts harder. The breakup of the Soviet Union left nuclear material dispersed throughout the newly independent states. The potential for theft of nuclear materials has increased. We face the prospect of organized criminals entering the nuclear smuggling business. Add to this volatile mix the fact that a lump of plutonium the size of a soda can is enough to build a bomb, and the urgency of the effort to stop the spread of nuclear materials should be clear.[1]

From the beginning of the Atomic Age, the nuclear weapons states assumed that the difficulty of producing or acquiring fissile materials would constrain nuclear proliferation. This is a key premise of the international safeguards system, and has shaped the debate on nonproliferation policy. Widespread knowledge of weapons design has increased the relative importance of protecting fissile materials from theft, but experts fear that worldwide safeguards may not be adequate to the task. This problem of inadequate security for fissile materials is particularly acute in the newly independent states (NIS) of the former Soviet Union, where social and economic change has outpaced

---

1. U.S. President Bill Clinton, address to the Nixon Center for Peace and Freedom Conference, Washington, D.C., March 2, 1995.

The author wishes to thank the Council on Foreign Relations, the Hoover Institution, and the MacArthur Foundation for funding this research; Nicholas Burns and Chip Blacker for providing encouragement to pursue these subjects; Jerry Dzakowicz for constant support; Matthew Bunn and Frank von Hippel for providing tutorials and the constant motivation to do more; the members of the MPC&A and Nuclear Smuggling Interagency Working Groups for insights on how government works; the many Russian and U.S. government officials who consented to be interviewed and provided comments on this chapter, especially William Alberque of the Department of Energy; and Tatiana Krasnopevtseva, for helping to formulate and translate questions for interviews in Moscow.

safeguards reform. Russian officials claim that the potential for insider theft has increased at many nuclear facilities. Kilogram quantities of stolen weapons-usable highly enriched uranium (HEU) have been recovered in Russia and in Europe, demonstrating the urgency of improving nuclear safeguards worldwide.

An ideal nuclear security system would contain three basic elements:

- *physical protection:* barriers, sensors, and alarms intended to deter, delay, and defend against both intruders gaining access and insiders removing material;

- *material control:* locked vaults for storage of nuclear materials, portal monitors equipped to detect nuclear materials to prevent workers from walking off the site with nuclear material in their pockets, continuous monitoring of nuclear-material storage sites with tamper-proof cameras, seals, and alarms, and prohibition of access to sites containing sensitive materials unless personnel enter in pairs, a procedure known as the two-man rule; and

- *material accounting:* a regularly updated measured inventory of nuclear weapons-usable material, based on regular measurements of material arriving, leaving, lost to waste, and remaining within the facility, including a measurement control program to ensure the accuracy of the measurement equipment.

These three elements together are referred to as material protection, control, and accounting (MPC&A). Other desirable elements of a nuclear security system include a system of personnel reliability (background checks, training, and reliable salaries for nuclear custodians) and regulation and inspection by an outside agency with real enforcement powers.

Assisting the NIS to reduce the dangers of nuclear proliferation resulting from the breakup of the Soviet Union has become one of the highest priority tasks on the U.S.-NIS nuclear agenda.[2] This chapter

---

2. As is explained below, beginning with the Fiscal Year (FY) 1996 budget request, U.S.-NIS MPC&A projects for nuclear materials will no longer be funded by the Department of Defense (DOD) Nunn-Lugar Cooperative Threat Reduction (CTR) budget. They will instead be funded out of Department of Energy (DOE) funds.

considers the extent to which U.S.-NIS cooperative programs for fissile material protection, control, and accounting, including joint projects between the United States and NIS governments and between U.S. and Russian national laboratories, have achieved this goal.

In order to make the assessment, it is necessary to appreciate the disarray in the NIS nuclear security system. This chapter begins by analyzing inadequacies in Russia's nuclear security, focusing especially on the inventory system. Similar problems exist at the dozen or so nuclear facilities located elsewhere in the NIS, but this assessment focuses on Russia because many more nuclear facilities, and a far greater quantity of weapons-usable nuclear material, are located there. This chapter then describes and evaluates the successes and key problems of ongoing joint efforts to increase NIS nuclear security, including U.S.-NIS government-to-government MPC&A programs and the U.S.-Russian lab-to-lab program. Of particular concern in this assessment are potential threats to the continued viability of the programs, including bureaucratic issues on both sides.

This chapter concludes that the MPC&A program is on the right track, but that success will depend on how quickly the projects are completed. As one proponent of the program inside the U.S. government has asked, "We are making good progress, overcoming many bureaucratic obstacles as they arise, but will we succeed soon enough to prevent something terrible from happening?" That is the question "that keeps me awake at night."[3] Ultimately, success will depend on four additional variables: (1) bureaucratic politics, including the ability of both sides to resist taking what is now a highly successful, flexible, but somewhat messy multipronged approach and transforming it into a single, comprehensive, and centrally-managed government-to-government MPC&A program; (2) the ability of NIS partners to overcome suspicions about U.S. motives, which hamper cooperation; (3) the proper long-term implementation, operation, and maintenance of upgraded MPC&A systems by NIS partners, which in turn depends on the development of a safeguards culture in these countries; and (4)

Conceptually, however, MPC&A remains part of Nunn-Lugar and must be addressed in any comprehensive treatment of the Nunn-Lugar initiative. MPC&A for warheads remains a DOD Nunn-Lugar program.

3. Author's interview with U.S. government official who requested anonymity, December 1995.

the U.S. administration's greater involvement in educating the American public and the Congress about the importance of these programs, in order to ensure their continued funding.

Inadequate MPC&A for Nuclear Materials

The Soviet system for protecting nuclear materials, which functioned effectively for five decades of Soviet rule, "was not designed for a democratic state," according to an official with the Russian Ministry of Atomic Energy (Minatom).[4] It was designed with two objectives: preventing terrorist attacks and keeping American spies from acquiring nuclear secrets. "Nobody even considered the possibility of workers stealing nuclear materials," this official acknowledged. Another Minatom official, in a recent published account, has described a system based on "regulations and ordinances which either no longer are in place or are not effective, and upon military discipline and a sense of responsibility which no longer exist."[5]

Civilian research facilities, even those that process or store weapons-grade materials, were not considered strategically important targets for potential foreign espionage and thus have only minimal security. Since the principal purpose of the Soviet system was to keep out American spies, and since many of the people who ran that system are still on the job, it is not surprising that American experts are viewed with suspicion. Convincing Minatom officials that Americans touring and inspecting Russian nuclear sites are part of the answer, rather than the problem, "has been a difficult sell that has required a prolonged period of socialization," in the words of a U.S. government official familiar with this process.

The Russian system of accounting for nuclear material was developed to maximize quality and quantity of the material produced. Inventories were conducted once a year using two forms, one for the

---

4. Author's interview with Minatom official who requested not to be identified, November 7, 1995. Much of the material in this chapter is based on interviews in Moscow between November 3 and 15, 1995, with officials of Minatom, the Federal Atomic Inspectorate, and other Russian nuclear security agencies who asked not to be identified by name.

5. Mark Hibbs, "Physical Protection Reportedly Eroding at Minatom's 10 'Closed Cities' in Russia," *Nucleonics Week*, January 2, 1995, p. 13.

Ministry of Finance and one for Minatom. For direct-use (weapons-usable) materials, inventories might be taken more frequently, depending on the site, according to officials at Minatom and at the Federal Atomic Inspectorate of Russia, known by two Russian acronyms, Gosatomnadzor or GAN.

Russian officials explain that the philosophy of the Soviet inventory system, which stressed production targets rather than security, led to practices that they now believe must be changed in order to bring the system up to international standards. First, as a rule, input materials or feed stocks are not measured; only output is measured.

A second important distinguishing feature of the inventory method is the system of "allowed losses." Officials at GAN and at Minatom explain that they do not measure "material unaccounted for" (MUF), as long as it is within a certain range. Someone who knows the quantity of allowed losses could steal a significant quantity of HEU or plutonium, provided he did so slowly, staying within that limit over months or years.

To illustrate the "allowed losses" system, one Minatom official describes a similar regime for truck drivers responsible for transporting vodka from the production plant to the store. The Ministry of Finance (MOF) instituted a system that allowed for a certain number of broken bottles per truckload, based on the average losses per truckload for all shipments. A truck driver was allowed to arrive at a store with $N-X$ bottles, where N was the truck's capacity and X was the allowed number of losses, say four bottles for illustrative purposes. No one was concerned whether those bottles were broken or stolen, as long as the amount of vodka delivered to the store was at least $N-X$. "You can be sure," this official said, "that every truck driver was exceedingly careful, and that those four bottles went straight into the truck drivers' pockets." The analogy illustrates the systemic problems in Russia's nuclear inventory procedures that, unless corrected, could continue to encourage thefts of material. In the words of this same Minatom official:

The system we need to put in place for a proper nuclear materials inventory is one in which the precise amount of missing or extra material is recorded. We cannot use the Ministry of Finance system of allowed losses. We need to bring our system up to the level of international standards. But nobody in this country has any idea of how to conduct a thorough inventory of all nuclear material because we have never done it.

There are only a handful of people in Russia who understand the concept of safeguards.... They are scientists who have worked for the IAEA. [6]

Several officials have recounted in interviews the case of nuclear material theft in Podolsk, in which a worker stole one and a half kilograms of HEU over a long period of time. The missing HEU was never detected during inventories because the worker knew how to stay within the allowed losses limit.[7] One official from the Russian National Security Council also confirmed in a recent interview what other Russian officials have said in the past: to ensure their ability to meet production quotas under the Soviet system, nuclear facilities often produced extra plutonium to have on hand in case of an inventory shortfall in future years. As much as ten percent of production might have been diverted without being entered into the accounting system, this official explained.[8]

This practice of excess production was not considered dangerous from the standpoint of theft since there was no market in Russia for HEU or plutonium. Now, however, there is a growing perception of a lucrative market for nuclear materials. These secret caches of material, likely to be found at many production sites, present a real danger in the current economic environment in Russia.

---

6. Author's interview with Minatom official who requested not to be identified, November 7, 1995.

7. Even the best possible inventory system (with no system of allowed losses) would not solve the problem of the determined, well-informed thief who knows to spread his thievery out over a long period of time, always staying within the technical limits of the accounting system. According to the Head of the Department of Arms Control and Nonproliferation of Russia's Federal Intelligence Service (SVR), General Gennadii Evstafiev, "No accounting system can detect losses of less than one percent of the total inventory. This is why it is important to install a comprehensive MPC&A system," that is, one that includes not only accounting, but also systems to detect attempts to remove even small amounts of nuclear material. Author's interview with General Evstafiev, November 14, 1995.

8. Author's interview with a senior member of Russian President Boris Yeltsin's National Security Council staff, November 8, 1995.

Inadequate Material Control and Accounting and Warhead Safety

Many (but not all) Russian and U.S. officials are more sanguine about warhead security than about nuclear materials security.[9] There is a basic "guards, gates, and guns" approach to warhead security. Unlike materials, in the words of one U.S. government official, "you can't use uncertainties in the accounting system to steal warheads, and you can't put them under your overcoat. It's clearly much harder to steal a warhead than to steal the materials to make one." [10]

Nonetheless, Russia's transition from an authoritarian, command economy to a struggling, chaotic democracy is subjecting the warhead security system to stresses it was not designed to withstand. Undisciplined, understaffed, and underpaid, the Russian military is facing a crisis. Troops desperate for hard currency routinely sell conventional weapons to private consumers, often with the *mafiya* as middleman. A new openness in Russia has reduced the distance between personnel with access to nuclear weapons and "those who may hope to profit from the theft of a nuclear weapon," a U.S. intelligence official has testified. Russian security procedures were not designed to counter well-planned insider threats to weapons.[11]

Stanislav Lunev, a former colonel in Russia's Military Intelligence Agency, the GRU, wrote recently that he believes some tactical weapons were lost in the immediate aftermath of the breakup of the Soviet Union:

Practically all army divisions located in the former Soviet republics and abroad had missile battalions and other military units capable of using tactical nuclear weapons. But nobody knows where these weapons went after the disintegration of the USSR. The Russian government doesn't know either, but still insists that there is nothing to worry about.[12]

---

9. See, for example, David Osias, testimony before the Senate Foreign Relations Committee, Subcommittee on European Affairs, August 22, 1995.

10. Author's interview with U.S. government official who requested anonymity, December 1995.

11. David Osias, testimony before the Senate Foreign Relations Committee, Subcommittee on European Affairs, August 22, 1995.

12. Stanislav Lunev, "Russia's Nuclear Safety Problems," *Prism*, Part 1, Vol. 1, No. 22 (October 20, 1995).

Lunev also claims that the Russian government is depending on custodians who are paid inadequately and whose role models are "corrupt senior officers" to protect the warheads from theft. Russian officials have repeatedly denied that any warheads are missing. U.S. officials also doubt the veracity of Lunev's claims, but, as one knowledgeable analyst has acknowledged, "we really don't know what to believe."[13]

In a November 1995 interview, General Evgenii Maslin, head of Strategic Forces of the Main Directorate of the Russian Ministry of Defense (MOD), repeated his assurances that an inventory of all Russian warheads, in which seals are removed and the warheads are physically inspected, takes place two times every year. However, a Minatom official who requested anonymity has claimed that the seals are removed only to assess the electronic equipment inside the warhead, not to verify the presence of nuclear material. One could easily replace a warhead with an "imitator," and the substitution would not be noticed for many months because the seals are of poor quality and can be falsified. In the view of this official, the MOD does not understand the requirements for a high-confidence inventory and instead uses a paper-based system prone to human error, in which warheads are counted *na pal'tsakh* (on the fingers).[14] Moreover, the system is not designed to deter insider threats. Like the system for materials, it was designed with two principal objectives: to keep out Western spies and to prevent intruders from obtaining access to the weapons.

With rare exceptions, the Russian government has officially denied that nuclear warheads are vulnerable to terrorist attack or to theft. Nonetheless, the government has taken steps to remove nuclear weapons from the volatile Caucasus region and to consolidate nuclear warheads in storage from over 600 sites in 1989, to 200 sites in 1991, to

---

13. Author's interview with U.S. government official who requested anonymity, December 1995.

14. Author's interview with Minatom official who requested anonymity, November 14, 1995.

fewer than 100 in 1995.[15] Moreover, General Maslin and other officials have admitted concerns about the security of the warheads in transit. For example, in a 1995 account, General Maslin is reported to have observed,

What is theoretically possible and [for] what we must always be prepared is train robbery, attempts to seize nuclear weapons in transit. We ran some modeling exercises at our facilities [to test our warhead security system].... And I must tell you frankly that as a result of those exercises, I became greatly concerned about a question that we had never even thought of before: What if such acts were to be undertaken by people who have worked with nuclear weapons in the past? For example, by people dismissed from our structures, social malcontents, embittered individuals?[16]

Russia's troubled economy, the government's inability adequately to pay custodians of both nuclear materials and warheads, the rise of organized crime and corruption, the KGB's loss of absolute power, and the absence of a "safeguards culture" have led to a dangerous situation *vis-à-vis* protection of nuclear materials and, perhaps to a lesser extent, of warheads.

The Problem of Nuclear Theft: Distinguishing Rumor from Fact

As early as 1991, Kurt Campbell, Ashton Carter, Steven Miller, and Charles Zraket warned that:

Economic disorder within the Soviet nuclear weapons complex ... creates a potential source of nuclear proliferation outside the Soviet Union unlike any ever faced by the nonproliferation regime. Nuclear materials, sensitive non-nuclear components of nuclear weapons, the talents of skilled bomb-

---

15. The figure of 600 storage sites for 1989 is from the testimony of Gordon Oehler, director of the Nonproliferation Center, Central Intelligence Agency, before the Senate Armed Services Committee, January 31, 1995, Senate Hearing 104-35, p. 4. In an August 1995 discussion with U.S. officials, General Maslin noted that there had been 200 sites in 1991.

16. Vladimir Orlov, "A Threat of Nuclear Terrorism Exists in Russia," *Moskovskie novosti*, No. 44 (June 25, 1995), p. 14.

builders, and even entire nuclear weapons might find their way onto world markets. [17]

Since the dissolution of the Soviet Union, increasing U.S. and international attention has focused on the question of clandestine transfers of fissile or other nuclear materials from poorly guarded nuclear facilities in former Soviet republics to foreign states or terrorist groups. A key analytical dilemma, however, has been to determine the real dimensions of the nuclear smuggling problem. As two experts on confirmed and alleged smuggling incidents have observed in a recent assessment, there are several difficulties in determining the scale and severity of the problem:

First, nuclear trafficking is sufficiently serious that intelligence agencies are rarely willing to confirm more than the broadest outlines.... Second, Russian sensitivities and the belief in some quarters in Moscow that the danger is being artificially exaggerated in order to put Russia's nuclear weapons under international control have added another element of uncertainty.... Compounding these difficulties is the prevalence of numerous 'con men' and 'scam artists' in the market. A high profile black market provides many opportunities for fraud.[18]

Most reports of alleged smuggling of nuclear weapons or weapons-usable components have been unreliable.[19] Nonetheless, a number of

---

17. Kurt Campbell, Ashton B. Carter, Steven E. Miller, and Charles A. Zraket, *Soviet Nuclear Fission: Control of the Nuclear Arsenal in a Disintegrating Soviet Union*, CSIA Studies in International Security (Cambridge, Mass.: Center for Science and International Affairs [CSIA], Harvard University, 1991), p. 125. Conversations between Ashton Carter and Senators Nunn and Lugar in the formulation of this book were a major factor behind the genesis of the Nunn-Lugar Program.

18. Phil Williams and Paul N. Woessner, "Nuclear Materials Trafficking: An Interim Assessment," *Transnational Organized Crime*, Vol. 1, No. 2 (Summer 1995), pp. 206–238.

19. Several technical aspects of the nuclear smuggling problem have been muddled in press reports. One of these is the distinction between nonfissile radioactive isotopes and fissile material used to make nuclear weapons. The former include medical isotopes which, although extremely toxic, cannot be used to create a nuclear detonation in a bomb. A second important distinction, relating to the isotopic purity of fissile material, is between "weapons-grade" material and so-called "weapons-usable" material, which could be used, albeit less efficiently, in a nuclear weapon. Strictly speaking, HEU is uranium that has been enriched to

reported smuggling cases warrant concern. The most serious cases are those few that have involved fissile materials that could be used to make nuclear devices.[20] While no single known case has involved enough material to manufacture a bomb, kilogram quantities of stolen

---

greater than 20 percent U-235. "Weapons grade" HEU refers to HEU that has been enriched to 90 percent U-235 or higher. U.S. and Russian bomb designers typically use weapons-grade fissile material in order to ensure a high degree of weapon reliability and efficiency, which also allows design of smaller weapons more easily transported by plane or in a missile warhead. However, HEU enriched to between 20 and 90 percent U-235, according to unclassified International Atomic Energy Agency (IAEA) data, can also be used in a weapon, although a lower level of enrichment will require a larger amount of material to make a detonable weapon, resulting in a proportionately heavier and larger weapon. Similarly, "weapons-grade" plutonium typically contains no more than seven percent Pu-240. However, relatively less pure plutonium, including reactor-grade plutonium, can be used to make a bomb, albeit with an assured yield of only one to a few kilotons for a simple, Nagasaki-type design, and a higher, but still reduced yield for more sophisticated designs. An understanding of these distinctions helps place the smuggling problem in some perspective: it is not as bad as many journalists would have the public believe, but it is far worse than many Russian government officials are willing to admit.

20. Often overlooked are the many cases of stolen medical isotopes and other radiation sources. These incidents are discounted because radioisotopes cannot be used to make detonable nuclear devices; MPC&A programs cannot possibly address the threat they pose. But they can be used by terrorists to draw attention to their cause, to wreak havoc, and to terrorize civilians. Shamil Basaev, the leader of the Chechen group who took more than 1,000 hospital patients hostage in June 1995, has claimed credit for placing a packet of radioactive cesium in Izmailovski Park in Moscow, a popular recreation spot for families, frequented by tourists as well as by Muscovites. Cesium-137, a radioactive isotope used in the treatment of cancer, is a waste product of nuclear reactors with a relatively long half-life, and areas contaminated with it require extensive cleanup. It can be absorbed into the food chain and is carcinogenic. Cesium is used in industry in photoelectric cells, for measuring the thickness or density of materials, and in gamma-radiography.

A related concern is the possibility of terrorism directed against nuclear power plants or other civilian facilities. Dzhokhar Dudaev, the former leader of the rebellious republic of Chechnya, who was killed in spring 1996, frequently threatened to attack Russian nuclear power plants or to commit other acts of nuclear terrorism. The Russian government formed an interagency group to address concerns about nuclear terrorism, including Dudaev's threats. The group ordered additional safeguards to be put in place at power plants, for example, but the effort was not serious, according to a Minatom official who requested anonymity. An intelligent terrorist could easily circumvent the beefed-up controls, he said.

weapons-usable HEU have been seized both inside and outside the Russian Federation. Examples include one and a half kilograms of 90 percent enriched HEU stolen from the Luch production facility at Podolsk in October 1992; nearly two kilograms of 36 percent enriched HEU stolen from a naval base in Andreeva Guba in July 1993; four and a half kilograms of 20 percent enriched HEU naval fuel stolen from the Murmansk shipyard in late 1993; three separate caches of weapons-usable HEU and plutonium, ranging in size from less than a gram to 350 grams, seized in Germany in the summer of 1994; and nearly three kilograms of 87.7 percent enriched HEU, seized in Prague in December 1994.[21]

Western officials believe that some of the materials seized abroad may also have come from Russia, although Russian officials deny this. The technical distinction between "weapons-grade" and "weapons-usable" nuclear materials has been an important issue in U.S.-Russian discussions about the smuggling problem. Russian officials have repeatedly denied that any smuggling case has involved weapons-grade uranium, which according to the strict definition, is uranium enriched to greater than 90 percent or plutonium with less than seven percent Pu-240. However, all the cases cited above involved nuclear materials which in fact could have been used in a nuclear weapon, albeit with a less efficient yield than weapons-grade material.

ARE THERE BUYERS FOR STOLEN NUCLEAR MATERIALS?

U.S. and Russian government officials claim that there is little evidence to suggest that countries or terrorist groups are actively seeking black-market nuclear materials.[22] This apparent lack of evidence notwithstanding, the prospect that terrorists or irresponsible leaders could acquire nuclear material from poorly protected facilities in the NIS is

---

21. For an excellent analysis of these incidents, see William Potter, "Before the Deluge? Assessing the Threat of Nuclear Leakage from the Post-Soviet States," *Arms Control Today*, October 1995, pp. 9–16. Experts speculate that the 0.8 gram cache of 87 percent enriched HEU seized in Germany may have come from the same source as the consignments seized in Prague, which were of similar isotopic content.

22. Thieves of nuclear materials tend to be amateurs who have no specific buyer in mind. Russian SVR General Gennadii Evstafiev has observed, "As a rule, the thieves hide the material with extreme care, often for a long time, and only then do they begin to search for a buyer." General Gennadii Evstafiev, "Nuclear Mafia in Russia: Truth and Myths," *Vek*, No. 37 (September 22–28, 1995), pp. 1, 10.

cause for serious alarm. One Russian official has privately expressed grave concerns on this issue: "I, like many nuclear custodians, would know exactly how to go about stealing nuclear materials. I am very afraid about the future—that a terrorist group either inside or outside Russia—will learn details about our poor level of MPC&A, the terrible economic situation ... that a group will find a way to pay off the relevant officials. Business in Russia is actually legalized stealing. Nearly everyone is corrupt; nearly anyone can be bought."[23]

There have been cases that appear to link buyers with sellers. Reports began to surface shortly after the dissolution of the Soviet Union that Iran had purchased nuclear weapons components, and even intact warheads, from Kazakstan. The U.S. government looked into the reports and concluded that they had no basis in fact.[24] Subsequently, reports emerged that Iran had approached Kazakstan in connection with enriched uranium located at the Ulbinsky (Ulba) Metallurgy Plant, a nuclear reactor fuel fabrication facility near Ust-Kamenogorsk in northeastern Kazakstan.[25] However, the veracity of these claims, made by a number of U.S. government officials, including Secretary of State Warren Christopher, has been the subject of some dispute. U.S. government experts, in confidential interviews, have recounted Kazakstani official claims that Iran had approached the Ulba plant about a possible purchase of low-enriched uranium (LEU), not HEU. In another reported case, Turkish police apprehended a professor in the act of selling two and a half kilograms of uranium of uncertain enrichment to three Iranians, reportedly agents for Sawama, the Iranian Secret Service. According to Turkish police, the uranium was brought

---

23. Author's interview with Minatom official who requested anonymity, November 14, 1995.

24. James Wyllie, "Iran Quest for Security and Influence," *Jane's Intelligence Review*, Vol. 5, No. 7 (July 1, 1993), p. 311.

25. In 1994, nearly 600 kilograms of HEU were subsequently airlifted from this poorly secured site to safe storage in the United States in a joint U.S.-Kazakstani operation dubbed Project Sapphire. For a complete description of this operation, the events that surrounded it, and the possible Iranian connection, see Chapter 16 by William Potter in this volume. See also Mark Hibbs, "Kazaks Say Iran Sought LEU for VVER Fuel, Not 'Sapphire' HEU," *Nuclear Fuel*, July 17, 1995, pp. 11–12.

to Turkey by visiting Russians.[26] The accuracy of this case has also been called into question, however. More recently, Konrad Porzner, head of Germany's Federal Intelligence Service (BND), told a German parliamentary committee in January 1996 that of the 32 cases of interested buyers registered by German intelligence in 1995, 16 involved states. Moreover, Porzner testified that he had definitive proof that Iran and Iraq had been seeking nuclear materials on the black market. The Iranian government has denied the charge.[27]

Although it remains unclear whether any transactions of fissile or other nuclear materials from former Soviet facilities have actually taken place, the risk of such transfers clearly exists. The consequences of this problem are sufficiently grave to warrant immediate action. The next section describes recent and ongoing cooperative efforts to address this threat.[28]

---

26. *Ankara Anatolia*, in English, 10:15 GMT, October 6, 1993, as reported in an unclassified cable, serial TA06 10103193; Istanbul *Turkiye*, in Turkish, October 7, 1993, as reported in an unclassified cable, serial NC0910082 693. Details of this incident are also based on a conversation by the author with Ozgen Acar, an editorial and special investigative reporter for *Cumhuriyet*, a major Turkish daily paper.

27. "Iran, Iraq Secretly Buying on Nuclear Market," Reuters World Service, January 18, 1996; "Iran Objects Over German Nuclear Charges," Reuters World Service, January 25, 1996. Czech press reports on the ongoing trial in Prague (in connection with the December 1994 seizure in that city) have revealed that, according to Czech police, the seized uranium had been obtained by Russian organized criminals and was ultimately bound for a country that was trying to develop nuclear weapons. Czech papers reported that the investigation had not yet confirmed that the radioactive cargo was bound for Iraq, as reported by the Italian newspaper *Corriere della Sera*. See CTK National News Wire, May 7, 1996. If these reports are true, they would directly contradict statements by both U.S. and Russian government officials that organized crime is not involved in nuclear smuggling and that nuclear thieves are amateurs—usually workers involved in opportunistic thefts.

28. The U.S. government has a comprehensive program to combat nuclear smuggling in addition to programs to enhance fissile materials protection, but space limitations preclude discussion of anti-smuggling initiatives in this chapter.

U.S.-NIS Joint Efforts to Address Inadequate Nuclear Security

The Nunn-Lugar Cooperative Threat Reduction (CTR) Program has been the Clinton administration's principal tool for working with the NIS to improve nuclear security. The original Nunn-Lugar legislation authorized the Department of Defense (DOD) to help former Soviet States to: (1) destroy weapons of mass destruction; (2) store and transport weapons slated for destruction; and (3) reduce the dangers of proliferation. The MPC&A projects, originally funded under the Nunn-Lugar Program, are the most important instrument for reducing the dangers of proliferation associated with weapons dismantlement and inadequate nuclear safeguards.[29]

Since 1992, the original Nunn-Lugar MPC&A program has evolved and expanded into several independent initiatives: the government-to-government MPC&A program (originally funded from DOD's Nunn-Lugar budget); the lab-to-lab program (principally funded from the budget of the Department of Energy but also receiving some funds from DOD); the DOE-GAN program (a new program funded under DOE's budget); and the warhead security program (funded from DOD's Nunn-Lugar budget). This section begins by describing the White House's involvement in the MPC&A initiative and then describes each of the four components of the program.

In January 1994, Presidents Clinton and Yeltsin agreed that reducing the risk of nuclear theft should be a "high priority," and agreed to expand cooperation to include fissile materials at both civilian and military facilities. In September 1994, they endorsed expanded cooperation, and in May 1995, they directed U.S. Vice President Al Gore

---

29. Beginning with the FY 1996 budget request, MPC&A projects for nuclear materials will no longer be funded out of DOD's Nunn-Lugar CTR budget. Instead, they will be funded by DOE. At the time of this writing, MPC&A projects paid for by DOD funds include: (1) the lab-to-lab program for FY 1995, which was funded by $15 million transferred from DOD to DOE in a one-time, top-line transfer; (2) government-to-government MPC&A projects through FY 1995, which were funded by $30 million allocated to DOD between FY 1992 and FY 1994 for the (then) Nunn-Lugar MPC&A program; and (3) some of the non-Russian NIS MPC&A projects. DOE is now the executive agent for the entire MPC&A effort for nuclear materials. Warhead transport and security remain a Nunn-Lugar program, however. Author's interviews with DOD and DOE officials, November 1995.

and Russian Prime Minister Viktor Chernomyrdin to provide a status report on progress in U.S.-Russian MPC&A cooperation.

After the START Treaty entered into force in December 1994, President Clinton began to focus surprisingly intensively on fissile material security issues. He raised the issue repeatedly in conversations with President Yeltsin and other foreign leaders, as well as in formal summit meetings. President Yeltsin responded by proposing a G7+1 conference[30] on nuclear safety and security, which took place in April 1996. The White House also established a Nuclear Smuggling Response Group, overseen by the Department of State, to coordinate U.S. government responses to significant smuggling incidents. On September 28, 1995, President Clinton signed a decision directive that called for an acceleration of joint U.S.-NIS programs to enhance security and accounting of nuclear materials and weapons, and an expansion in diplomatic, law enforcement, and intelligence efforts aimed at stopping nuclear smuggling.

THE GOVERNMENT-TO-GOVERNMENT MPC&A PROGRAM IN RUSSIA

On September 2, 1993, the United States and Russia signed a Nunn-Lugar implementation agreement that included up to $10 million for MPC&A activities. This agreement became known as the "government-to-government" MPC&A agreement to distinguish it from the less formal "lab-to-lab" agreements that were negotiated in separate fora, described below. Other government-to-government MPC&A cooperation agreements were subsequently signed with Belarus, Kazakstan, and Ukraine.

The purpose of the government-to-government program is to strengthen, in a timely manner, NIS national systems of MPC&A. MPC&A systems provide the capability to deter, detect, delay, and respond to possible adversarial acts or other unauthorized use of nuclear material and, if necessary, aid in recovering nuclear materials.[31]

---

30. As an observer at the June 1995 G7 summit in Halifax, Yeltsin proposed that a G7 summit convene in the spring of 1996 in Moscow, in commemoration of the tenth anniversary of the Chernobyl accident. The characterization "G7+1" was used by Russia prior to the April 1996 summit to strengthen its position as an up-and-coming partner of equal status with the G7 states.

31. Information provided by Department of Energy officials, December 1995.

Initially Russian government officials were highly suspicious of U.S. motives, and were reluctant to allow the U.S. side access to sensitive sites. The two sides had fairly different expectations. According to one DOE official familiar with the process, the U.S. side had hoped "to begin work right away and finish as soon as possible." The United States was forced to moderate its hopes, especially about the pace of the program, in the months and years that followed.

Russia at first agreed to allow MPC&A cooperation only at civilian sites; military sites were to be off limits. Moreover, Russia initially objected to cooperation with the United States at any sites, civilian or military, involving weapons-usable materials (plutonium or HEU that can be used to make nuclear weapons). Russia first suggested two demonstration MPC&A systems at the LEU lines at Elektrostal and at Novosibirsk. LEU does not pose a significant proliferation threat, however, and the U.S. side was determined to achieve more, insisting that security be improved at sites where weapons-usable materials were most susceptible to theft or diversion. However, the Russians were understandably reluctant to allow U.S. experts to inspect security vulnerabilities at these sites, many of which had broken-down fences and wholly inadequate controls. The suspicion that the United States had ulterior motives—to collect intelligence about Russian nuclear weapons programs—was extremely strong then and persists even now. After further discussions, the two sides agreed to an interim arrangement that included a single demonstration system at Elektrostal, as well as reciprocal visits to plutonium storage facilities at Hanford and Mayak as a first step toward greater cooperation.

After extensive negotiations, in January 1995, the MPC&A agreement was amended to include an additional $20 million in Nunn-Lugar funds, and an agreement by Russia to allow access to sites housing weapons-usable nuclear materials. Eventually the two sides agreed to cooperate at Obninsk, Dmitrovgrad, Podolsk, Mayak, and the HEU line at Elektrostal. However, delays and broken promises continued even through the first six months of 1995. The most frustrating problem was that, despite the January agreement, U.S. experts were repeatedly denied permission to carry out site surveys at agreed facilities, a necessary first step for putting MPC&A upgrades in place. Out of $30 million allocated to MPC&A between 1992 and 1994, the administration had spent only about $1.5 million as late as June 1995. The government-to-government MPC&A program appeared to be in serious trouble.

A long-awaited breakthrough was reached at a meeting of the Gore-Chernomyrdin Commission in June 1995. By the end of that session, DOE Secretary Hazel O'Leary and Minatom Minister Viktor Mikhailov signed an agreement calling for site surveys at all five of the agreed government-to-government program sites, thereby shifting the program into much higher gear. Background discussions between U.S. and Russian officials revealed that the delay in the first half of 1995 had been due in part to a bureaucratic battle within Minatom over responsibility for MPC&A, which had been largely resolved. Within two months, surveys were completed at all five Russian sites.[32] Since that time, a number of MPC&A activities have been ongoing at these facilities:

- U.S. and Russian experts conducted site surveys of Dmitrovgrad in August 1995 and again in February 1996, which included sites containing HEU and plutonium. Contracts were concluded for the first phase of the project, which included determining material balance areas. By the end of 1996, installation of physical protection upgrades was to be under way at all four Dmitrovgrad sites.

- At the Production Association Machine Building Plant at Elektrostal, DOE provided upgraded MPC&A equipment and MPC&A training at the LEU facility. Agreement was reached to begin upgrading MPC&A at the HEU fuel fabrication line as well. A joint working group agreed to strive to complete the upgrades by the end of 1996.

- At the Institute of Physics and Power Engineering (IPPE) at Obninsk, the two sides agreed to establish a Russian Safeguards Training and Methodology Center to train Russian MPC&A specialists. This is arguably the most important element of the entire MPC&A program in that it will help establish a safeguards culture in Russia. U.S. and Russian experts have also developed a plan to expand MPC&A cooperation at Obninsk, focusing on physical protection and access control.

---

32. Ibid.

- At the Luch Scientific Production Association in Podolsk, the two sides began upgrading MPC&A at two facility sites that house HEU. These upgrades were expected to be completed by the end of 1996.

- At the Mayak Chemical Metallurgical Combine at Chelyabinsk-65, experts have begun planning MPC&A upgrades for plutonium reprocessing sites. The two sides agreed to install MC&A equipment and physical protection system upgrades by the end of 1996.

- The Novosibirsk Chemical Concentrates Plant, Beloyarsk Institute for Energy Technologies (NIKIET), Beloyarsk Nuclear Power Plant, and Khlopin Radium Institute were added to the program at the sixth meeting of the Gore-Chernomyrdin Commission in January 1996. Initial site surveys were conducted at these facilities in May 1996.

By 2002, DOE hopes to have cooperative programs in place for nuclear materials in each of four sectors in Russia: the Minatom civil complex; the Minatom weapons complex; facilities processing fresh naval fuel; and non-Minatom civil nuclear facilities, such as research reactors. DOE plans to alter the program slightly in the near future according to the following rationale: civil facilities will be covered under the government-to-government program, the weapons complex will be covered under the lab-to-lab program, and non-Minatom civil facilities will be covered principally under the GAN program. DOE and the Russian Navy are working out a program to secure fresh fuel for naval reactors and icebreakers under the lab-to-lab program. DOE officials explain that the MPC&A program is designed to help Russia through a difficult transition until its nascent safeguards culture is more fully developed. These officials are hopeful that, by 2002, the two sides together will have put in place MPC&A upgrades at all of the most vulnerable nuclear sites, and that the program will then move on to a second phase, characterized by joint experiments, some of which are likely to be related to nonproliferation.

NON-RUSSIAN NIS
In general, government-to-government MPC&A projects have run more smoothly in NIS other than Russia. Compared to Russia, there are fewer nuclear facilities in these states, housing less nuclear material, and with

fewer bureaucratic obstacles to overcome. DOE has encountered some problems, however. In Ukraine and Kazakstan, some difficulty was encountered with state licensing of MPC&A technologies to be installed at nuclear facilities. Other problems experienced throughout the NIS relate to customs duties, taxes, and protection of proprietary information.

As discussed below, MPC&A programs are under way at four sites in Ukraine, four sites in Kazakstan, and one site in Belarus. DOE is also cooperating with other International Atomic Energy Agency members to upgrade MPC&A at sites in Latvia (Salaspils Institute of Physics), Lithuania (Ignalina Nuclear Power Plant), and Uzbekistan (Tashkent Institute of Nuclear Physics). There has been substantial progress at the site in Belarus, and the project in Latvia was completed in March 1996. In Georgia, DOE conducted a physical protection site survey in January 1996. While no decision has yet been made with respect to the permanent disposition of the material at this site, physical protection upgrades were implemented in May 1996. The programs for Ukraine, Kazakstan, and Belarus, unlike the programs for Latvia, Lithuania, Uzbekistan, and Georgia, have been funded principally under DOD's Nunn-Lugar Program. Future work will be carried out with DOE funding, with the one-time exception of $15 million from FY 1996 CTR funds for a project in Kazakstan.[33] DOE now has joint MPC&A programs in place at all sites known to house weapons-usable material in the non-Russian NIS.

UKRAINE. An MPC&A implementation agreement was signed with Ukraine in December 1993. Work is proceeding or planned at four sites.

- Kharkiv Institute for Physics and Technology. DOE completed a physical protection assessment report in September 1995, and has supplied hand-held metal and special nuclear material detectors, computer systems and accounting software. The project is expected to be complete by the end of 1997.

- Kiev Institute for Nuclear Research. The project includes provision of a variety of MPC&A equipment, including hand-held metal and special nuclear material detection equipment, portal monitors,

---

33. Ibid.

communications equipment, computer systems, a material accounting software system prototype, and seals. DOE provided MPC&A training in September 1995. A central alarm station, access control equipment, and intrusion detection equipment will soon be installed. Physical protection upgrades were expected to be complete by October 1, 1996, and MPC&A upgrades by November 1, 1997.

- South Ukraine Nuclear Power Plant. DOE has delivered a variety of MPC&A equipment (the same list as for Kiev above, as well as a personnel badge system) and continues to purchase and install MC&A equipment upgrades. Physical protection upgrades are in the design stage and are expected to be complete by late 1997.

- Sevastopol Naval Institute. A site survey was postponed due to negotiations over the future of the Black Sea Fleet and, until recently, complications involving access to a closed city.

KAZAKSTAN. An MPC&A implementation agreement was signed with Kazakstan in December 1993. Work is proceeding, or planned, at four sites. DOD agreed to a one-time allocation of $15 million in FY 1996 CTR funds to support a project at Aktau. DOE has used program funds to begin work at the other three sites.

- Aktau BN-350 Breeder Reactor. DOE conducted a site survey in November 1995, and planned to provide additional MPC&A training for reactor personnel in 1996. The Japanese government is cooperating with DOE in installing a spent fuel gate monitor.

- Ulba State Holding Company, Fuel Fabrication Plant. DOE has provided MPC&A equipment, MPC&A training, and a computer system for MPC&A activities.

- Almaty Research Reactor. DOE conducted a site survey in September 1995 and planned to provide MPC&A training in early 1996. Additional cooperation under discussion depends on the availability of funds.

- Semipalatinsk-21. DOE is providing physical protection training. Experts have discussed nuclear materials security upgrades.

BELARUS. An MPC&A implementation agreement was signed in June 1995. Work that began in advance of the agreement is proceeding at one site, the Minsk Institute of Nuclear Power Engineering (Sosny). The U.S. government agreed to cooperate with the Swedish and Japanese governments to carry out immediate physical protection upgrades at this site. U.S. experts cooperated with Swedish experts to conduct a site survey in April 1994, and provided recommendations for physical protection upgrades to the IAEA. A team of U.S. experts visited the site in August 1995 and again in November 1995. The United States agreed to fund upgrades at the central alarm station, MPC&A upgrades, training in physical protection, nondestructive assay, tamper-indicating devices, and other MPC&A equipment. All work at Sosny was expected to be complete by the end of 1996.

THE LAB-TO-LAB PROGRAM IN RUSSIA

While the government-to-government MPC&A program in Russia was temporarily faltering, the lab-to-lab program was proceeding on a parallel but much faster track. This program employs a "bottom-up" approach to MPC&A improvements, in which U.S. and Russian scientists have developed their own upgrade programs at individual facilities throughout Russia without, until recently, significant involvement by government officials. From its inception the program has been astonishingly successful, especially in comparison with the slow progress of the government-to-government MPC&A program until the summer of 1995.

A Joint U.S.-Russian Steering Committee made up of representatives of the participating U.S. and Russian laboratories began meeting in mid-1994 to set priorities for the joint program. By summer 1994, the two sides had drawn up work plans with contracts specifying concrete deliverables. The program includes installation of upgraded MPC&A systems at the most vulnerable sites, as well as joint projects to develop, demonstrate, and produce MPC&A equipment. By December 1994, the first tangible results were in evidence. The first project completed was at Building 116 of the Kurchatov Institute, one of the most poorly protected nuclear facilities in Russia. Seventy kilograms of HEU, used as fuel for zero-power criticality tests of a model space reactor, are stored at the Moscow site. Prior to the joint MPC&A improvement project, there was no equipment to prevent laboratory workers or others in the building from stealing nuclear materials or equipment.[34] Only two months after the two sides began working together, fences had been put up or repaired, video cameras continuously monitored sensitive areas, and portal monitors were installed to deter insider thefts. Much of the equipment deployed was Russian. By early 1995, an MPC&A demonstration system was also up and running at Arzamas-16. All this was achieved in the space of half a year, whereas the government-to-government MPC&A program, by that time, had been languishing for nearly two years. Programs are now under way at a wide range of sites throughout Russia's nuclear complex, including nuclear weapons facilities.[35]

The excitement and *esprit de corps* among U.S. scientists involved in the lab-to-lab program is palpable and has been extremely productive. Many factors explain this excitement: the opportunity to work jointly with Russia on a pressing security problem to which nuclear weapons scientists are particularly sensitive; the lure of a new program at a time of dwindling opportunities for weapons scientists; and the chance to work with their former enemies at places that hold a special fascination, such as Arzamas-16, the famous, ultrasecret nuclear weapons design laboratory.[36]

For their part, scientists at the Russian laboratories appear thrilled by the success of the lab-to-lab program. For example, at the Institute of Physics and Power Engineering at Obninsk, technicians proudly demonstrate to visitors a nascent inventory system, which will

---

34. Mark Hibbs, "Russia Improving Protection for Sensitive Nuclear Sites," *Nucleonics Week,* March 30, 1995, p. 12.

35. These include the Institute of Physics and Power Engineering Institute, Obninsk; the All-Russian Scientific Research Institute of Automatics; ELERON; the Kurchatov Institute; Mayak; Krasnoyarsk-26; Sverdlovsk-44; Arzamas-16; Chelyabinsk-70; Avangard, Penza-19, Sverdlovsk-45, and Zlatoust-36 dismantlement facilities; and Tomsk-7 (now called the Siberian Chemical Combine). Recent bureaucratic decisions have slowed work at the dismantlement sites, however. Information provided by Department of Energy officials, December 1995 and June 1996.

36. Arzamas-16 is located in a closed city straddling Nizhny Novgorod oblast and the Udmurt Republic. The first joint lab-to-lab project was initiated at this laboratory, which Russian scientists jokingly refer to as Los Arzamas, because it was partially modeled on Los Alamos. Public Affairs Office, Los Alamos National Laboratory, "Los Alamos Works with Russians on New Systems to Track Nuclear Materials," January 16, 1994.

eventually record the location, mass, and isotopic content of thousands of tiny plutonium and HEU disks used to fuel the fast critical assemblies at the site.[37]

Obninsk was once considered to be a prime candidate for insider thefts of nuclear materials, in part because of the easy portability of these disks. As a result of the joint work, workers have boarded up doors to minimize the number of exit points. Specialized doors fitted with sensors check workers' passes electronically as well as their weight. Video cameras continuously monitor all activities. The "two-man rule" applies in the plutonium storage facility: scientists can enter the facility only in pairs. All employees must pass through a portal monitor upon leaving the facility. "The Obninsk system is a showcase for the very best in U.S. and Russian protection, control and accounting capabilities," explains Mark Mullen, special assistant to the lab-to-lab program. "We're not only installing new equipment, but also helping spread the principles of nuclear materials safeguards in the most concrete way possible."[38]

Scientists at Obninsk are well qualified to judge the relative strengths of the lab-to-lab and government-to-government programs, as Obninsk is one of only two facilities so far to be targeted by both programs. There is unanimous agreement among scientists interviewed at the facility that the lab-to-lab program is more flexible and more efficient. Engineers explain that the lab-to-lab program allows them to change course quickly in midstream if doing so will improve results. For example, these engineers claim that under the lab-to-lab program they were allowed to switch vendors in the middle of a project when they discovered the existence of an alternative device that was demonstrably superior to the original—something they could not do under the more bureaucratic procedures of the government-to-government program. They especially welcome the lab-to-lab system of contracts, in which each side commits to a list of concrete deliver-

---

37. These observations are based on the author's tour of the Institute of Physics and Power Engineering at Obninsk on November 13, 1995. These disks, each of which weighs approximately five grams, could easily be slipped into a thief's pocket. There are tens of thousands of them at the site, totaling about eight metric tons of HEU and about 800 kilograms of plutonium.

38. Los Alamos National Laboratory Public Information Group News Release, "U.S., Russian Scientists Demonstrate Nuclear Materials Security System at Russian Power Institute," September 21, 1995.

ables. This system has now been incorporated in the government-to-government program as well. They, like their American counterparts, enjoy working directly with scientists who understand their problems, rather than with *chinovniki* (bureaucrats). Moreover, the lab-to-lab program affords them greater flexibility in choosing either Russian-or U.S.-manufactured MPC&A equipment or a combination of both.

In the words of one DOE official involved in the program, "We recognize that the key to consensus between the United States and Russia on MPC&A was the creation of an indigenous MPC&A capability. As Russian personnel have been empowered to create, maintain, and purchase MPC&A equipment and services, we have gained a resolute buy-in from Russian scientists and officials.... This has greatly increased the speed and scope of MPC&A cooperation."[39] Moreover, Russian officials are in a position to lobby for greater MPC&A funding, which will enable the program to expand still further.

Perhaps the most important outcome of the lab-to-lab program is that it has created a cadre of safeguards enthusiasts in the field. The U.S. government is eager to cooperate with Russia in upgrading MPC&A for all sites with weapons-usable material, while protecting legitimate secrets that both sides still have. DOE has drawn up a comprehensive plan for projects through 2002. The program will only be as good as the scientists, technicians, and guards charged with running it, however. The enthusiasm and pride exhibited by personnel at Kurchatov and Obninsk is an important first step in the development of an indigenous safeguards culture, which in turn will influence the ultimate success of the entire joint effort.

THE GAN PROGRAM

GAN is Russia's nuclear regulatory agency. In principle, it is responsible for inspecting and licensing all facilities that handle nuclear and other radioactive materials. In practice, it has been unable to enforce compliance at Minatom or at MOD facilities, at least so far. The MOD has done its best to prevent GAN, a civilian agency, from overseeing its nuclear stockpiles, much as DOD would fight the U.S. Nuclear Regulatory Commission (NRC) if the NRC had been given similar responsibilities. President Yeltsin repealed GAN's oversight over MOD

---

39. Author's interview with DOE official involved in the lab-to-lab program, November 1995.

facilities in July 1995.[40] GAN is still responsible for inspecting all Minatom facilities associated with production of nuclear materials, however, including plutonium production reactors and reprocessing facilities.

U.S. officials have tried to support GAN in its efforts to become an independent nuclear regulatory agency. In June 1995, DOE and GAN signed an agreement to cooperate on developing a national MPC&A system for Russia. The two sides met to begin planning their joint program in October 1995, and GAN came to the meeting with six proposals: to exchange experience in developing regulations; to work together to design elements of a federal MPC&A information system; to request equipment for GAN inspectors and to develop Russian prototypes of the equipment; to work together on an MPC&A Information Center; to request MPC&A training for GAN inspectors and operators; and to assess and upgrade MPC&A systems at six research reactors.[41]

By April 1996, DOE had conducted visits at all six sites, and memoranda had been signed agreeing to a plan of action for implementing MPC&A upgrades. U.S. officials were clearly excited about GAN's readiness to begin cooperation immediately, especially at the six sites, all of which were identified by GAN as high-priority sites needing MPC&A upgrades.

THE WARHEAD SECURITY PROGRAM

The warhead security program consists of two parts: transportation security and storage security. Both parts deal only with nuclear weapons that have been removed from Russia's stockpile. Nearly $60 million had been committed under this program through FY 1995, and $42.5 million was approved for FY 1996.[42]

---

40. Penny Morvant, "Gosatomnadzor Ceases Military Inspections," *OMRI Daily Digest*, Vol. 1, No. 179 (September 14, 1995). "Statute on Nuclear Radiation Safety Updated," *Rossiiskaia Gazeta*, August 2, 1995, p. 4.

41. Karpov Research and Development Institute of Physics and Chemistry, Obninsk; Institute of Nuclear Physics, Gatchina; Moscow Institute of Physics and Engineering, United Institute of Nuclear Research, Dubna; Tomsk Polytechnic University; and Nikel Combine, Norilsk.

42. Author's conversation with DOD officials, November 1995.

Under the transportation security program, DOD is supplying supercontainers to protect warheads in transport from terrorist attack; emergency support equipment, including communication and diagnostic equipment (the latter used to determine whether there has been a nuclear yield in the event an explosion occurs); and security upgrades for railcars for both nuclear cargo and personnel.

Under the storage security program, DOD is helping the Russian MOD to: (1) develop an automated inventory management system, the ultimate goal of which is to put tags on every warhead in storage; (2) implement storage site and guard force upgrades by supplying computers and guard force training; (3) improve the MOD's personnel reliability program to include drug testing and personality testing; and (4) enhance storage site security by providing generic fissile material protection and control equipment.

General Maslin has claimed that the program has "really improved nuclear warhead protection during transportation."[43] While DOD is understandably proud of this program, officials hope in the future to move to a systems approach, identifying a full range of vulnerabilities for all weapons slated for dismantlement, from "cradle to grave." The biggest challenge in moving forward with this program, as was the case for the government-to-government MPC&A program, is Russian sensitivity about revealing security vulnerabilities at these sites.

Prospects for the Viability of the MPC&A Program

A number of issues have emerged that may threaten the continued viability of the overall MPC&A effort. These include bureaucratic politics both between partners and within the U.S. and NIS governments; potential cuts in funding; and continuing suspicions of U.S. government motives, especially on the part of Minatom.

BUREAUCRATIC POLITICS: HURDLES IN THE UNITED STATES

Beginning in FY 1996, as a part of its effort to streamline the program, the Clinton administration transferred the MPC&A program from DOD to DOE. DOD had already transferred $30 million of FY 1992–94 funds to DOE, and in order to ease the transition, agreed to an additional top-

---

43. Interview with General Maslin in *Yadernyi Kontrol,* reprinted in *The Monitor,* Spring 1995, p. 13.

line transfer of FY 1995 funds.[44] DOE began making its own requests for MPC&A beginning in FY 1996, requesting $70 million for MPC&A activities (including for Russia and other NIS) for FY 1996, and $95 million for FY 1997. Non-Russian NIS programs have been covered under Nunn-Lugar funds allocated in prior years, including $22 million for Ukraine, $3 million for Belarus, and approximately $17 million for Kazakstan. DOE has funded MPC&A projects for Lithuania, Latvia, and Uzbekistan out of overhead.[45]

At the time, critics claimed that transferring authority for MPC&A to DOE, a symptom of what former National Security Council staff member Rose Gottemoeller has called the "balkanization" of Nunn-Lugar, would reduce White House involvement in MPC&A projects and might ultimately damage their budgetary prospects.[46] Precisely the opposite occurred, however, at least in the immediate aftermath of the decision.

Shortly after the decision was made to transfer the program to DOE, several steps were taken that worked to ensure interagency coordination and focus on the MPC&A problem. The National Security Council (NSC) established an MPC&A interagency working group charged with submitting the program to interagency review, ensuring that the sites most deficient in security were preferentially targeted for assistance, providing instructions to diplomatic delegations, and keeping the issue at the top of the NIS foreign policy agenda. National Security Advisor Anthony Lake recruited Ken Fairfax, a renowned expert on fissile materials and nuclear security, to focus exclusively on NIS fissile material security issues for the NSC. Moreover, the White House drafted a decision directive (described above) that directed agencies to devote substantial personnel, financial, and intellectual resources to NIS fissile materials security problems and to combating nuclear smuggling.

---

44. In addition, beginning in FY 1996, the Department of State assumed responsibility for the International Science and Technology Center (ISTC) as well as for several projects related to export control assistance to Ukraine, Belarus, Kazakstan, and Russia.

45. Author's conversation with DOE officials, November 1995.

46. This critique and the events surrounding the "balkanization" of Nunn-Lugar are explained in detail in Chapter 4 by Rose Gottemoeller in this volume.

Nor did balkanization adversely affect the program's budget, at least for FY 1996. DOE's budget request of $70 million for MPC&A projects, which was granted, was significantly higher than similar requests for any single previous year under the Nunn-Lugar Program. And Congressman David Obey (Democrat–Wisconsin) added an additional $15 million for FY 1996 at the time of the April 1996 Moscow Nuclear Summit. The remainder of the Nunn-Lugar Program did not fare so well: out of its $371 million FY 1996 budget request, DOD received $300 million for all projects remaining under Nunn-Lugar. DOE plans to request $95 million for FY 1997. [47]

Proponents of shifting the MPC&A program out of DOD and Nunn-Lugar, such as former Deputy Secretary of Defense Gloria Duffy, who until August 1995 was special coordinator for the Nunn-Lugar Program, have observed that because Senator Nunn planned to retire, the program would lose one of its strongest proponents in Congress and would need to attract a broader base of support. Dr. Duffy has argued that giving budgetary authority to the agencies responsible for carrying out individual parts of what formerly came under the Nunn-Lugar umbrella inevitably will attract a broader group of congressional supporters.

The long-term effects of balkanization of the program are difficult to predict, however. Ultimately, the success of the program will probably depend at least as much on the administration's willingness to build and sustain congressional and public support as on NIS partners' continuing willingness to cooperate. Although in principle it might be easier to promote a single, unified Nunn-Lugar Program than several related projects housed in separate agencies, the agencies that have been responsible for running the projects (DOE with respect to MPC&A; the Department of State with respect to the International Science and Technology Center) may be better suited to testify on behalf of the projects than is DOD.

BUREAUCRATIC HURDLES IN RUSSIA

The response of the Russian government to the problem of nuclear security is complicated. On the one hand, most official statements deny that Russia is the source of any of the weapons-usable material seized in smuggling incidents. Russian government officials tend to blame the

---

47. Information provided by U.S. government officials, November 1995.

nuclear smuggling problem either on German "provocateurs" or on journalists. For example, in a recent article, the head of the Department of Arms Control and Nonproliferation of Russia's Federal Intelligence Service (SVR), General Gennadii Evstafiev, argued:

With respect to the so-called leakage of nuclear materials from Russia, the Germans were the initiators. Following the Germans, the Americans also got involved. It is obvious that before October of last year the leakage was a problem of only one country—Germany. Ninety percent of the illegal nuclear-material consignments were seized on German territory.[48]

Russian officials claim publicly that the government has taken a thorough inventory of its fissile material stockpile and that nothing is missing. Minatom's spokesman has told a group of journalists that the material missing at Minatom facilities "is not in the realm of tons of kilograms, but grams. You might not agree with this, but it is a fact."[49] Before the spate of significant smuggling incidents beginning in 1994, however, senior Minatom officials claimed that many significant quantities of plutonium were missing from a single facility, the RT-1 plutonium separation plant in Chelyabinsk.[50]

Despite frequent official denials that Russia faces a nuclear security problem, the Russian government has actively sought assistance in establishing a modern fissile material inventory system and in upgrading physical security at nuclear sites. The Yeltsin administration also issued two important orders related to nuclear security. On September 15, 1994, President Yeltsin issued a decree On Emergency Measures to Perfect a System of Secure Storage of Nuclear Materials that charged a newly established interagency commission with developing a plan to improve nuclear security and accounting.[51] Subsequently, Prime Minister Chernomyrdin drafted a resolution on

---

48. General Gennadii Evstafiev, "Nuclear Mafia in Russia: Truth and Myths," *Vek*, No. 37 (1995).

49. Mark Hibbs, "Europeans Term 'Worthless' Minatom Claim that No HEU or Pu is Missing," *Nuclear Fuel*, Vol. 20, No. 7 (March 27, 1995), p. 12.

50. Ibid. The IAEA defines a "significant quantity" as eight kilograms of elemental plutonium and 25 kilograms of HEU enriched to at least 20 percent U-235.

51. Decree of the President of the Russian Federation on Emergency Measures to Perfect a System of Secure Storage of Nuclear Materials, September 15, 1994.

January 13, 1995, that ordered GAN, in consultation with other agencies, to develop and implement a state nuclear materials control and accounting system. It also ordered the Ministry of Finance to allocate the necessary funds "on a priority basis."[52]

More impressive is the fact that, in private conversations, lower-level Minatom officials acknowledge the seriousness of the nuclear material inventory problem. These admissions contrast sharply with interviews of more senior officials, and with the public statements of many Russian officials in the press. One mid-level Minatom official interviewed for this study who had worked for the IAEA was adamant in his belief that the problem was far worse than generally recognized.[53]

The most disturbing bureaucratic development that emerged in conversations with Minatom officials is that ministry's alleged plans to take over control of the lab-to-lab program. At least one senior Minatom official has expressed grave reservations about what he calls the "chaotic nature" of the lab-to-lab program. Some of these officials also remain deeply suspicious of U.S. motives and are convinced of the need to keep the system of physical protection a state secret. In the view of these officials, resistance to allowing Minatom more control over the program is only evidence that the United States has ulterior motives for working with the nuclear weapons laboratories.

However this potential crisis is resolved, these issues are bound to reemerge. Government agencies have a natural tendency to expand their territory, a characteristic that organizational theorists call "bureaucratic imperialism." Agencies are most likely to exhibit "colonizing" behavior when "boundaries are ambiguous and changing,"

---

52. Resolution of the Government of the Russian Federation on Priority Projects for 1995 to Develop and Implement the State Nuclear Materials Control and Accounting System, January 13, 1995.

53. Author's interview with Minatom official, November 14, 1995. This mid-level official refrained from blaming the smuggling problem on German provocateurs or on journalists exaggerating the problem to sell newspapers. Nor did he employ another tactic in vogue among more senior officials interviewed by this author, as well as in official statements in the press deflecting attention from the problem by focusing on Western failings in the nonproliferation arena, such as the West's alleged responsibility for the Pakistani, Israeli, South African, and Iraqi nuclear programs. This official was so determined that the urgency of the MPC&A problem be communicated that he asked to read over the author's written translation of interviews to ensure that no important points had been missed.

or when programs are new, with ill-defined owners.[54] If this theory is correct, it is possible that turf battles in both countries will continue into the indefinite future. This tendency must be resisted if the program is to be successful.

There is growing sentiment in some agencies in Moscow that Minatom is functioning as a "state within a state" and should be reined in. The root of the problem, in the view of one Ministry of Foreign Affairs official, is the system of closed cities that has overseen design and production of nuclear weapons. Over the past decades, Minatom has had all the responsibilities of a state in these cities, and it has grown accustomed to power and secrecy. Minatom currently controls agricultural production on a land mass the size of an oblast, and more than one million people work for the ministry, which translates to a large number of votes. The most egregious example of Minatom's apparent independence from the rest of the government was its attempt in 1995 to include enrichment equipment in the sale of a nuclear reactor to Iran.[55]

THE RESPONSE OF NON-RUSSIAN NIS GOVERNMENTS

Non-Russian NIS partners have generally been far more cooperative on MPC&A issues than Russia. As one DOE official has explained, "These are smaller countries with smaller governments. There are fewer bureaucrats able to set up barriers." Another important distinction is that Russia is the single nuclear weapons state in the NIS, with the largest amount of weapons-usable nuclear material and the most complicated fuel cycle. Moreover, as non-nuclear weapons states party to the NPT and subject to IAEA safeguards, the non-Russian NIS governments inevitably have fewer reservations about protection of classified, weapons-related information.

Obstacles in carrying out MPC&A projects have been fairly prosaic, including problems with shipping, customs, taxes, duties, and reporting. There have also been problems, as in Russia, with access to closed cities. An additional area of disagreement in the non-Russian NIS has been the definition of the scope of work. As another DOE

---

54. Graham T. Allison, *Essence of Decision: Explaining the Cuban Missile Crisis* (Boston: Little, Brown, and Co., 1971), p. 96.

55. Alexei Yablokov, "Atomic Energy Ministry Mixed Up Its Own Interests With National Ones," *Izvestia*, June 2, 1995, p. 3.

official explained recently, "While some countries have been slow to accept the extent of work necessary to upgrade indigenous MPC&A systems, others have requested and been turned down for assistance in areas outside our mandate, i.e., non-MPC&A upgrades (dry storage, fire protection, emergency response, etc.)." Despite these problems, MPC&A work with non-Russian NIS partners is expected to be completed by the end of 1997, five years earlier than the work in Russia.

CONCERNS ABOUT THE PACE OF THE PROGRAM

Critics have accused the Clinton administration of exceedingly slow progress in cooperative threat reduction in the area of MPC&A. As one prominent critic has claimed,

> The foot-dragging that has characterized much U.S. and Russian implementation of such measures ... is deplorable.... The responsible bureaucrats in both countries, most of whom appear to be in no hurry to get on with the job, need to be reminded in particular that protecting plutonium and highly enriched uranium ... represents not only one of the most urgent of arms control and nonproliferation tasks but also one of the most cost effective.[56]

Bureaucratic battles inevitably hamper the program. Government officials, especially in the United States and Russia, have allowed interagency and even interpersonal rivalries to stymie progress. Perhaps even worse is the danger that U.S. and Russian bureaucrats, in their zeal for control, will damage the program's greatest strength, which is its flexibility. The worst possible outcome would be if Minatom succeeds in taking control of the lab-to-lab program, especially if U.S. funds are required to go through Minatom, rather than directly to the facilities where MPC&A activities are taking place. This shift in control would significantly damage the program's flexibility, and could impair excellent working relationships that have developed over several years.

The principal obstacle to progress, however, is not bureaucratic infighting. It is the lack of trust. Lingering suspicions about U.S. motives persist, especially in Russia, despite the substantial progress already achieved through cooperative efforts. Alleged Minatom attempts to take control of the lab-to-lab program, for example, are

---

56. John Holdren, Nobel Lecture Delivered on Behalf of the Pugwash Conferences on Science and World Affairs, Oslo, December 10, 1995.

partly a symptom of this deeper problem. Activities related to nuclear weapons have always been the most closely held of government secrets, and development of trust inevitably takes time. Many Russian officials believe that the U.S. government is still insufficiently aware of Russian sensitivities. In the words of one Minatom official, "It is very important that you stress repeatedly that you have no intention of stealing secrets. You don't do this enough." U.S. officials might profitably heed this advice.

Conclusions

The MPC&A program, though only a few years old, is already fulfilling one of the principal objectives of the Nunn-Lugar Program: reducing the risks of proliferation resulting from the breakup of the Soviet Union. Ultimately, success will depend on four variables explored in this chapter: the development of trust among the U.S. and NIS government officials involved; bureaucratic politics in both donor and recipient countries, and the extent to which the flexibility of the program can be maintained and enhanced; continued congressional funding, which in turn depends on public awareness of the nuclear security problem; and, most importantly, the development of a safeguards culture in the recipient countries.

Until now, the MPC&A program has been unusually flexible, in that it incorporates parallel, mutually reinforcing components. The advantage of this multipronged approach—including projects managed from the bottom up as well as from the top down—is that when problems arise, as they inevitably will, cooperation may nonetheless proceed along an alternative route. This principle was illustrated most dramatically during the first two years of the government-to-government MPC&A program, when, try as it might, the U.S. government could not convince the Russian government to accept equipment it obviously needed. Meanwhile, lab-to-lab cooperation was proceeding at a rapid pace. The multipronged approach is the greatest strength of the MPC&A effort, and might usefully be incorporated into other parts of the Nunn-Lugar Program. Other useful innovations include contracting directly with NIS facilities and personnel for goods and services, thereby fostering indigenous capabilities.

While significant progress has been made at many NIS nuclear facilities, many sites are still vulnerable to theft. A convincing inventory of nuclear materials has yet to be taken in Russia, and the MPC&A

system for warheads is not yet adequate. These are among the most serious threats to international security, and deserve far greater U.S. funding than they have received so far.[57] The problem is sufficiently grave that government agencies in all the relevant countries cannot afford to conduct business as usual. To the greatest extent possible, interagency rivalries and lingering suspicions should be set aside. This effort, according to one of the program's most prominent proponents, U.S. Secretary of Defense William Perry, is neither an aid program nor a means to achieve unilateral Russian disarmament. It is "defense by other means," a particularly cost-effective way for taxpayers—in both the United States and the NIS—to protect future generations.[58]

---

57. For an excellent proposal on how future funds should be allocated for MPC&A activities, see John Holdren, "Reducing the Threat of Nuclear Theft in the Former Soviet Union: Outline of a Comprehensive Plan," unpublished proposal submitted to Senator Richard Lugar, November 1995.

58. Secretary of Defense William Perry, speech before the National Press Club, January 5, 1995. Secretary Perry was referring to the entire Nunn-Lugar effort. He said, "It's neither Russian aid, nor is it unilateral Russian disarmament. Indeed, for the United States, Nunn-Lugar is defense by other means, a particularly effective way to protect ourselves against nuclear weapons that were once aimed at our cities."

Chapter 16

Project Sapphire

U.S.-Kazakstani Cooperation for Nonproliferation

William C. Potter

Tom Clancy might well have crafted the story line for Project Sapphire: 600 kilograms of weapons-grade uranium left over and forgotten from a secret Soviet submarine program; rediscovery of the material by Kazakstani authorities at an ill-protected facility on the windswept steppes of Central Asia; a race against the onset of winter by a team of U.S. scientists and technicians to ready the sensitive cargo for airlift out of Kazakstan; the discovery in the room next to the one holding the weapons material of empty canisters with Tehran addresses; the successful removal of 104 percent of the declared inventory of highly enriched uranium from the vulnerable facility.

Notwithstanding its resemblance to a Hollywood thriller, Project Sapphire was a real-world nonproliferation success story. Its outcome, however, was not preordained. An analysis of the case indicates both the opportunities and challenges of post–Cold War diplomacy. It also suggests possible lessons about the problems of and prospects for nonproliferation in the former Soviet Union.

The Historical Context

At the time of its demise in December 1991, the Soviet Union maintained a vast complex of nuclear research, production, and storage facilities, in addition to an enormous nuclear weapons stockpile. Although little known in the West, this nuclear complex included the massive Ulbinsky (Ulba) Metallurgy Plant located 20 miles outside the city of Ust-Kamenogorsk, Kazakstan. Set up in 1949 and known simply as "Mailbox 10" prior to 1967, the plant served a number of different

---

The author is grateful to the many U.S., Kazakstani, and Russian officials who shared their insights about the conception and implementation of Project Sapphire. This chapter is based almost exclusively on their accounts.

missions over the years, including production of most of the uranium dioxide (UO_2) powder and fuel pellets fabricated in the Soviet Union.[1] The Ulba plant also was the principal producer in the Soviet Union of the dual-use nuclear-related metal beryllium and the metal tantalum. Only recently did the West learn that during the Brezhnev era the facility acquired the additional military function of fabricating highly enriched uranium (HEU) fuel for Soviet naval propulsion reactors as part of the Alfa nuclear submarine program.[2]

Fabrication of HEU appears to have ceased at the Ulba plant in the 1980s. However, a large inventory of HEU—approximately 600 kilograms—remained at the plant into the 1990s, most likely forgotten by officials in Moscow after the abandonment of the secret Alfa program.

It is doubtful that more than a handful of officials in the newly independent state of Kazakstan were familiar with the nuclear material cache either. The individual most likely to have known of its existence was Vitalii Mette, former deputy prime minister of Kazakstan, who probably learned of the material's presence when he became director of the Ulba plant in January 1989. Nursultan Nazarbaev also may have known about the use of HEU at Ulba prior to assuming the presidency, due to his long-time tenure as the number-two ranking party official in Kazakstan.[3] Little attention, however, appears to have been given to the significance of the HEU—if indeed its presence was recalled—until the

---

1. For a more detailed description of Kazakstan's nuclear heritage, see Oleg Bukharin and William Potter, "Kazakstan: A Nuclear Profile," *Jane's Intelligence Review*, April 1994, pp. 183–187.

2. It remains unclear precisely when the Ulba facility began to fabricate HEU. In a press conference on November 23, 1994, former plant director Vitalii Mette reported that the uranium airlifted from Ulba had been produced beginning in the 1960s and ending in 1976–77. See Steven Erlanger, "Kazakstan Thanks U.S. for Moving Uranium," *New York Times*, November 25, 1994. U.S. analysis of the recovered HEU, however, suggests that it was of more recent origin.

3. Dinmurkhamed Kunaev, head of the Communist Party of Kazakstan from 1960 until late 1986, almost certainly would have been briefed about the Alfa program. Kunaev died in August 1993.

newly appointed director of the Kazakstani Atomic Energy Agency, Vladimir Shkolnik, visited the site in 1992.[4]

U.S. knowledge of and interest in the Ulba plant also was very limited prior to Kazakstani independence. The facility was best known as the site of a large explosion in September 1990 which dispersed large amounts of toxic beryllium into the air. By mid-1992, however, the United States may have begun to pay closer attention to Ulba's nuclear-related activities. There are news reports, for example, that in August 1992 the CIA learned of a visit by Iranian nuclear experts to the Ulba plant.[5] There also are numerous accounts in the media of Iranian purchases of beryllium from Ulba in 1992 and 1993. Although these reports—denied by Kazakstani authorities—are difficult to corroborate, there are multiple indications that Iran was interested in Kazakstan's nuclear-related activities. It is known, for example, that by fall 1993, Iran had explored the possibility of opening a consulate at Aktau on the Caspian Sea—a site far removed from Ust-Kamenogorsk, but the location of Kazakstan's sole nuclear power plant, a BN-350 liquid metal fast-breeder reactor.[6]

It also is well documented that there were canisters at the Ulba plant, in the room next to that holding the HEU, bearing Tehran addresses. These particular canisters, probably filled with beryllium, were discovered in 1993 or 1994 and were not exported after the U.S. government expressed concern. But it is uncertain whether other exports to Iran from Ulba took place. More recently, Ergali Bayadilov, former director general of the Kazakstani Atomic Energy Agency, was reported to have acknowledged that Iran had formally approached Kazakstan in 1992–93 to purchase low-enriched uranium (LEU) and beryllium from the Ulba plant. This same report, based on a meeting of the Institute of Nuclear Materials Management at Palm Springs, California, in July 1995, indicates that U.S. officials confirmed an

---

4. The Kazakstani Atomic Energy Agency was established in May 1992. Shkolnik was appointed to head the agency in August 1992.

5. See Andrew Higgens, "Kazaks Tell How U.S. Flew Out Uranium," *The Independent*, November 26, 1994.

6. This reactor, usually fueled with uranium enriched to 20–25 percent, was designed to use uranium-plutonium mixed oxide (MOX) fuel as well. In the early 1990s, a series of experiments were conducted in which weapons-grade plutonium-based MOX fuel assemblies were loaded into the Aktau reactor.

Iranian initiative in Kazakstan, but agree with Bayadilov that it was limited to an attempt to acquire LEU.[7]

It is difficult from the public record to establish how much Iran knew about Ulba or whether it had actually succeeded in establishing trade relations with the Ulba plant. What is clear is that, at a minimum, Iran (and possibly other states) were familiar with at least some of Ulba's nuclear history and were probing to learn more.

The Kazakstani Overture

In February 1993, the International Atomic Energy Agency (IAEA) made a "pre-safeguards" visit to the Ulba plant. The trip was part of the agency's program to facilitate the introduction of international safeguards at the civilian nuclear facilities of the post-Soviet states. Conclusion of a safeguards agreement with the IAEA was something favored by Shkolnik and other Kazakstani nuclear officials who were anxious to receive technical assistance from the agency for their country's civilian nuclear power program. Although there are no clear indications that the IAEA gained any information about the presence of HEU at Ulba during its February visit, Shkolnik must have anticipated that inspectors from the agency would discover the uranium stocks on subsequent visits, and understood that Kazakstan would have an obligation to declare all of its nuclear holdings once it acceded to the Nuclear Non-Proliferation Treaty (NPT).[8]

By mid-1993, Kazakstan's leadership appears to have decided that it would be prudent either to upgrade national safeguards at Ulba or, alternatively, remove the HEU from the plant. Having reached this conclusion, President Nazarbaev authorized the communication to the United States of information about the existence of weapons-grade

---

7. See Mark Hibbs, "Kazaks Say Iran Sought LEU for VVER Fuel, Not 'Sapphire' HEU," *Nuclear Fuel,* July 17, 1995, pp. 11–12.

8. After May 1992, there does not appear to have been any serious discussion in Kazakstan about retaining nuclear weapons. The Kazakstani leadership, however, was in no hurry to formally accede to the NPT. This accession decision was made by the Supreme Soviet in December 1993, and two months later Kazakstan deposited its instrument of accession. For an analysis of Kazakstan's decision to remove nuclear weapons see William Potter, "The Politics of Nuclear Renunciation: The Case of Belarus, Kazakstan, and Ukraine," Occasional Paper No. 22, The Henry C. Stimson Center, April 1995.

nuclear material at Ulba. This information was passed to U.S. Ambassador to Kazakstan William Courtney in August 1993. That same month, the U.S. Department of State sought confirmation from Russia about this new nuclear information. Whether due to duplicity, ignorance, or a lapse of institutional memory, none of the Russian ministries that were contacted, including the Ministries of Atomic Energy (Minatom) and Foreign Affairs, acknowledged the existence of HEU at Ulba.

Despite the lack of confirmation by Russia, Ambassador Courtney received instructions from Washington to pursue the matter further with the Kazakstani government, and in October 1993 obtained more details from senior Kazakstani officials about the situation at Ulba. Among other things, Kazakstan conveyed its concerns about its ability to safeguard adequately the nuclear material and sought assistance from the United States in protecting the nuclear stocks. Kazakstan did not specifically request that the HEU be sent to the United States, but indicated that it should be removed from Kazakstan and placed under IAEA safeguards.

It remains open to question whether or not the United States was the first or only state approached by Kazakstan regarding the HEU at Ulba. According to most U.S. officials involved in Project Sapphire, Kazakstan was not anxious for Russia to learn of the situation at Ust-Kamenogorsk and feared that Moscow might try to block its safeguards initiative. The principal U.S. players in the operation also cannot recall any indication that Russia (or any other state) was offered the HEU before an overture was made to the United States. This information, however, is at odds with a number of Kazakstani and Russian public statements after the completion of the airlift. Former First Deputy Prime Minister Vitalii Mette, for example, has been quoted as saying at a press conference, "We offered to give it [the HEU] to Russia, but Russia refused."[9] A spokesman for Minatom also is reported to have claimed that Kazakstan first offered to sell a large quantity of uranium-beryllium alloy and uranium dioxide to Russia. "We didn't want this material," he maintained, "we produce enough of it ourselves."[10] These different recollections are not easy to reconcile. What does appear clear, however, is that if Moscow were approached first, it showed no interest

---

9. Cited by Higgens, "Kazaks Tell How U.S. Flew Out Uranium."

10. Vitalii Nasonov, cited by Barry Schweid, Associated Press, November 23, 1994.

in the HEU and most certainly was not prepared to pay Kazakstan for its relocation.

The U.S. Response

Ambassador Courtney's deliberations with senior Kazakstani officials in October 1993 set in motion U.S.-Kazakstani collaboration to remove the HEU. A number of important issues, however, had to be resolved before any concrete action could be taken. On the U.S. side, for example, it was necessary to (1) confirm that the material in question was indeed HEU; (2) decide whether to remove the material if it were HEU or, alternatively, to assist Kazakstan in upgrading safeguards at the plant; (3) determine the Russian reaction to alternative scenarios; (4) reach agreement with Kazakstan about compensation for the material if it were to be removed; and (5) reach interagency agreement on the final disposition of the material (an issue that was not without potential domestic political ramifications).

The United States treated the information that had been conveyed to Ambassador Courtney seriously, and the Office of Politico-Military Affairs in the Department of State was tasked with pursuing the matter. The issue, however, had to compete with a number of more public proliferation challenges, most notably those posed by North Korea's refusal to comply with IAEA safeguards and Ukraine's reluctance to surrender strategic nuclear weapons. As a consequence of this preoccupation with other proliferation threats and the need to assemble, essentially from scratch, information and expertise relevant to the Kazakstani issue, the United States was unable to get firsthand confirmation of the Ulba situation until February 1994. This confirmation finally was obtained in late February by Elwood Gift, a nuclear engineer from the Department of Energy's Oak Ridge Y-12 Plant, who was sent on a one-man reconnaissance mission to Ulba.

With the cooperation of Kazakstani authorities, Gift was able to examine the physical layout of the Ulba plant and discern how the material in question was stored and protected in three different vaults. He also was given 11 samples of the material, three of which were split and dissolved in nitric acid at the plant's lab in his presence. The mass spectroscopy analysis of the samples, observed by Gift, revealed assays of U-235 of approximately 90 percent: weapons-grade material!

An additional 11 samples of material were transported back to the United States for more detailed analysis. The preliminary findings obtained on-site by Gift, however, were sufficiently worrisome to prompt the United States to accelerate its response. Following a meeting in early March among the three senior U.S. nonproliferation officials—Robert Gallucci from the Department of State, Ashton Carter from the Department of Defense (DOD), and Dan Poneman from the National Security Council (NSC)—a decision was made to have DOD take the lead in coordinating U.S. efforts to secure the Ulba fissile material. An interagency "Tiger Team" chaired by Jeff Starr of DOD was set up to accomplish this objective.[11] At about the same time, the mission acquired the name "Project Sapphire."[12]

The Tiger Team held its first meeting on March 25, 1994. Although its formal instruction was to implement the decision to get the material out of Kazakstan on the basis of the assay performed at Ulba, the Tiger Team initially reviewed three options: (1) leave the material in Kazakstan, but protect it by means of upgraded material protection, control, and accountancy (MPC&A); (2) leave the material in Kazakstan and ignore it; or (3) get the material out.

The Tiger Team briefly reviewed and rejected the first option because it did not address the near-term physical protection threat (the material would remain relatively vulnerable until the MPC&A upgrade was completed). This option also was deemed undesirable because of the perception—possibly mistaken—that it would be extremely expensive and difficult to sustain over the long haul. The second option, to ignore the problem, was not given serious attention. Most of the first meeting, therefore, was devoted to the practical problems associated with getting the HEU out of Kazakstan. These problems

---

11. The Tiger Team usually was composed of representatives from the Departments of State, Defense, and Energy, the NSC, the Joint Chiefs of Staff, the intelligence community, and also other agencies such as the Office of Management and Budget, depending upon the focus of the particular meeting. The Tiger Team reported to a higher-level interagency group chaired by Rose Gottemoeller at the NSC.

12. The name was coined by an Oak Ridge scientist and had no special significance other than to connote that the object in need of safeguarding was valuable. The code name was proposed after the scientist had observed other government officials carrying folders conspicuously labeled "Kazakh HEU." The code name used by the U.S. Air Force was Phoenix Sapphire.

included the matters of compensation for Kazakstan and coordination with Russia.[13]

The Tiger Team agreed from the outset that Kazakstan should be given fair and appropriate compensation for the HEU, and in late March agreed to negotiate with Kazakstan on this subject. There was considerable interagency wrangling, however, over who should foot the bill. Unfortunately, Presidential Decision Directive No. 13 of September 1993, which authorized the United States to purchase nuclear material at the market rate when it would serve U.S. nonproliferation interests, offered little guidance. Although DOD was anxious to tap Nunn-Lugar Cooperative Threat Reduction (CTR) monies for the mission, it was not clear if some of the items requested by Kazakstan for compensation (e.g., hospital supplies and medical assistance) could legitimately be funded under the terms of the CTR Program. Thus, although there never was any question about the compatibility of the objectives of Project Sapphire and the CTR Program, a lack of consensus within DOD over what were appropriate CTR expenditures led the department to seek contributions from other agencies. An interagency debate over how to pay for Project Sapphire therefore ensued in tandem with U.S.-Kazakstani deliberations about the size and composition of the compensation package.[14]

Coincident with the interagency debate in early spring 1994 over compensation was a debate about whether or not to talk to Moscow. It revolved about a number of thorny issues including Kazakstani concerns that Almaty not get involved in a trilateral negotiation in which Moscow might make demands for compensation for "its HEU." The Tiger Team as a whole was wary of approaching Russia if this were likely to result in a veto of U.S. action. The team members disagreed, however, about the desirability of Russia serving as a repository for the material assuming that Moscow were so inclined. DOD in particular opposed that outcome, while the Department of Energy (DOE) was more favorably predisposed to a "Russian solution" because of concern

---

13. Other issues that needed to be negotiated before the mission could be executed were completion of an environmental assessment and indemnification for foreign nuclear activities.

14. Following an NSC meeting in early March 1994, the United States agreed to initiate discussions regarding compensation with Vladimir Shkolnik, who was scheduled to participate in a conference in Monterey, California, on nuclear safety problems in the former Soviet Union.

about possible domestic political fallout of transporting HEU to the United States. DOE was especially worried about protests by environmental groups and the potential opposition of state officials who might view the material as waste dumped on their doorstep.

Although the debate over the possible negative domestic side-effects of Project Sapphire continued until the summer of 1994, a decision was taken by the Tiger Team in early spring to approach Russia regarding the HEU at Ulba.[15] A cable was sent to the U.S. Embassy in Moscow with instructions to discuss the matter with senior officials at the Ministries of Foreign Affairs, Defense, and Atomic Energy. The U.S. message to the Russians was basically, "Last summer you would not acknowledge the presence of HEU at Ulba; now we know it's there. We have two options: you take it or we take it."

Although the principal U.S. players in Project Sapphire are not in perfect agreement about the Russian response, one can piece together the following account. All agree that the Ministry of Defense expressed disinterest in the issue—a pleasant surprise for the United States. Senior Minatom officials, it appears, were not available at first to respond to the U.S. inquiry. The Minatom staff person who did reply initially indicated that he assumed his superiors would not like the idea of the United States taking "their material."[16] The United States, however, persisted in getting a response from the head of the ministry, Viktor Mikhailov, who indicated that the material in question belonged to a foreign country and was a matter that should be handled by the Ministry of Foreign Affairs (MFA). The initial MFA response, it appears, was not regarded by the United States as either authoritative or clear, although it did not object specifically to the U.S. proposal to remove the HEU. A long silence—perhaps up to four weeks—then ensued before the MFA sent the United States a cable on the issue. Although the response was, "we don't want it," the DOE reportedly still pushed for having the Russians take the material.

---

15. The spate of German nuclear smuggling cases involving material of Russian origin in the late spring and summer of 1994 bolstered the arguments of those who insisted that Russia could not safeguard its own nuclear material, much less that of Kazakstan.

16. One Tiger Team member recalls the initial Minatom response as furious and negative. This recollection is challenged by other members, however.

In order to settle the issue of material disposition, U.S. Vice President Al Gore raised the subject directly with Russian Prime Minister Viktor Chernomyrdin during the visit of a high-level Russian delegation to Washington on June 21–22, 1994. According to one eyewitness to the event, a number of Russian officials chuckled when the issue was brought up by the vice president. Apparently the Russians recognized that there had been an internal U.S. bureaucratic battle on the subject since the matter was raised at a high level after an initial response had been sent through diplomatic channels. The U.S. side also could smile, however, because the Russian prime minister said that the United States could have the material.

The End Game

A major concern of the United States since it first learned of the presence of HEU at Ulba was how to prevent that information from reaching would-be nuclear weapons proliferants, terrorists, or black marketeers. In order to minimize the possibility of news leaks, the United States sought to keep the operation as low profile as possible and to conduct most of the negotiations through Ambassador Courtney in Almaty.

Keeping a lid on the project became more difficult as it moved into the operational phase. Fortunately, there already was a considerable amount of traffic between the United States and Kazakstan because of the CTR Program, implementation agreements of which had been signed by Kazakstan in December 1993. The United States also could attempt to mask its activities at Ulba under the guise of assisting Kazakstan to prepare for its IAEA safeguards obligations. It was one thing, however, to have one Oak Ridge engineer at Ulba—or even nine Y-12 Plant experts there for several days, as was the case in early August 1994—and quite another matter to inconspicuously maintain a team of 31 Americans at the Ulba facility for six weeks.[17] This large and long-term presence, however, was necessitated by the very difficult task of transferring the uranium in Ulba from 1,036 containers into 1,299

---

17. Nine Y-12 Plant experts were sent to Ulba August 4–6, 1994, to survey the HEU storage vaults and to gather technical and logistical information to support the packaging of the HEU for transport. Five to six U.S. Air Force personnel also were sent to the area to survey airfields at Ust-Kamenogorsk and Semipalatinsk, the nuclear testing site also located in the same general vicinity.

steel cans, which in turn needed to be placed into IAEA-approved transport drums.

On October 8, 1994, within hours of President Clinton's authorization of the airlift operation, 29 men and two women were en route to Ust-Kamenogorsk aboard three C-5 Galaxy cargo aircraft. The team, led by Oak Ridge scientist Alex Riedy, was composed of nuclear, chemical, and industrial engineers, health physicists, industrial hygienists, packing experts, criticality safety engineers, maintenance technicians, a physician, and three Russian-speaking interpreters. Most were Martin Marietta Energy Systems employees at the Oak Ridge Y-12 Plant in Tennessee; four were members of the military from the On-Site Inspection Agency. In addition to personnel, the airlift delivered 130 tons of equipment, including a sophisticated array of technical instruments, the components for a uranium assay laboratory, electrical power generators, satellite communications, and a maintenance depot.

Oak Ridge's National Security Program Office had been tasked by the DOE in March 1994 with developing a conceptual plan for the removal of the HEU from Ulba. This task was complicated by the manner in which the HEU was stored at the plant in Ust-Kamenogorsk and by the fact that the fissile material was present in a variety of forms, many of which were hazardous to handle. For example, about two-thirds of the stock of material designated for repackaging and transport, which totaled approximately 2.37 metric tons, was in the form of various beryllium-HEU alloys, including machine scrap and powder.[18] This material had originally been stored at the Ulba plant in over 1,000 containers that did not meet international transport standards. It was necessary, therefore, to remove the material from the original containers, and in some instances to bake, cut, and crush the different HEU products to make them easier and safer to handle and to get them to fit into 1,299 quart-sized stainless steel cans. These cans in turn were placed into 447 IAEA-approved 55-gallon transport drums.

---

18. The material consisted of 581 kilograms of HEU in a total material stock of 2.37 metric tons. The HEU was present in the form of HEU metal (168.7 kg), HEU oxides (29.7 kg), beryllium-HEU alloy machine scrap and powder (231.5 kg), beryllium oxide-uranium dioxide fuel rods (1.6 kg), graphite with trace HEU (.7 kg), and laboratory salvage (.2 kg). See Alexander W. Riedy, "Project Sapphire Briefing," meeting of the U.S.-German Study Group on Non-Proliferation, Bonn, June 12–13, 1995. A detailed analysis of the materials is provided in "Sapphire Sampling Plan," Oak Ridge Y-12 Plant, December 1994.

In addition to the difficult task of repackaging the HEU, the U.S. team, in collaboration with its Kazakstani partners, sought to cross-check the HEU being prepared for transport with that in the original Ulba inventory. This was not a simple exercise since all material accounting records at Ulba were maintained in paper form, rather than on computer. It also proved highly embarrassing to both sides when in the course of its inspection of Ulba's fissile material stocks, the U.S. team discovered a number of canisters that had not been tagged as part of the plant's HEU inventory.[19] Although it certainly was preferable from the standpoint of nonproliferation to discover that Ulba contained more rather than less HEU than was recorded in the Kazakstani inventory, it also highlighted the more generic problem of material accounting practices in the Soviet nuclear industry.

During the course of their six-week mission at Ulba, the U.S. team also had occasion to observe firsthand the underdeveloped state of physical protection at the Kazakstani facility. As with most post-Soviet nuclear installations, the principal security threat at Ulba was the risk of diversion by insiders, a danger that was a function of inadequate material control and accounting procedures, the dire economic situation of plant workers, and the absence of basic security measures (e.g., the use of wooden doors, some of which were not always padlocked, to safeguard the weapons-grade material). Thanks in part to their frequent interaction with U.S. nonproliferation specialists in conjunction with the CTR Program, Kazakstani officials had themselves become increasingly concerned about these safeguards' shortcomings. Their readiness to cooperate fully with the U.S. team at Ulba was remarkable and underscored the truly joint nature of Project Sapphire's nonproliferation mission.

Unlike U.S. and Kazakstani officials, the weather at Ust-Kameno-gorsk was not very cooperative. Slippage in the anticipated airlift date by several weeks resulted in the arrival of winter in the steppes of northeastern Kazakstan before the repackaging of the nuclear material had been completed. Despite the herculean efforts of the U.S. team,

---

19. According to a recent study by a team of Harvard researchers, the United States recovered 104 percent of the declared inventory at Ulba. See Graham T. Allison, Owen R. Coté, Jr., Richard A. Falkenrath, and Steven E. Miller, *Avoiding Nuclear Anarchy: Containing the Threat of Loose Russian Nuclear Weapons and Fissile Material*, CSIA Studies in International Security (Cambridge, Mass.: MIT Press, 1996), p. 38.

which labored up to 14 hours a day, six days a week, the uranium was only ready for transport in mid-November.

Because of inclement weather and impassable runway conditions, the first C-5 cargo jet did not arrive at the Ust-Kamenogorsk airport until November 19.[20] Its arrival set in motion a convoy of trucks in the early morning of November 20 carrying the first half of the shipment of the precious nuclear cargo on an 18-mile trek to the airport. Accompanying the HEU was half of the team of U.S. technicians and scientists, along with an escort of Kazakstani Special Forces personnel and police. Special precautions were taken to protect the cargo during transit to the airport since the process of repackaging the fissile material had also made it easier for anyone to handle and thus more attractive as a target for theft.

Although weather conditions were extremely poor at the airport, and truck-mounted jet engines were needed to clear off the ice and snow from the runway, the first C-5 was able to lift off by the afternoon of November 20. At about the same time, the second C-5 arrived, and the next morning another convoy from Ulba set off for the airport with the remaining HEU cargo. By noon of November 21 the cargo was airborne.[21]

After flights of more than 20 hours and two air-to-air refuelings each, the planes landed at Dover Air Base in Delaware. The Ulba cargo was then loaded aboard 12 unmarked but heavily defended DOE tractor-trailers for the remaining journey to Oak Ridge's Y-12 Plant.[22] Only after the material was secure at Oak Ridge was news of Project Sapphire made available to the public during an unusual joint press conference held by three cabinet officials, Secretary of Defense William Perry, Secretary of State Warren Christopher, and Secretary of Energy

---

20. An earlier C-5 group had been forced to turn back, and only one aircraft out of a subsequent group was able to reach Kazakstan. See John A. Tirpak, "Project Sapphire," *Air Force*, August 1995, p. 53. The DOD reportedly had difficulty in gaining overflight rights for the C-5s from some countries because of notification that they would be carrying hazardous cargo. See R. Jeffrey Smith, "Kazakstan Site Had Lax Security," *Washington Post*, November 24, 1994.

21. A third aircraft also landed on November 20 and departed the following day with the U.S. Air Force logistic elements.

22. The four three-truck convoys took different routes to Oak Ridge to minimize the threat of interception.

Hazel O'Leary.[23] According to Secretary Perry, the operation had kept the weapons-grade nuclear material—enough for over 20 nuclear bombs—from falling into the hands of "potential black marketeers, terrorists, or new nuclear regimes."[24]

The operational phase of Project Sapphire came to an end with the successful delivery of the HEU to Oak Ridge. A number of issues related to the project, however, remained to be settled, including final agreement on the nature of the compensation package and the ultimate disposition of the fissile material from Ulba.

The U.S. government had reached interagency agreement on the amount of compensation for Kazakstan in early September 1994. In subsequent discussions with Kazakstan, the two sides also were able to agree upon the total value and the general shape of the compensation package.[25] This initial agreement, however, began to unravel when later in the fall, Kazakstan requested changes in the types of in-kind assistance it would receive. This request, precipitated by a change in the governmental responsibilities of one key Kazakstani player in Project Sapphire, led to a lengthy negotiation that only was settled in late spring 1995.[26]

---

23. Despite at least two instances in which parties outside of the governments of Kazakstan, Russia, and the United States learned of the planned Sapphire operation, there were no major leaks to the news media until the day before the completion of the airlift mission. The prospect of news leaks had increased substantially prior to the actual airlift when the Tiger Team began to plan the November press conference. This planning entailed expanding the number of people who knew about Sapphire. It is estimated by one knowledgeable U.S. participant that at least 100 personnel at the Y-12 Plant and 100 U.S. Air Force personnel were involved in preparations or implementation of the project.

24. See R. Jeffrey Smith, "Kazakhstan Site Had Lax Security," *Washington Post*, November 24, 1994.

25. Kazakstan initially sought $25 million. Although the total assistance package remains classified, it is widely believed to be in the $10–20 million range and included both cash and in-kind assistance.

26. The Kazakstani official in question was Vitalii Mette who, in his new post as deputy prime minister, took a different perspective on desirable non-cash forms of assistance. These requests then had to be reconciled with the availability of materials at different U.S. agencies. New requests for high-tech equipment, in particular, posed problems for the United States, which had found it easier to draw upon its surplus stocks for items such as medical supplies.

The issue of what to do with the HEU from Ulba proved to be even more bedeviling than paying for it. DOD had briefly considered storing the fissile material at a military facility in the United States, but learned that this option was precluded by provisions of the Atomic Energy Act. At one point it also had contemplated and then rejected the possibility of shipping the material to a third country that might be interested in blending it down for use in commercial power reactors. In the end, DOD saw no real alternative to transferring the HEU to the Y-12 facility for interim storage before it was processed for use as commercial fuel.

It took longer for DOE to be persuaded. In addition to overcoming its concerns about the political risks of importing the material, it also was necessary to satisfy environmental impact statement (EIS) requirements of the National Environmental Policy Act. DOD's approach was to finesse this issue by attaching the Project Sapphire material to an EIS that already was being conducted for HEU at the Oak Ridge Y-12 Plant. Although DOE correctly anticipated opposition by state government to the import of the Kazakstani material, the Tiger Team succeeded in enlisting the support of Vice President Gore to reassure Tennessee authorities, who opposed the idea of storing any new HEU at Oak Ridge.[27]

DOE eventually acquiesced to the DOD position and agreed to store the Ulba material at Y-12 prior to its conversion to commercial nuclear fuel. U.S. officials reportedly also made verbal commitments to their Kazakstani counterparts to blend the Ulba HEU to low-enriched uranium within six to nine months after receiving the material.[28] Impurities in the Kazakstani material, however, made the blending process more complicated and costly than originally anticipated. A lawsuit filed by a local Oak Ridge environmental group in June 1995 also stalled DOE's plans to convert the HEU into commercial fuel.[29] As

---

27. At the November 23 conference, Energy Secretary O'Leary also sought to ease public concern over the issue by pointing out that the Sapphire shipment was not nuclear waste, but "non-irradiated material" and was only a fraction of the uranium stocks already at Oak Ridge.

28. Wilson Dizard, "Intervenor Lawsuit Blocks Blending of 'Sapphire' HEU from Kazakstan," *Nuclear Fuel*, July 17, 1995, pp. 12–13.

29. This suit filed by the Oak Ridge Environmental Peace Alliance sought to force DOE to prepare a complete EIS before it disposed of the HEU. See Dizard, "Intervenor Lawsuit."

a consequence of these unanticipated delays, the final chapter in the history of Project Sapphire was only recently written with the settlement of the suit in the favor of DOE, the removal of the HEU from Y-12, and its conversion into low-enriched fuel.[30]

Lessons Learned

Many of the circumstances present in Project Sapphire are peculiar to post-Soviet Kazakstan and are unlikely to be found elsewhere. One must be cautious, therefore, about making generalizations. Nevertheless, it is possible to derive a number of lessons from the Sapphire experience that may have broader applicability.

SHARED OBJECTIVES

Perhaps the most important lesson of Project Sapphire, which is reinforced by an analysis of the entire Nunn-Lugar CTR Program, is the critical role played by two factors in the successful implementation of denuclearization assistance: (1) the congruence of objectives between the United States and the CIS party (in this case Kazakstan), and (2) the true spirit of cooperation in the pursuit of shared nonproliferation objectives. In contrast to the frequently strained relationship between CTR donor and recipient countries, Project Sapphire was an example from the outset of how two states can forge what Graham Allison and his colleagues at Harvard University refer to as a "shared sense of mission."[31] Indeed, what is particularly striking in this case is that in interviews, more than a dozen U.S. participants from six different agencies all uniformly praised Kazakstani intentions and behavior in working to remove the fissile material from Ulba.[32] This symmetry in

---

30. EDITORS' NOTE: A postscript to Project Sapphire may yet need to be written as a consequence of news in late 1996 that the amount of HEU recovered in the operation was less than originally announced. See Wilson Dizard III and Dave Airozo, "Sapphire HEU Is Less than DOE First Claimed, Government Admits," *Nucleonics Week*, November 7, 1996, p. 15.

31. Allison, Coté, Falkenrath, and Miller, *Avoiding Nuclear Anarchy*, p. 87.

32. It is interesting to note that this spirit of cooperation was less noticeable in the characterization by some U.S. officials of their colleagues in other U.S. governmental agencies engaged in the Sapphire operation. Although Russia was sometimes viewed by U.S. officials as being less than forthcoming, its cooperation in not going

U.S.-Kazakstani objectives can be attributed to a number of factors, including the history of U.S.-Soviet cooperation on nonproliferation; the recognition by the small group of key Kazakstani participants that their country's security and energy needs were best served by embracing the global norms of nuclear nonproliferation; and the reinforcement of this nonproliferation sentiment by a program of denuclearization assistance in the form of the CTR Program.

THE BUYBACK BARGAIN

Today most programs funded by the U.S. government are under attack in Congress. This budget-cutting sentiment also applies to the CTR Program.[33] Project Sapphire, however, should be a lesson that the purchase of weapons-usable material such as that acquired from Kazakstan can be a prudent, cost-effective nonproliferation and defense strategy for the United States. Even if one assumes the high estimate of $20 million for the Sapphire compensation package and adds an additional $5 million in costs to mount the repackaging and airlift operation, Project Sapphire appears to have been a bargain from the standpoint of purchasing national security.[34] How much, one may ask, would the United States have to pay to defend against the weapons equivalent of the HEU that was present at Ulba, if it were to find its way to powers hostile to the United States?

HOW MANY OTHER ULBAS?

One of the most disturbing lessons of Project Sapphire is the need to recognize the possible existence of other caches of undeclared weapons-usable material in the former Soviet Union. It is estimated, for example, that Russia's nuclear material inventory alone—distributed over more than 50 sites—consists of approximately 1,100–1,300 tons of HEU and

---

public with the information or applying pressure on Kazakstan to halt the operation was appreciated.

33. See "U.S. Congress Readies to Finalize Funding Cuts for Soviet Weapons Dismantlement," *Post-Soviet Nuclear & Defense Monitor*, September 22, 1995, pp. 1–3.

34. One source places the cost of the airlift at roughly $3 million. See "U.S. Takes Charge of Uranium Cache," *Aviation Week & Space Technology*, November 28, 1994, p. 27.

165 tons of weapons-grade plutonium.[35] Although the bulk of the former Soviet Union's nuclear assets are concentrated in Russia, significant quantities of weapons-grade material also are present in Belarus, Kazakstan, and Ukraine.[36] Given the vast quantity of fissile material produced in the Soviet Union, the secrecy that surrounded the Soviet nuclear industry complex, and the generally underdeveloped state of material control and accountancy that persists, it should not be surprising to see the declared nuclear material inventories in a number of CIS states increase as IAEA inspections take place. Indicative of this phenomenon was the fivefold increase in weapons-grade uranium reported to the IAEA in 1994 at Ukraine's Khar'kiv Physical Technical Institute (from 15 to 75 g of HEU enriched to 90 percent U-235), and the IAEA's discovery during its February 1995 visit to Sevastopol of a previously undeclared research reactor at the Naval Academy of the Ukrainian Ministry of Defense.[37] These developments suggest that the relevant question to ask is not whether any more forgotten caches of fissile material exist, but how many there are and where they are located.

---

35. See Thomas B. Cochran, Robert S. Norris, and Oleg A. Bukharin, *Making the Russian Bomb: From Stalin to Yeltsin* (Boulder, Colo.: Westview Press, 1995), p. 51.

36. For more details on these sites, see *Nuclear Successor States of the Soviet Union. Nuclear Weapon and Sensitive Export Status Report*, Carnegie Endowment for International Peace and the Monterey Institute of International Studies, No. 3 (July 1995).

37. A senior Ukrainian nuclear official recalls that a proposal to offer HEU at Khar'kiv to the United States for compensation was considered briefly but rejected by his government prior to the public announcement of Project Sapphire. Author's interview, Washington, D.C., March 1995.

Chapter 17

U.S. Assistance to Russia's Chemical Demilitarization Efforts

Igor Khripunov

As the successor state to the Soviet Union, Russia has inherited the entire Soviet stockpile of chemical weapons (CW) as well as most of its former CW production facilities. Following the disintegration of the Soviet Union, Russia made an attempt to involve other members of the Commonwealth of Independent States (CIS) in its chemical demilitarization efforts; however, this effort never got off the ground. On May 15, 1992, most CIS countries signed an agreement under which the Russian Federation assumed an obligation to destroy chemical weapons "with due regard for its potential and in accordance with international agreements." Other parties to the agreement undertook to cooperate in CW destruction efforts including a joint funding scheme to be regulated by a separate future agreement.[1] However, like many other CIS arrangements, this separate agreement never materialized, and Russia took on the burden of destroying the entire Soviet CW stockpile by itself.

Throughout the 1980s, the Soviet Union actively participated in the Conference on Disarmament negotiations with a view to developing and adopting a global convention on the prohibition of chemical weapons (CWC). Both the Soviet Union and Russia have unambiguously committed themselves to the objectives of chemical disarmament. The Soviet Union unilaterally stopped CW production in 1987, and in 1993, Russia signed the CWC and withdrew its original reservation to the Geneva Protocol of 1925, a reservation that permitted the use of chemical weapons in retaliation to a CW attack. The Russian military doctrine of November 1993 leaves no room for CW use in the conduct of warfare. Moreover, there have been numerous statements at different levels of Russian leadership to the effect that chemical weapons are no

---

1. *Krasnaia zvezda*, May 23, 1992.

longer either politically or militarily acceptable and their destruction is in Russia's national interests.

As the Nunn-Lugar Program (later known as the Cooperative Threat Reduction [CTR] Program) was launched in 1991, CW destruction seemed to provide a much less controversial common objective than nuclear disarmament, which involved weapon systems that were far more sophisticated, whose security was extremely sensitive, and that were still at the core of U.S. and Russian defense postures. Both the United States and Russia ceased CW production and were prepared to dispose of existing stockpiles. Unlike nuclear weapons, which were originally deployed in three other former Soviet republics, the CW problem was largely a Russian problem. As a result, chemical demilitarization assistance could be targeted exclusively at Russia, substantially simplifying important political and organizational issues.

Chemical demilitarization cooperation was launched on a workable bilateral legal basis with the signing of two documents: the Wyoming Memorandum of Understanding in 1989, which provided for an exchange of data and visits, and the 1990 "Agreement on Destruction and Nonproduction of Chemical Weapons and on Measures to Facilitate the Multilateral Convention on Banning Chemical Weapons," which unfortunately never came into force despite intensive negotiations after its signing. The objective of this chapter is to evaluate the CTR Program's chemical demilitarization component and suggest ways to achieve more rapid and substantive progress in this area.

How Much to Destroy and at What Cost

Russia still must destroy its declared CW stockpile of 40,000 agent tons stored at seven sites within its national territory. Table 17-1 gives a breakdown of what quantities of CW agents are currently stored at these sites. Weaponized chemical agents, mostly organophosphorus, account for 80 percent of the entire stockpile. Chemical agents are stored in bulk at only two sites: Kambarka and Gornyi.

There is no exact or reliable data on the total tonnage of chemical weapons or agents produced by the Soviet Union throughout the many decades of the CW arms race. Anatolii Kuntsevich, former chairman of the Presidential Committee on Conventional CW and BW Matters, admitted while in his official capacity that not a single ministry or agency has complete information on the exact amounts produced or the

Table 17-1. Location and Agent Types of Russian CW Stockpile.

Location	CW Agent Types	Percent of Stockpile
Kambarka, Udmurt Republic	Lewisite	15.9
Gornyi, Saratov oblast	Mustard, lewisite, & their compounds	2.9
Kizner, Udmurt Republic	VX, sarin, soman, lewisite	14.2
Maradykovsky, Kirov oblast	VX, sarin, soman, mustard/lewisite compounds	17.4
Pochep, Bryansk oblast	VX, sarin, soman	18.8
Leonidovka, Penza oblast	VX, sarin, soman, phosgene	17.2
Shchuchie, Kurgan oblast	VX, sarin, soman, phosgene	13.6

sites where they were sunk or buried.[2] The CW stockpile of 40,000 agent tons formally declared by the USSR and then Russia is only a fraction of the approximately 100,000 to 200,000 tons produced overall, according to an independent estimate by Aleksei Yablokov, a well-known Russian environmentalist. At the end of 1995, Yablokov continued to insist that the figure of 40,000 agent tons is misleading and does not accurately reflect existing stockpiles. His major concern is that the balance, which has been dumped, buried, or sunk, represents "the underwater portion of the iceberg, which poses a more serious environmental threat than civilized CW destruction."[3] In the view of another specialist, Lev Fyodorov, chairman of the Union for Chemical

---

2. *Krasnaia zvezda*, October 22, 1993.

3. *Nezavisimaia Gazeta*, March 24, 1995.

Security, the total amount of CW produced over the past decades may be as high as 500,000 agent tons.[4]

The range of these estimates is an indication of how many toxic chemical substances were disposed of in a way similar to industrial and household waste because of the complete disregard for environmental concerns and the lack of understanding of the consequences of such actions for human health. The current critique of today's plans to destroy CW stockpiles is that they focus mostly on what is actually stored at CW storage facilities and largely ignore the immense task of cleaning up the sites of past dumpings and burials.

Funding government efforts to destroy CW stockpiles on a stable basis clearly will remain a serious problem for Russia's cash-strapped federal budget. Prior to 1996, the current chairman of the Presidential Committee, Pavel Siutkin, estimated the cost of CW destruction in Russia at $5–8 billion overall. The Federal Program for CW Destruction, approved in March 1996, was based on cost estimates of $3–4 billion. However, throughout the early 1990s Russia's chemical demilitarization efforts were chronically underfunded. From 1994 to 1995, only 30 percent of the required funds was allocated. In 1996, the Ministry of Defense (MOD) requested 587 billion rubles ($130 million) but received only 1.5 billion ($334,000).[5] This did not reflect well on the credibility of federal authorities trying to win regional support and launch the chemical demilitarization program. As German Frizorger, senior expert of the Udmurt Committee for Conventional CW Matters, commented bitterly in January 1995, contrary to all expectations, not a single ruble from the federal budget ever reached the Udmurt Republic in 1993 or 1994 to pave the way for CW destruction activities.[6] In 1995, the Ministry of Emergency Situations requested 1.5 billion rubles for emergency response and population protection measures in Kambarka and Gornyi but received no funding at all. In 1996, the ministry requested 50 billion rubles ($11.1 million) but expects to receive only 6 billion ($1.33 million).[7]

---

4. Lev Fyodorov, "Khimicheskoe oruzhie v Rossii: Istoriia, ekologiia, politika," Center for Ecological Policy of Russia, Moscow, 1994.

5. *Rossiiskaia Gazeta*, September 6, 1996.

6. *Izvestia*, January 20, 1995.

7. *Rossiiskaia Gazeta*, September 6, 1996.

Without regular and adequate allocations from the federal budget and direct support from the world community it is hard to expect significant progress in Russia's chemical demilitarization. Two supplementary funding options previously suggested in various government papers are unlikely to work. One was a long-standing project to reprocess at a profit lewisite stockpiles into super-pure arsenic, which can be used in the electronics industry. In the current set of documents approved for the Kambarka site this option is barely mentioned. The other idea was to establish a chemical disarmament fund with a view to raising private money through a special system of incentives. But in Russia's transitional economy and unattractive investment climate this concept is not taken very seriously by the parties concerned.

The Current Concept and Organization of CW Destruction

Originally, the Soviet and Russian governments opted as the most economical approach to build a regional destruction center involving extensive transportation from existing CW storage facilities. However, two such projects had to be put on hold. The first one, in Chapaevsk, Samara oblast, was halted in the late 1980s midway through construction, and another in Novocheboksarsk, Chuvash Republic, was halted in the early 1990s before construction even began. Both were put on hold largely because they had been rejected by local communities.

A new concept, based on agent destruction at individual storage sites, was formally announced in Russian President Boris Yeltsin's Decree No. 314 of March 24, 1995. This decree had several significant implications for Russia's chemical demilitarization efforts. First, it attempted to check the nearly yearlong bureaucratic tug-of-war between the Presidential Committee (set up in 1992 as the lead agency for CW destruction) and the MOD, which had been moving toward an unchallenged position in the interagency process. The decree sought to reverse this trend by elevating the Presidential Committee to an important role as overall coordinator. Accordingly, its director was authorized to assist then national security adviser Yuri Baturin, who was appointed chairman of the newly established Interagency Commission on Chemical Disarmament directly subordinate to President Yeltsin. This was certainly a blow to the military, which had hoped to develop and implement the CW destruction program with little input or interference from the outside. A second consequence of Yeltsin's

March 1995 decree was that chemical demilitarization was to be written into the federal budget as a separate line item, ensuring stable funding and stricter accountability. Until very recently, despite even meager funding allocations in annual federal budgets, CW demilitarization money was at best only partially released for designated projects either by the Ministry of Finance or the MOD. However, as subsequent events would illustrate, the bureaucratic infighting resumed and resulted in another resounding victory for the MOD, which continues to dominate the interagency process.

On March 21, 1996, the Russian government approved a program to destroy CW stockpiles. Under this program, destruction is to take place near the storage facilities, thus involving minimal transportation, and is to be completed by 2005. By 2009, all destruction and storage facilities should be decommissioned. Under the current distribution of roles and functions, the MOD is designated as the lead agency for developing and implementing a federal program of phased destruction of CW stockpiles. The MOD is also responsible for selecting optimal destruction technologies, designing and building CW destruction facilities and the social and medical infrastructure for areas where these facilities are located, as well as operating the facilities.

The Ministry of Foreign Affairs will take the lead, in cooperation with other government agencies, in formulating Russia's positions at bilateral and multilateral talks on the prohibition of chemical weapons and in conducting such talks. Another important player is the Committee for Chemical and Petrochemical Industries (incorporated into the Ministry for Industry as part of an August 1996 government restructuring scheme), which has the principal responsibility for actually developing CW destruction technologies and relevant hardware and instrumentation. In cooperation with other agencies, the committee will be involved in equipment installation and start-up operations at future CW destruction facilities. The Ministry for Defense Industries will mostly deal with the disassembly of CW munitions and destruction or utilization of their components. Development of environmental and health standards and subsequent monitoring of compliance were to be handled originally by three other agencies: the Ministry of Health and Medical Industries (Federal Directorate for Medical-Biological Problems), the State Committee for Sanitary and Epidemiological Oversight, and the Ministry for Environmental and Natural Resources Protection, which were also affected by the August 1996 restructuring of the government. The Ministry for Civil Defense and Emergency

Situations is tasked with developing accident response measures and their implementation.

The legal basis for Russia's chemical demilitarization efforts is to be provided by a law on CW destruction, which the government submitted for the Duma's consideration and approval in the fall of 1995 after yearlong discussions at the interagency and regional levels. Although a draft of the law was reviewed and rejected by the Duma in November 1995, it passed the first reading in December 1995 despite strong opposition from the Duma Committee on Environment. It was also criticized for not adequately reflecting the important role to be played by local authorities throughout the entire chemical demilitarization process.[8]

The Federal Program for CW Destruction prioritizes the disposal of lewisite, mustard, and compounds of these agents stored in bulk at Kambarka and Gornyi. The old steel tanks in which these agents are stored are corroding and getting thinner every year, making them unsafe and preventing any major overhaul. At the same time, the Russian military believes it can ensure long-term storage of munitions filled with organophosphorus agents. Although the service life of most aerial bombs and artillery shells (ten years on average) has expired and many of them have already been stored for more than 15–20 years, there is no danger, according to the military, of chemical munition self-detonation. The MOD is on record as assuring the public that after all preventive work is completed, most chemical agent-filled munitions can wait at least five to ten more years for their orderly dismantlement and destruction.

There may be a number of reasons why the MOD chose to start destruction efforts with old blister agents. However, the most plausible one is that both the Gornyi and Kambarka communities had already granted permission to serve as destruction sites for stored chemical agents, while the Kurgan oblast agreed conditionally and the others withheld consent. Saratov oblast has hosted several CW-related facilities for many years, including the Shikhany test range and the Technological Institute of Organic Synthesis in the town of Volsk. By the end of 1994, the federal government had successfully negotiated a set of documents opening the way to CW destruction there. As an

---

8. EDITORS' NOTE: The law passed the last reading in the State Duma in December 1996.

incentive, Government Decision No. 1470, dated December 30, 1994, provided for 36 billion rubles (in June 1994 prices) for the development of Gornyi's infrastructure.

The Udmurt government is the only one out of all the other regions slated to become CW destruction sites to have laid down the groundwork for seriously considering chemical demilitarization options and adopting workable solutions. It has set up its own Udmurt Committee for Conventional CW Matters as well as two working groups with a mandate to select appropriate sites for destruction facilities in both the Kambarka and Kizner areas. In 1994, the committee sponsored a trip for the representatives of these two areas to visit neighboring CW storage sites at Gornyi and Shchuchie to coordinate bargaining positions *vis-à-vis* the federal government. Several faculty members at Udmurt State University at Izhevsk participated in the MOD-sponsored project, the objective of which was to assess the risk and select the most environmentally safe and effective CW destruction technologies.

As a result of the close coordination between the federal and Udmurt governments, the highly emotional and negative initial response in Kambarka gave way to a more realistic consideration of existing options. A joint meeting of the Kambarka city and *raion* councils held on November 3, 1993, adopted a resolution in support of hosting a destruction facility in exchange for commitments to fund several projects that would benefit the local communities. According to an appendix to Russian Government Decision No. 289 of March 22, 1995, on the destruction of lewisite in Kambarka, most of the demands had been met. About 6 billion rubles (in June 1994 prices) were planned to be invested in Kambarka's infrastructure, including improved gas and water supplies and new sewage treatment facilities. According to the government decision, local construction and other companies were to be granted priority in contracting required services.

Prioritizing Gornyi and Kambarka would also mean considerably reduced up-front costs compared to other sites where weaponized organophosphorus agents are stored. Destruction of old agents kept in bulk at Gornyi and Kambarka is expected to be less technologically demanding and costly, which could allow demonstration of a CW destruction "success story" in a relatively short amount of time. Such success stories will be a much needed commodity in future attempts to secure consent from other local communities throughout Russia.

There is reason to believe that the next phase would involve destruction efforts at Shchuchie, where the United States is scheduled to build a pilot destruction facility expandable into a full-scale model. The previous public relations experience could easily be applied to the remaining five sites, but with one important caveat. The population in Gornyi and Kambarka would hardly have the capability to safely reload and transport chemical agent stockpiles that have been stored there in aging, large-capacity containers, whereas taking CW munitions out of storage sites for subsequent destruction elsewhere may be viewed by other communities as a viable alternative.

In addition, there are serious complications regarding most of the remaining storage sites. For example, a questionnaire circulated at Pochep indicated that the overwhelming majority of respondents were absolutely opposed to the idea of CW destruction *in situ*. In the spring of 1995, the oblast assembly adopted a resolution banning CW destruction in Bryansk oblast. This is not surprising since Bryansk oblast, particularly its agricultural sector, suffered considerably from the Chernobyl disaster. More than 39,000 hectares were phased out of the farming sector, and a considerable amount of timber is still banned from any economically significant use due to its radioactivity. There was mass resettlement of people from the heavily affected areas, including 28 villages. Also, Bryansk oblast is in close proximity to Ukraine and Belarus, both independent states with legitimate concerns about the safety of CW operations. The Kizner CW storage site is located within the city limits. As directed by a decision of the Udmurt government, work is under way to build health resort facilities in Kizner to take advantage of recently discovered mineral waters and curative muds. According to the estimates of MOD officials, it may take, on average, up to three years to launch a public outreach campaign for a given site and wrap up relevant talks with local communities to get their consent to host a destruction facility.

Destruction Technologies

Destruction technology is the key to successful chemical demilitarization. Russia did not accept the direct incineration method proposed by the United States and embarked on a selection process. Sixty destruction technologies were under consideration by a group of government experts that was established by a February 1994 protocol between the MOD and various institutions to evaluate alternative technologies. For the destruction of organophosphorus agents, a two-stage approach, in which agents are first neutralized to a low toxicity mass and then either destroyed or converted, was the preferred method. The final choice was a neutralization/bituminization approach. Alternative technologies included one-stage thermal disintegration of agents inside munitions and direct disintegration inside munitions by catalysis. Biodegradation was also still very much under consideration: the MOD claimed that strains of microorganisms have been developed that are capable of destroying sarin, soman, VX, and other CW compounds.

Four destruction (reprocessing) technologies for lewisite were submitted for consideration to the expert group. The first, developed by the Institute of Organic Chemistry and Technology, was based on alkaline hydrolysis followed by electrolysis. The second, proposed by the University of Nizhny Novgorod, involved lewisite disintegration under the impact of gaseous ammonia. The third technology came from the Obninsk branch of the Karpov Institute of Physical Chemistry and was based on direct restoration of lewisite into elementary arsenic. The fourth was lewisite alcoholysis, developed by the Volsk Technological Institute of Organic Synthesis. In rating these four technologies, the experts were requested to follow instructions prepared by the MOD. The first technology scored maximum points and was recognized as the most acceptable. There was consensus among Russian experts that indigenously developed technologies offer more advantages than any Western ones. For example, the German technology developed by the Metallgesellschaft is effective and safe only if used to destroy small amounts of weaponized lewisite. This technology is useless in Kambarka where lewisite is stored in bulk and where hard-to-destroy sediments already account for one percent of its total tonnage.

Another destruction technology considered in the selection process was nuclear explosion. This technology was developed in the late 1980s by what is now the Federal Nuclear Center (Arzamas-16). In 1991, this project was approved and supported by the Military-Industrial Commission. Some components of the project were implemented on a contractual basis with the MOD in cooperation with the Research Institute for Organic Chemistry and Technology and other institutions. Experimental work was performed using sarin and soman at the MOD's Shikhany test range. However, since the signing of the Comprehensive Test Ban Treaty in September 1996, the Russian government has concluded that this option is no longer politically viable.

U.S. Assistance to Russia's Chemical Demilitarization Efforts

Foreign assistance has been generally recognized as an indispensable part of Russia's chemical demilitarization efforts. After the shift to a more costly configuration of CW destruction at individual storage sites became inevitable, former Chairman of the Presidential Committee Anatolii Kuntsevich estimated that the share of foreign inputs in the CW destruction budget should range between 30 and 40 percent of the total. International cooperation is recognized as a vital component of the Federal Program for CW Destruction and includes the following:

- assessment and international evaluation of foreign and domestic CW destruction technologies including joint experiments and manufacture of pilot plants for testing safety features and demonstrating them to the local population;

- development, manufacture, and delivery of technological and other equipment, instruments and monitoring systems for building pilot plants and destruction facilities, as well as supplying equipment for analytical laboratories;

- development of safety systems for CW storage and destruction facilities; and

- training of CW destruction facility personnel and inspectors to verify compliance with international requirements.

Despite some warnings from nationalist quarters about Russia's unilateral disarmament and possible dependence on Western technologies, a majority of the Duma supports using as much outside funding and experience for chemical demilitarization as possible. Sergei Yushenkov, former chairman of the Defense Committee, is on record as suggesting the establishment of a CW parliamentary group that would approach other parliaments to request such funding and would see to it that available assistance was efficiently used. There are only four Western countries involved in providing assistance: Germany, the Netherlands, Sweden, and the United States. They may soon be joined by Finland, which is planning to team up with the Netherlands for work on the Kambarka project. The United States is the largest donor to chemical demilitarization, with a total of $68 million in proposed and actual obligations, and several hundred millions more under discussion.

The first step toward full-scale assistance under the U.S. Nunn-Lugar Program was made in July 1992 when both sides signed the "Agreement Concerning the Safe, Secure and Ecologically Sound Destruction of Chemical Weapons." Like several similar U.S.-Russian agreements in the nuclear field, this document was an outgrowth of the 'Agreement Concerning the Safe and Secure Transportation, Storage and Destruction of Weapons and the Prevention of Weapons Proliferation' (the U.S.-Russian umbrella agreement) of June 17, 1992.

The negotiating process for the CW Destruction Agreement involving Russia's CW experts was very brief because it borrowed most of its provisions from the umbrella agreement that another Russian team had agreed upon earlier: the CW negotiators essentially faced a *fait accompli*. Discussions focused on Article III, which provided for assistance worth not more than $25 million and specified two distinct categories of cooperative arrangements. Under the first category, the U.S. Department of Defense (DOD) committed itself to develop a concept plan with the Presidential Committee, provide detection and alarm systems, establish a familiarization program for Russian experts at U.S. facilities, organize visits to U.S. destruction facilities, and demonstrate protective equipment.

The Russian side objected from the outset to the idea of U.S. involvement in developing a concept plan, claiming that Russia's CW community could adequately do this job itself, and insisted on removing the phrase that placed the second category of assistance projects at "DOD discretion." The second category was viewed as substantively more important because it involved such arrangements as creation of national laboratory complexes, provision of technical equipment for destruction sites, joint experimentation related to destruction, and other activities. Under the pressure of the deadline for signing, the two sides agreed not to change the text, assuming that Article VI, which allowed amendments and extensions by written agreement, would enable them to modify the scope of work if necessary.

In the months that followed, this agreement went through a difficult period of implementation. The main controversy was over U.S. involvement in a concept plan which, to make things even more difficult, was interpreted differently by each side. The ensuing differences centered on the divergent, if not conflicting, work approaches based on the cultures and traditions of each country. The Russian draft program for the first stage of the demilitarization program (destruction of 43 percent of the entire CW stockpile), which was prepared by the Presidential Committee and submitted to the Supreme Soviet in the fall of 1992, consisted of only about 20 typed pages and was no match in terms of substance and detail to the parallel U.S. document which numbered hundreds of pages. The Russian side also showed very little enthusiasm for working on a concept plan based on Western methodology that was little understood and appreciated in Russia. Moreover, Russia denied the United States access to sensitive information without which any planning and design efforts would be meaningless.

Another disappointment for the Russian side was the two-year delay (1992–94) in selecting a U.S. contractor (a major initial contract was awarded to a consortium of four U.S. companies headed by Bechtel in May 1994). The Russian side consistently promoted the idea of a major general contractor on the U.S. side committed to working for the duration of U.S. involvement. Instead, and to the surprise of its Russian counterparts, DOD preferred to stick to its traditional contracting rules and regulations, effectively rejecting the general contractor concept and breaking the process into separate stages for which new U.S. contractors would be sought and selected on a competitive basis.

For its part, however, DOD was understandably in no position to ask the U.S. Congress for money to implement specific projects in the absence of any Russian program approved by the national legislature. Moreover, the U.S. administration and Congress indirectly linked progress in assisting chemical demilitarization to Russian compliance with CW and other arms control agreements. Yet Russia delayed submission of data required by the Wyoming Memorandum of Understanding and was not responsive to U.S. efforts to accelerate the entry into force of the 1990 Agreement on CW Destruction and Nonproduction.

Credit for developing a better understanding of the intricacies of Russian politics and finding relevant compromises should be given to U.S. Assistant to the Secretary of Defense Dr. Harold Smith. As a result of his efforts, a CW Destruction Support Office was established in Moscow on June 15, 1993, and is currently staffed by the U.S. Army Corps of Engineers, the On-Site Inspection Agency, and U.S. contractors. On March 18, 1994, the Agreement of July 30, 1992, was amended to increase the $25 million maximum to $55 million. Although not specified in the amendment, up to $30 million was to be used to finance a project to provide a central CW destruction analytical laboratory.

U.S.-Russian work plans for 1994 and 1995 were signed following laborious and tough negotiations. They provided for many of the elements of the necessary concept plan (called the Comprehensive Implementation Plan), such as development of a public outreach and education plan; development of methods to select CW destruction technologies; a program of Russian internships at U.S. facilities related to chemical weapons destruction; development of design criteria for CW destruction facilities; recommendations on a comprehensive emergency preparedness plan; demonstration of technologies for CW destruction; and other activities. In September 1994, the MOD proposed a joint technology evaluation program to evaluate the Russian two-step CW destruction process. An agreement on the conduct of this joint technology evaluation was concluded in January 1995 and included in the 1995 work plan finalized on April 3, 1995. The laboratory tests were performed in designated U.S. and Russian laboratories to obtain data on the chemical reactions and reaction products and to verify the suitability of the Russian two-step chemical neutralization and bituminization process for destroying Russia's organophosphorus agents. This joint evaluation was also intended to generate data required to design a destruction facility for organophosphorus chemical weapons. The work was successfully completed by the end of 1995, and final recommendations were positive.

The year 1994 was characterized by increased MOD clout in chemical demilitarization matters as a result of the removal of Presidential Committee Chairman Anatolii Kuntsevich, who had dominated the scene as chief Russian negotiator in this area. He was replaced temporarily by one of his low-profile deputies, and the interagency process tipped heavily toward the MOD. The military negotiators immediately informed the United States of their grievances and displeasure with some of the oral and written agreements consummated by Kuntsevich. The focus of MOD criticism was the Comprehensive Implementation Plan, which it characterized as redundant and inappropriate for bilateral cooperation. Apparently the MOD believed that getting the United States involved in developing Russia's chemical demilitarization program and sharing additional information would stretch the limits of transparency too far. Moreover, the MOD preferred to have U.S. assistance in the form of funding actual design and construction of demilitarization facilities.

As a result, DOD began to reshape the entire U.S. assistance program for Russian chemical demilitarization in a major way. There has been a dramatic shift in emphasis away from addressing Russia's chemical demilitarization program in its entirety (with the Comprehensive Implementation Plan as the focus), and toward a project the sole objective of which will be to design and construct a single, full-scale chemical destruction facility in Russia. Shchuchie was designated by MOD as the site where such a facility would be built. This narrowly focused approach was effectively reflected in the 1995 work plan.

This very significant change was accepted with some misgivings by DOD. On the positive side, it would result in the creation of a visible destruction facility in Russia, conducting actual chemical demilitarization activities, by about 2004. (The United States has changed its concept of Nunn-Lugar assistance from that of an open-ended program to one of finite duration, of about five more years.) There was a very important downside to this change in approach, however. The previous U.S. assistance plan followed the Western practice of not embarking on a major, multibillion-dollar project without having a well-developed master plan showing costs, schedules, locations, manpower and resource requirements, environmental impacts, verification of technologies, and so on. By contrast, now U.S.-Russian joint efforts would construct a facility with little knowledge of how Russia's overall program is progressing and no control over its implementation.

The DOD strategy and objectives are not always clearly understood or shared in the U.S. Congress. For example, in 1995 the House National Security Committee denied a request for the design and construction of a CW destruction facility in Russia because, in its view, this project was "premature."[9] The committee's position was supported by the full House of Representatives. On the Senate side, the Armed Services Committee preserved the DOD request for CTR almost in its entirety, although the release of most of the funds for the chemical demilitarization component was conditional on presidential certification of Russia's compliance with the Biological Weapons Convention.

Those in the House who denied funding for the construction of a CW destruction facility cited at least five areas of concern. First, Russia had refused to agree to destroy the most lethal and militarily useful

9. House of Representatives, National Defense Authorization Act for Fiscal Year 1996. Report of the National Security Committee on H.R. 1530, June 1, 1995, Washington, D.C., pp. 256–257.

stocks of chemical weapons first. Second, Russia has refused to accept U.S. plans to build an incinerator to burn its chemical weapons stocks and instead insisted on a questionable two-step destruction technology involving neutralization. Third, there were many other relevant issues to be resolved before the requested large-scale funding could be undertaken. Fourth, Russia had yet to ratify the CWC and might still be developing new chemical weapons. Fifth, a comprehensive implementation plan had yet to be signed to govern these activities.

Upon close examination, all of the above points had some validity and were sources of legitimate concern, but they were hardly grounds for jeopardizing bilateral chemical demilitarization cooperation by withholding money. Under these circumstances, a lack of clear commitments by the United States to large-scale funding of Russia's chemical demilitarization would be counterproductive. The relatively unopposed nature of the FY 1997 budget request and its consideration, leading to more money for CW destruction in Russia, are indicative of broader bipartisan support for chemical demilitarization.[10]

Conclusions and Recommendations

Continued outside assistance and support are important ingredients to ensure progress toward actual CW destruction, without which Russia cannot comply with its international obligations. As stated in DOD's April 1995 report on the CTR Program, "without substantial technical and monetary assistance from the United States and other countries, Russia will have difficulty complying with the Chemical Weapons Convention (CWC) destruction schedules."[11] There is little chance that the Federal Assembly will ratify the CWC without firm commitments by the government to specific CW destruction arrangements supported by adequate and long-term funding.

---

10. AUTHOR'S NOTE: As a result, on December 3, 1996, the U.S. Army Corps of Engineers awarded a contract to the Ralph M. Parsons Corporation for engineering and management support of a CW destruction facility in Shchuchie. No dollar amounts have been set, but the total estimated value of the task orders to be issued is $600 million.

11. U.S. Department of Defense, *CTR: Cooperative Threat Reduction* (Washington, D.C.: April 1995).

Chemical demilitarization assistance to Russia, if carefully coordinated and responsive to Russian needs, may provide a much needed "success story" in the area of demilitarization and threat reduction. A major prerequisite for such a success will be for the United States to understand that this is a Russian program and that it must be tailored to Russian national needs and interests. Hence any U.S. attempt to impose values and approaches that are poorly understood or not shared by Russia will be counterproductive. The Russian side, for its part, should realize that the U.S. offer of assistance is a unique chance to deal effectively with the ticking time bomb of aging CW stockpiles that are near the end of, or well beyond, their service life.

There are several steps which, if implemented, could enhance the effectiveness and acceptability of U.S. chemical demilitarization assistance.

GREATER COORDINATION BETWEEN U.S. AND INTERNATIONAL AGENCIES

Russia's chemical demilitarization efforts involve not only CW destruction but also development of transportation, social infrastructure, and other projects. Although CTR funds can be spent only on the former, other related projects may be important enough to be funded on a selective basis from other U.S. sources, thus improving their prospects for quick execution. This money might come from foreign aid, the U.S. Department of Agriculture, and other institutions, both governmental and private. With Russia joining the Partnership for Peace program, there are grounds to expect that other Western countries may set up national programs for assisting Russia's chemical demilitarization efforts. If the United States is to retain its position as the lead donor, it will be only natural for the United States to assume a coordinating role for other countries' assistance, with a view to channeling the money to prioritized projects.

SELECTION OF AN INTEGRATING CONTRACTOR

Russian chemical demilitarization efforts function in a much more complex environment than a typical U.S. domestic program, which involves multiple small projects and separate competitions by a number of companies for small contracts. The Russian environment makes it imperative to minimize the number of participating companies by assigning the bulk of the work to one integrating contractor with experience in doing business in Russia. An integrating contractor would be authorized by DOD to maintain independent contacts with relevant entities throughout the country and be part of ongoing government-to-government negotiations. Another compelling reason for an integrating contractor is that government decisions regarding Gornyi and Kambarka have set an important precedent of awarding most of the contracts to local firms. If the same approach is taken with the U.S.-funded facility at Shchuchie, an integrating contractor would have to demonstrate continuity and hands-on experience in dealing with a wide range of local companies. As in the past, personal contacts rather than written agreements, particularly with local players, will matter most.

A COMPREHENSIVE IMPLEMENTATION PLAN

Despite MOD's continuous opposition to a comprehensive implementation plan, it is important to encourage Russia to move ahead with such a plan, patterned on Russia's traditions and approaches but still providing necessary landmarks and cost estimates. Moreover, this plan has been requested by the Duma before it releases money for large-scale destruction projects. It is also required by the U.S. Congress as the basis for evaluating specific DOD requests for money to be channeled to Russia's chemical demilitarization projects.

DELINKAGE FROM OTHER ARMS CONTROL OBLIGATIONS

If the ultimate objective is to ensure Russia's compliance with bilateral CW agreements, the best way to achieve this objective is to accelerate Russia's ratification of the CWC. Delaying U.S. chemical demilitarization assistance to Russia will delay Russia's CWC entry into force, which could otherwise be a powerful multilateral lever for Russian compliance with most of its bilateral obligations. Linking U.S. assistance to compliance with other non-CW-related arms control obligations (such as for biological weapons) would paralyze any progress in the CW-related arms control area.

INVOLVEMENT IN PUBLIC OUTREACH EFFORTS

Under past work plans, DOD shared its experience with Russia on developing public outreach policies to win trust and consent from local communities to host CW destruction activities. However, the current emphasis on building a CW destruction facility at one storage site is pushing the U.S. team into a more direct role. This makes the case for an integrating contractor even stronger. Helping local authorities create a more attractive climate for private investment in the economy and developing mutually beneficial contacts with the local business community would be an effective U.S. contribution to public outreach efforts.

SUPPORT FOR THE GORNYI AND KAMBARKA PROJECTS

Although, understandably, the U.S. administration is primarily interested in destroying weaponized organophosphorus agents, which have the highest military utility, it must not distance itself from the projects dealing with old blister agents stored in bulk which are the first to be destroyed in the Russian program. Ways may be found to support some of the most vital components of these projects while retaining the emphasis on destroying organophosphorus agents. If the Gornyi or Kambarka efforts failed or were considerably delayed, this would inevitably reflect on any U.S.-sponsored projects at other sites. Alternately, if the two projects move ahead successfully, DOD may accumulate enough experience to deal effectively with a more complex working environment elsewhere.

ESTABLISH A JOINT U.S. CONGRESS–FEDERAL ASSEMBLY COMMISSION

The Russian Federal Assembly has shown a keen interest in acquiring oversight of the use of foreign sources of funding. Both the United States and Russia would benefit from a joint U.S. Congress-Russian Federal Assembly commission on CW destruction. It would not only facilitate a direct exchange of information on the status of CW destruction in each country, but would also help the U.S. Congress develop a better understanding of Russia's needs for non-Russian sources of funding.

Conclusion

CTR funding is in no way a charitable operation, but rather an important program that supports U.S. national security interests. Accordingly, its implementation must be more flexible and innovative than ordinary foreign and domestic assistance programs.

Starting virtually from scratch in 1992, the CTR Program's chemical demilitarization component has not shown major visible initial results because of its longer-term and programmatic orientation. Unlike the CTR Program's nuclear projects, which were originally relatively short-term and stand-alone projects (except the storage facility), chemical demilitarization assistance has played a role in shaping the entire

Russian CW destruction program. The value of U.S. chemical demilitarization assistance can best be measured by the remarkable series of steps it has encouraged the Russian government to take to move ahead with its own program, drawing, where appropriate, on the U.S. experience. Dealing with the government of a country in transition is a challenge, and any evaluation of the CTR Program's performance in the chemical demilitarization area should take this into account. Again, unlike the nuclear area where the Ministry of Atomic Energy and its Minister, Viktor Mikhailov, are firmly in control, the chemical demilitarization area has been for some time filled with a number of players competing with each other and speaking to the U.S. government in different voices.

A major achievement so far is the creation of an unprecedented U.S.-Russian dialogue through the presence in Moscow of a DOD office staffed with Pentagon officials and U.S. contractors. These continuous contacts, the initial U.S. funding, and the persistent pressure on the Russian decision-makers were clearly the driving forces that led to an important series of actions by the Russian government in 1995 and 1996. Barring sudden upheavals in the Russian political scene, the current momentum may lead to more dynamic chemical demilitarization efforts, hopefully accompanied by Russia's ratification of the CWC. The current period, which follows the passage of Russian presidential elections, represents a propitious moment for the U.S. administration to establish a dialogue with new players, demonstrating its willingness to live up to earlier commitments to provide chemical demilitarization assistance. Successful implementation of the chemical demilitarization assistance program in the current and subsequent stages will provide an important impetus to political relations between the United States and Russia in general, as well as to global efforts to halt the proliferation of and eventually ban chemical weapons.

Conclusions, Next Steps, and Future Directions

Chapter 18

Cooperative Assistance

Lessons Learned and Directions for the Future

John M. Shields & William C. Potter

In a remarkable instance of legislative foresight, U.S. financial and technical resources were mobilized in late 1991 to aid the newly independent states (NIS) of the former Soviet Union in countering a variety of disarmament challenges and proliferation threats. Under the aegis of the Nunn-Lugar Cooperative Threat Reduction (CTR) Program, as of June 1996, over $1.5 billion had been appropriated to assist Belarus, Kazakstan, Russia, and Ukraine to eliminate or reduce weapons of mass destruction and to modernize and expand proliferation safeguards in the NIS. In addition to the CTR Program, other initiatives have been undertaken since 1992 by numerous U.S. government agencies, other governments, and multinational organizations to supplement the CTR Program's activities and to pursue areas of assistance not specifically addressed under CTR.

Since its inception, the CTR Program has achieved some noteworthy accomplishments but also has been marked by missteps and important missed opportunities. A number of these problems are the product of "growing pains" that emerge in any novel venture, and many have been corrected as programs have matured. However, CTR and other assistance programs to the former Soviet Union now confront a more fundamental challenge to their existence that requires immediate attention. This challenge is of a political and economic nature that results from a sea change in U.S. domestic politics. The erosion of bipartisanship in the U.S. Congress, that body's obsession with cost-cutting and disdain for any program perceived to be "foreign assistance," and the rise of anti-Russian sentiment have combined to make the CTR Program an increasingly tough sell. Unfortunately, the erosion of the broad consensus of support for the CTR Program in the United States has been matched by growing anti-Western sentiment and hostility to cooperative assistance activities in the Russian Parliament.

Contributing to the challenge now facing the CTR Program is its growing complexity. Over the life of the program, it gradually has expanded beyond the bounds of its original mandate. One result of this expansion—what some critics would characterize as "mission creep"—has been a loss of consensus by U.S. decision-makers and legislators on the focus and key priorities of U.S. denuclearization assistance to the NIS. Disagreements over the appropriate focus on the U.S. side in turn have, on occasion, poisoned the U.S.-NIS working relationship established under the CTR process. NIS recipients in some cases have developed inflated expectations of the purpose and scope of the CTR Program and have come to see it as an entitlement or spoils system rather than a partnership.

The intensity of the criticism directed at the CTR Program and the urgency of the work that remains to be done make it imperative to rebuild consensus for assistance and to complete time-urgent projects. In particular, there is a need to reexamine the goals, scope, and priorities of U.S. assistance to determine which priorities are achievable in the current political and budgetary climate and to define a strategy to achieve these goals. Among these measures, there is a special requirement for rebuilding a base of support for assistance to the NIS in both U.S. and NIS national legislatures and among the public at large.

A necessary step in rebuilding U.S. and NIS support for the CTR Program is to identify the key factors that have been responsible for the relative success or failure of its constituent program parts. Understanding why some projects have worked and whether these factors can be applied to other areas may be critical to building support for priority projects and carrying them forward. The remainder of this chapter draws upon the insights presented by other contributors to this volume in order to discern lessons which may be a guide for future action.

Accomplishments of CTR Assistance

The CTR Program and related assistance efforts have been responsible for or have helped to facilitate a number of significant achievements since 1992. The most important achievement has been to help underwrite the elimination of former Soviet strategic weapons deployed outside Russia, effectively preventing the emergence of three new *de facto* nuclear weapons states after the breakup of the Soviet Union. A major accomplishment in this regard was to provide incentives to NIS states to accede to arms reduction and nonproliferation agreements. The CTR Program provided additional incentives to Ukraine, Belarus, and Kazakstan to carry out their Lisbon Protocol commitments and to relinquish control of nuclear weapons residing on their territory. Technical and financial assistance promised under the U.S. program played a key role in encouraging Ukraine, for example, to sign the January 1994 Trilateral Statement agreeing to withdraw all strategic warheads on its territory to Russia for dismantlement. The program also was instrumental in encouraging these countries to accede to the Nuclear Non-Proliferation Treaty (NPT) as non–nuclear weapons states.

Moreover, U.S. technical and financial assistance has provided some assurance to all four recipient states that they will be able to meet the requirements of transporting, dismantling, and/or securing strategic nuclear weapons and their delivery systems, thus facilitating signature and ratification of the START agreements by these states. U.S. assistance has expedited Russia's compliance with START by helping to eliminate more than 200 submarine launched ballistic missile (SLBM) launchers, more than 350 intercontinental ballistic missile (ICBM) silos, 25 heavy bombers, and more than 1,300 ballistic missiles, and by removing more than 1,000 strategic warheads from deployed systems. As of spring 1996, the CTR Program had facilitated the return to Russia of more than 2,500 strategic warheads from Belarus, Kazakstan, and Ukraine, most of which will be dismantled in Russia. The program has also funded the design and partial construction of a secure, centralized storage facility in Russia for fissile material from dismantled nuclear weapons. Although not without problems, including delays in delivery of appropriate equipment, both the U.S. Department of Defense (DOD) and the Russian Ministry of Defense (MOD) generally regard positively their experiences in technical cooperation to transport, secure, and dismantle Russian nuclear weapons.

CTR Program assistance has also played a crucial role in ensuring that Belarus, Kazakstan, and Ukraine have been able to carry out their commitments to become nuclear-free. The program has helped Kazakstan to remove all 1,410 nuclear warheads from its territory and transport them safely to Russia. In June 1996, the last of more than 4,000 strategic and tactical nuclear warheads deployed in Ukraine were transported to Russia as well. In Belarus, the remaining 18 nuclear warheads, deployed on SS-25 ICBMs at Lida and Mozyr, were expected to be removed, with CTR technical assistance, before the end of 1996.[1] U.S. technical support is aiding dismantlement of SS-24 and SS-19 ICBMs in Ukraine, destruction of the 176 ICBM silos on its territory, and environmental restoration of these sites. The CTR Program is providing technical support to the destruction of SS-18 ICBM silos in Kazakstan. It has also assisted the removal to Russia of 72 road-mobile SS-25 ICBMs from Belarus and is helping Belarusan officials destroy SS-25 launch facilities and dispose of missile propellant in an environmentally sound manner.

U.S. CTR assistance also has provided the means for more unconventional threat reduction projects. One such success story is Project Sapphire, which was partially financed with CTR funds. Under this project, carried out over a period of months in 1994, the United States and Kazakstan, in consultation with Russia, cooperated in the removal of 600 kilograms of highly enriched uranium (HEU) from Kazakstan to more secure storage in the United States. This initiative addressed a core nonproliferation problem, preventing the possible diversion of a cache of inadequately secured fissile material that might have fueled literally dozens of bombs in a clandestine weapons program. Project Sapphire was a model of U.S.-NIS cooperation and demonstrated how a relatively small amount of resources could yield enormous dividends for demilitarization and nonproliferation. However, it also revealed the enormity of the fissile material security and accountancy problem in the former Soviet nuclear complex.

The CTR Program has acted as a catalyst for other U.S. assistance programs in the areas of fissile material protection, control, and accounting (MPC&A), defense conversion, export controls, and defense personnel retraining, among other activities. One example is the lab-to-lab program of the Department of Energy (DOE) between DOE laboratories and equivalent research facilities in the NIS, which promotes scientific activities with commercial applications. In addition to its efforts in defense conversion, a principal focus of the lab-to-lab program has been to institute improvements in MPC&A at NIS facilities. While representing a relatively small amount of resources, the lab-to-lab program has been widely praised as an important threat reduction effort instituted at the grass-roots level. The International

---

1. EDITORS' NOTE: The last nuclear warheads were withdrawn from Belarus in late November 1996.

Science and Technology Center (ISTC), a project established under the CTR Program but now overseen by the State Department, is another example of a low-cost initiative that has begun to make an impact in the area of demilitarization. Although hampered by bureaucratic delays in its infancy, the ISTC has grown to become a powerful tool to help redirect former weapons scientists in NIS states to commercial and civilian ventures. As of summer 1996, more than 230 scientific and technical projects, employing more than 12,500 former weapons scientists in the NIS, had been sponsored by ISTC funds.

Beyond the specific contributions that U.S. assistance has made to threat reduction, nonproliferation, and demilitarization, it has also had an important ancillary achievement. Combined, the CTR Program and other assistance efforts have served as a key mechanism for deepening bilateral relations between the United States and Belarus, Kazakstan, Russia, and Ukraine. In the midst of political and military upheaval in the former Soviet Union, the CTR Program provided an important, stable channel for communication and improved understanding between the United States and emerging NIS states.

Outstanding Problems

Despite the number of accomplishments brought about by CTR and associated programs, NIS officials have voiced a number of complaints about the management and implementation of U.S. assistance. Key concerns among NIS participants *vis-à-vis* implementation of assistance include:

- the slow pace of implementation, both at the top decision-making levels and between DOD and contractors on the ground in the NIS;

- a lack of management flexibility on the part of the United States, and the imposition of U.S. accounting procedures, work plans, and schedules on NIS participants;

- the high level of bureaucracy on the U.S. side, including multiple or redundant points of contact for CTR activities and the large number of "consultants" who consumed CTR resources but contributed little to specific projects;

- the use of mostly U.S. contractors and U.S.-supplied equipment to perform CTR tasks, often at higher cost and with longer delays than equally qualified NIS contractors and suppliers;

- the lack of timely and consistent information from the United States about current funding obligations and schedules for delivery of goods and services under the CTR Program; and

- the amount of "nuclear tourism" by U.S. officials and others around NIS facilities that did not seem to result in any subsequent real improvements.

Some implementation problems, particularly early in the CTR Program, probably were unavoidable given the complexity of the program. DOD officials also have argued that the slow pace early in the CTR Program was warranted to watch closely how money was spent, even at the risk of losing unobligated funds. Other delays in the flow of assistance can be attributed to the postponement by NIS states in signing CTR umbrella agreements, after which the pace of activity increased dramatically. In some cases, even when projects had been approved at the national ministerial level in the NIS, lower-echelon bureaucrats in the customs service or local administration officials delayed actual delivery of CTR goods and services. Additional problems, such as in the management and oversight of particular projects, have been acknowledged by U.S. officials, who have made efforts to correct them. For example, DOD is streamlining contractor oversight of its remaining projects in the NIS, giving contractors on the ground in these countries greater autonomy to make and execute decisions.

A complaint of project planners in both the United States and NIS countries has been the lack of information-sharing and coordination on a number of cooperative assistance ventures. U.S. officials have noted that few, if any, identifiable NIS government documents exist detailing NIS weapons destruction and demilitarization objectives, schedules, and needs. Similarly, NIS officials have long complained of a lack of official U.S. sources of information on amounts of assistance spent on given projects. Nor is it clear to NIS participants that DOD-reported expenditures match manpower and materials that have actually arrived in recipient countries. Moreover, there is a mutual lack of understanding of the decision-making and project execution process on each side, a state of affairs that merely breeds uncertainty and suspicion. The lack of transparency and resulting misperceptions on both sides have aggravated the problems of understanding NIS requirements and matching U.S. assistance to specific NIS needs. More important, the lack of transparency has complicated the vital task of making an effective case to legislatures and to the public at large for continued cooperation.

Many of these implementation problems can be addressed through relatively simple administrative changes. A much more profound problem, however, is the growing disagreement between the United States and its NIS partners as to the scope and purpose of the CTR Program and other forms of assistance. Many NIS officials have developed a firm belief that demilitarization assistance, through the CTR Program or some other vehicle, should encompass not only military-technical tasks, such as weapons destruction and fissile material control, but also economic and social issues in demilitarization, such as conversion of defense production plants and retraining and housing of former strategic weapons officers and defense industrial personnel. Others have suggested that more attention should be paid to environmental issues, including the remediation of former weapons production facilities. Key NIS decision-makers have argued that an assistance strategy that addressed the social and economic dislocations of moving to a commercial, civilian economy would ease the perception in the NIS that the CTR Program is simply a means for the United States to disarm NIS states and erode their scientific and industrial infrastructures. At the same time, many in the U.S. Congress believe that DOD funds should be used only to dismantle and destroy weapons that pose a clear threat to the United States.

This widening gap in perceptions is due in part to the internal politics in the United States and the post-Soviet states regarding NIS assistance. It is also testimony to a failure on the part of U.S. policymakers to communicate to their NIS counterparts the limitations on what the CTR Program can or was meant to accomplish.

The purpose of the original Nunn-Lugar Program, as defined in the Soviet Nuclear Threat Reduction Act of 1991, was "to (1) destroy nuclear weapons, chemical weapons, and other weapons, (2) transport, store, disable, and safeguard weapons in connection with their destruction, and (3) establish verifiable safeguards against the proliferation of such weapons."[2] The program was subsequently expanded to address defense conversion, environmental cleanup, military housing, retraining, and a host of other problems in NIS states, not all of which were obviously security-related. Although there had been some congressional opposition to the CTR Program from the outset because of its alleged diversion of focus and funds from traditional DOD missions, this sentiment grew markedly after the Republican landslide in the 1994 congressional elections. The new conservative majority in Congress was less inclined than either its Democratic predecessor or the Bush White House to perceive the CTR Program as an appropriate tool for inducing good arms control behavior or facilitating the transition from defense-based commercial economies to market-oriented ones. Moreover, even among those members of Congress who, in principle, support U.S. assistance to the NIS for purposes of defense conversion, environmental cleanup, and personnel retraining, many object to having these activities funded out of the DOD budget. The 1995 decision to disaggregate CTR functions and to redistribute noncore weapons elimination tasks to other governmental agencies was therefore probably prudent from the standpoint of retaining congressional support for the CTR Program in the short term, notwithstanding the possible long-term costs of harnessing the different program components in pursuit of national, as opposed to departmental, foreign policy objectives.

The initial budgetary results of the transfer of CTR activities from DOD to other agencies appear to have been successful. DOD retained $298 million in Fiscal Year (FY) 1996 funds for the central CTR tasks associated with weapons elimination. DOE received $70 million in funds for its MPC&A activities in the NIS, and the State Department also received about $25 million to support work on NIS export controls

---

2. Public Law 102-228, Section 212. For a discussion of the Soviet Nuclear Threat Reduction Act, see Theodor Galdi, "The Nunn-Lugar Cooperative Threat Reduction Program for Soviet Weapons Dismantlement: Background and Implementation," Congressional Research Service report (December 29, 1993). An account of the earlier unsuccessful effort by Congressman Les Aspin and Senator Sam Nunn to provide similar assistance through an amendment to the defense authorization bill is provided by Sam Nunn and Richard Lugar, "The Nunn-Lugar Initiative: Cooperative Demilitarization of the Former Soviet Union," in Allan E. Goodman, ed., *The Diplomatic Record 1992–1993* (Boulder, Colo.: Westview Press, 1995), pp. 139–156.

and the International Science and Technology Center. This total of $393 million compares favorably with the $400 million in CTR funds received by DOD in FY 1995 and in previous years. For FY 1997, the CTR program also was funded at the amount requested by DOD, $327.9 million, without significant legislative restrictions on the use of the funds. In addition, new legislation co-sponsored by Senators Nunn, Lugar, and Pete Domenici (Republican–New Mexico), known as "Nunn-Lugar II," will provide an additional amount, approximately $90 million, for CTR-related activities in the former Soviet Union.[3]

The relative success of DOD, DOE, and the State Department in securing funding for their threat reduction and demilitarization programs provides reason for optimism. And the opening of a "second front" to supplement these activities by Senators Nunn, Lugar, and Domenici is an especially encouraging development. Nonetheless, the long-term trend is still one of congressional hostility to all kinds of foreign assistance, and particularly aid to Russia. Ominously, the House defeated by only a very narrow margin a Republican amendment to the FY 1997 Defense Authorization Act that would have placed a number of restrictive conditions on aid to Russia and Belarus, effectively killing CTR assistance to these countries.

A key task, therefore, is to identify and prioritize a set of U.S.-NIS cooperative threat reduction activities. A new consensus is required, not only among U.S. policymakers but between the United States and recipient countries in the NIS, as to what assistance is required and, more important, what is possible to achieve with limited resources. Given the limited resources available, a second task is to identify and learn from past successes and mistakes. In today's more adversarial climate, U.S.-NIS cooperative efforts cannot waste precious political capital or fiscal resources. Identifying those factors that have made some past or ongoing projects successful may help planners on both sides reshape current projects and design future efforts to be more efficient.

---

3. At the time of this writing the administration had not yet decided how to allocate the "Nunn-Lugar II" funds. The $90 million that was approved was far less than the $235 million sought by Senators Nunn, Lugar, and Domenici in their amendment to the FY 1997 Defense Authorization bill.

Factors Contributing to Success

A review of those assistance projects that have been most successful reveals a number of common factors. They include a symmetry of interests and objectives on the part of U.S. and NIS participants, truly joint contributions, good communications, minimal bureaucratic intrusiveness, and cost consciousness.

SHARED INTERESTS AND GOALS

An important lesson from the first four years of CTR and related assistance is the need for a symmetry of interests and objectives between U.S. and NIS participants. One of the factors that distinguishes successful projects from more problematic areas of cooperation is the high priority that both the United States and its NIS partners place on the task at hand. The strained relationship between U.S. and NIS participants in some areas is due in many cases to the perception by NIS participants that they have been pressured to engage in an activity important to the United States but of relatively less importance to them.

One consequence of this lesson is that U.S.-NIS assistance efforts may have to coalesce around a smaller number of cooperative projects where there is strong agreement by all parties on the importance of the work. Areas of assistance that are important to NIS states but for which there is little interest or political support on the U.S. side—particularly such social issues as officer housing and retraining—may have to await other, non-CTR or nongovernmental solutions. By the same token, it is likely to be difficult to sustain, much less expand, projects that are of relatively greater importance to the United States unless means are found to coopt powerful NIS critics (e.g., the Ministry of Atomic Energy [Minatom]).

Regardless of the number of projects, U.S. and NIS participants must begin with a clear understanding of the scope, time frame, and goals of agreed efforts. Statements by NIS officials since 1992 suggest that NIS participants have sometimes had expectations for CTR and other projects that far exceeded the intentions or understanding of U.S. administration planners or congressional appropriators. Better communication between U.S. program managers and their NIS counterparts could help prevent such disconnects and the ensuing feelings of bad faith on both sides.

PARALLEL INVOLVEMENT

A related issue is the need for shared, equal, and active involvement by both U.S. and NIS participants. The most successful projects have been those in which the U.S.-NIS relationship is one of partners, rather than donor and recipient. Initiatives such as Project Sapphire and lab-to-lab efforts have been propelled by the sense of *esprit de corps* and "jointness" that came from close cooperation between like-minded individuals such as U.S. and NIS military officers or scientific personnel at national laboratories. By contrast, many projects in which NIS participants perceived themselves as principally passive objects of assistance or token participants were marked by roadblocks and inertia.

An important, cost-effective way to develop this kind of parity and build goodwill may be to rely more heavily on local NIS contractors and personnel to provide manpower, equipment, and materiel for demilitarization and nonproliferation projects. U.S. technology and expertise has filled a number of critical gaps for technical tasks in several joint efforts. However, there have also been examples in which U.S. or other foreign equipment was imported at higher cost and with longer delays to perform demilitarization projects when similar or superior equipment was available from local contractors. This appears to be especially true in the case of cutting tools, heavy-lift equipment, and other machinery imported to dismantle and destroy strategic delivery vehicles. Besides giving NIS partners a more active role in the denuclearization process, such a local investment strategy could lower overall costs and stretch limited resources by utilizing "off-the-shelf" technologies, expertise, materials, and manpower that frequently would otherwise be idle. It also would reduce transport costs and stimulate the local economy. Unfortunately, the lab-to-lab projects and, to a lesser extent, the ISTC are among the few examples in which NIS partner countries have been able to see direct, real-time benefits for local personnel of cooperation with the West.[4]

REGULAR CHANNELS OF COMMUNICATION

Not surprisingly, successful areas of cooperation in the past have been marked by frequent, routine opportunities for communication and exchanges of information and ideas. The feeling of being "left in the

---

4. It is true that the original Nunn-Lugar legislation calls for use of U.S. technology "where feasible," but it makes little sense to insist that virtually all equipment come from the United States.

dark" and not knowing the status of current projects have frequently raised suspicions of bad faith by both NIS and U.S. participants. Communication in particular projects has frequently been a function of the personalities involved. The strong working relationship that developed in military-to-military efforts to transport nuclear weapons back to Russia securely was due in part to the regular discussions of needs and technical problems between high-ranking and mid-level military officers in DOD and the Russian MOD.

There is a critical need to create and improve channels of communication in U.S.-NIS assistance programs at a variety of levels. As in more successful programs, there needs to be some regular means, formal or informal, of communicating ideas, problems, and questions between U.S. planners and their NIS counterparts on a bilateral basis in such a way that a timely response is possible. More rigorous procedures for reporting funding decisions, contract announcements and awards, and delivery of goods and services to recipient states could raise the level of trust and understanding in these countries. Improving bilateral communication (and thus coordination) may first require developing a joint framework to track the level and schedule of assistance disbursements and the delivery of goods and services to recipient states. At a minimum, this would require a common understanding of accounting rules for tracking these disbursements. NIS officials have in the past had a difficult time deciphering such DOD budgetary jargon as "notified," "agreed," "obligated," and "disbursed"—accounting terms that are part of DOD's way of doing business, but which do not clearly correspond to observable deliveries of CTR goods and services. Coordination would also be greatly improved by more systematic, reciprocal reporting of current activities, requirements, and needs by NIS partner countries.

Such reciprocal bilateral documentation could improve the timing of U.S. and NIS budget development and requests, helping planners to better match U.S. resources to gaps in NIS budget allocations for eligible activities. By demonstrating how U.S. expenditures were directly filling NIS budget gaps for demilitarization and other activities, such documentation could help U.S. officials make a stronger programmatic case to Congress for near-term and future funding. To the extent that better bilateral communication would help make U.S. budgetary and decision-making processes more transparent to NIS officials, these officials may come to have a better understanding of the realm of the possible where U.S. funding is concerned.

MINIMAL BUREAUCRACY

The need for reduced red tape is a truism of any complex enterprise, particularly for such a time-urgent venture as the cooperation between the U.S. and NIS countries. A perennial complaint of many NIS participants is the excessive level of bureaucracy on the U.S. side. This has been particularly true of government-to-government MPC&A projects, in which U.S. partners at Minatom, the Federal Atomic Inspectorate (GAN), and other Russian agencies have been perplexed by U.S. auditing and reporting requirements. Some delays in implementing projects, particularly early on, may have been unavoidable given the complexity of the new program. The lab-to-lab program, however, has demonstrated that it is possible to implement MPC&A projects in a timely fashion with less intrusive oversight and still retain adequate program control. This model needs to be applied more widely, and is likely to be as CTR projects transition from DOD oversight and complex DOD acquisition procedures to those of other agencies.

COST CONTROL AND COST SHARING

In the current political climate, program decisions are largely budget-driven. Large, expensive assistance efforts will remain a magnet for criticism. As a consequence, there is a need to devise creative means to attract new capital both from private business and from other national governments and international lending agencies. The United States or a consortium of Western countries, for example, might purchase additional surplus Russian weapons-grade HEU for blending down into low-enriched uranium fuel. A portion of the payments could be earmarked for MPC&A improvements and/or to assist in the conversion away from plutonium activities of Russia's three "plutonium cities," Tomsk-7, Krasnoyarsk-26, and Chelyabinsk-65.

The CTR Program also needs to look increasingly to the NIS as a resource for more cost-efficient implementation of threat reduction activities. Local sourcing of technical manpower, materiel, and equipment for cooperative projects has the potential to reduce overall CTR costs while simultaneously stimulating local economies. If applied creatively, a move toward greater indigenousness also might contribute to U.S.-NIS nonproliferation objectives by stemming the "brain drain" of technical expertise from former Soviet defense industries. A step in the right direction is the recently established MPC&A training center in Obninsk. This center will reinforce indigenous MPC&A efforts by educating a new generation of specialists who will serve as practitioners and instructors. Ideally, one might draw upon the ISTC to identify relevant scientific talent for both MPC&A training and research purposes.[5] One can imagine similar cost-effective ways to utilize the ISTC to train experts in and to conduct research on other CTR and nuclear threat problem areas (e.g., chemical weapons destruction, export controls, environmental cleanup, and nuclear safety). Past CTR success stories also offer valuable clues for controlling costs and achieving multiple goals in a single project. One of the more creative ventures under the CTR Program was not only to demobilize Russian and Ukrainian military facilities but to use a marginal amount of resources to purchase and install U.S.-made modular housing equipment at these facilities and retrain former military personnel to manufacture housing for former Strategic Rocket Forces officers. By taking advantage of the synergism of the program, this particular project was able to kill multiple birds with one stone, addressing some of the defense conversion and social welfare concerns of NIS partners as well as CTR's core demilitarization objectives with a minimum of additional resources.

Priorities for Future Work

There is little doubt that a new consensus is needed on the goals and scope of future U.S.-NIS threat reduction cooperation. The United States must strive to reach a consensus internally on its key priorities for future demilitarization and nonproliferation cooperation with its NIS partners; it must then consider what type of assistance it is willing to offer. Recipient countries, for their part, must better appreciate the political context within which the CTR Program is administered in Washington, and modify their objectives accordingly.

MATERIAL PROTECTION, CONTROL, AND ACCOUNTING
The highest priority today is to ensure the security and accountability of all nuclear weapons and weapons-usable materials in the post-Soviet states. Ironically, this task has been complicated by the success of CTR

---

5. Although the ISTC has reviewed more than 640 scientific and technical projects by former Soviet scientists, and funded more than 230 of these proposals, only one project has been related to the protection, control, and accounting of fissile material

weapons dismantlement activities which has created an enormous influx of materials requiring secure storage and control.[6] The Department of Energy has an extremely ambitious program, which, if implemented on schedule, should go a long way toward reducing the potential for diversion of nuclear materials. Under current plans, by the end of 1997 the United States expects to provide the resources to: (1) upgrade significantly MPC&A at all sites in the non-Russian successor states where weapons-usable material is present; (2) upgrade MPC&A at all the major civilian sites in Russia that handle weapons-usable material; (3) initiate MPC&A upgrades at a wide range of additional Russian sites, including a cross-section of those within the Minatom weapons complex; (4) establish the basis for MPC&A cooperation at all Russian nuclear material sites, including those in the weapons complex and at civilian and naval propulsion reactors; (5) facilitate the development of a national nuclear material accounting system; (6) foster the growth of an effective national regulatory program in Russia; and (7) facilitate a sustainable indigenous Russian MPC&A program.

These are all vital steps that deserve the highest level of political support in both countries. The estimated cost of approximately $70–90 million a year to implement the program through FY 1997 is a modest amount to pay for improved physical protection and fissile material control.

However, not all safeguards problems are amenable to technical fixes. Probably most difficult to correct, but also significant for the long-term security of Russia's nuclear assets, is what may best be called an "underdeveloped safeguards culture" among the staff and custodians of the post-Soviet nuclear industry. In part, this tendency to undervalue physical protection rules and regulations is the product of the Soviet political and economic system, which bred such work and management practices as the avoidance of individual initiative and responsibility and the neglect of employee safety. These habits persist, even though many Russian nuclear industry officials acknowledge that plant security and material control improvements must be made.

---

6. The most comprehensive discussion of this issue is provided by John P. Holdren, "Reducing the Threat of Nuclear Theft in the Former Soviet Union," *Arms Control Today*, March 1996, pp. 14–20. See also William Potter, "Before the Deluge? Assessing the Threat of Nuclear Leakage from the Post-Soviet States," *Arms Control Today*, October 1995, pp. 9–16.

Changing attitudes and instilling a new philosophy cannot be done easily or quickly. Nor will an influx of money alone solve the problem. A sustained educational effort is required. This is a task that nongovernmental organizations (NGOs) are particularly well suited to perform, and there is a need for a much greater partnership between the U.S. government and NGOs in the provision of such educational assistance. In addition, efforts to nurture the development of strong and independent nuclear regulatory bodies in the post-Soviet states should be intensified.

EXPORT CONTROLS

The development of more effective export controls in the NIS also is vital to combat nuclear leakage and should proceed in tandem with steps to strengthen MPC&A. Unfortunately, progress in providing meaningful export control assistance under the CTR Program has been uneven at best.

Although there have been some positive developments in Belarus, Kazakstan, and Ukraine, for all practical purposes CTR assistance on export controls has been stalled in Russia due to bureaucratic political battles in Moscow and Washington, disputes over auditing requirements, and very different perceptions in the two capitals of the nature of export control problems. The situation has been aggravated by organizational turf disputes in both countries, including the reluctance of responsible parties in the Department of State to routinely make good use of their own country desk officers who better understand the economic and political context in which NIS export controls are evolving.

Outside of Russia, the development of export controls has been stymied principally by the absence of high-level political commitment to stringent controls. The effectiveness of Russia's export controls also is undermined by the absence of effective customs controls between Russia and the other post-Soviet republics. These factors, combined with a lack of equipment for monitoring illicit nuclear trade, mean that sensitive defense goods—including nuclear material and technology— can pass readily from Russia or Ukraine to other post-Soviet states, and from there to countries of major proliferation concern. If anything, this problem of the "weakest link" will increase if recent agreements to establish customs unions and unregulated trade between Belarus and Russia and between Russia and Kazakstan are implemented. To be effective, export control assistance must therefore be directed to all of the post-Soviet states, not only the "big four."

CHEMICAL WEAPONS DESTRUCTION

The early promise of U.S.-Russian cooperation in chemical weapons (CW) destruction has, until recently, been held hostage to a number of problems and disagreements regarding destruction of Russian bulk and weaponized CW stockpiles. Destruction of thousands of tons of Russian CW agents has been delayed by disagreements between the United States and Russia on the technical means of destroying these stockpiles; disagreements over proposed work plans, schedules, and contracting mechanisms to oversee destruction; and bureaucratic disputes in Russian national and local governments over the lines of responsibility for CW demilitarization. A central issue has been the immense cost of this enterprise, including not only design, construction, outfitting, and operation of CW destruction facilities, but also the related costs of transportation, environmental cleanup, and other infrastructure problems.

Although these difficulties will not be overcome easily, the U.S. commitment to assist Russia in financing CW destruction technology development and destruction facility operation has been the driving force behind the Russian government's own efforts to move ahead with chemical demilitarization and to support a joint comprehensive implementation plan for CW destruction. Reduction or abandonment of this commitment would be a jarring obstacle to progress in reducing the Russian chemical weapons threat, both military and environmental, and might doom prospects for Russian ratification of the Chemical Weapons Convention (CWC).

INFORMATION SHARING

In order for a new consensus to emerge on the goals and scope of future CTR activities, it is vital to improve communications and coordination among NIS states. At present, these states have few means of comparing experiences, airing grievances, and sharing information. Bilateral discussions are useful, but are too often held hostage to bumps in bilateral relations between the United States and individual countries. Establishing a multilateral forum that would meet at regular intervals, such as a "group of four" or "four plus one" arrangement, would assist U.S. partner states to work jointly on a common set of problems and perhaps generate creative solutions.

Similarly, there is an urgent need to improve the level of communication with national legislatures and the public at large about the accomplishments and status of cooperative assistance. Given the charged political discourse in the United States against such foreign assistance, there is a special requirement now for effective outreach and "public relations" that graphically demonstrates not only the value of this cooperation but the implications for national and international security should this cooperation be derailed. Representatives of NIS partner countries have a special role to play in such a public communication strategy. These officials are likely to make a much more effective case for future assistance and the consequences of assistance ending than their U.S. counterparts. New channels of communication must be developed that allow these NIS officials to take their case directly to Congressional leaders and other U.S. decision-makers not favorably disposed to assistance.

Such a dialogue would allow NIS states to make their case more directly to those controlling the purse strings of assistance. At a minimum, this would help NIS representatives draw a distinction between Russian actions and "misbehavior" and other NIS states that have abided by congressional preconditions for aid. Similar contacts could be established between U.S. officials and national legislatures in the NIS republics and perhaps also with local legislatures and governmental bodies in NIS regions directly involved in cooperative assistance projects. This kind of dialogue might help erase the problems encountered in CTR chemical demilitarization and MPC&A projects whereby local NIS bodies have objected to or sought to frustrate decisions made at the national ministerial level.

The Consequences of Inaction

It is unrealistic to expect implementation of the CTR Program to proceed independently of the broader sphere of U.S.-Russian relations. Regrettably, recent changes in the political climate in the United States and in NIS states, particularly Russia, have raised the stakes for continued threat reduction efforts, even as they have posed a fundamental challenge to cooperation of any sort. CTR and other cooperation programs have become the target of intense political criticism and are in danger of becoming a political liability in both donor and recipient countries. In the United States, the dominant trend is anti-foreign, anti-aid, and anti-Russian. In the NIS, early expectations and perceptions of the program have been disappointed not only because of exaggerated expectations and implementation problems early on, but also because of the program's failure to address the tremendous social and economic dislocation arising from demilitarization. Increasingly, U.S. assistance programs are perceived, cynically, as a means for the United States to disarm NIS states militarily and to erode their technological and industrial base.

U.S. Secretary of Defense William Perry's characterization of the Russian nuclear complex—as a hydra whose (war)heads could grow back if the entire beast is not destroyed—is often cited by Russian critics of the CTR Program as proof of the U.S. aim.[7] Reinforcing this interpretation is the Russian perception that the United States has imposed punitive tariffs on Russian nuclear exports, excluded Russia from the North Korean nuclear deal, sought to scuttle Russian-Iranian nuclear cooperation, and encouraged publicity that ridicules Russian nuclear reactor safety and material security. These views find many adherents in the reconstituted Russian Duma where economic reform and cooperation with the West have small and declining constituencies.

Disputes over Russian military intervention in Chechnya, expansion of NATO to include former Warsaw Pact states, Russian sales of nuclear technology to Iran, Duma opposition to the START II Treaty, and credible allegations of continued Russian biological weapons research could potentially derail continued assistance to Russia and may affect assistance to all NIS states. The inability or unwillingness of some NIS states to meet their arms control obligations also could further erode political support for the CTR Program in the United States.

These problems are more than simply "bumps on the road" of U.S.-NIS relations. They will not be solved without serious, high-level lobbying that demonstrates both the rewards of past cooperation and the dangers of failing to cooperate in the future. It is worth considering what might happen if bilateral disagreements are allowed to derail

---

7. See, for example the interview with Viktor Mikhailov in "Nuclear Cooperation with Iran: The View from Ordynka," *Priroda* (August 1995), pp. 3–11. In fairness to Perry, who has been a tireless promoter of the CTR Program, the hydra analogy was intended to convey the need to support less popular program components such as conversion of defense facilities and retraining of defense personnel, rather than just to support destruction of weapons. See Secretary of Defense William Perry, address to the National Press Club, January 5, 1995.

U.S.-NIS cooperative assistance entirely. Many of these activities, particularly fissile material control and chemical weapons stockpile destruction, are at critical stages of development after overcoming a number of prior obstacles. The immediate impact of reductions or elimination of assistance would be to increase dramatically the danger that nuclear and other sensitive weapons material technology and expertise would be diverted to the global arms market. Critics of the CTR Program should consider the potential costs of buying security against future adversaries armed with former Soviet weapons of mass destruction compared to the present expense of eliminating these weapons. They also would do well to contemplate how cessation of U.S. CTR assistance would affect the ability of the NIS states to continue fledgling political, military, and economic reforms.

As representatives from Ukraine, Belarus, and Kazakstan have suggested either implicitly or explicitly, cuts in or elimination of U.S. assistance could threaten the special relationship that these countries have come to feel they have with the United States. Arriving at a consensus in these countries on defense and foreign policy issues, particularly nuclear issues, has in some cases been a long, arduous journey. There are political forces at work in these countries that are ready to seize on a sudden downturn in relations with the United States to reopen debate on the NPT, adherence to START, and other security issues. Likewise, it is clear from the tone of political discourse in Russia that the end of the Cold War has brought about tremendous social and economic dislocations. Major cuts in or elimination of assistance to ongoing demilitarization efforts will only further aggravate this situation, creating more disarray and emboldening those in Russia who are suspicious of the West and wish to reverse the course of disarmament and reform.

These developments could have a chilling effect not only on bilateral U.S.-NIS disarmament efforts, but on global efforts to stem the spread of weapons of mass destruction. Multilateral agreements, particularly the Chemical Weapons Convention and the Nuclear Non-Proliferation Treaty, could be undermined by the failure of the United States and Russia to come to terms on destruction of chemical weapons stockpiles and to meet their NPT obligation to further reduce their nuclear weapons stockpiles. In short, derailment of U.S.-Russian threat reduction cooperation might adversely affect other countries' decisions to sign and/or abide by the terms of the CWC and the NPT. In the words of an unusual joint statement on the CTR Program by the deputy foreign ministers of Belarus, Kazakstan, and Ukraine, one should:

Consider carefully the worldwide impact of the future of the Nunn-Lugar program. Will it serve as a positive stimulus for the so-called 'threshold' nuclear countries to give up their national nuclear weapons ambitions? Or will it provide a justification for the ill-founded, but unfortunately widespread perception, that only those possessing weapons of mass destruction are treated with international respect?[8]

---

8. Kostyantyn Hryshchenko, Bulat Nurgaliev, and Andrei Sannikov, "The Nunn-Lugar Program Should be Increased, Not Reduced," *The Nonproliferation Review* (Winter 1996), pp. 67–68.

Appendix

CTR Funding by Country (July 1, 1996).

Program Areas and Projects	Notified	Agreed	Pending Agreements	Other Support	Obligated	Disbursed
		Russia				
Chain of Custody						
Armored Blankets	$5,000,000	$5,000,000	$0	$0	$3,244,083	$2,905,156
Fissile Material Storage Facility	$75,000,000	$75,000,000	$29,000,000	$0	$57,043,122	$11,697,703
Fissile Material Containers	$50,000,000	$50,000,000	$0	$0	$48,377,859	$16,457,011
Fissile Material Storage Facility Design	$15,000,000	$15,000,000	$0	$0	$14,999,458	$14,466,333
Weapons Security Transportation	$46,500,000	$46,500,000	$0	$0	$24,709,600	$1,933,474
Weapons Security Storage	$28,000,000	$28,000,000	$0	$0	$2,489,675	$300,726
Emergency Response Training/Equipment	$15,000,000	$15,000,000	$0	$0	$14,384,129	$12,589,038
Railcar Security Enhancements	$21,500,000	$21,500,000	$0	$0	$21,200,000	$19,272,383
Material Control & Accounting	$45,000,000	$30,000,000	$0	$15,000,000	$42,844,260	$17,802,839
Export Control	$2,260,000	$0	$0	$2,260,000	$1,517,447	$38,215
Demilitarization						
Industrial Partnerships	$38,000,000	$40,000,000	$0	$0	$37,308,119	$12,099,517
Defense Enterprise Fund	$10,000,000	$0	$0	$10,000,000	$10,000,000	$10,000,000
International Science & Technology Center	$35,000,000	$0	$0	$35,000,000	$34,685,462	$31,625,451
Research & Development Foundation	$10,000,000	$0	$0	$10,000,000	$10,000,000	$5,000,000
Defense & Military Contacts	$15,548,000	$0	$0	$15,548,000	$8,964,604	$4,920,466

Destruction & Dismantlement						
Strategic Offensive Arms Elimination	$236,000,000	$231,000,000	$5,000,000	$0	$132,000,383	$93,779,891
Chemical Weapons Destruction	$68,000,000	$68,000,000	$0	$0	$37,946,201	$28,062,487
Other						
Arctic Nuclear Waste	$30,000,000	$0	$0	$30,000,000	$29,876,051	$16,364,941
Total Russia	$745,808,000	$625,000,000	$34,000,000	$117,808,000	$531,590,453	$299,315,631
Belarus						
Chain of Custody						
Emergency Response Training/Equipment	$5,000,000	$5,000,000	$0	$0	$4,979,687	$4,094,163
Material Control & Accounting	$3,000,000	$3,000,000	$0	$0	$2,890,583	$488,374
Export Control	$16,260,000	$16,260,000	$0	$0	$9,980,813	$6,375,127
Demilitarization						
Industrial Partnerships	$20,000,000	$20,000,000	$0	$0	$19,699,849	$11,161,765
Defense Enterprise Fund	$5,000,000	$0	$5,000,000	$0	$5,000,000	$5,000,000
Science & Technology Center	$5,000,000	$0	$5,000,000	$0	$4,950,000	$488,000
Defense & Military Contacts	$3,524,000	$0	$3,524,000	$0	$741,083	$364,413
Destruction & Dismantlement						
Strategic Offensive Arms Elimination	$33,900,000	$28,900,000	$5,000,000	$0	$2,394,647	$78,323
Continuous Communication Link	$2,300,000	$2,300,000	$0	$0	$1,058,241	$789,806
Site Restoration (Project Peace)	$25,000,000	$25,000,000	$0	$0	$19,425,597	$10,752,371
Total Belarus	$118,984,000	$100,460,000	$18,524,000	$0	$71,120,500	$39,592,342

Program Areas and Projects	Notified	Agreed	Pending Agreements	Other Support	Obligated	Disbursed
		Kazakstan				
Chain of Custody						
Emergency Response Training/Equipment	$5,000,000	$5,000,000	$0	$0	$2,792,051	$780,865
Material Control & Accounting	$23,000,000	$23,000,000	$0	$0	$7,718,434	$2,272,953
Export Control	$7,260,000	$7,260,000	$0	$0	$4,028,445	$2,383,273
Demilitarization						
Industrial Partnerships	$15,000,000	$15,000,000	$0	$0	$14,909,042	$5,887,195
Defense Enterprise Fund	$7,000,000	$0		$7,000,000	$7,000,000	$7,000,000
Science & Technology Center	$9,000,000	$0		$9,000,000	$8,950,000	$640,000
Defense & Military Contacts	$1,900,000	$0	$0	$1,900,000	$338,424	$57,404
Destruction & Dismantlement						
Strategic Offensive Arms Elimination	$78,500,000	$78,500,000	$0	$0	$35,452,220	$1,244,927
Government-to-Government Communications Link	$2,300,000	$2,300,000	$0	$0	$980,175	$668,072
Nuclear Infrastructure Elimination	$23,500,000	$22,500,000	$0	$1,000,000	$6,799,780	$2,881,055
Total Kazakstan	$172,460,000	$153,560,000	$0	$18,900,000	$88,968,571	$23,815,744
		Ukraine				
Chain of Custody						
Emergency Response Training/Equipment	$3,400,000	$5,000,000	$0	$0	$2,919,802	$1,381,051
Multilateral Nuclear Safety Initiative	$11,000,000	$11,000,000	$0	$0	$11,000,000	$8,857,746
Material Control & Accounting	$22,500,000	$22,500,000	$0	$0	$21,520,716	$2,995,197
Export Control	$13,260,000	$13,260,000	$0	$0	$6,919,032	$5,535,865
Demilitarization						
Industrial Partnerships	$55,000,000	$55,000,000	$0	$0	$54,103,347	$37,750,809
Science & Technology Center	$15,000,000	$0	$0	$15,000,000	$14,931,659	$2,374,194

Destruction & Dismantlement

Strategic Nuclear Arms Elimination	$242,700,000	$244,700,000		$0	$181,477,420	$92,022,445
Government-to-Government Communications Link	$1,000,000	$2,400,000		$0	$760,586	$459,576
Nuclear Infrastructure Elimination	$23,400,000	$23,400,000		$0	$900	$0
Total Ukraine	$396,288,000	$377,260,000		$24,028,000	$296,362,345	$152,465,438
Other Program Support						
Defense Enterprise Fund	$7,670,000	$0	$0	$7,670,000	$7,670,000	$7,670,000
Industrial Partnering Program	$10,000,000	$0	$0	$10,000,000	$0	$0
Other Assessments/Administration Costs	$50,900,000	$0	$0	$50,900,000	$28,573,843	$21,031,579
Total Other	$68,570,000	$0	$0	$68,570,000	$36,243,843	$28,701,579
Grand Total	$1,502,110,000	$1,256,280,000	$34,000,000	$247,830,000	$1,024,285,712	$543,890,734

SOURCE: CTR Program Office, U.S. Department of Defense.

Contributors

Oleg Bukharin received his Ph.D. in physics in 1991 from the Moscow Institute of Physics and Technology (MIPT). He also studied international security issues at Princeton University, where he currently serves as a Research Staff Member of the Center for Energy and Environmental Studies. Dr. Bukharin is the co-author, with Thomas Cochran and Robert Norris, of *Making the Russian Bomb: From Stalin to Yeltsin.*

Richard Combs served for six and one-half years on the staff of the Senate Armed Services Committee and 23 years as a Department of State Foreign Service Officer before joining the Monterey Institute of International Studies (MIIS) in December 1996. He is currently Associate Director of the MIIS Center for Russian and Eurasian Studies and Director of the Center for Nonproliferation Studies' NIS Nonproliferation Project. Dr. Combs received his Ph.D. from the University of California at Berkeley.

Gloria Duffy is currently a Visiting Scholar at the Center for International Security and Arms Control at Stanford University and Chief Executive Officer of the Commonwealth Club of California. From 1993 to 1995, as Deputy Assistant Secretary of Defense and Special Coordinator for Cooperative Threat Reduction, Dr. Duffy headed the Nunn-Lugar Program. She also served as Deputy Head of the Safe and Secure Dismantlement (SSD) delegation in 1993–94, and in 1994–95 she led negotiations of Nunn-Lugar agreements. She holds Ph.D., M.Phil., and M.A. degrees in political science from Columbia University.

Dastan Eleukenov is Chief of the Division of International Security and Arms Control in the Kazakstani Ministry of Foreign Affairs. Prior to assuming this post in 1996, he served as Deputy Director of the Kazakstan Institute for Strategic Studies under the Office of the President of the Republic of Kazakstan. Dr. Eleukenov graduated from Moscow State University and received a Ph.D. in physics from the Institute for Nuclear Research in Kiev.

Rose Gottemoeller is Deputy Director of the International Institute for Strategic Studies in London. From January 1993 to December 1994, Ms. Gottemoeller was the Director for Russia, Ukraine, and Eurasia on the

National Security Council staff with responsibility for denuclearization issues.

Kostyantyn Hryshchenko is Deputy Foreign Minister of Ukraine. Prior to assuming this post in 1995, he served as Head of the Arms Control and Disarmament Directorate of the Ukrainian Ministry of Foreign Affairs. A graduate of the Moscow State Institute of International Relations, Dr. Hryshchenko served in the UN Secretariat and subsequently in the Soviet Ministry of Foreign Affairs. His international relations expertise has focused on the countries of the Asia and Pacific region, Africa, and the Middle East.

Katherine E. Johnson is a staff member in the Office of the Deputy Assistant Secretary of Defense for International Security Policy (Russia, Ukraine, and Eurasia). From 1992 to 1995, Ms. Johnson served as the representative of the Office of the Secretary of Defense (OSD) to a number of multilateral nuclear nonproliferation regimes, including the preparatory committees to the 1995 Non-Proliferation Treaty Review and Extension Conference and the Nuclear Suppliers Group. In 1996 she completed a one-year assignment from the Defense Department at the Center for International Security Affairs, Los Alamos National Laboratory (LANL), which coordinates all LANL interactions with the states of the former Soviet Union and with China.

Oumirserik T. Kasenov is Director of the Kazakstan Institute for Strategic Studies under the Office of the President of the Republic of Kazakstan. In 1992, he served as Adviser to the Vice President on foreign policy and national security issues. Dr. Kasenov graduated from the Moscow State Institute of International Relations and received a Ph.D. in history from the Academy of Social Sciences in Moscow. Dr. Kasenov's current research interests include defense conversion, nonproliferation, nuclear security, and other foreign policy and security issues of particular importance to Kazakstan.

Igor Khripunov is Associate Director for NIS Programs at the Center for East-West Trade Policy at the University of Georgia. He is also co-director of the Center's NIS Export Control Project, which conducts policy-oriented research and service on nonproliferation export controls and normalization of East-West trade and technological relations. Prior to joining the Center in 1992, Dr. Khripunov served as First Secretary of the Political-Military Section at the Soviet (later Russian) Embassy in Washington, D.C., and participated in the INF and START talks and the Soviet-American Standing Consultative Commission.

Murat Laumulin is Senior Researcher at the Kazakstan Institute for Strategic Studies under the President of the Republic of Kazakstan. From 1993 to 1994, he was a staff member of the Department of International Security and Arms Control in the Ministry of Foreign Affairs of the Republic of Kazakstan. Previously he was a professor at the Al-Farabi Kazakstan National University in Almaty. He received a Ph.D. in history from the Institute of History of the Kazakstani Academy of Sciences.

Evgenii P. Maslin is Chief of the Nuclear Weapons (Twelfth) Main Directorate of the Russian Ministry of Defense. The Twelfth Main Directorate is responsible for the maintenance, transportation, and security of all Russian nuclear weapons. General Maslin has worked with nuclear weapons in the Soviet and Russian military since 1959 and in April–May 1995 he was a member of the Russian delegation to the NPT Review and Extension Conference.

R. Adam Moody is a Senior Research Associate on the Monitoring Proliferation Threats Project at the Center for Nonproliferation Studies. Prior to receiving an M.A. in International Policy Studies from the Monterey Institute of International Studies in 1994, he served in the Military Intelligence Corps of the U.S. Army as a tactical electronic warfare systems operator and a nuclear/biological/chemical weapons defense specialist.

Michael H. Newlin is a former career diplomat who is now a private consultant on nonproliferation issues in the former Soviet Union. Prior to his retirement from the U.S. Department of State in 1994, Ambassador Newlin was involved in implementing Nunn-Lugar programs in Russia, Ukraine, and Kazakstan. In 1993, he served as Deputy Executive Chairman of the UN Special Commission (UNSCOM) on Iraq. Prior to this assignment, Ambassador Newlin was U.S. ambassador to the International Atomic Energy Agency and other UN bodies in Vienna.

Sam Nunn was first elected to the U.S. Senate in 1972, and is the ranking Democrat on both the Senate Armed Services Committee and the Senate's Permanent Subcommittee on Investigations. Senator Nunn has become one of the leading figures in American government and an internationally recognized expert on economic policy, defense, and national security. He attended Georgia Tech and Emory University, as well as Emory Law School, where he graduated with honors.

Vladimir A. Orlov is Director of the Center for Policy Studies in Russia (PIR Center) as well as Editor of the journal *Yadernyi Kontrol* (Nuclear control). From 1990 to 1994, he was a political analyst with the weekly *Moscow News*, on whose board he now sits. Prior to joining *Moscow News*, Mr. Orlov graduated from the Moscow State Institute of International Relations, where he studied international relations and journalism.

Vyachaslau E. Paznyak is Director of the International Institute for Policy Studies in Minsk. He also is Editor-in-Chief of *The Vector*, a Belarusan journal of international affairs. Previously he served as Director of International Programs at the Minsk Center for Nonproliferation and Export Control, Director of the International Security Project at the National Centre for Strategic Initiatives, and an Assistant Professor of Political Science at the Minsk State Institute for Foreign Languages. Dr. Paznyak graduated from the Minsk State Institute for Foreign Languages in 1976 and received his Ph.D. from the Belarusan State University in 1988.

Alexander A. Pikayev is a senior researcher with the Russian Institute for World Economy and International Relations, where he received his Ph.D. Since 1994, he has also served as Director of the Committee for Critical Technologies and Nonproliferation, an independent nongovernmental organization in Moscow promoting research in the field of arms control, nonproliferation, and weapons technology controls. Dr. Pikayev also serves as Counsel to the Defense Committee of the Russian Duma.

William C. Potter is a Professor and Director of the Center for Nonproliferation Studies at the Monterey Institute of International Studies (MIIS). He also directs the MIIS Center for Russian and Eurasian Studies. His books include *Nuclear Profiles of the Soviet Successor States, Nuclear Power and Nonproliferation, Soviet Decisionmaking for National Security,* and *The Nuclear Suppliers and Nonproliferation.* Dr.

Potter has served as a consultant to the Arms Control and Disarmament Agency, Lawrence Livermore National Laboratory, the RAND Corporation, and the Jet Propulsion Laboratory. He served as an adviser on the Kyrgyz delegation to the 1995 NPT Review and Extension Conference.

John M. Shields is a Senior Analyst with the NIS Nonproliferation Project at the Center for Nonproliferation Studies at the Monterey Institute of International Studies, where he conducts research on U.S.-NIS security cooperation and on nuclear, chemical, and biological weapons proliferation worldwide. Mr. Shields was previously an analyst with Science Applications International Corporation in McLean, Virginia, conducting assessments of global trends in the diffusion of advanced weapons technologies and of U.S. defense planning, regional security policies, and counterproliferation strategies.

Jessica Eve Stern is currently writing a book on nuclear, biological, and chemical weapons terrorism under the auspices of the MacArthur Foundation Research and Writing Program. In 1995–96 she was a National Fellow at the Hoover Institution on War, Revolution, and Peace at Stanford University. In 1994–95 she was a staff member on the National Security Council (NSC), where she had responsibility for fissile material protection, control, and accounting and nuclear smuggling issues. Prior to joining the NSC, Dr. Stern was a staff member at Lawrence Livermore National Laboratory. She received her masters degree in chemical engineering/technology policy from the Massachusetts Institute of Technology and a Ph.D. in public policy from Harvard University.

Index

Center for Science and International Affairs
Graham T. Allison, Director
John F. Kennedy School of Government
Harvard University
79 JFK Street, Cambridge MA 02138
(617) 495-1400

The Center for Science and International Affairs (CSIA) is the hub of research and teaching on international relations at Harvard's John F. Kennedy School of Government. CSIA seeks to advance the understanding of international security and environmental problems with special emphasis on the role of science and technology in the analysis and design of public policy. The Center seeks to anticipate emerging international problems, identify practical solutions, and encourage policymakers to act. These goals animate work in each of the Center's four major programs:

- The International Security Program (ISP) is the home of the Center's core concern with international security issues.

- The Strengthening Democratic Institutions (SDI) project works to catalyze international support for political and economic transformations in the former Soviet Union.

- The Science, Technology, and Public Policy (STPP) program emphasizes public policy issues in which understanding of science, technology, and systems of innovation are crucial.

- The Environment and Natural Resources Program (ENRP) is the locus of interdisciplinary research on environmental policy issues.

Each year CSIA hosts a multinational group of approximately 25 scholars from the social, behavioral, and natural sciences. Dozens of Harvard faculty members and adjunct research fellows from the greater Boston area also participate in CSIA activities. CSIA also sponsors seminars and conferences, many open to the public; maintains a substantial specialized library; and publishes a monograph series and discussion papers. The Center's International Security Program, directed by Steven E. Miller, publishes the CSIA Studies in International Security, and sponsors and edits the quarterly journal *International Security*.

The Center is supported by an endowment established with funds from the Ford Foundation and Harvard University, by foundation grants, by individual gifts, and by occasional government contracts.